RECOVERING HISTORY, CONSTRUCTING RACE

The Indian, Black, and White Roots
of Mexican Americans

by Martha Menchaca

University of Texas Press

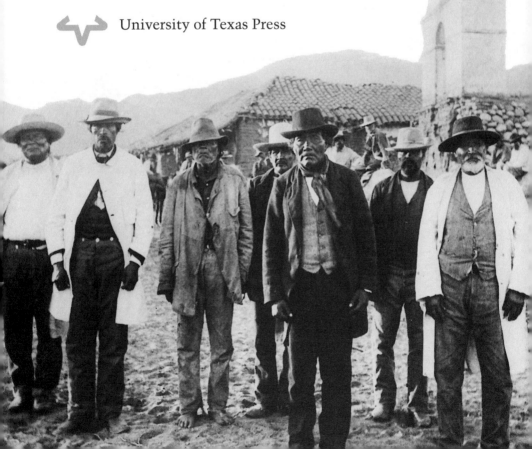

Parts of chapters 2, 8, and 9 previously appeared in Menchaca 1993, "Chicano Indianism: A Historical Account of Racial Repression in the United States," *American Ethnologist* 20 (3): 583–603.

Portions of the history of schooling in the Southwest discussed in chapter 6 and on the Treaty of Guadalupe Hidalgo and citizenship discussed in chapter 8 appeared in an earlier version as "The Treaty of Guadalupe Hidalgo and the Racialization of the Mexican Population," in *The Elusive Quest for Equality: 150 Years of Chicano/Chicana Education,* ed. José F. Moreno (Cambridge, Mass.: Harvard Educational Review, 1999), pp. 3–29. Copyright 1999 by the President and Fellows of Harvard College. All rights reserved.

Ninth paperback printing, 2016

Library of Congress Cataloging-in-Publication Data
Menchaca, Martha.
Recovering history, constructing race : the Indian, black, and white roots of Mexican Americans / by Martha Menchaca. — 1st ed.
    p. cm.
  Includes bibliographical references (p.   ) and index.
  ISBN 978-0-292-75254-2 (pbk. : alk. paper)
    1. Mexican Americans—Race identity. 2. Mexican Americans—Ethnic identity. 3. Mexican Americans—History. 4. Racially mixed people—United States—History. 5. United States—Race relations. 6. United States—Ethnic relations. 7. Racism—United States—History. 8. United States—Relations—Mexico.
  9. Mexico—Relations—United States. I. Title.
E184.M5 M46 2001
973'.046872—dc21   2001033309

doi:10.7560/752535

For my family

Contents

Illustrations

Maps

Photographs

Acknowledgments

In this book I examine the racial history of the Mexican Americans. It is the culmination of many years of historical research. One of the major theoretical frameworks influencing my work has been Michael Omi and Howard Winant's theory of racialization. In weaving this anthropological history, I hope to illustrate that knowledge of history can be used to understand our racial present. I would like to take this opportunity to express my thanks to archaeologist Fred Valdez, who in many of our conversations helped me theorize the relations between land and race. I am also indebted to historian Ricardo Romo, who in the initial conceptualization of this book shared valuable insights into the Black heritage of the Mexican Americans. I am indebted to Diego Vigil, who over the years read my manuscripts and encouraged me to continue my historical research. I am also grateful to the National Research Council/Ford Foundation Postdoctoral Program for Minorities for the financial support I received in the early years of this research project. I extend my appreciation to the Center for Mexican American Studies at the University of Texas at Austin for the financial support I received to visit library archives and to the University Co-operative Society Subvention Program for funds used to complete this book.

I want to thank my husband, Richard R. Valencia, my sisters-in-law, Betty Valencia-Cruz and Martha Gonzalez, and my niece, Elena Gonzalez, for allowing me to use their family histories to exemplify how oral traditions merge history and ethnography.

Recovering History, Constructing Race

Introduction

In this book it is my intent to write about the Mexican American people's Indian, White, and Black racial history. In doing so, I offer an interpretive historical analysis of the experiences of the Mexican Americans' ancestors in Mexico and the United States. This analysis begins with the Mexican Americans' prehistoric foundations and continues into the late twentieth century. My focus, however, is on exploring the legacy of racial discrimination that was established in the aftermath of the Spanish conquest and was later intensified by the United States government when, in 1848, it conquered northern Mexico (presently the U.S. Southwest) and annexed it to the United States (Menchaca 1999:3). The central period of study ranges from 1570 to 1898.

Though my interpretive history revisits many well-known events, it differs from previous histories on Mexican Americans and on the American Southwest because the central thread of my analysis is race relations, an area of study that is often accorded only secondary significance and generally subsumed under economic or nation-based interpretations. It also differs because I include Blacks as important historical actors, rather than denying their presence in the history of the Mexican Americans. Finally, as part of this analysis I demonstrate that racial status hierarchies are often structured upon the ability of one racial group to deny those who are racially different access to owning land. This process leads to the low social prestige and impoverishment of the marginalized. I close my analysis with commentaries on contemporary United States race relations and auto/ethnographic observations of Mexican American indigenism. Auto/ethnography is used as a method to illustrate how historical events influence racial identity.

This form of intellectual inquiry emerged from my conversations with archaeologist Fred Valdez. In 1986 Fred and I were both hired as assistant professors in the Anthropology Department at the University of Texas at Austin. It was the first time that I had met a Mexican American archaeologist. We were both fascinated by the ethnohistory of the indigenous peoples of the Americas and shared the unconventional view that Mexican Americans were part of the indigenous peoples of the American Southwest. Following endless conversations on the indigenous heritage of the Mexican Americans, we decided to study the indigenous groups of the Southwest that had been conquered by Spain and Mexico. Our objective was to identify the groups that had become subjects of Spain and, later, citizens of Mexico. This research was used to prepare an undergraduate class on the "Indigenous Heritage of the Mexican Americans." We were pleasantly surprised that our class became very popular, as evidenced by the large enrollments. In general, students were interested in knowing about their heritage, while many others were interested in seeking specific information about the mission Indians from whom they were descended.

For me, this academic endeavor converged with the publication of Michael Omi and Howard Winant's classic book *Racial Formation in the United States: From the 1960s to the 1980s* (1986). Their work influenced me to reassess the significance of studying the racial heritage of the Mexican Americans, given that my interest until that point had been solely to outline their indigenous ancestry. According to Omi and Winant, the significance of studying race is not to analyze the biological aspect of a people's heritage, but rather to understand the politics and processes of racial categorization. They urgently call upon social scientists to study race as a central source of societal organization, because in multiracial societies race has been used historically by those in power to share social and economic privileges with only those people who are racially similar to themselves. Omi and Winant do not urge scholars to explore the origins or psychology of this inclusive-exclusive behavior, but rather to provide a historical context, showing how those in power use race to rationalize the distribution of wealth.

I also found Omi and Winant's discussion on racial ideology very insightful and useful in understanding the dynamics of historical shifts in the area of national racial policy. Though they offer a macroanalysis of state systems, their interpretation is dynamic. They propose that in most multiracial countries only one racial group ascends to power. When the state encodes racial policies, the views of the dominant racial group are converted from ideology into practice. Such racial policies are legislated to order and regulate racial interaction. Although those in power control the legislation of racial policies, Omi and Winant propose that each generation adopts a new racial ideology that is reflected in legislation. Generational views about race are premised upon the meaning and value people ascribe to bodily characteristics (e.g., color, physical features). Over a generation, some racial attitudes may be reproduced, while others may be discarded. In sum, Omi and Winant propose that changes in racial ideologies are manifested in policy that can intensify or diminish racial boundaries and status hierarchies. Though they argue that the dominant racial group prescribes racial policy—which they label "racial dictatorship"—they also propose that racial minorities and dissenting dominant group members can spark ideological changes by initiating social movements. When this happens, the state is forced to change its racial legislation.

Notwithstanding the dynamic theoretical framework proffered by Omi and Winant, they concur with Pierre Bourdieu that major institutional changes are difficult to implement. Bourdieu (1992) posits that shifts in social policy can be promoted either by groups or by individuals. Because individuals are a product of society, however, they are habituated to internalizing externality. This leads to a social outlook that promotes the maintenance of the status quo. Indeed, this notion of institutional stability is a pessimistic interpretation of historical change. It nonetheless persuasively explicates the reproduction of racial and class strata and outlines why those who are dominated remain in subaltern positions for generations. I must also add that my research on Mexican Americans verified Bourdieu's historical reproduction thesis: I found that over time the legal system has been the most effective method of reproducing institutional stability and indoctrinating people to accept their prescribed racial roles. Under the governments of Spain and the United States, the reproduction of racial inequality was instituted through a legal process I call "racialization."[1] Spain and the United States used their legal systems to confer social and economic privileges upon Whites and to discriminate against people of color. Racial characteristics were effectively used to categorize people into groups meriting privilege, while dissimilar groups were deemed unworthy and instead were expected to serve the meritorious. Racial meritocracy was founded upon real and presumed racial differences.

In part my interest in writing this book was prompted by personal inquiries, in particular exploring the Mexican Americans' Black history. Throughout my life I had observed that many Mexican Americans had facial features that markedly or faintly resembled those of Black Americans. When I moved to Texas to begin my professorship, I noticed that Black facial characteristics were more common among Mexican Americans there than I had observed elsewhere. This obviously was a result of intermarriage. When this blending took place I had no idea or hypothesis. These observations caused me to reflect upon my own family history. As a child I recall asking my mother why my father's hair and nose resembled those of Black Americans. My father, Lauro Menchaca, had faintly Black facial characteristics, yet his skin was White, with a rosy pigment. My mother, Isabel Esparza Menchaca, responded that my father's distinct nose was a marker of our Roman heritage and his curly black hair a characteristic inherited from Spaniards of mixed Arabic blood.

I was satisfied with my mother's response, as her explanation was combined with mythological accounts of how our family descended from Chichimec Indian royalty and Spanish *conquistadores* (conquerors). I did not question her account because we had gone to Mexico many times and stopped each time to visit the pyramids in Chicomoztoc, Zacatecas, where my mother related stories of our royal Chichimec lineage. During our visits, however, I could not understand why we did not visit one of my father's brothers, Uncle José, who lived a short distance by car from Chicomoztoc. I finally met my uncle when he came to visit my father in Santa Paula, California. When I met Uncle José I began to doubt my mother's stories about our Spanish-Indian heritage, since by U.S. conventions my uncle and one of his sons were clearly Black. I finally realized that my mother was omitting part of my history. My suspicions were confirmed when I traveled to Mexico as a young adult and stopped to visit my father's side of the family in the state of Zacatecas. During my visit to Jerez I discovered that many of my relatives were fair-skinned *afromestizos* of White, Indian, and Black ancestry. Some had only faintly Black features like my father, while others were *moriscos* (three-quarters White and one-quarter Black) or *coyotes* (half Indian, one-quarter White, one-quarter Black). When I returned home and asked my mother if this was true, she responded that my father was not of Black descent, but that

Uncle José had married into a Black family. I did not doubt her explanation, as his wife was a *mulatta* (half White and half Black), but I also knew that her story was incomplete.

When I asked my father about his *afromestizo* relatives, he knew very little because his parents had divorced when he was about five. His father, Lauro, moved to Texas or Chihuahua and no longer had contact with his family. My father did not recall what Lauro senior looked like because he had seldom seen him. After my father was born in 1911, one year after the Mexican Revolution started, Lauro senior joined the revolutionary forces. When the major battles had been fought (by 1914) and the process of disarming the victorious army began, my grandfather did not settle down and instead remained in Pancho Villa's army; consequently he did not live with my grandmother, Delfina Robles. My grandmother's family, considering her a disgraced and abandoned woman, forced her to seek a divorce. Soon afterward my grandmother died in an epidemic in Zacatecas; or at least that was the story my father was told.

My father believed his Black ancestry came from his father's side of the family and not from his mother's. To illustrate his story, he showed me photographs of his family. Although he did not have pictures of his parents, he had photographs of his father's sisters and mother's brother, Eulalio Robles, the man who had raised him. In one photograph his aunts are well dressed; two of them are very good looking women who appear to be of mixed Indian and Black descent (see Photograph 1). The other photograph is of his uncle Eulalio, a White man (see Photograph 2).

Though my father acknowledged that he was of partially Black descent, he like my mother emphasized that our family's heritage was Indian and White (see Photograph 3). He did not know family accounts of our Indian heritage, however. The only stories he knew well were those about the Mexican Revolution and about his uncle Eulalio's ability to remain neutral when the revolutionaries and the government soldiers passed through their home in Zacatecas, Zacatecas. Apparently Eulalio gave the soldiers anything they wanted, and they left his family alone. Unlike my father, my mother knew countless stories about our family's past. She was proud of having listened attentively to her grandparents' oral histories. My mother's stories about Indians and pyramids eventually inspired me to love history and become an anthropologist, in particular her stories about Chicomoztoc, Zacatecas.

My mother's parents also died during the Mexican Revolution, when

Photograph 1. My Father's Aunts

Photograph 2. My Father's Uncle, Eulalio Robles

Photograph 3. My Father, Lauro Menchaca Robles (seated)

typhoid spread throughout the state of Zacatecas. My mother was raised by her grandparents. On her grandmother's side of the family our relatives came from Spain: my mother's grandmother, Doña Hermeñita, was born there. Doña Hermeñita immigrated to Mexico with her parents, an aunt, and an uncle. Her grandmother's family settled in Monte Escobedo, Zacatecas, where Doña Hermeñita met her husband, Don Domingo. On my mother's side of the family our Spanish and indigenous fusion took place when Doña Hermeñita married Don Domingo, who was part of Monte Escobedo's landed elite. When I was a child I traveled to Monte Escobedo and stayed on the estates of my mother's relatives. Don Domingo told my mother that he was a full-blooded Indian and a native of Monte Escobedo. His family had owned thousands of acres in Monte Escobedo for generations. Don Domingo claimed that his ancestors were Chichimec Indians from Chicomoztoc, Zacatecas. He told my mother that hundreds of years ago his tribe had left Chicomoztoc and spread throughout the state of Zacatecas.[2] Don Domingo's clan finally settled in the mountains of Monte Escobedo to work the land. One of his ancestors became the village *cacique* (regional political boss), and the political governance of Monte Escobedo remained in his family's lineage until Don Domingo's death. Monte Escobedo is located approximately four hours by car from Chicomoztoc.

My mother recalled that when she was a young child Don Domingo took her to Chicomoztoc and told her the same stories he had been told. Interestingly, this oral tradition was kept alive by my mother as she repeated the same accounts to my brothers and sisters. Chicomoztoc is located in the municipal district of Villa Nueva, near the Hacienda de la Quemada. Archaeologists propose that Chicomoztoc was founded around A.D. 1164 by Chichimec Indians (Rodríguez Flores 1976:46). It is considered to be the first city of the people of Zacatecas. A few years after Chicomoztoc was established, many of its inhabitants dispersed throughout Zacatecas and San Luis Potosí. Other groups migrated to the Atlantic coast of Mexico. Historian Emilio Rodríguez Flores proposes that the people from Chicomoztoc came from Aztlán, a homeland north of the Gila River and west of the Colorado River, in what is today California. During one of my childhood visits to Chicomoztoc, as my mother and I walked through the ruins she pointed to rooms situated on the high platforms and claimed that our ancestors must have lived there (see Photograph 4). These were the sites archaeologists identified as the quarters of the indigenous elite. These remarks caused my brothers to laugh and tease my mother by saying, "If we are the descendants of indigenous royalty we must have come from the royal line of *barredores* [street sweepers]."

Over the years, after my mother repeated her stories I commonly asked: "Mamá, if we came from Mexico's landed elite, why did we leave Mexico and migrate to the United States?" My question saddened her, and she always apologized for having been unable to pass down the property she had inherited from her grandfather. When she reached adulthood, her grandfather gave her two ranches, and throughout her youth she led an affluent lifestyle. When she was twenty-six, her first husband died during an epidemic. She was left widowed with six children. To support her family, my mother sold most of her property, yet she did not lose all of her investments. Seven years after becoming a widow, she met and married my father. Together they invested their money in two bakery stores

Photograph 4. A Family Visit to Chicomoztoc, Zacatecas

and a theater. The bakeries did well, yet the expenses in maintaining the theater eventually led the family to bankruptcy.

My father decided to move to the United States until we weathered the storm. Within six months of announcing his plan we obtained immigration papers for our entire family, and in 1962 we arrived in Santa Paula, California. I was five years old at that time. My father alleged that our family had quickly obtained immigration visas because unlike most Mexican immigrants we were financially stable. We had come to the United States to start a business and not to work in the fields. Though our financial stability no doubt was an important factor in helping us meet U.S. immigration requirements, my interpretation of this event differs. At this time, the U.S. government practically had an open door policy toward Mexican immigrants because agribusiness needed farm workers (Galarza 1964). In any case, my family lost the property, and when this occurred my father had to find a job. Since there were plenty of jobs available in the United States, we moved in search of a better life and in an attempt to remain part of the middle class.

As I have shared with you, my intent in writing this book was partly academic (embarking on a historical project) and partly personal (finding out about my racial background). I was also motivated, however, by my interest in exploring my husband's family history. Unlike myself, my husband and my twin sons descend from California American Indians. My husband, Richard Valencia, identifies himself as a Mexican American of Chumash descent. On his mother's side they are Chumash, and on his father's side they are Mexican. My husband's parents divorced, and he lost contact with his father's side of the family. Verónica Ruiz, my husband's mother, was at least three-quarters Chumash, from the Barbareño subdivision (Santa Barbara). Richard's family, though dispersed throughout the United States, remains closely knit. They do not share the same ethnic or racial identity, however. Some identify themselves as Chicano *mestizos* (Spanish and Indian descent) of Chumash descent, while others identify as Chumash Indians of partial Mexican descent. Furthermore, some live on the Santa Inés reservation, while others live in ranches near the reservation, and most relatives live in Santa Barbara. Their family's racial history is discussed in the Epilogue, which illustrates how racial and ethnic identities are conditioned by historical events.

In narrating the racial history of the Mexican Americans, I use the first-person voice, because this is also my history, a positioned history. It is an interpretive history that revisits many events previously described by borderland historians Herbert E. Bolton, Hubert H. Bancroft, and David Weber, yet departs from this tradition because my focus is on understanding the politics of race relations and not on the growth of the Spanish Empire in the Southwest. My quest is to shed light on the economic and political factors pushing conquered *mestizos, afromestizos,* and Indians to join forces with their Spanish colonizers against the Indians of the Southwest—a conquest that culminated in the integration of thousands of southwestern Indian villages into Spanish and later Mexican society.

My account also differs because I do not focus on the achievements of Spaniards and Anglo Americans in the making of their nations; instead I examine how their nations legislated unfair racial laws to ensure that people of color would remain subservient subjects or second-class citizens. Specifically, because I position my discourse as one that privileges racial politics as the central focus of analysis and I disclose that this history is as much about myself as it is about Mexican Americans, I acknowledge that my narrative is situated, because it examines historical events from the position of the subaltern. To historicize is to interpret events; when scholars interpret, their voice is situated, because their analysis cannot be separated from their positions in society as members of a racial group, a social class, and a gender. Being situated does not nullify historical objectivity; it merely stresses that the author stages what s/he perceives to be the main events (see White 1992). In my case I offer a history of those people who lost the Mexican American War of 1846–1848 and became incorporated as U.S. racial minorities. Though my account of major events will not differ greatly from those of mainstream historians, it will be more inclusive of unpleasant happenings, because conflict takes center stage when the focus is on race.

I must also emphasize that my narrative is about Mexican Americans and not exclusively about the American Indian experience. Though both peoples' histories are interrelated, my analysis focuses on those indigenous groups who were conquered by the governments of Spain and later by the United States.[3] I do not intend to insult anyone by using the term "Indian" rather than "Native American." I am aware that anthropologists prefer the label "Native American" as a means of stressing the Indians' antiquity in the United States. This label is inappropriate here, however, because the term "Native American" is an ethnic identifier for the indigenous peoples of the United States and does not apply to groups from Latin America. I must also add that my analysis of the interrelations between Indians and *afromestizos* is incomplete, for this history has largely been ignored by historians. This silence has led to devaluing the accomplishments of Black people in Mexico and the U.S. Southwest and erased a heritage shared by many. Though I offer just an outline, it is the most comprehensive analysis to date of the experiences of *afromestizos* in the Southwest. This history is also dialogic: I am aware that the interpretations of many of these undisclosed events that I have found in library archives can be reinscribed from multiple positions. I introduce only one interpretation that I have carefully analyzed and proffer an overview so that such events will no longer lie unrevealed.

My account begins with the Mexican Americans' Indian, White, and Black racial foundations. The second chapter examines the Spanish conquest of Mexico and the introduction of Black slaves from Africa. My focus is on how Mexico's racial order, *la casta*, was rationalized and institutionalized. The third and fourth chapters examine the northward migration of Indians, *mestizos*, and *afromestizos* into the Southwest, drawn by promises of a relaxed racial order where people of color would be given some of the economic opportunities only enjoyed by Whites in the interior of Mexico. These chapters also outline the privileged legal positions of Whites and examine how Indians, *mestizos,* and *afromestizos* reacted to this unfairness. As part of these discussions, I explore the conquest of many indigenous groups of the Southwest and their conversion to Christianity.

Chapter 5 discusses the settlement of California and the end of the Spanish period. The Mexican War of Independence was a central event in ending Spain's racial order; it was not solely a revolution about the formation of a modern nation—it was also a racial revolution.

Chapter 6 examines how the newly formed Mexican Republic adopted the United States' constitutional structure and moved a step further by giving citizenship to people irrespective of race. This liberal idea, though philosophically ahead of its time, resulted in the forced acculturation of many Indians of the Southwest. This chapter also delineates the migration of Anglo-American immigrants into the Southwest and examines how Mexico's land and antislavery policies sparked revolutionary movements in Texas. I argue that the Texas War for Independence was largely a struggle over slavery.

Chapter 7 analyzes the Mexican government's attempt to dismantle Spain's racial order and improve the economic position of its citizens of color in the Southwest. Converting them into property owners was one of the main policies used to empower them, but this process adversely affected the Christian Indians. This chapter also examines the events leading to the U.S. government's taking possession of the Southwest.

Chapter 8 discusses the Treaty of Guadalupe Hidalgo, which brought closure to the Mexican American War of 1846 to 1848, and the racial laws instituted by the U.S. government. Mexicans of color returned to a racial order where they had few civil rights, and most were denied citizenship. Under the U.S. legal system Mexicans were distinguished on the basis of race and were ascribed the legal rights accorded to their respective racial group. Matters were worse in Texas, as slavery had been reinstituted. This chapter also delineates how U.S. racial laws were used by government officials to determine which types of Mexicans were eligible to retain their Spanish and Mexican land grants. In particular, the U.S. government denied Mexican Indians property rights if they continued to practice tribal customs, coercing them into adopting a Mexican public identity as a means of escaping the reservation policies of the period. Under

U.S. law, Mexicans who were identifiably *afromestizo* were legally differentiated and were subjected to the laws applied to Blacks.

Chapter 9 brings us to the present, with an overview of the racial laws affecting Mexican Americans into the late twentieth century (e.g., marriage, citizenship, *de jure* segregation, affirmative action) and the common struggles facing Mexican Americans, African Americans, and other people of color. This section is based upon my previous publications in *American Ethnologist* and the *Harvard Educational Review*. My historical analysis ends with an overview of current social movements which are attempting to repeal the liberal legislation of the 1960s, in particular the civil rights laws extending to racial minorities many of the legal rights enjoyed by Whites. In the Epilogue I employ auto/ethnographic methods, offering my husband's family history as a concluding reflection on the influence that historical events have had on peoples' racial identities.

My historical analysis is based on primary and secondary sources. The primary sources include Spanish, Mexican, and U.S. government documents such as court cases, naturalization documents, property and census records, archival documents on Texas civic government, U.S. congressional legislation, international treaties, constitutional legislation, photographs, state and national racial laws, and ethnographic interviews. The secondary sources include historical writings on the exploration, conquest, and colonial settlement of Mexico and the American Southwest as well as literature on the institutionalization and breakdown of social segregation in the United States. I hope that this book provides a comprehensive analysis of the Mexican Americans' racial history and an outline of the influence *afromestizos* have had in the Southwest. My ultimate goal is to historicize for the purpose of contextualizing the present: I believe race does matter and has mattered throughout history.

1

Racial Foundations

Textual Politics

I begin the Mexican Americans' racial history with an overview of their racial foundations. First, however, I offer a critique on why academics have dismissed this theme as a significant area of research. My aim is to illustrate the textual politics of neglect.

The recovery of the Mexican Americans' prehistory has largely been neglected due to lack of interest on the part of mainstream archaeologists and anthropologists. In 1988, when Dr. Fred Valdez and I began teaching our class on the indigenous heritage of the Mexican Americans, the only anthropological source we found that specifically made interconnections between Mexican Americans and prehistorical peoples was the text by James Diego Vigil, *From Indians to Chicanos: The Dynamics of Mexican American Culture* (1980/1984).[1] Vigil was part of the first cohort of Mexican American anthropologists who obtained doctoral degrees in the early 1970s and initiated the recovery of the Mexican Americans' history and prehistoric past. Prior to that time, only a few Mexican Americans had been admitted to U.S. universities (Rosaldo 1985). Among the first to obtain doctoral degrees were Octavio Romano-V and Thomas Weaver (American Anthropological Association 1999). They were soon joined by Renato Rosaldo, Carlos Vélez-Ibáñez, and James Diego Vigil. These pioneering anthropologists approached the study of Mexican Americans from a historical perspective and began challenging the social science assumption that poverty among Mexican Americans was an outcome of their dysfunctional culture.

In a 1968 article Octavio Romano-V urgently called upon Mexican American students—and any person who opposed racism—to contest stereotypic and racist propaganda against his people. In "The Anthropology and Sociology of the Mexican-Americans: The Distortion of Mexican American History," Romano-V asserted that Anglo-American scholars were generating deficit-thinking discourses in efforts to blame Mexican Americans for the social and economic problems generated by Anglo-American racism. He charged that these scholars, particularly anthropologists, ignored the way in which racism historically had been used by Anglo Americans to obstruct the social, economic, and political mobility of Mexican-origin people. Romano-V argued that Mexican Americans were studied ahistorically in order to ignore the vestiges of Anglo-American racism—such as segregation, employment discrimination, racist laws, and police violence. By treating Mexican Americans ahistorically, he asserted, anthropologists conjured an image of them as an immigrant and peasantlike group who had not contributed to the nation's infrastructure culturally, technologically, or architecturally. Their antiquity in the Southwest was strategically ignored. Romano-V's article was widely read and influenced the future direction of Mexican American scholarship (Paredes 1978; Rosaldo 1985). Since then most social scientists, including anthropologists, have approached the study of Mexican Americans from a historical and (post)structural perspective, examining the impact of institutional discrimination on the Mexican American family, individual, and ethnic group.

Though Romano-V and other scholars successfully dismantled most social-scientific myths claiming that familism, Catholicism, honor, and machismo were the basis of the Mexican Americans' economic problems, the number of Mexican American graduate students accepted into anthropology doctoral programs did not steadily rise. The traditional failure of anthropology departments to recruit and admit Mexican American graduate students is reflected in the ethnic composition of the discipline. In 1996 less than 3 percent of full-time faculty in anthropology departments were of Hispanic descent, and most of these were not of Mexican origin (Givens and Jabloski 1996:5). To this day there are still few Mexican American anthropologists, and Vigil's book continues to be the only anthropological source on the Mexican Americans' ancient origins.

In his book entitled *The Spanish Frontier in North America* (1992) historian David Weber offers observations similar to those of Octavio Romano-V: though abundant literature on the U.S. Southwest has been produced, traditional mainstream scholars have distorted or neglected to recognize the Mexican Americans' historic roots in the Southwest.

Weber argues that this omission has been the result of a political act and a reflection of the power Anglo Americans have in the production of United States history. According to Weber, since the early nineteenth century Mexicans and Spaniards have been historically situated as villains and savage overlords of the southwestern Indians. This portrayal allowed nineteenth and early twentieth century Anglo-American historians to justify the U.S. government's annexation of Mexico's northern territories (after the Mexican American War of 1846 to 1848) and to perpetuate the myth that Mexican Americans' presence in the Southwest was insignificant. Weber writes:

> In the late eighteenth and early nineteenth centuries, Englishmen and Anglo Americans who wrote about the Spanish past in North America uniformly condemned Spanish rule. . . . Anglo Americans had inherited the view that Spaniards were unusually cruel, avaricious, treacherous, fanatical, superstitious, cowardly, corrupt, decadent, indolent, and authoritarian—a unique complex of pejoratives that historians from Spain came to call the Black Legend, *la leyenda negra*. . . . Americans who wrote about the Southwest before midcentury interpreted the past in a way that justified their nation's expansionist aims. (Weber 1992:335, 336, 339)

To make matters worse, not only were the historical contributions of the Mexican Americans ignored, but when their ancestors were identified, the descriptions were essentialized, posing an alleged singular truth that all Mexican *mestizos* were enemies of the Indians. This monolithic construction failed to describe the colonial encounter accurately. A nominalist fiction was passed on as historical fact, and no room was left to account for the different types of relations that developed between the *mestizo* colonists and the Indians, including conflict, mutual exploitation, social distance, and peace.

Weber adds that in the early twentieth century Anglo-American historians began criticizing their predecessors' narratives and a new southwestern historiography was introduced, less politically motivated by the aim of glorifying the superiority of the Anglo-American people. In 1911 Herbert Eugene Bolton and his cadre of doctoral students contested past distortions (Weber 1992:353). Immersing themselves in Spanish and Mexican archives, they generated a new image of the Southwest: they credited

Spaniards for the infrastructure they had built and depicted the Indians as noble savages whose complex societies had been disturbed by the arrival of the Europeans. But the Boltonians continued to ignore the multifaceted and complex social relations that had evolved between the *mestizo* colonists and the native peoples of the Southwest. Little attention was given to the fact that by the turn of the nineteenth century a large part of the *mestizo* colonial population was of southwestern American Indian descent. Weber argues that *mestizos* were depicted by Boltonian historians as uncultured Mexicans and "gente baja" (lower-class people) and were distinguished from the noble savages and the glorious Spaniards (see Bolton 1960:14). This led to the denigration of the *mestizos* and the perpetuation of the assumption that *mestizos* and Indians did not have anything in common. In essence, the Boltonians shared the view that to be Indian an individual must be culturally and ethnically pure and not influenced by Spanish or Mexican culture. A fictional border was drawn between *mestizos* and southwestern Indians, tacitly denying *mestizos* their historic roots in the Southwest. Weber writes:

> The Bolton school dominated American historical scholarship on the borderlands until the 1960s. . . . Bolton himself simultaneously celebrated "Spain's frontiering genius," while suggesting that Mexican "half-breeds—mestizoes or mulattoes" were naturally vicious and unruly. In Bolton's day, social scientists who studied living Mexican Americans explained the group's relative poverty as a pathological condition caused by cultural deficiencies, including passivity, laziness, and an inability to look beyond the present. At best the fantasy heritage split the history of Hispanics in the Southwest into two disconnected parts, tacitly denying Mexican Americans their historic roots in the region. At worst, it implied that long-time residents with strong Indian features, or immigrants from Mexico, were inferior aliens in a new land. (Weber 1992:354, 356)

By the late 1960s Mexican American and Anglo-American scholars were contesting Boltonian interpretations and questioning the quasi-monolithic history that had been written (Weber 1992:357). Although Weber disagrees with some of the interpretations presented by Mexican American political activists who assert that most Mexican Americans have ancient roots in the Southwest, he concurs with the more moderate view presented by Mexican American historians. That is, many Mexican Americans with strong Indian features owe their indigenous roots to the Indians of the Southwest (Gutiérrez 1991). Weber attributes the lack of knowledge on this issue to Anglo-American historians' reluctance to value the history of the Mexican Americans. Ending his critique on a positive note, Weber posits that post-Boltonian Anglo-American historians have begun to find historical value in the view introduced by Mexican American historians that many Mexican Americans are part of the indigenous peoples who have historic roots in the Southwest. According to Weber, this area needs to be researched in order to write a more accurate history of the Southwest that does not focus solely on the Spanish elite, but rather examines the social relations between the *mestizos* and the colonized Christian Indians. Once this history is reconstituted, it can then be contested, perhaps revised, and eventually accepted as historical fact.

I concur with Weber, but must add that additional research on the Mexican Americans' prehistory also needs to consider their ancient past in Europe and Africa, because Mexican Americans are a racially mixed people with a complex history of conquest. Thus, I begin with an outline of their prehistory that delineates their racial origins. The prehistorical analysis is based upon various sources, starting with nineteenth-century studies that attempted to describe the racial characteristics used to differentiate people and offer historical trajectories of the periods when contact occurred between the peoples of Europe, the New World, and Africa. Historical literature provides an overview of the peopling of Spain and the influence of the Phoenicians, Greeks, Romans, and Muslims on Spanish civilization. Archaeological and ethnohistorical studies provide information on settlement patterns in Spain, Mexico, the U.S. Southwest, and Africa. In essence, I have assembled literature that offers a composite overview of the Mexican Americans' prehistory. The analysis of the arrival of Black people in Mexico closely follows the pioneering ethnohistorical research of anthropologist Alfonso Aguirre Beltrán and those scholars who have built upon his work. The account of the Indians is limited to the cultural complexes identified by archaeologists as having significantly influenced the cultural development and social organization of Mexico and the U.S. Southwest.

Aztlán: History, Myth, or Mythologized History?

Mexican Americans are a people with a multiracial prehistorical past (Aguirre Beltrán 1946; Vigil 1984). Their White heritage began in Spain, the Indian in Mexico and the U.S. Southwest, and the Black in West Africa. Most Mexican Americans are a predominantly *mestizo* people: after Spain conquered Mexico in 1521, widespread intermixture of Spaniards and Indians occurred (Meyer and Sherman 1995:126). As David Weber notes, however, not all Mexican Americans are *mestizo*, since many Spaniards chose not to intermarry. To unravel this account I begin with an analysis of the indigenous background of Mexican Americans.

The intellectual recovery of the Mexican Americans' racial history started with the production of oral texts by working-class Mexican American college students. Exploring their indigenist roots was the primary concern of many social activists who had turned to the study of race as a means of contesting dehumanizing views that alleged that Brown people were poor because they were culturally deprived and racially inferior. They also entrenched themselves in the study of race to contest the racial aesthetics of the period, which elevated "being White" as the standard of beauty and viewed all Black and Brown phenotypes as markers of abnormality. On 31 March 1969 the Crusade for Justice, a Mexican American civil rights organization, organized the Chicano Youth Liberation Conference held in Denver, Colorado, where Alberto Baltazar Urista, professionally known as Alurista, recited the "Epic Poem of Aztlán" and introduced the seminal outline of the Mexican Americans' indigenous foundations. His poetics challenged the politics behind the racial aesthetic philosophy of the period (Keller 1972:xiii; Rendón 1971:337).

The conference was organized as a meeting place for Mexican American students to discuss how Anglo-American racism had shaped the Mexican experience in the United States. It was part of a larger national political movement—the Civil Rights Movement—in which people throughout the United States participated in hundreds of organizations to contest racial discrimination, in particular the forced social segregation of racial minorities (Omi and Winant 1994). As part of the Civil Rights Movement, Mexican Americans organized their own organizations to address the particular problems affecting their communities. Demonstrations, boycotts, strikes, and sit-ins became political vehicles that brought to national attention the Mexican-origin people's poverty level, the farm workers' struggle against unfair wages and working conditions, and perceived inequalities (e.g., police brutality, limited access to higher education, school segregation). Such ethnic consciousness was also manifested in the birth of the self-imposed label "Chicano" (Gómez-Quiñonez 1978) and the national mobilization of Mexican Americans into local and regional civil rights organizations, such as the United Farm Workers, the Alianza Federal de Pueblos Libres (Federal Alliance of Free City States), the Crusade for Justice, and the Brown Berets. The Chicano Movement was the national term used for the political organizations founded by Mexican Americans.

The Chicano Youth Liberation Conference was instrumental in mobilizing student groups to political action: when students returned to their colleges and communities, they energized local civic organizations. The conference was also instrumental in the production of historical knowledge. By the time of the Chicano Movement, Mexican American students were aware that the poverty experienced by many members of their ethnic group was a result of multiple problems, including racism, school segregation, their social class background, the recent immigrant status of many Mexicans, and a devastating high school dropout rate (Valencia 1991). During the conference, they discussed these issues as well as strategies to engage the federal government in their resolution (Rendón 1971; Ybarra-Frausto 1978). Though mobilizing for ethnic politics was the goal of the conference, sparking the participants' sense of peoplehood was also central. When Alurista recited the "Epic Poem of Aztlán," he outlined the Mexican Americans' historic roots in Mexico and the U.S. Southwest, asserting that they were a Brown people with a long history in the Americas.

Alurista, influenced by sixteenth-century Aztec oral histories collected by Fray Diego Durán, revised and appropriated the Aztec version of Aztlán (Keller 1972). He was one of the first Chicano scholars, if not the first, to have been well versed in Pre-Columbian history. Alurista created a narrative mixed with poetry, fiction, and archaeology to give Mexican Americans a source of pride in their indigenous heritage. This was his attempt to invert the stigma attached to being a Brown people living in the United States and transform that racial heritage into a legacy of pride. It was also Alurista's attempt to dispute the myth that Mexican Americans were solely a recent immigrant group in the United States and therefore had not contributed to the growth of the nation. He asserted that the first settlers of the Americas were indigenous people and that Mexican Americans were descendants of the Indians. He claimed that thousands of years ago the ancestors of the Mexican Americans left their homeland in Aztlán, a place located somewhere in the Southwest, hidden in sands and riverbeds. By situating Aztlán in the Southwest, rather than northwest Mexico as most scholars propose (see Ganot and Peschard 1995), Alurista identified a location that fit the Mexican American experience. Mexican Americans were a people with an indigenous history in both Mexico and the United States. Sadly, after Alurista revised the Aztec origin myth, many scholars considered his historic analysis to be more fiction than fact (see Weber 1992; Ybarra-Frausto 1979).

The concept of Aztlán originated in Mexico, and since its introduction scholars have debated whether it is myth, history, or mythologized history (see Gillespie 1989; Tibón 1983). In the aftermath of the Spanish conquest of Mexico, Spanish scholars became interested in the Aztec notion of Aztlán (Gillespie 1989). During the mid-sixteenth century, the Catholic Church initiated a historical recovery project to investigate what Aztlán was about. Spanish chroniclers, working with indigenous intellectuals in what is today Mexico City, interviewed hundreds of Aztecs and asked the intellectuals to record their history. Aztlán emerged as one of the most important historical concepts. When the Aztec transmitted their accounts of Aztlán, they conceived it as reality and acknowledged it as their ancient past. They claimed that Aztlán was the place of their birth as a people. No one knew where Aztlán was located; they merely indicated to sixteenth-century cartographers that it was to the north of the Valley of Mexico (see Map 1).[2] Though several accounts of the migration out of Aztlán were recovered, all versions share the central idea of a southward migration of the Chichimec people. The Chichimec were the ancestors of many of the indigenous peoples of Mexico, including the Aztec (León-Portilla 1975).

Since the recovery of the oral testimonies, scholars have debated whether Aztlán is based on an actual event or is solely a mythologized story. The dominant perspective proposes that the journey of the Chichimec from Aztlán is based on actual events and persons (Gillespie 1989). Aztlán is perceived as a distorted historical message, however, because it has been revised over time and allegedly fictive accounts have been

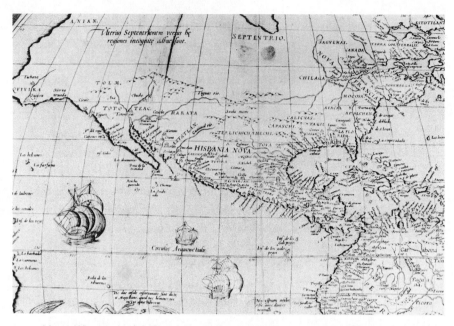

Map 1. Where Is Aztlán? Map of America by Abraham Ortelius, 1575. Courtesy of the University of Chicago Libraries, Special Collections.

added. Though some people in Mexico believe it is a myth and others that it is historical fact, today Aztlán is part of Mexico's official national folklore and indigenous history (Rodríguez Flores 1976). And the sign that Huitzilopochtli gave the Chichimec to mark the place where they should stop migrating—an eagle perched upon a cactus sprouting from a rock—became the emblem of Mexico's flag.

In a series of poems written during the 1960s Alurista strategically revised the Mexican version of Aztlán and added a concluding event that better fit the Mexican American experience in the United States (Alurista 1969, 1970, 1972; see Keller 1972). Since then many Mexican American scholars have maintained Alurista's central concepts, yet adopted their own particular interpretation of where Aztlán was located (Leal 1985; Rendón 1971; Valdez 1972). All Mexican American versions share the story of the epochs during which the Chichimec migrated south toward central Mexico. The account begins with their departure from Aztlán, after their deity Huitzilopochtli expelled them from their homeland (León-Portilla 1975; Rendón 1971; Valdez 1972). Mexican American scholars, however, disagree on whether Aztlán was located in Arizona, New Mexico, Colorado, or California. No version claims that Aztlán was located in Texas. The Chichimec migrated for four epochs and only stopped moving when Huitzilopochtli told them to settle and establish villages. When they settled, they built temples to venerate him. As they traveled through northern and central Mexico, the Chichimec met other indigenous peoples with whom they intermarried and who afterward joined them in their southward migration. Huitzilopochtli finally told them to stop migrating when they saw an eagle perched upon a cactus sprouting from a rock. This site is the current location of the center of Mexico City. Huitzilopochtli then ordered the Chichimec to settle, propagate, and establish cities.

Until this point, the Mexican American versions of Aztlán are very similar to the Mexican accounts. The Mexican American versions, however, continue the story, ending after Huitzilopochtli has destined the descendants of the Chichimec to return to Aztlán and reclaim their homeland. This notion of a return migration was introduced by Alurista in 1969 during the Chicano Youth Liberation Conference (Rendón 1971:10). At the conference Alurista poetically declared:

> In the spirit of a new people . . . we, the Chicano inhabitants and civilizers of the northern land of Aztlán, from whence came our forefathers, reclaiming the land of their birth and consecrating the determination of our people of the sun, declare that the call of our blood is our power, our responsibility, and our inevitable destiny. . . . With our heart in our hand and our hands in the soil, we declare the independence of our *mestizo* Nation. We are a bronze people with a bronze culture. Before the world, before all of North America, before all our brothers in the Bronze Continent, we are a Nation. We are a union of free pueblos. We are Aztlán. (cited in Rendón 1971:10)

At the conference Alurista subtly presented the philosophical base to argue that Mexican Americans, even if they were not born in the Southwest, had a historic claim to Aztlán as part of the original tribes to settle the Southwest. Obviously, his interpretation was a brilliant piece of political poetics, because after the conference, through word of mouth, it became part of the Mexican Americans' oral tradition (Ybarra-Frausto 1978). During political rallies, cultural festivals, and sit-ins, students used the image of Aztlán to instill a sense of pride in the audiences and to teach Mexican Americans how to respond when they were told their people were foreigners. After the conference, Alurista himself traveled to forty-one universities and community colleges reciting his "Epic Poem of Aztlán" (Keller 1972:xxix).

For many Mexican American academics, Aztlán has become a symbolic trope used to promote racial and cultural pride among college students taking courses on Mexican American studies (see Contreras 1998). Its legacy also continues in textual form: in the last two decades it has been inscribed by literary scholars and preserved for future generations to read, enjoy, and share with others (Leal 1985). Today many of Alurista's writings on Aztlán are archived at the University of Texas at Austin in the Nettie Lee Benson Latin American Collection, where I was privileged to find his original manuscript entitled "The History of Aztlán" (Alurista Box II, Part II, Folder 3). His poetic essay was written in 1969; oddly, it was never published in its entirety. Perhaps Alurista was apprehensive about being criticized for using archaeological facts incorrectly. His account is written poetically and, unlike earlier works, is anthropological in content, citing dates and locations. What is fascinating about the manuscript is the near accuracy of the events and the pioneering interconnections he makes between the prehistoric peoples and Mexican Americans. Alurista's anthropological poetics begins:

> aztlán, aztlán
> a legend of the people
> long ago
> 50,000 years ago . . .
> Embodied by the sun
> the Toltec master artists
> and laborers of earth
> meet the nomadic
> Chichimecs from Asia
> southbound following
> the great mastodon
> and other pre-historic
> game which crossed
> the Bering Straits
> (Alurista 1969:1)

Alurista then unravels events after the Chichimec arrived in the Valley of Mexico. He proposes that several centuries afterward some Chichimec groups returned to Aztlán and mixed with the peoples of the Southwest:

> the children of these
> Toltecs and Chichimecs
> the Tribal Nations of the North
> Four nations
> followed the Toltec path
> of human ways:
> the Rio Grande Nation
> the Zuñi Nation
> the Hopí Nation
> and the Pima Nation
> Four nations
> followed the Chichimec path
> of warlike ways:
> the Apache Nation
> the Ute Nation
> the Navajo Nation
> and the Comanche Nation . . .
> aztlán, aztlán
> very old dream
> of Nationhood
> North of Mexico
> in today's California,
> Arizona, New Mexico
> Colorado & Texas
> (Alurista 1969:2, 3)

Alurista's anthropological poetics advanced a seminal outline that can be of aid in unraveling the Mexican Americans' indigenous prehistory. As an anthropologist whose focus is cultural history, rather than poetics, however, I am critical of Alurista's analysis. Yet I agree with him that the Mexican Americans' indigenous past is situated both in Mexico and in the Southwest—a central historical issue that Alurista introduced and that cannot be disputed today. I will develop this central issue throughout my narrative.

My main critique of Alurista's analysis is that Mexican Americans owe their historic roots less to the preconquest migratory movements from Aztlán to Mexico and more to the subsequent Spanish invasion of the Southwest. Aztecs, Toltecs, and Chichimecs did return to the Southwest, but not in the manner Alurista proposed; sadly, they returned as conquered subjects, in a Spanish invasion launched by the royal crown and rationalized by the Catholic Church. Our historic roots are embedded in a history of conquest, when Mexican *mestizos*, Tlaxcalans, Aztecs, Otomís, and other Indians from central Mexico joined the Spanish in the conquest of the Gran Chichimeca and the Southwest. Our historic legacy in the Southwest includes conquering Indians, subduing them, lusting over indigenous women, Christianizing them, and establishing mission communities. My aim in the following historical interpretation of the Mexican Americans' indigenous antecedents is to support Alurista's assertion of the Mexican Americans' prehistoric past in Mexico and the Southwest and to show what aspects of the concept of Aztlán are supported by archaeological and ethnohistorical sources.

The Peoples of Mexico and the American Southwest

Though the concept of Aztlán accurately captures the idea of an indigenous migratory southern movement, archaeologists and ethnohistorians propose that Aztlán is about a recent past and not about the origin of the indigenous peoples in the Americas. The migratory movements contained in the account of Aztlán have been dated to approximately A.D. 925 to A.D. 1111, while the date of the arrival of the Indian peoples in the New World is much earlier (Berdan 1982:2; León-Portilla 1975:121).

Indigenous peoples began migrating from the Old World to the New World about 30,000 years ago, during the Ice Age (Fagan 1991:139; Vigil 1984:11). Scholars have classified these ancient peoples and their descendants as Indians (Brinton 1890; Fagan 1991).[3] The first people of the Americas crossed over the Bering Strait, a landmass connecting the Old and the New World. Most likely they migrated from Siberia, crossed the Bering Strait, passed through Alaska into Canada, and dispersed themselves throughout North and South America. Migratory movements from the Old World continued for close to 10,000 years (Fagan 1991:138). They stopped at the end of the Ice Age, when the Bering Strait was once again submerged.

In the Southwest and Mexico the earliest sites inhabited by humans are found in California's Mohave Desert, Lewisville, Texas, and Texpepan, a community on the outskirts of Mexico City. The sites are archaeologically labeled paleo-Indian. The Mohave Desert site dates to approximately 9000 B.C. (Aikens 1978:135), while both the Lewisville and Texpepan sites date between 11,000 B.C. and 8000 B.C. (Hester 1989b: 192; Meyer and Sherman 1995:5; Newcomb 1986:9). By 6000 B.C. paleo-Indians had spread throughout central and southern Mexico, leaving evidence of village dwellings and animal butchering sites (Fagan 1991:196). A few sites of that age have been discovered in the Southwest (see Lipe 1978:335–337), including the California sites in San Diego County and in the Santa Barbara Channel Islands (Aikens 1978:135; Forbes 1982:24–25; King 1990:30). In Texas sites with a similar antiquity are located in Lubbock, Lipscomb, Plainview, Midland, and near the Trinity River in Henderson County (Newcomb 1986:10–11). Several sites in southern Arizona have been identified, such as the Cochise cultural complex (Lipe 1978:337).

Sites in central Mexico indicate that an agricultural revolution had begun by around 5000 B.C. (Meyer and Sherman 1995:6). Cultivated corncobs were first discovered in the Tehuacán Valley. From there farming techniques diffused throughout Mexico, subsequently sparking a sedentary village lifestyle. Approximately 2,000 years later, Indians from Mexico introduced farming into the Southwest and influenced many ancient cultures to lead a sedentary lifestyle (Lipe 1978:50). If people were to be successful farmers, they had to settle down and tend their crops.

Around 1500 B.C. one group of Indians in Mexico, the Olmec, reached a sophisticated level of social organization (Vigil 1984:17). They inhabited the lowland region south of Veracruz, along the eastern coast of Mexico. The Olmec established many villages in the present states of Tabasco and Veracruz. There they built stone temples, established commercial networks, began a maritime canoe culture, and built a large pyramid in La Venta serving the surrounding population. The La Venta region is estimated to have reached a maximum population of 18,000 (Meyer and Sherman 1995:9). The Olmec also invented calendrical systems to mark religious and agricultural events as well as a system of writing and mathematics. These more developed forms of social organization were diffused by conquest or by trade to the surrounding regions, helping other groups reach a similar level of social development.

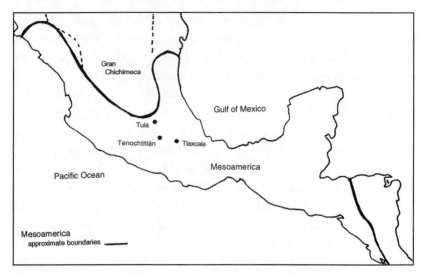

Map 2. Mesoamerica. Sources: Gillespie 1989; Meyer and Sherman 1995; Powell 1952.

After the Olmec, thousands of Indian groups participated in the making of Mesoamerica, including a zone in Mexico distinguished by archaeologists as exhibiting advanced forms of cultural organization (see Map 2). Mesoamerica has been characterized as a cultural area where the majority of indigenous societies practiced a centralized form of political government (a chieftainship, theocracy, or state system). There it was common for people to establish cities or villages; build pyramids, temples, altars, houses, bureaucratic centers, walkways, and ball courts; and practice large-scale agriculture. These communities were also socially stratified according to occupation, gender, age, and ancestral lineage. This level of social organization, however, coexisted with less highly organized ones; not all groups chose to replicate a Mesoamerican lifestyle. In particular, north of the state of Hidalgo many groups did not live in permanent villages, refused to be governed by a single leader, and did not erect stone monuments (Newcomb 1986; Powell 1952; see also Spicer 1981).

By 200 B.C. the largest ancient urban center of the Americas had been founded near present Mexico City (Meyer and Sherman 1995:20). Teotihuacán covered eight square miles and consisted of avenues, plazas, markets, temples, palaces, apartment buildings, and complex drainage and agricultural systems. Elites lived in the center of the city, and commoners were dispersed in farms throughout the outskirts. Teotihuacán exported its technological and architectural knowledge to other cities through commercial networks or military conquest. By A.D. 650 Teotihuacán had 120,000 to 250,000 inhabitants (Meyer and Sherman 1995:20; Stuart 1995:8). Strangely, around this time the city was burned and abandoned. Most likely it was destroyed by powerful enemies. Its collapse contributed to the rise of other complex societies because when the city was abandoned its population dispersed. Government functionaries, priests, and artisans established new villages or settled among other people, teaching them their ways. In this manner the culture of Teotihuacán was transported throughout Mexico. While Teotihuacán rose and fell, other indigenous peoples established similar complex societies in Oaxaca, Cholula, and various places on the Yucatán Peninsula (Gutiérrez 1992; Meyer and Sherman 1995; Tibón 1983). Among these people were the Maya, Zapotec, Cholulan, and Mixtec. They built impressive cities, left hieroglyphic texts, practiced long-distance trade, and also conquered many of their neighboring villages.

In the Southwest, during the same time span as Teotihuacán, around 200 B.C. to 300 B.C., the Hohokam, a people living in present Sonora, Mexico, migrated further north and settled in southern Arizona (Lipe 1978:342; Molitor 1981:32).[4] They became an influential culture, introducing irrigation techniques and contributing to the technological improvement of the region's agricultural production. At several sites, including Snaketown in Arizona, they introduced Mexican material cultural traits such as mirrors, conch shells, copper bells, formalized town plans, and ball courts (Kelley 1995; Reyman 1995). After the Hohokam peoples entered the Southwest, they dispersed throughout New Mexico and Arizona, where they constructed irrigation ditches, manufactured pottery, erected pit houses on raised superstructures, and built adobe houses above ground (Fish, Fish, and Madsen 1992; Haury 1992b; Molitor 1981).

Approximately a century after the Hohokam entered the Southwest, the Mogollon people settled north of them, inhabiting several sites in Arizona and northern New Mexico (Haury 1992a; Lipe 1978). There they established cultural complexes that were clearly distinct from the Hohokam or Mesoamerican. Their material culture was distinguished by the use of pit houses, kivas, burial traditions, and several ceramic traditions. They did adopt farming techniques from the Hohokam, however, and contributed to the growth of sedentary village life. A few centuries later, the Anasazi migrated to the Southwest, settling north of the Mogollon (Fagan 1991; Lipe 1978). Anasazi sites have been found in northern New Mexico, southwest Colorado, southeast Utah, and northeast Arizona. In these sites people had domesticated turkeys and adopted farming either from the Hohokam or from the Mogollon. They established villages and erected ceremonial centers and irrigation systems. There is also strong evidence supporting the hypothesis that they established long-distance trade with Indians from central Mexico (Fagan 1991; Kelley 1995; Lipe 1978). Mesoamerican copper bells, conch shells, ceramics, and mirrors have been found in Anasazi sites.

In New Mexico the Anasazi cultural complex was widely dispersed, and within a few centuries of their arrival they came to dominate their Mogollon neighbors (Dean 1992; Haury 1992d; LeBlanc 1992). This led to regional consolidation and the concentration of large urban centers ranging in size from 2,000 to 200 inhabitants (Fagan 1991; Haury 1992c, 1992d). Between A.D. 1100 and A.D. 1450, however, the Hohokam and Anasazi-Mogollon cultural complexes began to break down into several ethnic subdivisions and new art forms, pottery styles, and subsistence traditions appeared (Fish, Fish, and Madsen 1992:19; Forbes 1982:26; Lipe 1978:357). The Pima and Papago emerged from the Hohokam, and the Western Pueblo from the Mogollon or the Anasazi.[5]

During this period, a subdivision of the Hohokam or Mogollon migrated into Texas. The Jumano Indians, who are believed to be related to a village-dwelling culture, appeared in Texas in approximately A.D. 1000 to A.D. 1250 and settled in the area from El Paso to Big Bend (Haury 1992a:403; Newcomb 1986:230). They also settled along the Río Conchos in Chihuahua, Mexico. Since divisions of the Jumano practiced farming and a sedentary lifestyle, archaeologists propose that they must have migrated from New Mexico or Arizona, where such a lifestyle was common.[6] Many Jumano Indians established farming villages throughout southwestern Texas and constructed adobe houses with roofs and wall frames made out of wood (Morfí 1780, 1935; Newcomb 1986; Spicer 1981). They also produced various ceramic traditions for utilitarian and luxury consumption. To supplement their harvests, these Jumano groups hunted animals for food and used skins for clothing. Their villages were governed by a chief. Though many Jumano groups were farmers, they coexisted with Jumano groups that were nomadic and had less complex forms of social organization. Most prehistoric peoples in Texas left scant trace of their material culture, and thus very little is known about them (Hester 1989a). Most of the information we have on the Indians of Texas dates to the historic period and is based on sixteenth-century Spanish accounts.

In contrast to the scarce information on the material culture of the pre-historic peoples of Texas, cultural complexes have been well documented in California, indicating that during prehistoric times it was the most widely populated territory in the Southwest (Aikens 1978; Forbes 1982; Heizer and Almquist 1977). Parts of present San Diego County have been continuously populated since around 6000 B.C. and the Santa Barbara Channel Islands for nearly as long (Aikens 1978:134, 148; Fagan 1991:196; Forbes 1982:22).

One of the largest prehistorical cultural complexes of California was that of the Hokan. Due to differences found in their material culture, the Hokan are subdivided into several ethnic subdivisions. The largest sub-division was the Chumash, who inhabited hundreds of villages through-out present Santa Barbara, Ventura, and Santa Maria counties. There were eight Chumash subdivisions: Barbareño, Cuyama, Emigdiano, Island Chumash (San Miguel, Santa Rosa, and Santa Cruz Islands), Obispeño, Purisimeño, Santa Inés, and Ventureño (King 1990; Swanton 1984). Doubts have been raised, however, regarding the kinship relationship of the Island Chumash, because they practiced a specialized maritime subsistence lifestyle that emphasized fishing and sea mammal hunting, in contrast to the subsistence patterns of the inland Chumash (Fagan 1991; Forbes 1982). The Chumash who occupied the inland territories sub-sisted on the animals they hunted and the seeds and roots they gathered. Neither group farmed. Archaeologists estimate that before the arrival of the Europeans, the Island Chumash numbered 3,000, while the rest of the Chumash ranged from 15,000 to 30,000 (Aikens 1978; Fagan 1991; Forbes 1982).

Though the Chumash have been identified as one of the first groups to settle in California, the date and place of entry are uncertain. One hypothesis challenging the Hokan classificatory scheme proposes that the Chumash were an ethnic subdivision of the Hohokam or some other northern Mexico cultural group (Castetter and Bell 1951; Spicer 1981; Spier 1933; Swanton 1984). This hypothesis is supported by archaeologi-cal data indicating that the Chumash exhibited northern Mexican Indian traits (e.g., in their chieftain political structure, art forms, and bone and wood artifacts). A competing hypothesis proposes that the Mexican traits must be attributed to the effects of trade or intermarriage (Fagan 1991; Forbes 1982). The eight subdivisions of the Chumash may not share a common ancestral prehistory, as only the Island Chumash left material remains dating to 6000 B.C. (Aikens 1978:134). These questions about the origins of the Chumash remain for future scholars to examine. Although this prehistory needs to be explored, we do know that some of the oldest prehistoric remains are found in the islands inhabited by the Chumash.

The Shoshone are another major cultural group with ancient historic roots in California (Hurtado 1988; Steward 1933). Several ethnic subdivisions were spread throughout eastern California. Two competing hypotheses attempt to explain the Shoshone settlement patterns. One posits that they migrated from northern Mexico approximately 3,000 years ago and settled along the present Arizona-Sonora border (Fowler 1972:110; Lamb 1958:98–99). Approximately a thousand years later they settled in Utah and California (Aikens 1978; Fowler 1972; Lamb 1958, 1964). This hypothesis is supported by seventeenth-century Spanish accounts, which reported that most Shoshone groups in California spoke an Uto-Aztecan language similar to the languages spoken in central Mexico (Steward 1933). The alternate hypothesis concurs on their date of arrival in California, but posits that they migrated from the central or northern plains of the United States rather than from Mexico (Simpson 1986). This hypothesis is supported by similar cultural complexes yielding earlier dates that have been found in Wyoming, Montana, Idaho, Utah, Nevada, and Oregon (Aikens 1978).[7]

The Penutian cultural complex was spread throughout northern and central California (Costello and Hornbeck 1989; Hurtado 1988). They entered California around 2500 B.C. (Fagan 1991:207). Many ethnic subdivisions of the Penutian family practiced a lifeway based on hunting and gathering and did not recognize a central leader (Aikens 1978). Most groups who inhabited the coast, however, lived in sedentary villages and practiced a more complex form of social organization. They subsisted on fishing, practiced burial ceremonies, and were governed by chiefs.

The archaeological data found in Mexico and the Southwest indicate that these areas were populated as early as 11,000 B.C. (Hester 1989b:192; Meyer and Sherman 1995:5; Newcomb 1986:9). Though migration patterns in Mexico and the Southwest have been difficult to trace and are currently the center of archaeological debates, scholars agree that indigenous groups moved south. The questions of where they came from and what relations evolved between different groups are under investigation. What is certain is that farming first appeared in central Mexico and was later diffused into northern Mexico and finally into the southwestern United States. Villages were established throughout both zones, while urban centers were more common in Mesoamerica. Long-distance trade developed between the peoples of Mexico and the Southwest after the Hohokam appeared there, but it probably was minimal, because only a few Mexican artifacts have been found in southwestern villages. The exact kinship connections between the peoples of the Southwest and Mexico are uncertain.

The Chichimec and the Aztec

Outside of the borders of Mesoamerica, most of the land north of present Mexico has been labeled the Gran Chichimeca. Thousands of groups inhabited this region, and the majority of them were Chichimec.[8] On the periphery of Mesoamerica, where the present states of Zacatecas and Durango lie, a cultural complex belonging to some of the earliest Chichimec peoples has been identified. Archaeologists call this cultural complex Chalchihuites and date it to around A.D. 200 (Kelley and Kelley 1971:3). By A.D. 950 the number of Chalchihuites sites radically declined. This reduction has been attributed to outmigration and to their absorption within other indigenous societies (ibid., 176). Though many Chichimec people remained in Zacatecas and Durango, others continued a southward migration (Rodríguez Flores 1976).

Around the same time that Chalchihuites sites decrease, a group of Chichimec Indians appeared in the Valley of Mexico, led by Mixcóatl. This branch of the Chichimec has been distinguished as the Toltec-Chichimec (Meyer and Sherman 1995). They settled a few miles north of the ancient city of Teotihuacán. While they were there, they learned from the descendants of the Teotihuacán people their ceramic art, philosophy, astronomy, architectural knowledge, and in particular hieroglyphic and iconographic writing. After living nearly twenty years near Teotihuacán, Mixcóatl's people were expelled for being hostile and barbarian intruders. They departed to the north and built their own community, incorporating the skills they had learned. The Toltec-Chichimec called their new settlement Tula and erected temples, pyramids, bureaucratic offices, and enormous statues called butterfly warriors to venerate their deity Quetzalcoatl. Glyphic texts were inscribed on buildings and monuments. The city did not last long; a century later, the inhabitants abandoned it and moved on, thus continuing a migratory pattern.

The fate of the people from Tula is uncertain. Archaeologists propose that some migrated north, while another branch sailed south, landing in the Yucatán Peninsula and eventually conquering a group of Maya people (Adams 1991; Meyer and Sherman 1995). Those who settled among the Maya are believed to have contributed to the renaissance of Chichén Itzá. Maya mythology as well as wall paintings in Chichén Itzá depicting a Toltec-Chichimec invasion support this theory. Toltec-Chichimec iconography and three-dimensional bas-relief sculptures found in Chichén Itzá offer further supporting evidence (Gillespie 1989; see also Tibón 1983). Though convincing data support the Maya-Toltec-Chichimec connections, archaeologists have been unable to prove or disprove this claim, and the debate continues. Similar diffusionist hypotheses have been advanced about other peoples in the Valley of Mexico, Veracruz, and Michoacán (Tibón 1983).

What is historically certain is that a Chichimec group called the Mexica claimed their homeland was Aztlán and identified the Toltec-Chichimec as their ancestors. The Mexica were one of the seven Chichimec tribes of northern Mexico that migrated south and settled in the Valley of Mexico in approximately A.D. 1111 (Meyer and Sherman 1995:56). Most of the fertile land was already inhabited by many peoples organized into kingdoms, and the Mexica were treated as intruders. They were allowed to settle in Chapultepec, but their neighbors soon expelled them for their allegedly barbarous ways. They collected their belongings and sought refuge in the Kingdom of Chulhuacán (Gillespie 1989). The Chulhuacán people protected them because they acknowledged a distant kin relation, and their king allowed them to settle in Tizaapan. In return for this hospitality the Mexica were expected to act as mercenaries and attack the enemies of the Kingdom of Chulhuacán. Over several generations the military efficiency of the Mexica became well known, which led to their acceptance in the area. Mexica warriors began to marry members of the royal families of the Valley.

Mexica prestige continued to rise, and around A.D. 1325 Achitometl, king of Chulhuacán, allowed the leader of the Mexica, Tonachca, to marry his daughter Yaocihuatl (Berdan 1982:7). In this way, Tonachca became part of the royal family of Chulhuacán. Achitometl claimed to be a direct descendant of the last Toltec-Chichimec king of Tula. Once Yaocihuatl had been given to Tonachca, a Mexica priest received a vision from Huitzilopochtli ordering them to kill her and remove her skin from her body. Afterward her father was asked to join Tenochca and Yaocihuatl in a ceremony. To Achitometl's shock, a priest dressed in his daughter's skin appeared and danced in front of him. Horrified by the barbarous cruelty committed against his daughter, Achitometl immediately expelled the Mexica from Tizaapan. They refused to leave the Valley and instead settled in the middle of Lake Texcoco, on uninhabited land infested with snakes and insects. To the surprise of their neighbors, the Mexica adapted and incorporated snakes and insects as part of their basic cuisine. This further stigmatized them, yet ironically it also aided them, because they became a feared people. The Mexica flourished, increasing their population and continuing to strengthen their military.

Knowing they were feared and unwelcome in the Valley, the Mexica began a war of conquest, attacking their neighbors. By A.D. 1430 they had formed alliances with the kingdoms of Texcoco and Tlacopan (Berdan 1982:10). With this military aid, the Mexica conquered the entire Valley. Those conquered kingdoms who vowed allegiance to the Mexica were incorporated as allies and came to constitute a confederacy of states which subsequently became the Aztec Empire. The Mexica became the ruling kingdom and their king the emperor. Each allied kingdom was allowed to retain its king, but was obliged to follow the rules of the Mexica, participate in the confederacy's military, and pay tribute. After the Mexica subdued their neighbors, they embarked on the conquest of the peoples outside the Valley of Mexico.

Anthropologist Susan Gillespie (1989) argues in *The Aztec Kings: The Construction of Rulership in Mexica History* that when the Mexica ascended to power they removed the stigma of their humble roots by appropriating the account of Aztlán, which was believed to be the homeland of some of the most powerful groups in the Valley of Mexico.[9] She attributes the survival of the oral account of Aztlán to the Aztec. Under Aztec rule it became part of the official history of the people of the Aztec Empire.

There is much more to say about Aztlán, but I must stop here. For me personally, Aztlán has been an ideological site since I was a child, although I am still undecided about whether it is a mythological or historical location. I do know that it has given me a source of pride and is part of my oral tradition that was handed down to me by my brother, Blas

Menchaca, who was very active in the Chicano Movement. Blas, who was present at several of Alurista's poetry readings, shared the account of Aztlán as a historical fact. Though I learned the Chicano version from my brother, my parents taught me that Aztlán was a myth. To them, Aztlán was a story about unity and nationhood. To Blas, Aztlán was one of the most important public historical memories that Spain had been unable to erase after defeating the Aztec. My parents disagreed and did not view Spaniards in the same way. On the contrary, they taught me to value my White heritage—which came from Spain.

Spain: A History of Whiteness?

Spaniards traditionally have been classified as White. This point is extremely significant in analyzing the Mexican Americans' racial history. Throughout history the Mexican Americans' Spanish ancestry protected them many times from the full impact of racial discrimination because they were part White.

The racial schema of the peoples of the world was introduced in 1684 (Banton and Harwood 1975:15). By the early 1700s scholars classified the native inhabitants of Europe as Caucasian, the term used to refer to people with White skin (with brown, yellow, or rosy undertones), a narrow and prominent nose, a prognathic (protruding) or orthognathic (straight) jaw, and blond or brunet hair (Brinton 1890; Stanton 1966). Caucasian peoples were subdivided into four family stocks: Teutonic-Aryan, Cymric, Celtic, and Euscarian (Bravo Lira 1970; Brinton 1890; Feagin and Feagin 1999; Stanton 1966). The four families exhibited variations in appearance, yet preserved the aforementioned color and facial structure. The Teutonic-Aryan people were credited with having been the first settlers of northern Europe (Gossett 1977; Hechter 1977; Howe 1989). The Celtic people were indigenous to Ireland and England and the Cymric and Celtic people to parts of France and the border of northern Spain. The Euscarians were indigenous to central Spain and to parts of France, Italy, and Greece.

During the late eighteenth century, the term "Caucasian" fell out of popular academic use and was often replaced by the term "White" (see Brinton 1890; Stanton 1966). Many scholars preferred to use skin color as a racial classifier because the term "Caucasian" had come under scrutiny when scholars charged that its correct linguistic definition applied to a hybrid Asian and White people. Linguistic disagreements over which word was more appropriate to describe the indigenous peoples of Europe persisted. It was generally accepted, however, that the term "Caucasian" metaphorically referred to people who had no Black, Indian, or Asian ancestors, such as the four family stocks indigenous to Europe. "White" became a more inclusive term applied to the family stocks indigenous to Europe and to the Hamitic and Semitic peoples who were also part of these subdivisions, but were racially mixed.

The flexible definition that scholars assigned to the term "White" continues in use today (Feagin and Feagin 1999). Within the legal domain, however, each country encodes its own definition based on the meaning accorded to biological characteristics (Omi and Winant 1994). In the United States identifying people on the basis of race continues for various academic and legal record-keeping purposes. Over the generations the legal intent for using racial categories has varied, ranging from denying people citizenship to enumerating the U.S. population for census purposes. Mexican Americans are one of the peoples of the world who are of mixed racial origins. This racial background has historically placed Mexican Americans and their ancestors in ambiguous social and legal positions—they are discriminated against because they are only partly White, yet they have been spared the full impact of discrimination because they descend from Spaniards, one of the White peoples of Europe.

Spain and Portugal today occupy the Iberian Peninsula, which was first populated by Tartessians. The ethnic affiliations of the Tartessians are unknown; scholars disagree as to whether they entered the Iberian Peninsula from Asia, North Africa, or other parts of Europe. Though the Tartessians' point of origin is uncertain, eighteenth-century scholars overwhelmingly proposed that they must have been White and thus classified them as Euscarian. This hypothesis is supported by Phoenician inscriptions on ceramics and hieroglyphic texts (Blazquez 1975). Their date of arrival in the peninsula is also uncertain, although it is estimated to have taken place between 40,000 B.C. and 20,000 B.C. (Altamira 1988:71; Vinces Vives 1972:2). About 7000 B.C. the Tartessians' social organization began to change radically (Vinces Vives 1972:6). They spread throughout the peninsula, and most abandoned their cave dwellings in favor of huts. In a few areas some people began farming and preferred a sedentary village life over nomadism. Accompanying this shift was the production of ceramics, arrows, and lances. During the same period, maritime cultures with a similar sedentary village lifestyle flourished along the coast. By 2500 B.C. the coastal regions of Catalonia, Valencia, and Andalusia exhibited the most complex forms of social organization (Vinces Vives 1972:8). Chieftainship (leadership by one individual) became the standard form of political governance, which in turn stimulated many technological innovations, such as the large-scale construction of stone buildings with iconographic art and a metal tool industry (e.g., hatchets, knives, lances, and swords).

About 1000 B.C. to 500 B.C. Iberians and Basques entered the peninsula (Altamira 1988:73; Bravo Lira 1970:30).[10] They have been classified as part of the Euscarian stock (Lynch 1964; Nott and Gliddon 1857). Bernardino Bravo Lira (1970), however, questions this classification, arguing that the Basques came from Morocco in North Africa, a highly diversified region of racially mixed Euscarian and Hamitic groups. Hamitics were classified by eighteenth-century scholars as a mixed stock branching from Euscarian and Black peoples. Bravo Lira's hypothesis is based upon Phoenician legal records describing the Basques as a heterogeneous people. Part of the population was fair-skinned, while others were dark, indicating a Black racial influence.

The Iberians moved throughout the peninsula. Many settled near Tartessian villages, where intermarriage commonly took place. In Spain's present southern region of Andalusia, Iberians built fortified cities, wove fine textiles, produced ceramics, and introduced new agricultural techniques. Many Tartessian villages began adopting their Iberian neighbors' cultural traditions (Blazquez 1975; Bravo Lira 1970; Carpenter 1925). Unlike the Iberians, the Basques retained their distance from the Tartessians and Iberians, finally settling in northeastern Spain (Bravo Lira 1970; Brinton 1890; Lynch 1964).

During this same period, Phoenician soldiers conquered many Tartessian villages along the southern and eastern coasts and established military posts that lasted for nearly 400 years (Blazquez 1975). Local chiefs were allowed to retain power as long as they paid tribute and did not revolt. The Phoenicians influenced architecture and textile production in Cádiz as well as the artistic production of jewelry and ceramics; they also introduced hieroglyphic writing and a monetary exchange system. Their hieroglyphic writings contain historical information on the populations living in southern and eastern Spain, in particular drawings of the Tartessians (Altamira 1988; Blazquez 1975). Though their presence in Spain was long-lasting, the Phoenicians, who have been classified as Hamitic (Brinton 1890), did not intermarry with the local inhabitants in great numbers.

In 600 B.C. the Phoenicians were overthrown by their subjects; within a few years, the Greeks conquered the eastern coast as well as several inland Tartessian villages (Altamira 1988:73). Along the eastern coast they established military outposts (Carpenter 1925). Rhys Carpenter (1925) and Bernardino Bravo Lira (1970) propose that intermarriage between the Greeks and the Tartessians was highly unlikely, as the new invaders' purpose was to extract tribute and not to mix with the natives. Scholars have concluded that the Greeks belonged to the Euscarian stock; thus they would not have introduced any new racial mixture into the peninsula even if they did intermarry with the local population (Brinton 1890; Nott and Gliddon 1857). After less than forty years of domination, the Greeks were defeated by Tartessian chieftains and forced to leave. They had a radical influence on the conquered zones, however, giving these regions a distinct Hellenic cultural style in sculptures, ceramics, mosaic paintings, and architecture (Altamira 1988; Carpenter 1925), especially in Valencia (Wetterau 1994). Greek theater was also introduced.

Following the Greeks' exodus, the Celtic people arrived, not as conquerors but as refugees. Most Celtic groups came from present-day England (Altamira 1988; Wetterau 1994), pushed out of their homeland by a Teutonic invasion. Celtic groups first settled in northern Spain between Basque and Iberian villages (Bravo Lira 1970). Peaceful alliances evolved between Iberian and Celtic villagers, leading to large-scale intermarriage and eventually influencing the culture of many Iberian villages. The Celtic people did not intermarry with the Tartessians or the Basques in any significant numbers.

In approximately 236 B.C. the Iberian Peninsula was once again invaded (Altamira 1988:82; Livermore 1971:11). The southern and eastern coasts came under the military control of Carthaginian groups from present-day Morocco. The Carthaginians were ousted by Romans a few decades later. Roman rule lasted for over 600 years (Bravo Lira 1970; Fletcher 1992; Glick 1979). The Romans, a Euscarian people, conquered most of the peninsula, but intermarriage with the local population was uncommon. The Romans instituted structural changes, the most important modification being a centralized form of government and a standard legal system in the areas of local government, property, marriage, and inheritance. Local chiefs were allowed to retain control of their villages as long as they adopted Roman laws, pledged allegiance, and paid tribute to the emperor. Many chiefs revolted and subsequently lost their power; their positions were awarded to loyal chiefs. This led to political centralization of larger regions under the control of fewer chiefs (Bravo Lira 1970).

The political innovations introduced by the Romans were accompanied by a rigid tax system. Chiefs were expected to collect a set quota irrespective of the conquered subjects' ability to pay tribute. During times of drought or when the harvest seasons were poor, the Romans did not lower their quotas, and people were left near starvation. This inhumane practice generated intolerable economic stress and eventually sparked political turmoil. In A.D. 409 the peoples of the peninsula revolted, with the assistance of their new neighbors the Visigoths; together they overthrew the Romans (Altamira 1988:96; Bravo Lira 1970:125). The Visigoths had recently entered the peninsula as part of a military movement to challenge Roman rule in Europe (Altamira 1988; Bravo Lira 1970; Vinces Vives 1972). They offered military assistance to local chiefs who changed allegiances and accepted Visigoth rule. In exchange the local leaders were promised greater autonomy and reduced taxes. In the southern and coastal regions many local chiefs changed allegiances, whereas in the central and northern regions most Tartessian and Basque chiefs resisted.

During the next three hundred years, the Visigoths' hold over the peninsula spread, and most villages fell under their rule. Thousands of Visigoths left Germany and settled in the occupied zones. Unlike the Romans, who had retained their social distance from the indigenous inhabitants, the Visigoths intermarried with the locals, adding to the peninsula's racial mixture (Bravo Lira 1970). Though most Visigoths have been classified as Teutonic-Aryan, they were diverse; some of the migrating peoples had Asian ancestors (Brinton 1890; Nott and Gliddon 1854).

In A.D. 711 Visigoth political hegemony was challenged by several Muslim dynasties from North Africa (Altamira 1988:114; Bravo Lira 1970: 176). These people have been classified as Semitic and Hamitic. The Hamitic stock is a Euscarian and Black blend and the Semitic is White with Black and Asian influences. Though Muslim peoples, under the leadership of the Syrians, took control of the southern region, the Basque northeast and the Tartessian central regions remained independent.[11] Continuous political battles against Muslim rule forced Basque and Tartessian chiefs to consolidate tribal alliances and unify regions. By A.D. 1085 the threat of a Muslim invasion sparked by the military intrusion of the Moroccan Almoravid Dynasty further accelerated the consolidation of regions. Navarre, Castile, Portugal, León, Valencia, Catalonia, Aragon, Asturias, and Vizcaya evolved into fortified kingdoms (see Glick 1979:32–46), with Aragon, Castile, and Portugal emerging as the most powerful ones. Though kingdoms arose throughout Spain, the Almoravid Dynasty entrenched itself in the southern region, further strengthening the Muslim presence in Andalusia and Granada.

In 1469 Queen Isabella of Castile married King Ferdinand of Aragon and united their kingdoms, making them the most powerful monarchs of the Iberian Peninsula (Lynch 1964:1). Their marriage led to the unification of the kingdoms of Castile, Aragon, Catalonia, Valencia, and León into the Empire of Spain.[12] The centralization of power under imperial rule resulted in a powerful military consolidation. In 1492 Queen Isabella and King Ferdinand defeated the Muslims in the battle over Granada and ended their rule. The southern region was immediately annexed to the Spanish Empire (ibid., 19).

Although Muslims lost economic and political power, the crown allowed them to remain in their homes if they converted to Christianity.[13] Most people refused to abandon their Islamic faith and were soon expelled to Morocco. The refugees settled in the present cities of Tangiers and Rabat. Those who remained behind were predominantly part of the gentry and chose not to flee in order to retain their estates.[14] Though the lands of converted Muslims were to remain in their hands, within a few generations they lost most property through an unfair tax system. Nonetheless, in Granada a hybrid Castilian-Muslim culture evolved, becoming evident in architecture, cuisine, and music.[15]

The same year the Muslims were defeated, Queen Isabella commissioned Christopher Columbus to explore and conquer new lands in her name and on behalf of the Catholic Church. Columbus's voyage proved to be the most important event of that century and perhaps of the millennium. On his voyage Columbus encountered the peoples of the Caribbean and led the pathway to interaction with the peoples of Mexico and Latin America. For Spain the discovery of the Americas led to economic prosperity, but for the people of the Americas it marked the demise of their civilizations and a legacy of discrimination based on racial difference. Thousands of Spaniards crossed the Atlantic in search of wealth and land.

A few years after Columbus's voyage to the Caribbean Islands, Cuba became Spain's colonial center in the New World and Diego Velázquez was appointed as its governor. From Cuba the sea voyage explorations of Mexico were launched. Francisco Hernández de Córdoba reached the Yucatán Peninsula in 1517 (Díaz del Castillo 1963:17). Two years later Velázquez commissioned Hernán Cortés to explore Mexico and to conquer the Indians (ibid., 57). Cortés and his army of approximately 508 soldiers began their trek into Mexico on the Island of Cozumel, near the tip of the Yucatán Peninsula, and moved by sea and land throughout the eastern coast. Within a year, Cortés was joined by Captain Pánfilo Narváez and 1,400 men sent by Velázquez to take command of the military conquest of Mexico.

After many battles and coerced treaties, the Spanish *conquistadores* reached Tenochtitlán, the capital of the Aztec Empire, on 8 November 1519 (ibid., 219). By then Cortés had solicited the alliance of the most powerful enemies of the Aztec, the Tlaxcalans, who lived about 100 miles to the south. When Cortés's army arrived in Tenochtitlán, the Aztec emperor Moctezuma Xocoyotzin ordered that they be treated cordially. They were given gifts and comfortable quarters. Relations began to worsen after Moctezuma's generals decided that Cortés was a military threat. Approximately eight months later, the Aztec military conspired and rebelled against Moctezuma. They attacked and forced the Spanish to retreat to Tlaxcala. Several months later, Cortés and his captains returned, fortified by an army of Tlaxcalan soldiers. They attempted the siege of Tenochtitlán, but were repeatedly defeated. After approximately a year of ongoing battles, Cortés's army and 10,000 to 15,000 Tlaxcalan warriors defeated the Aztec, and Tenochtitlán fell on 13 August 1521 (Meyer and Sherman 1995:126, 128; cf. Díaz del Castillo 1963:326).

This event changed the course of history: the Spanish Empire was now successfully entrenched in building a colony. To do so, it was necessary to send thousands of Spaniards and a sizable slave population. Nearly 200,000 Black slaves from Africa were exported to assist in the restructuring of Mexico (Aguirre Beltrán 1944:431). This Black population was comparable to the number of migrants from Spain.

West African Heritage: The Malinké

Mexico's participation in the slave trade peaked between 1542 and 1650 (Aguirre Beltrán 1946:10–39).[16] The exact number of Black people brought from Africa is uncertain because the count of slaves was based on their health and age. A healthy adult was counted as one piece, children as one-quarter piece, and others were counted on the basis of a full piece depending on their health and whether their bodies were undamaged (Cortes 1964). Estimates of the number of Black slaves introduced to Mexico range from 150,000 to approximately 200,000 (Aguirre Beltrán 1944:431; cf. Meyer and Sherman 1995:215).

Registries indicate that throughout Mexico's participation in the slave trade the majority of slaves were Malinkés from the Kingdom of Mali and spoke the Mandé-Tan language (Aguirre Beltrán 1946; Thornton 1996). Mali was located on the inland coast of West Africa. Because the primary function of slaves in Mexico was to perform domestic duties and serve in occupations in the cities (Cope 1994; Seed 1988), Spaniards preferred to import Malinké slaves.[17] In particular, they preferred slaves trained in the North African island slave factories of Cape Verde and San Tomé. Though the Spanish recorded linguistic variances among Malinké captives, noting that slaves spoke different versions of Mandé, people who spoke similar languages (such as the Soninké of Songhay, who spoke Mandé-Tamu) were often registered as Malinké. Throughout the sixteenth and seventeenth centuries the Malinké continued to be Mexico's main slave source; however, Wolof and Soso slaves also began to appear in large numbers during the 1600s (Palacios 1988). These two peoples were also from West Africa and lived in close proximity to the Malinké. By the 1700s, when the main source of slaves shipped to Latin America shifted to the African Congo, in particular present Angola, Mexico's participation in the slave trade had nearly ceased; less than 3,800 Bantu slaves arrived in Mexico (Palmer 1981:104).

West Africa

The Malinké are a Black people indigenous to West Africa (Levtzion 1973; Stocking 1968). The first written accounts of the Malinké date to approximately A.D. 800, when North African Muslim scholars wrote about the

Kingdom of Ghana and the peoples of West Africa (Levtzion 1973; Oliver and Fagan 1975). Though Ghana is believed to have been the first West African society that evolved into a kingdom, it benefited from the technological innovations of earlier societies.

Archaeologists propose that agriculture was first practiced in West Africa by 2000 B.C. (Oliver and Fagan 1975:19). The technology to cultivate crops may have been diffused from northeast Africa, near the Nile River region, as agriculture was practiced there over 4,000 years earlier (Desmond 1973:54).[18] Agriculture may have developed independently in West Africa, however. The first farmers in the area were the Kintampoo people. Though they lived in the same region where the kingdoms of Ghana and Mali arose thousands of years later, it is uncertain if they were ancestors of the Malinké. The Kintampoo people introduced innovations to this part of West Africa: they domesticated cattle and goats, developed a microlithic axe/tool technology, lived in mud houses, and occupied permanent settlements (Oliver and Fagan 1975).

Around 1000 B.C. another region in West Africa exhibited similar forms of social organization (McIntosh 1995:377). Near the coast of the Upper Guinea River and north of the Senegal River, the Tichitt people manufactured pottery, cultivated plants, performed burial ceremonies, and developed a subsistence-base herding economy. By A.D. 100 farming and a subsistence herding economy had become common in West Africa (ibid.). Most peoples also manufactured copper and metal utensils. Few were hunters and gatherers. In particular, the Upper Inland Niger Delta north of the Niger River was heavily populated. People lived in towns, which were not unified under a state system. The largest town was Jenné-jeno, which by A.D. 300 had become an important trading center for the surrounding region and had established trade relations with North and West African peoples (ibid., 377, 390, 397). Most notable were the Berber-speaking traders from the present-day North African states of Mauritania and Morocco. In A.D. 800 the Kingdom of Ghana became the most powerful state in West Africa (Levtzion 1973:22). No one knows when the peoples of Ghana organized their kingdom. Tenth-century Muslim scholar Muhammad ibn Yūsuf al-Warrāq wrote that North African Berbers were told by people from Ghana that eight generations of kings had ruled Ghana before that time (Levtzion 1973).

The Soninké were the ruling ethnic group of Ghana. A confederacy of Soninké chiefs controlled a region extending from the bend of the

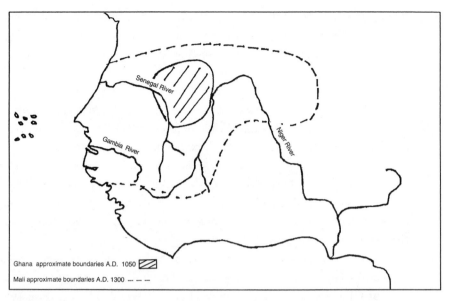

Map 3. Ghana A.D. 1050 and Mali A.D. 1300. Sources: Cortes 1964; McIntosh 1995; Oliver and Fagan 1975; Thornton 1996.

Niger to the headwaters of the Senegal (ibid., 2; see Map 3). The Malinké were ruled by Soninké chiefs and lived in villages dispersed between Soninké settlements. They were also forced to pay tribute. Co-existing with the Kingdom of Ghana were the neighboring kingdoms of Song-hay and Kanem. Songhay was also a Soninké kingdom, while the Sao lived in Kanem. These kingdoms were not as powerful and experienced political flux when they were conquered by Ghana. Songhay and Kanem retained independence most of the time, but many villages were unable to resist domination and were continuously forced to pay tribute to Ghana. The Wolof and Fulani, who lived south of Ghana in the Kingdom of Takrur, were able to maintain their independence, however (Levtzion 1973; Oliver and Fagan 1975). Jenné-jeno and most of the towns in the Upper Niger Inland Delta also retained their independence.

Scholars have attributed Ghana's political hegemony to the rulers' ability to unify Soninké villages and maintain a cohesive confederacy of chiefs under the command of one king. Ongoing raids launched by North African Berbers searching for gold and slaves also served to maintain Ghana's unification. Though many North African groups raided the kingdom throughout its existence, Ghana developed alliances with one

Berber people—the Magrib. Many Magrib Berbers established trade relations with Ghana chiefs and lived among their allies. Several trading posts were established in the Soninké villages near Kumbí, the main center of Ghana, as well as in the south and north of the Gambia River (Levtzion 1973:24, 28, 104). Other major Ghana trading posts included Timbuktu, Wagadugu, Gundiuru, and Awdaghustic. Magrib Berbers traded horses, brass, copper, glassware, beads, leather, textiles, tailored clothing, and preserved food to the Soninké in exchange for gold, ivory, cloth, pepper, kola nuts, and sometimes slaves. In these trading centers it became common for Magrib Berbers to marry Soninké women. Furthermore, the alliances between Ghana chiefs and Magrib Berbers helped Ghana retain its domination over Malinké and Songhay villages; when revolts erupted, the Magrib Berbers assisted their allies.

By A.D. 1076 the Magrib Berbers demanded that the Soninké people convert to Islam (Levtzion 1973: 44; Oliver and Fagan 1975:166). The king of Ghana complied, yet many villages resisted. The pressures to convert increased when Sanhaja tribes from various regions of North Africa united in a religious movement to convert people to Islam and attack those who resisted. The Sanhaja, like the Berbers, were a racially mixed Hamitic people, who were unified under the religious Almoravid Movement, centered in Morocco. Unlike the Magrib Berbers, the Sanhaja were enemies of Ghana and took over some of the Magrib Berber trading posts. Many Soninké villages converted to Islam as a means of averting Islamic attacks. This did not stop the Sanhaja from demanding tribute from Ghana villages and taking people as slaves. By A.D. 1250 the Almoravid Movement had provoked conflict and religious factionalism in the Kingdom of Ghana (Levtzion 1973:51; Oliver and Fagan 1975:169). Most Ghana chiefs refused to convert to Islam and instead chose to end the confederacy.

Many successor states emerged out of Ghana. By this time a large part of West Africa had converted to Islam. The Soso, who had been conquered by Ghana, emerged as the most powerful kingdom. They conquered many Soninké villages and also began preying upon the Malinké villages, which were not unified under one kingdom. Some Malinké villages were able to retain their independence and were subsequently unified by a man called Sundjata. Sundjata then launched a successful military campaign against the Soso people and replaced them as the military power of West Africa. By A.D. 1250 Malinké chiefs had united in a confederacy, with Sundjata as their king (Oliver and Fagan 1975:169). Sundjata's clan, the Keita, became the ruling family, and his confederacy evolved into the Kingdom of Mali. The power of the Kingdom of Mali expanded, and it came to encompass the entire region that had formerly been Ghana (see Map 3). The Malinké also conquered the peoples from the Kingdom of Songhay. Mali prospered as the most successful trading kingdom of the time, its main commodity being gold. Malinké villages became successful farming communities, and their towns and cities became known for textile production.

By the 1400s Mali had come under sustained attacks by rival North African groups attempting to take over trade routes (Levtzion 1973:94–96; Oliver and Fagan 1975:174–179). Mali's attention was diverted to defense, rather than maintaining control of the peoples it had conquered. The people of Songhay and others took advantage of Mali's weakened position and launched successful wars of independence. Unfortunately for Mali, these liberation movements coincided with a drought that affected many Malinké villages and thus prompted thousands of people to migrate in search of food. The Kingdom of Mali disintegrated, and Malinké villages became independent. Some villages formed regional military alliances, however. By 1540 the Kingdom of Songhay had emerged as the military power of West Africa and conquered most of the Malinké people (Levtzion 1973:97). Only one Malinké region near the Niger River remained fortified and independent of Songhay.

The ecological disaster and military attacks experienced by the Malinké converged with a worse threat—organized Portuguese slave expeditions. The Portuguese first made contact with a Malinké group in 1445 when João Fernandes sailed into the mouth of the Gambia River on an exploratory trip (Levtzion 1973:94–95). Within ten years Portuguese pirates descended upon the west coast of Africa, capturing people. In 1487 the royal crown of Portugal commissioned its military to commence a large-scale slave project in West Africa, as the European slave trade had become a lucrative business (Cortes 1964:57; Levtzion 1973:94–95). The Malinké, with no unified military state system, fell prey to the activities of Portugal and other European countries who joined in the exploitation of Africa.

The fall of Mali and the institutionalization of the Portuguese slave trade converged with Spain's discovery of the New World. Spain began to import thousands of slaves for its domestic population and for its New World colonies. Slaves were needed to work on the newly founded plantations in the Spanish Caribbean as well as to work as domestics. Black slaves first arrived in Mexico in 1519 as part of the Pánfilo Narváez expedition (Díaz del Castillo 1963:282; Meyer and Sherman 1995:214). It is uncertain whether they assisted Hernán Cortés in the conquest of the Aztec Empire. We do know that Esteban, one of the slaves introduced by Narváez, participated in the first expedition to set foot in Texas (see Chapter 3). Now we must turn to the aftermath of the conquest and examine how race relations unfolded in Mexico.

2

Racial Formation

In the aftermath of the conquest, the Spanish military strategy of "divide and conquer" effectively created disunity among the Indians of central Mexico and opened the path to a new social order. At first, the Spanish left the indigenous economy and lifestyle relatively undisturbed, allowing elites who pledged allegiance to the crown of Spain to continue governing their peoples (Díaz del Castillo 1963). About twenty-five million Indians inhabited central Mexico at that time (Borah 1983:26; Meyer and Sherman 1995:212; Miller 1985:141). Within fifty years of the conquest, Spanish-Indian relations were redefined and race became a principal factor in the social and economic organization of Spanish colonial society. Exemptions were made for the Indian nobility, and this tokenism effectively served to entrench a racial order that solely benefited White people. Interracial political and marital alliances commenced the restructuring process (Gibson 1964; Liss 1975). My focus here is on central Mexico, because during the sixteenth century Spaniards concentrated their efforts on populating and stabilizing this zone before launching their assault upon the present southwestern United States. Most of central Mexico constituted the former Aztec Empire.

Shifting Political Alliances

After the conquest, the Spanish chose present Mexico City as their principal administrative center and placed their Tlaxcalan allies in positions of power throughout Mexico (Frye 1996). Tlaxcalans were given land formerly belonging to the Aztec Empire as well as the right to govern the people living in those regions. To further undermine the political confederacy established by the Aztec, the emperor was killed and the regional kings were replaced when they did not accept Spanish rule (Liss 1975; Lockhart 1991). These kings were called *tlatoques* (singular *tlatoani*) and under their command was a *cacique* cadre that directly governed the villages. The *cacique* was in charge of overseeing one or more villages, depending on his relation with his *tlatoani*. The *tlatoques* resided in the *cabeceras*, the regional capitals. After the conquest, the *tlatoques* who were loyal to Spain were allowed to continue governing and collecting tribute from the villages and towns they controlled (Gibson 1964). If their *caciques* were also loyal, they in turn were allowed to continue to oversee the communities they supervised (Aguirre Beltrán 1991; Vigil 1984). When a *tlatoani* rebelled, it was common for the royal government to replace him and reconfigure the political boundaries of that region. Often the governance of a region was broken apart and distributed among several lower-ranking *caciques*. In this way the Spanish crown rewarded its most faithful Indian subjects.

To demonstrate their loyalty *tlatoques* and *caciques* often repressed anti-Spanish political revolts (Gibson 1964; Powell 1952). Through this process of repression, the Spanish were able to create a "middleman" political infrastructure to govern the masses. Though it was sometimes necessary to replace *tlatoques* with *caciques*, the Spanish knew that it was more effective to co-opt rulers, as this generated a semblance of legitimate rule and political continuity. Spaniards rewarded their allies and outfitted the *tlatoques'* armies with weapons and horses (Powell 1952).

The Spanish also retained the *tlatoques'* families—the indigenous nobility—in power as a means of averting regional revolts (Vigil 1984). By retaining the Aztec nobility in positions of power they placated the masses. Political continuity created a facade, hiding from the people the fact that the ruling families were under the control of Spain (Aguirre Beltrán 1991; Lafaye 1974). In most places the nobility accepted the lifestyle introduced by the Spanish and the political transition. For them, accommodation became a survival strategy and a safety net to maintain the privileges their families had enjoyed for centuries. In return for their postconquest complicity members of the indigenous nobility were allowed to retain control of their property and were awarded additional land (Gibson 1964). They were also exempt from paying tribute to the Spanish crown and were given gifts including clothing, furniture, literature, utensils, and other European commodities.[1]

The Noble Savage: Ideology and Practice

After the defeat of the Aztec, the royal crown rewarded the *conquistadores* by giving them *encomiendas* (Meyer and Sherman 1995), agricultural estates carved out of land occupied by Indians. As part of their reward, Spaniards also received tribute from the Indians living in the *encomiendas* in the form of free labor and material goods such as money, crops, farm animals, textiles, ceramics, and beverages. Of most importance to the *conquistadores* was Indian labor, since land was useless unless it had people to farm, construct buildings, and work as domestic servants. The *encomienda* system was clearly an abuse of the Indians' property rights, but was rationalized under the pretense that it was the most effective method of acculturating them. Such a rationalization was necessary because in 1512 the Spanish crown passed the Laws of Burgos, establishing the procedures and laws to govern Indians (Hanke 1949:24). These laws decreed that Indians, like orphans, widows, and the wretched, would be protected and Christianized.[2] Indians were legally declared wards of the crown and church. The laws also contained additional stipulations with respect to Indian laborers and the acculturation process they would be subjected to.[3] Though the *encomiendas* were beneficial to the *conquistadores*, many clergy opposed them and charged that in effect they were a legal method of enslaving Indians and dispossessing them of property. The Catholic Church, after hearing many complaints from New World clergy, launched a campaign to limit the growth of the *encomiendas* and to delineate the legal rights of the Indians. Such a legal battle was necessary to avoid their enslavement, for unless Indians were legally declared human Spaniards could treat them as beasts of burden.

Ginés de Sepúlveda, a juridical scholar, became the most influential spokesman in Spain arguing in favor of enslaving Indians. Sepúlveda wrote several inflammatory books demonizing Indians; his most famous text, *Democrates Alter*, received a favorable reception throughout Spain (Hanke 1949). He asserted that Indians were savages without souls—a view that countered the Catholic Church's interpretation of Indians as descendants of the lost tribe of Israel (Lafaye 1974). The divergent positions of the church and Sepúlveda came to be known as the Noble Savage debate (Stocking 1968). Although Sepúlveda and his followers concurred that Indians probably were from the "promised land," he argued that on their exodus from Israel they came in contact with the devil and entered a stage of demonic savagery, citing the iconography found in hieroglyphic texts and on buildings as proof of his assertions. He claimed that Spaniards in the New World therefore had the right to enslave these savages.

On the other side of the debate was Father Francisco de Vitoria, who challenged Sepúlveda's demonization of Indians. Vitoria has been credited with having been the most influential legal philosopher to persuade the Catholic Church and crown to classify Indians as humans and thus to bestow on them the legal rights of human beings (Borah 1983; Hanke 1949). These rights included not being enslaved, being able to marry anyone they chose, being Christianized, being allowed to own property, and being allowed to live in towns and villages. Essentially, Vitoria argued that Indians had the right to pursue happiness. His philosophy was reflected in the political activism of other clergy, such as Father Bartolomé de Las Casas, who moved from theory to activism by obtaining field evidence to support the position that Indians were rational beings with souls.

In 1502 Las Casas arrived in the New World in Hispaniola (present-day Haiti and Dominican Republic) and later observed the mistreatment of the Indians throughout Latin America (Haring 1963:10–11). In his travels he observed the colonists overworking the Indians and treating them as animals. In essence, the colonists were breaking the religious and labor laws by denying Indians time to rest and to learn Christian doctrines (see *Recopilación de leyes de los reynos de las Indias* 1774, Book 1, Title 1, Laws 3, 5, 9, 10, and 12). Most of the atrocities were committed by *encomenderos*.

Although in theory the *encomiendas* were acculturation sites to civilize and Christianize Indians, they became unofficial slave institutions (Vigil 1984). Many missionaries who were concerned about the suffering of the Indians intervened. They sent countless complaints to the Spanish king and began to lobby to end the *encomienda* system (Borah 1983). The king sent investigators to the New World to determine whether Indians were indeed being mistreated. Las Casas became the most outspoken critic of the *encomiendas* and launched an attack on them. Knowing that he needed evidence to prove the Indians' humanity if Sepúlveda's claims were to be discredited, he refined the hypothesis that the Indians had migrated from Israel to the New World by adding a cognition argument. Las Casas's main argument centered on the Indians' capacity to learn Christian doctrine. He asserted that since Indians were able to learn Christian doctrines and many were able to read Spanish, they had the capacity to think abstractly, thus proving they were human (Wagner and Parish 1967).[4] As a consequence of the Las Casas research, Vitoria successfully obtained the legal classification of the Indians as human beings.

The enslavement of Indians became illegal in 1537, when Pope Paul III, in the papal bull *Sublimis Deus,* proclaimed Indians to be human, with the rights to be Christianized and to own property (Hanke 1949:72–73). The Spanish crown endorsed the proclamation and over time imposed additional protectionist legislation. The liberal position taken by the Catholic Church and crown was not shared by the entire Spanish population or by most of the countries of Europe (Menchaca 1997). Not until 1859 did most European countries accept that Indians and other people of color were not animals (Menchaca 1997:30).[5]

Although the church succeeded in obtaining the legal status of human being for the Indians, it also endorsed the crown's position that they must be governed and protected. The crown therefore named the church the Indians' legal protector and gave it the responsibility of Christianizing and converting them into loyal tax-paying subjects (Cutter 1986; Polzer 1976; *Recopilación de leyes de los reynos de las Indias* 1774: Book 1, Title 1, Laws 1, 3, and 9).[6] These legal rights, which came to be known as Vitoria's Natural Laws, in theory became standard practice in Mexico by 1550 (Hanke 1949:150–154; Liss 1975:38–43). As long as Vitoria's Natural Laws did not conflict with the crown's colonization plans, officials were instructed to extend Indians their legal rights; if Indians resisted colonization, however, they were not to be given any legal rights and could be enslaved (*Recopilación de leyes de los reynos de las Indias* 1774: Book 1, Title 1, Law 1).

Changing Intermarriage Laws: The Eve of a Racial Hierarchy

Though forming political alliances with the *tlatoques* became the primary manner in which Spaniards maintained control of the masses in central Mexico, intermarriage was also an effective and peaceful approach to accomplish a similar goal. It was an important practice used to solidify alliances, serving as a public testimonial of the Spaniards' trustworthiness (Liss 1975). In many societies where intermarriage served a utilitarian function, as in Mexico, this practice became a symbolic gesture to attest that Indians and Spaniards had good intentions toward each other. Claude Lévi-Strauss (1982) proposes that in precapitalist societies intermarriage has traditionally been used to form enduring alliances between political groups. The ritual of marriage becomes a public testimonial to assure communities that they are safe during a period of political transitions when mistrust between allies is common. Intermarriage becomes a stabilizing factor. Lévi-Strauss also suggests that members of the dominant group will accept wives as a symbol of peace, but will not exchange their own women. Apparently, this practice was replicated in Mexico: the Indians offered their women kin, but the Spanish did not return this symbolic gesture (Meyer and Sherman 1995).

To encourage intermarriage between Spaniards and Indians in central Mexico, the Spanish crown awarded military officers and soldiers more acreage than was commonly assigned (Meyer and Sherman 1995:209). In 1524 the crown publicly demonstrated its support of intermarriage by officially decreeing such unions to be legally valid (*Recopilación de leyes de los reynos de las Indias* 1774: Book 6, Title 1, Law 8). Moreover, the crown increased its pressures on Spanish men to marry Indian women by penalizing those who had concubines and refused to wed. A soldier who had a concubine was required to marry within three years of receiving his *encomienda* or risk losing the property (ibid.). To support the legal penalty placed on the soldiers, the church ardently professed that concubinage was a sin and temporarily refused to baptize *mestizo* children born out of wedlock (Seed 1988). These pressures were necessary if the colony was to be stabilized and the children of these unions were to be raised to identify with Spain. By having the father live with his family, Spanish culture and the Catholic faith could be transmitted to his children and to his wife's kinfolk.

Fray Bernal Díaz del Castillo offered a glimpse of the widespread practice of concubinage in his account of the conquest of Mexico. Concubinage potentially posed a danger to the stability of the colony because Indian *caciques* did not welcome this behavior. Díaz del Castillo informs us that after Tenochtitlán fell Indian *caciques* visited Hernán Cortés and complained that his soldiers had forcibly taken many Indian women:

> *Guatemoc* and his captains complained to Cortés that many of our men had carried off the daughters and wives of chieftains, and begged him as a favor that they should be sent back. Cortés an-

swered that it would be difficult to take them from their present masters. . . . So he gave the Mexicans permission to search in all three camps, and issued an order that any soldier who had an Indian woman should surrender her at once if she of her own free will wished to return home. (Díaz del Castillo 1963:408–409)

Encouraging intermarriage also had an economic function for the church, since under the Laws of Burgos it was responsible for taking care of orphaned children (Haring 1963; Miller 1985). By 1527 the Catholic Church concluded that its efforts were succeeding: many *encomenderos* in central Mexico were marrying their concubines (Liss 1975; Meyer and Sherman 1995). Orphaned children, however, continued to be a problem because most *encomenderos* had more than one concubine and many children were not provided for (Bonifaz de Novello 1975). This forced the church to open orphanages throughout central Mexico.

In southern Mexico, nearly two decades later, the Maya peoples of the Yucatán Peninsula, who had remained independent after the Aztec Empire fell, also surrendered to representatives of the Spanish crown. All regional revolts had been suppressed in the Yucatán Peninsula by 1542, and Spain expanded its empire (Perry and Perry 1988:20). The process of restructuring Maya society replicated the colonial policies of central Mexico. Disloyal Indian chiefs were replaced and loyal Mayan nobles allowed to continue overseeing their communities. Unlike the situation in central Mexico, however, where Spaniards established residences, few *conquistadores* chose to settle permanently in the Yucatán Peninsula. Only in Mérida, Campeche, and Valladolid were *encomiendas* established at this time. The Maya masses were governed via the Maya nobility, the Spanish military, and a few Catholic missionaries. The process of *mestizaje* among the Maya was gradual and occurred much later than it did in central Mexico because few Spaniards lived there.

Throughout the colonial period the Catholic Church continued to encourage Spaniards to marry their Indian concubines. In 1575, however, the royal government reversed its liberal position on intermarriage and began to institute antimiscegenation laws (*Recopilación de leyes de los reynos de las Indias* 1774: Book 2, Title 16, Law 32). The royal crown passed a decree penalizing Spaniards of high social standing who wished to marry Indians. Viceroys, presidents, mayors, and all fiscal officers and their families were prohibited from marrying Indians. If any section of the decree was disobeyed, the crown required immediate dismissal of the official. Within a few years, the government expanded the decree to include all its employees; only military personnel were exempt. This exemption may have been necessary because the crown was in the process of conquering lands in northern Mexico and stabilizing its colony in the Yucatán Peninsula; thus intermarriage was still a useful military strategy.

Interestingly, the enactment of the first marriage prohibition law coincided with the growth of an elite Spanish class that was of noble birth and economically prosperous in comparison to the soldiers and first Spanish immigrants. By 1560 there were 20,211 Spaniards in Mexico, and a large number of them were recent immigrants (Meyer and Sherman 1995:208). Unlike most of the *conquistadores*, who had commoner origins, the new colonists were well educated, and many were from distinguished noble families. A large number of these colonists came at the request of the royal crown, because they were needed to administer the government, while other Spanish elites came to oversee the agricultural estates granted to their families. These two groups became the crown's favorite subjects and were given political, economic, and social advantages not available to other colonists. These special privileges, however, were dependent upon their loyalty, including obeying the marriage prohibitions. The passage of the marriage prohibition laws also coincided with another event in Mexico City. All political movements to overthrow the Spanish had been repressed by the allies of the Spanish crown, and the rebels from Tenochtitlán, Texcoco, and Tacuba had finally been placated (Gibson 1964). These regions had previously constituted the political center of the Aztec Triple Alliance and had been zones of periodic political outbreaks.

In 1592 the crown added a harsher amendment requiring government employees to marry spouses born in Europe (*Recopilación de leyes de los reynos de las Indias* 1774: Book 7, Title 3, Law 5). Once again, breaking the decree meant immediate dismissal. By this time, the crown was not solely interested in creating a White elite class; it had become necessary to form a loyal class with limited social commitment to the inhabitants of Mexico. For this purpose, the crown needed to extend privileges to those Whites who were born in Spain (Miller 1985). Ironically, while the royal government was forming an elite ruling class and passing laws to ensure their racial purity, it had to continue encouraging low-ranking soldiers to marry Indian women in order to entrench Spanish culture via intermarriage. In 1627, with the approval of the Catholic Church, the crown facilitated the marriage of its lower-ranking military personnel by allowing married men with wives in Spain who did not have any children to annul their marriages and remarry in Mexico (*Recopilación de leyes de los reynos de las Indias* 1774: Book 3, Title 10, Law 28). By 1646 sexual relations between Spaniards and Indians had produced a *mestizo* population estimated at 109,042 (Aguirre Beltrán 1946:221), and approximately half of the children were born in legitimate marriages (Cope 1994:68; Seed 1988:25).

In retrospect, the marriage laws passed in Mexico signify the initial formation of a racial order where race and nativity became the basis of ascribing and denying social and economic privileges. The crown had begun to use the legal system to entrench a hierarchical racial order and place Whites as the gatekeepers.

Factionalism among the Indian Nobility and the Epidemics of Central Mexico

By 1570 the political restructuring implemented by the administrators of the Spanish government in central Mexico had fueled political and territorial disputes between many *tlatoques* and *caciques* (Vigil 1984). To reward the most faithful *tlatoques* Spanish administrators expanded their political regional control and likewise reduced the regions overseen by disfavored *tlatoques*. This caused factionalism among the Indian nobility and spurred a sense of distrust among the masses. When a *tlatoani* was demoted, the local people did not recognize his replacement as their legitimate governor. Factionalism among the nobility was further exacerbated when the judicial function was stripped from the *tlatoques* and assigned to other administrators. To decentralize the power of the *tlatoques*, the role of *juez gobernador* (judge) was assigned to influential *caciques* (Gibson 1964:166–167). Though *tlatoques* were not dispossessed of their lands, this led to their political downfall and to the political ascent of many *caciques*. *Caciques* now had the power to adjudicate civil and property manners, a very important political function that for centuries had been solely the domain of the *tlatoques* (Aguirre Beltrán 1991).

Throughout central Mexico the *tlatoques*' political influence further eroded during the disastrous epidemics of 1576 to 1581 (Gibson 1964:6, 138). Due to these widespread epidemic outbreaks, the Indian population of central Mexico radically declined. By 1581 the Valley of Mexico's population had been reduced to approximately 70,000 (Gibson 1964:6, 138);[7] as the epidemics spread, central Mexico's population was reduced to 1,075,000 by 1605 (Meyer and Sherman 1995:212). During this time the epidemics did not affect the Yucatán Peninsula; yet within four decades disastrous diseases also broke out there, generating similar devastations. As villages were depopulated in central Mexico, those who survived moved. Many villages were abandoned as Indians recongregated and new communities were formed. As a result of these changing settlement patterns, the new communities refused to pay tribute to the regional *tlatoques* because they did not consider them to be their legitimate governors. In contrast, the *jueces gobernadores* became more powerful politically; only in places where a *tlatoani* held both titles did his power remain intact.

To respond to the depopulation crisis the crown instituted a reorganization of Indian tribute and land. The *tlatoques, encomenderos,* and *caciques* lost the right to obtain tribute from the Indians (Gibson 1964; Liss 1975). Only the crown and church retained that right. Part of the land that had been depopulated was reserved for the Indians under the *corregimiento* system. Sadly, a large part of the abandoned land was retained by the crown or given to influential Spaniards. In this way, many Indians in Mexico lost the land they had inhabited for centuries.[8]

Under the *corregimiento* system, the crown retained legal title to the Indian lands, yet it recognized their occupational use rights (e.g., farming, pasture) and ability to transfer land use rights from one generation to the next. Families were not given alienation rights to sell their land, however, unless they obtained permission from the crown or church. The crown also reserved communal land for the Indians (Borah 1983). Part of this communal land was to be used to erect civic buildings, the rest for communal agriculture or pasture.[9] Although it was a liberal practice to reserve a large part of the depopulated land for the Indians, the crown nonetheless sold or granted most of the acreage to Spaniards (Gibson 1964). Many wealthy *caciques* also took advantage of the crisis and purchased large tracts of land.

Once the land was reallocated, the new landowners needed workers to farm their estates. In response to this demand, the royal administrators allowed influential Spaniards to tap into the *repartimiento* system, which was a rationed and rotational labor system instituted to construct buildings for the church and crown (Gibson 1964). Since 1555 Indian communities had been required to organize crews able to work on any project commanded by the crown (Gibson 1964:224–235). Because Indian labor became scarce after the epidemics, the *repartimiento* system was increasingly exploited, as Indian labor was virtually monopolized for private use. Because Indian labor was insufficient to fulfill labor demands, many landowners also turned to slave labor (Aguirre Beltrán 1944, 1946; Pi-Sunyer 1957). Mexico's slave traffic grew dramatically, and the large-scale importation of Black slaves began. Nearly half of the slaves who entered Mexico during its entire history came between 1599 and 1637, totaling approximately 88,383 (Aguirre Beltrán 1946:220).

During this labor crisis, the church did not stand by idly as Indian labor was increasingly used for private purposes. When New World missionaries complained to the royal crown of the abuses, agents were sent to investigate matters. On 1 January 1633, after reviewing the evidence presented by the church, the crown concurred that the *repartimiento* system was corrupt and ordered its termination (Gibson 1964:235). This forced landowners to hire workers, and many supplemented their labor needs with slaves. Spaniards who had entirely relied on the *repartimiento* system went into bankruptcy shortly after its termination. They were unable to bear the costs of switching to a different type of agricultural production. The Spanish landowners, *caciques,* and *tlatoques* who had previously hired wage workers or purchased slaves were able to make the transition, however (Liss 1975). Many of these successful landowners supplemented their labor needs with tenant farming, allowing people to live on their estates and farm a tract of land in return for a percentage of the harvest. Because the amount to be turned over was set by the landowners, the tenant farmers' profits were often minimal, providing only a subsistence income. By the mid-seventeenth century the majority of the Indian population in central Mexico worked for Spaniards or *caciques* (Gibson 1964:255). Only those Indians who owned land or remained in the *corregimientos* were not under the control of the landed elite.

Malinké Slaves

The importation of Black slaves to Mexico from Africa began in 1527 (Aguirre Beltrán 1946:8). It started as a trickle, became a torrent during the epidemics in central Mexico, and dwindled by the mid-1600s

(Aguirre Beltrán 1944:426, 1946:10). After the turn of the seventeenth century only a few thousand slaves entered Mexico. The last large shipments of slaves arrived between 1715 and 1738 (Palmer 1981:104). During that time, 3,816 Bantu slaves were sold in Veracruz and were then transferred throughout Guatemala and Mexico. Scholars estimate that 150,000 to 200,000 Black slaves were imported to Mexico during its entire history (Aguirre Beltrán 1944:431; cf. Meyer and Sherman 1995:215). Most slaves shipped to Mexico came from West Africa, and the vast majority of them were registered as Malinké (see Chapter 1). Dispersed among the Malinkés were other West African peoples, including Soninkés, Sosos, and Wolofs. Though slaves were sold throughout Mexico, they were shipped to four main areas: Mexico City, Tlaxcala-Puebla, Michoacán, and Zacatecas (Aguirre Beltrán 1946:209; Love 1971:79, 80; Roncal 1944: 534). Mexico City received more than 50 percent of the slaves imported throughout the country's history (Aguirre Beltrán 1946:209, 212, 220, 221, 224). Slaves were used for varied tasks, including farm labor, mining, and household domestic work.

By the mid-1600s Mexican residents had nearly ceased importing slaves, largely due to the political activism of the Catholic Church. Since 1573 New World missionaries had condemned the slave trade and urged the crown to prohibit the sale of slaves in the New World (Palacios 1988: 9). The crown and the royal administrators in Mexico initially refused to comply. After Mexico recovered from the epidemics and Indian labor was once again plentiful, however, the administrators in Mexico began to pay attention to the church's views on the immorality of the slave trade. Many royal administrators discouraged people from purchasing slaves and enforced the labor codes prohibiting the physical abuse of slaves. Feeling the pressure from the Catholic Church, the crown reluctantly followed suit and discouraged Spanish entrepreneurs from investing in slave trade expeditions. It did not, however, issue a proclamation discouraging people from purchasing slaves—quite the contrary. The crown was not prepared to end the slave trade and instead circumvented its agreement with the church by contracting with Portuguese and British businesses to export slaves to Mexico. In this way Spaniards were not directly involved in capturing slaves. The crown was not about to end the slave trade in Mexico, because the profits from the sale of licenses to slave traders as well as the tax revenues collected from ships docking in the Americas went directly to the royal family.

Though the Catholic Church clearly was influential in decreasing the importation of slaves to Mexico, it was prompted by political self-interest. If the slave trade did not end, the church would alienate a large number of its wealthy patrons (Aguirre Beltrán 1946; Palacios 1988; Palmer 1981). During the depopulation crisis in central Mexico, the importation of a massive number of slaves altered the traditional Indian-Spanish racial composition of the country. Mexico's national census in 1646 indicates that there were 130,000 people of Black descent and only 114,000 to 125,000 Spaniards, most of whom were *criollos* born in Mexico (Meyer and Sherman 1995:208).[10] Though both racial populations were relatively small in comparison to the 1,269,607 Indians in 1646, Blacks as a group were sizable enough to influence the racial composition of Mexico (Aguirre Beltrán 1946:221).[11] Continuation of the slave trade would place the church in a politically precarious position because it had obtained the reluctant support of the crown and of many influential Spaniards to free the children of slaves and allow them to marry whomever they wanted. If more slaves were imported, their children could one day convert Mexico into a nation of *mulattos* (half Black and half Spanish) or *lobos* (half Black and half Indian).

Why the Children of Black Male Slaves Were Born Free

When Mexico was first colonized, the Catholic Church supported the royal crown's position on slavery (Blackburn 1998). Enslaving people imported from Africa was considered a necessity if the colonies in the New World were to prosper. It was a popular belief that a Black person could equal the labor output of four Indians (Aguirre Beltrán 1946; Palacios 1988). Spaniards, however, acknowledged they were enslaving human beings and chose to accord them some legal rights (see Cortes 1964). For example, people who were one-sixteenth Black were legally classified as Spaniards (Aguirre Beltrán 1946:174; Love 1971:79–80). Furthermore, under the *Siete Partidas* law code slaves were granted the right to select their spouse and slave masters were prohibited from intervening (Aguirre Beltrán 1946:261–262; Love 1976:135). This legislation was of monumental importance because it became the gateway for the children of slaves to gain their freedom. Due to the lobbying efforts of the Catholic Church the children of Black male slaves and Indian women were declared free and given the right to live with their mother. Unfortunately, the children of Black women were not given a similar privilege and were not emancipated.

Throughout Mexico's colonial history, slave owners attempted to convince the royal crown to annul the slave marriage code, arguing that their investments were lost within one generation, as most male slaves married Indian women. Indeed that was the case: marriage registries between 1646 and 1746 in Mexico City and Veracruz indicate that 52 percent of the Black population married Indians (Love 1971:85). The slave masters' zeal to enslave the children of Black males heightened during the depopulation crisis of central Mexico. In 1585 masters launched a lobbying campaign to change the law and convert such children into chattel (Aguirre Beltrán 1946:257). The church protested and overwhelmingly triumphed in its counter-lobbying efforts. The crown failed to annul the slave marriage code and instead issued a warning to slave masters. If a priest could demonstrate that a master had tried to prevent his slave from selecting a marriage partner, that master would be penalized financially. Slave masters were also prohibited from separating married couples (Aguirre Beltrán 1946; Love 1971).

For the church it was important to protect the rights of Black slaves, because this also affected the Indians and *mestizos.* Throughout Mexico Black slaves, Indians, and *mestizos* met while working as household domestics, and many subsequently married. In particular, this was the case in Mexico City, where a major part of the slave population worked as servants and produced a large *afromestizo* population (Cope 1994; Roncal 1944; Seed 1982, 1988). By 1742 the national census indicates that there was a population of 266,196 free *afromestizos,* a general term used to indicate a racially mixed person of partially Black descent (Aguirre Beltrán 1946:225).

The Racial Order and the Move North

Spain instituted a racial order called the *casta* system through which Mexico's population came to be legally distinguished based on race. This system was used to deny and prescribe legal rights to individuals and to assign them social prestige. In particular, distinguishing the population on the basis of parental origin became an adequate legal method of according economic privilege and social prestige to Spaniards (Lafaye 1974; Mörner 1967; Vigil 1984).[12] The Spaniards included both *peninsu-*

lares, individuals of full European descent who had been born in Spain, and *criollos,* who were also of full European descent but had been born in the New World. As miscegenation increased among the Spanish elite, the *criollo* category eventually came to be redefined. The *castas* were *mestizos* and other persons of mixed blood. The Indian category included only people of full indigenous descent.

Of the various racial groups, the Spaniards enjoyed the highest social prestige and were accorded the most extensive legal and economic privileges. The legal system did not make distinctions between *peninsulares* and *criollos.* Nevertheless, the Spanish crown instituted policies requiring that high-level positions in the government and Catholic Church be assigned to *peninsulares,* with the rationale that only *peninsulares* were fervently loyal (Haring 1963). If the crown could not find *peninsulares* willing to accept appointments in the colonies established along the frontier, it made exceptions to the decree for those areas and appointed *criollos,* although they had to be the sons of *peninsulares.* As a rule, *peninsulares* were appointed to positions such as viceroy, governor, captain-general, archbishop, and bishop, whereas *criollos* were appointed to less prestigious positions, such as comptroller of the royal exchequer, judge, university professor, and mid-level administrative positions in the church (e.g., priests or directors of schools) (Haring 1963). Furthermore, only *peninsulares* could obtain commercial licenses for direct trade between Spain and Mexico. *Criollos* were limited to the domestic commercial market.

The social and economic mobility of the rest of the population was seriously limited by the legal statuses ascribed to their ancestral groups. In theory, many Indians were economically more privileged than *mestizos* because they held title to large parcels of communal land protected by the crown and the Catholic Church (Haring 1963; Mörner 1967). Despite their claim to property, however, the Indians were accorded little social prestige in Mexican society and were legally confined to subservient social and economic roles regulated by the Spanish elite. Most Indians were forced to live in a perpetual state of tutelage controlled by the church, state, or Spanish landowners.

Mestizos enjoyed a higher social prestige than the Indians, but were considered inferior to the Spaniards. They were also often ostracized by the Indians and Spaniards and did not enjoy certain legal privileges accorded to either group. For example, most *mestizos* were barred by royal decree from obtaining high and mid-level positions in the royal and ecclesiastical governments (Haring 1963; Mörner 1967). Throughout the colonial period they were prohibited from becoming priests, except in the frontier zones, where Indians and *mestizos* would be their parishioners (Haring 1963:201). Moreover, the Spanish crown did not reserve land for the *mestizos* under the *corregimiento* system as it did for the Indians. The best economic recourse for most *mestizos* was to enter the labor market or migrate toward Mexico's northern and southern frontiers. Each migrant who was the head of a household was awarded land and exempted from taxation for a period of approximately ten years (León-Portilla 1972; Rubel 1966; Weber 1982). If they chose to move to the frontier, they were prohibited from being members of the town councils or generals of presidios or garrisons; these privileges were reserved solely for Spaniards (Poyo 1991a; *Recopilación de leyes de los reynos de las Indias* 1774: Book 3, Title 10, Law 12).

Free *afromestizos* were accorded the same legal privileges as the *mestizos*. Because they were of partially African descent, however, they were stigmatized and considered socially inferior to Indians and *mestizos* (Love 1970, 1971; Pi-Sunyer 1957; Seed 1988). For example, *afromestizos* were subjected to racist laws designed to distinguish them from *mestizos* and to impose financial and social penalties upon them. An *afromestiza* who was married to a Spaniard or was of noble birth was forbidden to use the traditional clothing of a Spanish woman or person of high social standing (*Recopilación de leyes de los reynos de las Indias* 1774: Book 7, Title 5, Law 28). She could not wear gold jewelry, a pearl necklace with more than one strand, or silk clothes, and her *mantilla* (veil) could not pass her waist. If she broke any part of this decree, it was lawful to humiliate her in public and confiscate the items.

Furthermore, free *afromestizos* were forced to pay special taxes because they were part Black (McAlister 1957; Pi-Sunyer 1957; *Recopilación de leyes de los reynos de las Indias* 1774: Book 7, Title 4, Law 3; Roncal 1944). To levy taxes local authorities kept registries of the *afromestizos*. When they traveled or lived outside of their communities for extended periods they were required to reregister and pay additional taxes. *Afromestizos* were also legally prohibited from walking on roads at night (*Recopilación de leyes de los reynos de las Indias* 1774: Book 7, Title 5, Law 14) and from carrying weapons, unless they were a *peninsular*'s private guard (*Recopilación de leyes de los reynos de las Indias* 1774: Book 7,

Title 5, Law 15). Most heinous of all, if free *afromestizos* in Mexico City were unable to pay their bills or became paupers they could be placed in indentured servitude (Cope 1994).

Although the racially mixed populations increased in number throughout Mexico's colonial era, the governing class in Mexico remained exclusively White, or at least its members professed that they were White (Meyer and Sherman 1995).[13] Notwithstanding this fact, there were economic and prestige differences among the *mestizo* and *afromestizo* populations. Their social positions varied and were highly dependent upon the father's social position and whether a child was born in a legitimate marriage (Seed 1988). Children whose Spaniard fathers were of high social standing but whose mothers were women of color were often fictively referred to as *criollos* and included as part of the White population. A similar exemption, however, was seldom available to the commoner classes. Though by law the *criollo* racial category was reserved for Whites, it was common for parish priests to register *mestizo* children of means as *criollo* by including in the baptismal registry only the race of the father (Meyer and Sherman 1995; Seed 1988). In this way no record was left of the mother's race. This also applied to *afromestizo* children who did not appear to be Black. If children's baptismal records indicated they were *criollo*, they were granted the legal privileges of Spaniards. Furthermore, it was also possible to register a child of means who was born out of wedlock as a *criollo*.

The case of the children of Hernán Cortés illustrates this scenario. Don Martín Cortés and Doña Isabel Moctezuma Cortés were born outside of a sanctioned marriage. Martín was the son of Doña Marina, Hernán Cortés's Indian translator and concubine throughout the conquest of Mexico, while Isabel was the daughter of Isabel Moctezuma and the granddaughter of Emperor Moctezuma Xocoyotzin (Chipman 1977; Meyer and Sherman 1995). Both were treated as *criollos* and were considered noble. Martín was taken as a young boy to Spain's royal court and treated as part of the noble class. After completing his education, he returned to Mexico and was granted an estate and a royal endowment to lead the lifestyle he was accustomed to.

Though not all *mestizos* were as fortunate as Martín, racially mixed women who were fair-complexioned were highly valued as marriage partners. Such fair-skinned women were called *castizas* because they were the daughters of Spaniards and *mestizas* (Chapman 1916; Liss 1975; Weber

1992). By the late 1600s there were sufficient *castizas* for *peninsulares* and *criollos* to marry, and it was no longer necessary for them to marry darker-toned women (Meyer and Sherman 1995:210). Although some *criollos* and *castizas* were incorporated into the social circles of Whites, similar privileges were unavailable to the rest of the non-White population. Most *mestizos, afromestizos,* and Indians continued to experience racial discrimination (Menchaca 1993). Blatant racial disparities became painfully intolerable to the non-White population and generated the conditions for their movement toward the northern frontier, where the racial order was relaxed and people of color had the opportunity to own land and enter most occupations.

3

The Move North

THE GRAN CHICHIMECA AND NEW MEXICO

For Mexican Americans the Spanish settlement of the territories that would become the U.S. Southwest was a singular event of monumental consequence. Many of the peoples inhabiting these territories were conquered and came to have a direct influence on the racial history and heritage of the Mexican Americans. In 1598 Spaniards, *mestizos*, Indians, and *afromestizos* moved north toward Mexico's frontier (Hammond 1953:17). Thousands of people left central Mexico in search of land and wealth; for those of color this migratory movement was also highly motivated by the opportunity to flee the restrictions imposed upon them by the *casta* system (Menchaca 1993; Poyo and Hinojosa 1991). Although people of color were not in charge of the racial projects instituted by Spain, they participated in the conquest of the indigenous peoples they encountered.

I concur with Marshall Sahlins (1985) that certain historical moments, such as the settlement of the Southwest, set off a chain of events changing the course of history. Sahlins calls this type of event a historical conjuncture, for it creates ruptures in people's everyday lives and generates the conditions to restructure social relations. The colonial movement and settlement of the Southwest initiated a social restructuring of the lives of many indigenous peoples and interjected race as a central source of social organization. In areas where indigenous peoples were conquered, the colonists created alliances, instituted technological changes, intermarried with many indigenous peoples, and instituted a racial hierarchy. These practices commenced an era of colonization which Edward Spicer (1981) has called "cycles of conquest." The first cycle was launched by Spain and the second by Mexico, culminating in the third cycle, when the United States took possession of most of Mexico's northern frontier.

I use the term "Southwest" here to refer to the territories where Spanish settlements were founded in New Mexico, Texas, Arizona, and California. I do not examine the entire North American region claimed by Spain, because Nevada, Utah, parts of Colorado, and small sections of Oklahoma, Kansas, and Wyoming remained under the control of indigenous peoples. My purpose in this chapter is to begin to delineate the political conditions that generated the outmigration of people seeking to better their social position. The irony of this seemingly liberating event was that the colonists of color were able to find a place where the quality of their lives indeed improved, at the cost of entrenching the same colonial order that oppressed them. *Afromestizos* played a minimal role in the conquest of New Mexico, because they did not migrate in large numbers until the colonization of Texas.

The Gran Chichimeca: Indian Resistance

Following the fall of the Aztec Empire, the Spanish *conquistadores* sought to conquer new lands to the north and south. Though militias were commanded by Spanish officers, the vast majority of the invading forces were composed of Indian warriors (Powell 1952). *Tlatoques* and *caciques* headed the auxiliaries, under the command of Spanish officers who in turn planned and executed the military maneuvers. In the conquest of the territories lying north of central Mexico the main Indian peoples assisting the Spanish were Tlaxcalans and Tarascans, both longtime enemies of the Aztec (Meyer and Sherman 1995).[1] They acted as soldiers, scouts, and intellectual strategists and also served as cartographers, identifying vulnerable villages that could easily be subdued and used as stepping stones to move further north. Otomí soldiers also assisted the Spanish; their most important function was to translate, since they were a multilingual people competent in the languages of many northern Mexican tribes (Gibson 1964). The Otomís were the most recent immigrants in the Valley of Mexico, having migrated after the Mexicas. Their bilingualism served the Spanish well in initiating contact with several of the northern tribes. To repay their allies' services, the Spanish confirmed the *tlatoques* titles of nobility and outfitted their armies with Spanish horses and European military artillery (Forbes 1994; Powell 1952). Indian commoners who proved to be valuable assets were also rewarded by being promoted to *tlatoques* or *caciques*.

The Spanish derogatorily called the northern region between the Valley of Mexico and the present United States–Mexico border the Gran

Chichimeca (see Map 2). The word "Chichimeca" meant the land of uncivilized dogs (Powell 1952). The people inhabiting this region were ge-
nerically termed Chichimec. The Gran Chichimeca did not include the
northwestern or northeastern coasts (Alonzo 1998; Chipman 1992).[2] For
the Spanish it was of utmost importance to vanquish the Chichimec
people, who posed a military threat because they inhabited thousands of
villages in the territories bordering the Valley of Mexico. The valley had
to be protected, since the Spanish had established their administrative
center in Tenochtitlán and renamed it Mexico City. It was also necessary to conquer the Chichimec villages because they obstructed the Spaniards' northward movement. Sea voyage explorers had identified lands
beyond the Gran Chichimeca (Powell 1952:32). To reach these unknown
areas, however, the Spanish had to establish land routes through the Gran
Chichimeca. They also had to overcome ecological problems in this vast
and arid region (Meyer and Sherman 1995). Ironically, the vastness of the
Gran Chichimeca eventually became the Chichimec Achilles' heel, since
the villages along its southern border were vulnerable to military attacks.
The proximity of these border villages to Mexico City hindered their
fortification because they lay closer to settlements under Spanish control than to other Chichimec villages. Nonetheless, these border villages
would prove to be difficult for the Spanish to conquer since the thousands
of peoples who lived there were prepared to stop the northern invasion
(Lafaye 1974).

The first Spanish *entradas* (official invasions) took place in the early
1520s (Chipman 1992:44–45). A temporary outpost was established in Culiacán, Sinaloa. Because the Spanish did not form alliances with the local
Indian population, however, the outpost was recurrently attacked and
did not become a stable site until much later (Chipman 1992). Throughout the 1530s it was virtually impossible to befriend the Indians of the
Gran Chichimeca (Engelhardt 1929:19–20). Only one official land expedition, headed by Franciscan friars in 1533, was able to move successfully
through the southwestern border of the Gran Chichimeca and establish
peaceful relations with Indians from the present state of Jalisco (ibid.).
There were also several unofficial expeditions led by impatient *encomenderos* unwilling to wait until the royal crown issued official orders to invade the north (Powell 1952). In the meantime it became necessary to explore the distant north by sea. One of the most famous sea expeditions
was commanded by Pánfilo Narváez in 1528 (Weber 1992:42).

Alvar Núñez Cabeza de Vaca and the Exploration of the Southwest

After Spaniards conquered the Aztec Empire, they were informed by Aztec nobles that greater mineral resources lay to the north (Lafaye 1974). In an attempt to verify this news Spain launched a series of sea voyage expeditions from Mexico as well as from the Spanish Caribbean Islands (Salinas 1990).[3] One of these expeditions was commanded by Captain Pánfilo Narváez. In 1528 he was commissioned to explore Florida and to initiate trade relations with the Indians (Weber 1992:42). An earlier report prepared by Juan Ponce de León had identified Florida as a region where friendly Indians could be contacted. Narváez was given command of three ships containing six hundred men. Alvar Núñez Cabeza de Vaca had been appointed as the secretary of the expedition, in charge of chronicling the exploration and maintaining an account of any goods obtained from the Indians. The Spanish sailors encountered a series of misfortunes. After disembarking in Florida, many of the men were ambushed and killed by the Indians (see Weber 1992). The sailors also suffered from ocean illnesses. The most devastating event, however, occurred when a series of ocean storms demolished the ships (Cabeza de Vaca 1922). Less than twenty men survived after constructing makeshift crafts. Cabeza de Vaca and several of his companions were among the survivors. Their craft was swept away and finally landed near present-day Galveston, Texas (Weber 1992). Within a few days of their arrival, most of the castaways met their deaths at the hands of the Indians. Cabeza de Vaca, Andrés Dorantes, Alonso del Castillo, and Dorantes's slave Esteban were among the survivors. Although their lives were spared by the Indians, they were taken captive. The four castaways were separated and sent to different villages.

Cabeza de Vaca was released several years later and allowed to leave. He decided to go south in an attempt to reach Mexico City. On his trek he encountered his fellow castaways (Bannon 1970). Together, the four men walked in a southwesterly direction along the coast of Texas and inland toward the Lower Rio Grande River, where they met several hostile and peaceful indigenous groups.[4] In 1536 they reached an Indian village near present-day Presidio, Texas (near El Paso), where they found evidence of European contact (Chipman 1992:32). They continued to move south, into the present state of Sonora. Esteban and Cabeza de Vaca temporarily left their companions and went south in search of Spanish soldiers. Somewhere in present northern Mexico, the two men found a Spanish military camp. The soldiers were camping while exploring the north. Cabeza de Vaca and his companions were soon reunited and taken to Culiacán.

Cabeza de Vaca immortalized his journey in 1542, when he wrote the first book about the Indians of North America (Chipman 1992:243), entitled *Naufragios y comentarios* (Cabeza de Vaca 1922). He recounted his experiences among the Indians of Texas, noting that the coastal Indians of Texas were hostile toward their neighbors and practiced hunting and gathering; most groups were politically organized into bands (this probably refers to the Karankawa Indians). Indians along the Lower Rio Grande, however, were peaceful and appeared to practice a more complex political organization, resembling rulership by committee. These Indians lived in villages most of the year, formed alliances with neighbors, practiced religious rituals, and mourned their dead. Some of the Indian groups also cultivated crops. Cabeza de Vaca described the Indians near Presidio as the most advanced group he met. They lived in adobe houses, harvested crops, and wove cloth; the women covered their bodies with skins and cotton blouses. Anthropologists have identified the last group encountered by Cabeza de Vaca as Jumano.

Cabeza de Vaca's journey sparked interest in Mexico's far northern frontier, and in the late 1530s the Spanish crown commissioned a series of sea and land explorations (Chipman 1992:39–42).[5] By this time, temporary passageways had been established through the Gran Chichimeca. Between 1539 and 1543 Spaniards explored the Southwest and other parts of the present United States (ibid.).[6] Spanish soldiers and missionaries claimed this land on behalf of Christianity and the Spanish crown during four major expeditions. In 1539 Fray Marcos de Niza was commissioned to lead the first expedition; Esteban, Cabeza de Vaca's former companion, acted as the guide and advance scout (Lafaye 1974). Fray Marcos and his companions set camp on the Río Mayo of Sonora, Mexico, while Esteban moved onward (Bandelier 1990; Bannon 1970). Esteban, walking two days ahead of Fray Marcos, became the first non-Indian to set foot in Arizona and New Mexico. Esteban was probably a Malinké, because Spain was importing Malinké slaves at this time (Aguirre Beltrán 1946). He was certainly an experienced explorer and adept in nautical sciences (Dubois

1975), skills that Malinké sailors were experts in before becoming captives (Thornton 1996). Their homeland in West Africa, Mali, encompassed a region with three major rivers, the Niger, Gambia, and Senegal. The Senegal and Gambia emptied into the Atlantic Ocean.

Esteban was killed in Cíbola, in present-day New Mexico, and the region was more fully explored several months later by Francisco Vásquez de Coronado. In a second expedition the Spanish crown commissioned Coronado to investigate Fray Marcos's report of Cíbola. Accompanied by Fray Marcos, Coronado explored the region and then moved east into Texas and north to the area currently known as Oklahoma and Kansas (Bannon 1970; Chipman 1992). A third expedition was commanded by Hernando de Soto. He began his trek in Florida and moved west to discover what is now known as Georgia, Alabama, Mississippi, Louisiana, and Arkansas (Chipman 1992). After three years in the field, De Soto was struck by a raging fever that took his life. He appointed Luis de Moscoso Alvarado to complete the expedition. Moscoso then explored present-day Arkansas and Texas. A fourth expedition was commissioned to explore the territory west of New Mexico (Bolton 1921). On this expedition, Juan Rodríguez-Cabrillo was the first European to reach California. Rodríguez-Cabrillo died during the voyage; his second-in-command, Bartolomé Ferrelo, completed the exploration of the coast of California and Oregon.

These early expeditions gave Spaniards the necessary information to initiate settlement projects. Sedentary villages located in ecologically rich environments were identified as possible colonization sites. New Mexico in particular became the favored site. Although the Spanish were able to explore the Southwest, their settlement plans were put on hold, because the Mixtón Wars broke out and the Chichimec villages blocked further intrusion into the far north (beyond Querétaro). When the wars began, it became impossible to establish land routes to launch a colonization plan in the U.S. Southwest.

Chichimec Resistance under the Leadership of Tenamaxtle

When the era of Spanish exploration and conquest began in the north of Mexico, it was the *tlatoques, caciques,* and their Indian warriors who provided most of the forces (Gibson 1967; Powell 1952). Their complicity clearly delineates the political restructuring that Spain instituted in Mexico and shows that Indian elites were willing to practice accommodative politics to retain their positions of power. Don Nicolás de San Luis, Don Juan Bautista Valerio de la Cruz, and Don Hernando de Tapia were the most powerful *tlatoques* aiding the Spanish (Powell 1952:160). Although the Spanish had formed a strong military alliance with many *tlatoques* from central Mexico, the Chichimec people were not easily vanquished.

The level of Chichimec political organization ranged from chiefdoms to autocephalous villages. Six powerful chiefdoms, however, controlled the central and southern regions of the Gran Chichimeca: the Guamares, Pames, Guachichiles, Zacatecos, Caxcanes, and Tecuexes. The Caxcanes were an independent nation that had branched from the Zacatecos.[7] The people of these chiefdoms were difficult to conquer because they were unified and prepared for war. Scattered within the territories controlled by the six nations, however, were independent villages that could easily fall.

In 1536 the first successful Spanish invasions were launched (Powell 1952:3). The first villages to be subdued were located in the present cities of Guadalajara and Querétaro. Spaniards made alliances with many Indian groups there and in turn used these relations to befriend other Indians. Defeated villages were assured that no harm would come to them if they helped the Spanish vanquish other groups. As a further enticement to side with Spain, Indians were given tools, cooking utensils, and clothing. Through this divide and conquer process the Spanish gradually gained support from some Indian groups and began to move further north, each village becoming a stepping stone in the northern invasion.

The movement north, however, came to a halt when the Chichimec nations united for purposes of self-defense. Tenamaxtle became the head of the coalition (Powell 1952). He was the tribal chief of several Caxcan *rancherías,* and his people often intermarried with Zacatecos and Tecuexes. In 1541 he was able to unite over 60,000 warriors under his command (Rodríguez Flores 1976:74). Second in command was Citlacotl, a Caxcan Indian from Mixtón, a *ranchería* in Jalpa. Between 1541 and 1542 the Chichimec Indians fought the Mixtón War and successfully defeated their enemies (Forbes 1994:24; Powell 1952:30). Their uprising was massive and spread outside the Gran Chichimeca, reaching villages in northwest Mexico. The only Spanish northwestern garrison in Culiacán was temporarily abandoned after the local Indians joined the Chichimec rebellion (Chipman 1992; Spicer 1981).

Ironically, although the Chichimec forces were able to stop the north-ward invasion, Tenamaxtle's army suffered a severe blow when Citlacotl betrayed him (Rodríguez Flores 1976). Citlacotl secretly made a treaty with Captain Miguel Ibarra in exchange for the protection of his people. About 1,000 Caxcanes and Zacatecos were to be secretly relocated to Guadalajara. In return Citlacotl revealed Tenamaxtle's military plans to Ibarra. On 26 December 1541 Tenamaxtle's army was ambushed and a large number of his warriors were killed. With a nearly depleted army Tenamaxtle was temporarily forced to retreat. This demoralized his troops (Rodríguez Flores 1976:79).

Although Tenamaxtle's army was defeated, other Chichimec tribes continued fighting. The fighting force changed from a well-organized military army to independent battalions led by hundreds of village chiefs. In particular, small Zacateco villages took up arms. The Tecuexes, one of the smallest nations of the Gran Chichimeca, began to unify the village chiefs and brought order to the attacks launched against the Spanish. Surprisingly, the Tecuexes, who did not have a well-trained army, fought many successful battles against the Spanish. Tenamaxtle's spirit to continue fighting rose when he heard that village chiefs and the Tecuexes, who were among the weakest military tribes in the Gran Chichimeca, had taken over the fighting and refused to be vanquished. No longer demoralized, Tenamaxtle took charge and once more recruited a massive army. Captain Ibarra, seeing that the Chichimec forces were once again unified under one leader, quickly attempted to bribe Tenamaxtle by promising him wealth in return for the surrender of his people. The captain sent a letter to Tenamaxtle informing him that Spain was prepared to enact a treaty if his people surrendered. Tenamaxtle boldly responded to the audacity of Ibarra's request and stated that his people would defend their land to the death. The land rightfully belonged to them and not to the intruders: "Surely you must be insane, or you must want us to kill you, if you think that we will give you our land and not defend it; who do you think you are, and who has asked you to come here?" (Rodríguez Flores 1976:76; my translation).[8]

Spain's military losses and inability to push northward led the royal government to reconsider its colonization plan and retreat temporarily. Economically it was no longer expedient to attack the Gran Chichimeca when financial investments were more fruitful elsewhere, such as among the Maya along the southern frontier, where the region had been stabilized (Perry and Perry 1988). If Spaniards or Indian *tlatoques* chose to continue fighting after the Mixtón Wars, they had to fund their own battles. For a short period both sides reduced their attacks.

Silver Mines and the Conquest of the Gran Chichimeca

In 1546 social conditions began to change in the Spaniards' favor after Captain Juan de Tolosa discovered silver in the present state of Zacatecas (Frye 1996:43; Powell 1952:10–11). Tolosa obtained the support of three wealthy war veterans, and together they took on the royal crown's challenge. They decided to recruit a large army and finance three mining camps in Zacatecas. Tolosa, Captain Cristóbal de Oñate, Diego de Ibarra, and Baltasar Temiño de Bañuelos were prepared for any challenge. They had previously benefited financially from successful campaigns against rebellious Indians. To them the north was a land of opportunity, a potential patrimony that could ensure their families' wealth for generations to come. They knew the cost of fighting the Chichimecs could ultimately be their deaths, yet the rewards for conquering the north exceeded the risks.

Before silver could be extracted from the mines it became necessary to increase the fortification of Zacatecas. For two years the Chichimecs left the camps alone and the four entrepreneurs gave the new frontier its first stability; they held on when others thought the job was impossible or not worth the risk (León-Portilla 1972). Within a few years, the news that silver had been discovered in Zacatecas prompted a large migration of settlers. Moreover, with the arrival of thousands of colonists in Zacatecas, they now had the forces to launch a fatal attack against the Chichimecs. As a result of the mining activities, the four investors were among the wealthiest men in the Americas and were prepared to finance the establishment of more mining camps. With increasing numbers of people prepared to settle in the north, Mexico's viceroy Don Luis de Velasco was willing to finance new colonies. After 1555 the settlements in the present state of Zacatecas grew into towns and mining camps were founded in the present states of Chihuahua, Coahuila, and Durango (Forbes 1994:32; León-Portilla 1972:90).

As more colonists settled in the north the Chichimecs responded by launching several attacks and temporarily causing many to abandon their camps outside of the heavily fortified region in Zacatecas. The Spanish retaliated, forcing the Indians to retreat. Once the Spaniards had re-stabilized the region north of Zacatecas, the colonists returned, but only for short periods, because the Indians launched counterattacks. Miguel León-Portilla describes this process of settlement and abandonment:

> To assure communications between Zacatecas and Mexico City, the authorities began to establish new towns, missions, and forts. Soon, too, new deposits were discovered where other mining centers were established: Guanajuato in 1555, Sombrerete in 1556, Fresnillo and Mazapil in 1568. Frequent assaults and rebellions on the part of the Chichimecs, although they were subdued time after time, made constant precaution and defense necessary. However, the zeal to exploit the gold and silver deposits from that time on prevented the abandonment of what had been achieved and, furthermore, im-pelled new attempts at penetration. (León-Portilla 1972:90)

By 1561 the Chichimecs had killed over 200 Spaniards and *mestizos* and 2,000 Indian colonists (Powell 1952:61).

A few years later the royal government responded to the setbacks by instituting radical military policies. The new viceroy, Don Martín Enríquez de Almanza, authored several enslavement policies allegedly to pacify the north. The policies of "guerra a fuego y a sangre" (war by the sword) were instituted in 1569 (Powell 1952:105–107). The intent was to promote factionalism and dissuade Indians from fighting, for if they continued challenging Spain the captured villagers would be enslaved for thirteen years and forced to work in the mines. Though the enslavement policies conflicted with Mexico's New Laws of 1542–1543, which prohib-ited Indian slavery, an exemption was made for the Chichimec captives (Hanke 1949:4). Among the first Indians to be enslaved were villagers near the mining camps of Zacatecas and Santa Bárbara in Chihuahua. Slaves were later captured from various villages in Guaynamota, Sina-loa, and Nuevo León (Powell 1952:110). People were captured, sentenced, distributed among the colonists, and then forced to work in the mines (Lafaye 1974; Forbes 1994). Many Indians were transported to Mexico City and sold at auction. After the first groups were enslaved, surrounding communities feared a similar fate and ended their revolts. The viceroy's campaign of terror was effective and coerced many to form alliances. The zone under Spain's control gradually grew.

In response to the enslavement activities, many Chichimec villages launched several battles against the Spanish from 1570 to 1580 (Powell 1952:37, 109). The main targets were the garrison and mining camps in Zacatecas. Travel north of the fortified regions in Zacatecas and Durango became very dangerous. With the exception of the mining camps in Santa Bárbara and San Bartolomé, Chihuahua, which were under the control of a handful of wealthy mining entrepreneurs and soldiers, very few settlers ventured past Zacatecas (Alonso 1995; Chipman 1992).[9] In an effort to hasten the colonization of the north, Viceroy Enríquez petitioned the royal government to provide more incentives for the settlers. He asked that all settlers be given Indian slaves and the right to retain them for life.

At first, many New World clergy supported the viceroy, because temporary slavery was an effective policy. When he asked that Indians be enslaved for life, however, the church protested and instead offered a more humane solution. Rather than instituting a war policy, the church proposed that a pacification strategy be implemented through a large-scale missionization program (Engelhardt 1929). They would build missions among the Chichimecs and entice Indians to relocate there, a process replicating the Maya mission system. The proposed plan would begin with the aid of Indian allies. Each mission would have at least three Christian Indians who in turn would convince others to move to the missions (Engelhardt 1929). If Indians did not want to live in the missions but were willing to become allies, they would be asked to relocate their villages near the missions (Polzer 1976; Spicer 1981). This policy was called *reducción*. The church also suggested that Indians from central Mexico be asked to form colonies, as this type of settlement would be less threatening to the Chichimecs (Bannon 1970).

The royal government responded favorably. King Philip II ordered a reduction of the armed forces, funded the mission program, and passed the royal Ordinance of Pacification of 1573, which nullified the enslavement policies (Chipman 1992:55; Cutter 1986:28). Although the king sided with the church, many colonists continued capturing and illegally enslaving Indians (Chipman 1992; Forbes 1994; Gibson 1964).[10] After many more battles, and the ongoing arrival of colonists and missionaries, the Chichimecs reduced their fighting. In 1591 the north was declared safe and ready for large-scale settlement (Powell 1952:194). The Chichimec Indians were no longer unified and did not pose a threat.

The Mission System

The settlement of Mexico beyond Zacatecas proceeded by way of missions and Indian towns. The royal crown considered these type of settlements to be less threatening to Indians unaccustomed to state systems. Once regions were stabilized, Spaniards and *mestizos* would follow. To unravel this colonial process I need to provide a brief overview of Mexico's mission system.

The first large-scale conversion of Indians occurred in 1523 among the Tlaxcalans (Engelhardt 1929:11). It was successful, as many Indians welcomed the fathers. The following year twelve Franciscans came to central Mexico to spread Christianity. Three years later Dominicans arrived, followed by Augustinians in 1533 and Jesuits in 1572 (ibid., 3). The Christianization of the Indians of central Mexico succeeded. In the north the first religious *entrada* began in 1533 among the Indians of Jalisco. A few Indians converted. Throughout the sixteenth century the church tried to Christianize the Indians of the north, but repeatedly failed. Most missionaries were forced to retreat, and those who remained behind were killed.

In central Mexico the Christianization of the Indians took place in the *corregimientos,* Indian pueblos, and *encomiendas.* There they were taught religious doctrines during their catechism lessons. Since the Indians were not under the constant supervision of the fathers, Fray Juan de Zumárraga proposed to the crown that missions be established to accelerate Indian acculturation. A few years after the conquest a small number of Indians in central Mexico were removed from the *encomiendas* and placed in experimental missions (Perry and Perry 1988). The church and the crown, however, decided that it was not necessary to construct missions in central Mexico because most Indians were already accustomed to the social order imposed by state governments. Isolating Indians for purposes of acculturation was expensive and unnecessary. Missions were to be established only in newly pacified frontier zones where other types of colonial settlements were not functional.

According to this plan, after a frontier region had been pacified and friendly Indians had been identified, a parish would be constructed as well as dormitories for the fathers and Indians. Acculturating Indians in missions was seen as a strategic method to entice people to live under the control of Spaniards. Most missions also were to contain rooms for religious instruction, occupational production (e.g., crafts, weaving, candles, winery), and other functions as well as stables (Engelhardt 1929). Missions located in dangerous zones would be protected by soldiers and a military center built for self-defense (with an office, jail, and soldiers' dormitories).

The chiefs of tribes who were allies of the fathers but were unwilling to live in the missions would be asked to move their villages near the missions. In this way, Indian villages would become part of the mission communities without threatening the social distance preferred by the people. The first frontier mission was built in 1542 at Nachi Cocom among the Mayas of the Yucatán Peninsula (Perry and Perry 1988:20). Within forty years, 22 Maya missions were established as well as 186 *visitas*, Indian villages regularly visited by missionaries to officiate mass, baptize Indians, and teach catechism (ibid., 35). In the Yucatán, and later throughout Mexico, it became common for mission communities to begin as *visitas* and later be elevated to missions (Polzer 1976).

The first missions in northern Mexico were established in 1590 in the present states of Sinaloa and Durango (Engelhardt 1929; Polzer 1976).[11] The large-scale construction of missions did not take place until after the Gran Chichimeca was pacified. By the early 1700s missions had been constructed in Baja California, Florida, Sinaloa, Sonora, Durango, Jalisco, Nuevo León, Nayarit, Querétaro, San Luis Potosí, Tamaulipas, and the U.S. Southwest. Throughout the frontier zones the missions proved to be essential in the pacification of hostile Indians. In the Gran Chichimeca, missions served that purpose, but they were also accompanied by Indian pueblos. The church and crown decided that the conquest of this region had been delayed long enough and that the missions alone could not rapidly acculturate the Indians. For that purpose Tlaxcalan Indians were ordered to help the mission fathers settle the Gran Chichimeca.

The Tlaxcalan Indians

After the Chichimec revolts ended, missions and Indian pueblos were founded throughout northern Mexico (Frye 1996). The first Indian colonists were Tlaxcalan. They founded the first towns and populated the first missions. At least three Tlaxcalan Indians lived in each mission (Bannon 1970:73; Bolton 1960:15; Simmons 1964:102, 103). All settlements were established near the largest Indian villages. In this way, the Tlaxcalans and the fathers had access to large communities and a place to retreat quickly when the other Indians became hostile.

Four hundred Tlaxcalan families set out to settle the north on 4 March 1591 (Hernández Xochitiotzin 1991:3).[12] The families were accompanied by Tlaxcalan captains Don Lucas Téllez, Don Buenaventura de la Paz, Don Lucas Montealegre, and Don Francisco Vásquez. These captains acted as guides and temporary civil judges. The head of the expedition was Miguel de Caldero, a Tlaxcalan *mestizo* who was well acquainted with the Indians of the north. Father Jerónimo de Mendieta and Indian scholar Don Diego Muñoz Camargo were appointed to chronicle the expedition and record events. Several other Franciscan friars were also among the settlers. In addition to these volunteers, twenty-five Tlaxcalan slaves accompanied the settlers (letter of Tlaxcala governor Martín López de Guana, 1591). These Indians had been condemned to slavery for having protested and attempted to prevent the march north. The idea that the north was to be settled by Indians had caused considerable turmoil in the city of Tlaxcala. Over 925 people, divided into four groups, left the present state of Tlaxcala (Hernández Xochitiotzin 1991:5).[13] The colonists rode in 111 covered wagons. Once they arrived at their destinations they were under the command of Captain Don Rodrigo del Río y Loza and Captain Don Agustín de Hinojosa y Villacencio.

The Spanish crown granted the colonists the title of *hidalgos libres,* designating persons who were the founders of a colony and deserved special privileges, including exemption from paying tribute and the right to receive land grants with alienation rights (the right to sell their property) (Alessio Robles 1934:4).[14] Interestingly, all *hidalgos,* regardless of their social standing, were also allowed to wear Spanish clothing, ride horses, and carry arms in public. This indeed was an honor, as these privileges were reserved for Indian nobles and Indian soldiers.

Overall, Tlaxcalans founded at least eight towns, and some of the settlers moved to the town of Zacatecas. The newly founded towns were located in the present states of Jalisco (San Luis de Colotlán), San Luis Potosí (San Miguel de Mixquitic, Tlaxcalilla, Agua de Venado Chanaca, Agua Hedionada, San Luis Potosí), and Coahuila (Saltillo, San Esteban de Nueva Tlaxcala).[15] Once established, the towns in Coahuila became the furthest northeastern colonies and strategic stepping stones in the settlement of Texas (Alessio Robles 1934; Baga 1690; Gibson 1967). Shortly after the arrival of the Tlaxcalans, thousands of Spaniards, *mestizos,* and *afromestizos* followed. Ironically, after Tlaxcalans helped to stabilize the north their political significance declined, and they were stripped of all political power (Frye 1996). By 1646 the Spanish Empire was entrenched in the Gran Chichimeca. Over 127,891 colonists and Christianized Indians became subjects of the crown: 102,289 Christian Indians, 16,230 Spaniards, 1,082 *mestizos,* and 8,290 *afromestizos* or Blacks (Cook and Borah 1974:197, 198, 200).[16] Nearly half of the Christian Indian population lived in or near the missions.

The Racial Politics behind the Settlement of New Mexico

By the time the colonization of the Southwest began, the Spanish crown and the Catholic Church had passed laws to protect the Indians (see Chapter 2). After Indians were subdued or befriended they were to be peaceably colonized in missions or in Indian villages under the judicial control of the Spanish, as ordered by the royal Ordinance of Pacification of 1573 (Cutter 1986; Polzer 1976). The church became their legal protector and the main agent of cultural change (Cutter 1986; Polzer 1976; *Recopilación de leyes de los reynos de las Indias* 1774: Book 1, Title 1, Laws 1, 3, and 9). As long as Indians accepted colonial rule, their land rights were validated; otherwise their property rights were abolished (Hanke 1949). The royal government also had the right to set the boundaries between Spanish and Indian settlements and to claim land on behalf of the colonists. In theory, this was the legal philosophy; in practice, many settlers disobeyed the royal orders and abused the legal rights of the Indians.

Spanish settlement of the Southwest began in 1598 when Juan de Oñate led over 400 male settlers to New Mexico; 130 of these men were accompanied by their wives and children (Prince 1915:139; Villagrá 1933: 103).[17] Plans for the northward movement began in 1595, after viceroy Luis de Velasco approved Oñate's petition (Hammond 1953:1). Oñate was selected to head the first colony in the Southwest due to his family's frontier legacy. He was an experienced frontiersman and the son of one of the wealthiest men in Mexico, Cristóbal Martín de Oñate, a war veteran who had pacified the Indians of Zacatecas and founded the frontier city of Guadalajara. Eventually Oñate spent over 400,000 pesos of his own funds to pay for the journey (Bannon 1970:41). Although Velasco approved Oñate's petition, the movement north had to wait several years, because the viceroy was removed from office.

When Don Gaspar de Zúñiga y Acevedo, count of Monterrey, was appointed the new viceroy he rescinded Oñate's commission, choosing instead Don Pedro Ponce de León. The viceroy allegedly disapproved of Oñate because of the dubious company he kept and the character of the colonists he had recruited. In a letter to the crown on 11 June 1596 he supported his decision by questioning the colonists' civility:

> ... it is very important that the people taken by Don Juan de Oñate be orderly and disciplined and cause no harm, and that they be corrected and punished if they cause any trouble ... we may well fear that when these people cross the provinces of New Galicia and New Vizcaya, great injury and damage will result to the cattle ranchers of those provinces, and also to the mining establishments, by which these people must of necessity pass. (letter of Don Gaspar de Zuñiga y Acevedo in Hammond and Rey 1953:98)

The viceroy's motives were highly suspect, as Oñate was a second-generation war veteran and one of the wealthiest entrepreneurs of Mexico. Why the viceroy instead selected a *peninsular* unaccustomed to the frontier is uncertain, but racial politics were obviously involved. At that time the loyalty of *criollos* was highly suspect, and commissioning *mestizos* for high-level positions was against the law (Haring 1963; Menchaca 1993). Oñate's political loyalty was in doubt because there were many substantiated allegations that he was a *mestizo* assuming the legal status of a *criollo* (Cornish 1917:459). Even Oñate's friends questioned his racial purity. Gaspar Pérez de Villagrá, one of the chroniclers and later a captain in Oñate's expedition, wrote about the rumors and investigated the family's genealogy, claiming that on his mother's side Oñate was a descendant of Moctezuma II (Villagrá 1933:73). Villagrá and many others proposed that the *peninsular* woman recorded as Oñate's mother could not have been his mother because she lived in Spain at the time of his birth (Cornish 1917). Adding to the viceroy's consternation, it was a well-known fact that Oñate's wife, Doña Isabel de Tolosa Cortés Moctezuma, was not White: she was the daughter of Juan de Tolosa (one of the founders of Zacatecas), the granddaughter of Hernán Cortés, and the granddaughter of Emperor Moctezuma II (Chipman 1977; Cornish 1917).

Despite these questionable associations, Oñate triumphed in the end. His wealth and political connections served him well: the royal crown disagreed with the viceroy and interceded on Oñate's behalf. On 2 April 1597 King Philip II personally approved his petition on the grounds that he was a frontiersman well suited for the commission (letter of King Philip II, in Hammond and Rey 1953:196).

Oñate was immediately granted the titles of captain-general and governor of New Mexico. This gave him the right to govern the colony and assign land grants to the settlers. On 26 January 1598 Oñate's colonists departed from Santa Bárbara, Chihuahua,[18] with 83 wagons and some 7,000 head of stock, accompanied by 10 Franciscans, 8 priests, and 2 lay brothers (Bannon 1970:36; Engelhardt 1929:14; Weber 1992). Fray Alonso Martínez was in charge of all religious matters and was appointed to begin the mission program (Hammond 1953:16). Oñate's colonists were also well prepared to launch a military attack if necessary; they brought horses, swords, shields, daggers, cannons, harquebuses, lances, spears, helmets, gunpowder, saddles, horseshoes, leather jackets, corsets, beaves, cosques, and halberds (Uolla Inspection, in Hammond and Rey 1953:136–137; Salazar Inspection, in Hammond and Rey 1953:225–227). Indeed they were equipped with the most advanced technology of the time.

Who Were the Colonists?

The members of Juan de Oñate's colony were recruited from different regions of Mexico and included *peninsulares, criollos, mestizos,* Indians, and approximately five Blacks (Bannon 1970:41; John 1975:39–43; Salazar Inspection, in Hammond and Rey 1953:514–519; Uolla Inspection, in Hammond and Rey 1953:94–168). Those who were born in Spain came primarily from Castille, Estremadura, Laredo, and Biscay, while the majority of those who were born in Mexico came from Zacatecas, Mexico City, and Puebla (Salazar Inspection, in Hammond and Rey 1953:514–519; Uolla Inspection, in Hammond and Rey 1953:94–168). Very few records remain describing the settlers. The main accounts are based on military inspections conducted by Lieutenant Captain Juan de Frías Salazar and Don Lope de Uolla. The inspections were conducted in several of the mining camps in Chihuahua. Unfortunately, the royal government ordered that detailed information be collected only on the White soldiers. We thus have little information on the colonists of color, who were merely asked to appear for roll call and register their belongings. General descriptions indicate that the colony was racially diverse. It is unclear why so little information was collected.

Nonetheless, one of Salazar's roll calls, conducted on 8 January 1598, contains valuable racial information (Salazar Inspection, in Hammond and Rey 1953:287). On the day of the inspection, in the mining camp of Todos Santos, Salazar ordered all the White soldiers to assemble inside the church. They were to be counted, declare where they were born, and identify their father. Salazar warned the soldiers that any person who attempted to impersonate a Spaniard would be severely penalized. He ordered that "no Indian, *mulatto* or *mestizo* present himself at the review unless he clearly states that he is such, under penalty of death, so that, with this knowledge, that which best suits the service of his majesty may be done" (ibid.).

Salazar faithfully executed the viceregal order and compiled a list of 117 Spaniards (Salazar Inspection, in Hammond and Rey 1953:289–300). He also identified which of the Spaniards were married, but did not report the race of the spouses. Interestingly, it appears that on one occasion Salazar doubted the ancestry of one Spanish officer but did not pursue the matter. He carefully described Captain Alonso de Sosa Peñalosa, a wealthy man who was accompanied by his wife: "Captain Alonso de Sosa Peñalosa, native of Mexico, son of Francisco de Sosa Albornoz, 48 years of age, of dark complexion, somewhat gray, with his arms; the other arms which he had declared he had given to a soldier" (ibid., 290).

Perhaps it was expedient to overlook Peñalosa's color and not inquire into his paternity, because he was a valuable asset to the colony. Among Peñalosa's registered supplies were jewels, silver, silk, 35 horses, 30 steers, 80 milk cows, 500 sheep, and 80 goats (Salazar Inspection, in Hammond and Rey 1953:241).

Although Salazar's inspection provides little demographic information on the colonists of color it is an extremely valuable record because the exclusion of information is itself significant. The historical erasure of racial information indicates a hesitancy on the part of the royal government to keep records of the activities of the people of color. Anthropologist Michel-Rolph Trouillot (1995) argues that this practice was quite common during the sixteenth through nineteenth centuries. Chroniclers consciously distorted events by deliberately ignoring the accomplishments of people of color or by documenting events in generalities to hide specific information. This was not done out of malice but emanated from a historiographic tradition that did not consider the heroic acts of people of color to be possible or of value. Nonetheless, another registry by Don Lope de Uolla provides some information on the nativity and racial composition of the settlers. Together the two inspections indicate that most of the colonists were not *peninsulares*. The Uolla registry taken between 10 and 17 February 1597 gives detailed information on all of the soldiers, not solely on those who were White. It also provides a few glimpses of the women.

Uolla registered a total of 228 enlisted men (Uolla Inspection, in Hammond and Rey 1953:150–168). Because nativity, rather than race, was used as one of the main variables to describe the soldiers, the registry obscures the racial background of the men born in Mexico; thus it is uncertain how many of the men were non-White. Of the men registered by Uolla 126 were *peninsulares* and 77 were either *criollos* or *mestizos* (ibid.). The registry indicates that 15 male servants accompanied their *peninsular* masters and were fully equipped with military gear (ibid., 94–168). The race of the servants was not recorded.

We also learn from various sources that a few Blacks were part of the expedition. Uolla's registry indicates that Oñate's personal servant was Black (Uolla Inspection, in Hammond and Rey 1953:129). In addition, Salazar's supply registry notes that Francisco de Sosa Peñalosa brought four female slaves and one male slave (Salazar Inspection, in Hammond and Rey 1953:247). Captain Gaspar Pérez de Villagrá reported in government documents that there were Blacks among the settlers and that Oñate felt comfortable socializing with them (Hammond 1953:15). On one occasion Villagrá noted that Oñate and his Black companions mocked Inspector Salazar. Uolla and Salazar provide little information on the women. We learn more about them from Villagrá's chronicle on the founding of the colonies in New Mexico. The notes on the women primarily indicate that many soldiers were married and many spouses came from Tlaxcala (Uolla Inspection, in Hammond and Rey 1953:151–168). In sum, though most of the information in the records refers to the *peninsulares*, the inspections, the roll calls, the letters sent by the viceroy, and Villagrá's account clearly indicate that Oñate's colony was racially mixed.

The Journey to New Mexico and the Pueblo Indians

On 26 January 1598 Oñate's colonists assembled and left Santa Bárbara, Chihuahua, commencing their trek toward New Mexico (Bannon 1970: 36; Chipman 1992:59). Along the way, they stopped in present-day El Paso, where they met two Indians from central Mexico named Tomás and Cristóbal. The two men were former scouts from an earlier expedition that had passed through New Mexico who had chosen to remain in El Paso and live among the Pueblo Indians. Oñate convinced them to accompany the party and serve as translators, as both men were familiar with some of the languages spoken by the Pueblo peoples (John 1975:40, 41). A bilingual chain of translation was immediately organized through Caso Barahona, a member of the colony who spoke Spanish and one of the Indian languages known by Tomás and Cristóbal.

When Oñate passed through villages, he greeted the Indians and announced that they had become vassals of the king of Spain. He informed them that if they voluntarily complied they would live in peace, justice, and orderliness, but if they resisted they would be severely punished. To repay the Indians for their allegiance, Oñate promised to protect them and to enrich their culture by teaching them Spanish traditions, trades, and farming technology. He then offered gifts as a token of peace and a confirmation of their conquest, including knives, necklaces, combs, scissors, *tomines*, shoemaker needles, mirrors, glass bottles, hats, bells, tin images, beads, headdresses, rosaries, lace edgings, fans, rings, thimbles, anklets, and flutes (Uolla Inspection, in Hammond and Rey 1953:134–135). Allegedly, the Indians accepted the gifts courteously and agreed to become vassals, or at least that was Oñate's assumption. What the Indians thought of this ritual is uncertain. We know only what Oñate wrote. These colonial contracts survived for centuries and became legal statutes validating the Pueblo Indians' land rights.

Some of the colonists finally arrived at an Indian village called Caypa on 11 July 1598, and the missionaries renamed the village San Juan de los Caballeros (Hammond 1953:17).[19] The village was occupied by Tewa Indians (Hodge 1953:365). The main body of Oñate's colony reached San Juan approximately a month later. For several months the colonists and Indians of San Juan lived in peace until news arrived in early December that Captain Juan de Zaldívar and twelve of his men, who had left San Juan in search of food, had been killed by Acoma Indians (Villagrá 1933:214;

John 1975:47). Oñate immediately declared war against the Acoma and ordered his men to prepare for battle. The Indians of San Juan, frightened by a change of affairs, cautioned their neighbors about the potential danger the Spanish posed. After the soldiers left for Acoma, some of the Indians from San Juan and from the surrounding villages became hostile. Oñate, who had remained behind, ordered his soldiers to launch a counterattack. With insufficient men to defend the colony, it became necessary for the women to arm themselves. Acting like veteran soldiers, the women hid on the housetops and positioned themselves to shoot their enemies. Doña Eufemia, the wife of Francisco de Sosa Peñalosa, organized the women. Villagrá chronicled the women's defensive attack:

> The general was in his quarters when the Indians raised an alarm that all the neighboring tribesmen were in arms and marching to destroy all the Spaniards. The pueblo of San Juan was so situated that it formed an immense square with four entrances. The general posted his men and guns at each of these approaches. . . . The Indians continued their alarms. The men were all well stationed and ready to defend the capital when the general noticed that all the housetops were crowded with people. He quickly sent two captains to investigate who they were and what they meant. They returned soon, informing him that Doña Eufemia had gathered all the women together on the housetops to aid in the defense. Doña Eufemia had stated that they would come down if the general so ordered, but that it was their desire to be permitted to aid their husbands in the defense of the capital. Don Juan was highly pleased at this display of valor coming from feminine breasts, and he delegated Doña Eufemia to defend the housetops with the women. They joyfully held their posts and walked up and down the housetops with proud and martial step.[20] (Villagrá 1933:223–224)

Finding San Juan well fortified, the Indians decided to retreat. While trouble brewed in San Juan, Oñate's soldiers arrived in Acoma and defeated the Acoma Indians after several days of fighting. Cannons and other artillery were used to disable them. The Acoma forces surrendered, but they refused to identify which Indians had killed Zaldívar and his companions. The Indians were then rounded up and placed in bondage. Some resisted and tried to hide in the kivas, while others escaped through underground passages.

At this point there are two distinct accounts of what transpired. According to Acoma descendants, their oral tradition says that their people surrendered because they knew if they resisted the entire tribe would be massacred (Forbes 1994:89–90). A conflicting account was advanced by Oñate's soldiers. Oñate's report claimed that, although many Indians surrendered, a large number resisted, and in defense his men set Acoma on fire (cf. Hammond 1953:21).[21] Based on these two contradictory versions of events it is uncertain what happened; but the Spanish destroyed Acoma and captured approximately 80 men and 500 women. The hostages surrendered and were charged with the murder of Zaldívar and the other Spanish soldiers. Oñate ordered a trial, appointing Captain Alonso Gómez Montesinos as their defense attorney. The Acoma captives were found guilty, and Oñate pronounced their sentences. Men over twenty-five years of age were condemned to have one foot cut off and were placed in servitude for twenty years. Males between twelve and twenty-five years of age and women over twelve were sentenced to twenty years of servitude. Boys and girls under twelve were placed under the supervision of the colonists. The boys were to live under the command of Spanish officers, and the girls were turned over to the missionaries (Bannon 1970:36; Hammond 1953:21). Unfortunately, these girls became the first mission neophytes of the Southwest.

The Colonists Rebel

Life for the colonists continued to be difficult. Six months later they left San Juan and resettled a few miles north in Yukewingge among another Tewa people (Hodge 1953:371). Oñate renamed the village San Gabriel. Though conditions in San Gabriel improved, many colonists found life there unbearable and asked Oñate to allow them to leave New Mexico. He rejected their petitions and cautioned everyone that they were prohibited from leaving under penalty of law. Abandoning the colony was treason. While problems brewed in New Mexico, Captain Juan de Sotelo was on his way with a new colony. The settlers arrived in San Gabriel on 24 December 1600 (Hammond 1953:24). Most of de Sotelo's colonists were from Puebla and Mexico City. A more detailed record was left of these colonists. There were a total of 110 registered members:[22] 46 *peninsulares*, 39 *mestizos* or *criollos*, 2 Black servants, 20 Indians, and 3 young women whose race and parentage were not noted (Gordejuela Inspection, in Hammond and Rey 1953:514–579). Most of the female colonists were women of color. There were 14 Indian females, 9 *criollas* or *mestizas*, 1 Black woman, 5 *peninsulares*, and 3 others (ibid., 557–566). Within a year, Oñate's troubles worsened, as the new colonists also wanted to leave. A few of the families deserted. Most, however, remained behind and dispersed themselves in the two colonial settlements already established in San Gabriel and San Juan (Prince 1915).

Although life was difficult for the colonists, relations with the Indians gradually improved. Stability was achieved through the missionaries' ability to befriend the Indians. As more communities welcomed the fathers and allowed them to live in their villages, amicable social networks developed. Memories of the Acoma affair became less divisive as friendships developed between the colonists and Indians. By 1608 the friars reported a total of 4,000 Christian converts (Bannon 1970:39).

Though the Spanish colonies were finally getting a foothold, Oñate was forced to resign his post as governor of New Mexico and his son, Cristóbal, was denied the privilege of becoming the new governor. The Council of the Indies, a branch of the royal government that oversaw the New World colonies, charged Oñate with three major crimes. First, he had sentenced deserters to death without giving them a trial. Second, the sentencing of the Acomas and the crimes committed against them were considered improper. Third, Oñate had disregarded his obligations as governor and spent excessive time exploring New Mexico, rather than assuring the welfare of the colonists. On 24 August 1607 Oñate resigned his post, and Don Pedro Peralta became the new governor (Hammond 1953:33).

After replacing Oñate, the council changed its indifferent policies and began taking steps to ensure the survival of the colony by increasing financial support and sending more missionaries. The council also decided that it was time to build a capital in New Mexico. In 1609 some of the settlers were ordered to move from San Gabriel to Santa Fe, where the capital was founded (Bannon 1970:41). By 1630 Santa Fe had 250 residents claiming pure Spanish ancestry and approximately 700 Indians and *mestizos*. There were also over 50 friars serving 25 missions (ibid.; Prince 1915:46–48). A large number of the residents in Santa Fe were Tlaxcalan Indians, as a colony of Tlaxcalans had been established in New Mexico between 1600 and 1605 (Prince 1915:86; Simmons 1964:108–110). It is uncertain how many Tlaxcalans migrated to New Mexico and later resettled in Santa Fe. Mission fathers, however, reported that by 1680 there were close to 500 Tlaxcalan Indians living in Analco, a neighborhood of Santa Fe (Forbes 1973; Gibson 1967; Prince 1915:88).

The Great Pueblo Rebellion and the Settlement of El Paso Valley

A large number of Pueblo villages in New Mexico had a corporate government structure, resembling the political systems of the Indians of Mexico's central valley (Gibson 1964; Hall 1989). Many Indians lived in towns and small cities governed by theocratic councils, with judicial systems that set penalties and fines when laws were broken (Deloria and Lytle 1988). This level of political development had been one of the main attractions leading the royal government to select New Mexico as the first place of settlement in the Southwest (Spicer 1981). The crown's representatives in central Mexico had found that it was more convenient to colonize people who were organized under a central government, who, once conquered, would already be socialized to obey laws, pay fines, and most important of all pay tribute.

Spaniards conquered most Pueblo Indians by using military force and then coercing alliances. Pueblo villages which were militarily stronger were able to keep the Spanish at a distance, however, and resist the vassalage conditions imposed upon them. Such was the case of some Hopi villages (Lomawaima 1989). The Tewa, Tiwa, Jemez, Piro, and Keresan Pueblo villages were militarily weak and were subjected to heightened forms of exploitation (John 1975; Kessell 1989). The governors of New Mexico forced these Indian peoples to pay tribute and accept the construction of missions adjacent to their villages (Bronitsky 1987; Hall 1989). Many of these Indians were also forced to move to Santa Fe and work as servants or farm laborers. Though few scholars question that Indians were coerced into making alliances, intertribal warfare also prompted the Pueblo Indians to retain alliances with the colonists (Kessell 1989; Spicer 1981; Swanton 1984). Most Pueblo villages were enemies of the Navajo, who resided in present northern Arizona, and the Apache, who were dispersed throughout Arizona and New Mexico. Warfare frequently broke out when Apaches and Navajos raided Pueblo villages in search of food. To keep them at a distance and to protect crops during harvest season, Pueblo villagers often sought the military aid of their colonial neighbors.

As the region under Spanish control grew, the settlers were able to disperse themselves throughout northern New Mexico, where they established ranches and farms. A settlement pattern emerged. *Mestizos* and Indians were given small plots of land in the region north of Santa Fe, which came to be known as Río Arriba (Scholes 1937:139–140). Many of the ranches were established near Pueblo villages. Indian-colonist relations were relatively peaceful, and the Pueblo and settlers banded together when under Apache and Navajo attack (Hall 1989; Swadesh 1974). In Río Abajo, where *peninsulares* and *criollos* concentrated their settlements and were awarded large agricultural estates, colonial relations became very exploitative (Swadesh 1974). This region consisted of the town of Santa Fe and the surrounding ranches. Many soldiers and elites were awarded *encomiendas* in the Santa Fe zone and needed labor to work their fields. Tiwas and Tewas were often removed from their villages and forced to live under a peonage system, while Apaches were illegally enslaved under the pretense that they were dangerous and needed to be civilized (Kutsche 1979). It became common for colonists to raid Apache settlements and capture children, converting them to slaves.

As a result of the harsh treatment experienced by the Indians of Río Abajo, seeds of discontent were planted. Missionaries began to lose their followers. In many villages the fathers were no longer welcomed and were forced to leave. The fathers complained to the royal government and won a partial victory in 1641 when the third governor of New Mexico, Luis de Rosas, was replaced (Scholes 1937:142). Rosas was hated by the Indians because he allowed the settlers to capture Indians and enslave them for personal use (Forbes 1994). Upon reviewing the church's report warning of the potential threat that slavery posed to the stability of the colony, the royal government ordered that all slaving activities immediately end. Under subsequent governors slavery decreased, yet it did not entirely cease; a peonage system that nearly replicated a slave system became commonplace in Río Abajo. Many Indians were forced to work in the fields of the colonists without being paid wages. The actions of the colonists against the Indians continued to worsen, leading to political disorder (Forbes 1994:121; Gutiérrez 1991:107). Pueblo alliances with the colonists completely broke down, motivating the Pueblo Indians to seek Apache and Navajo support. Finally, in 1680, Pueblo Indians, Apaches, and Navajos temporarily united, launching an attack called the "Great Pueblo Rebellion" (Bannon 1970:80). Their motive was to force the colonists to leave. Over 401 colonists were killed, and approximately 2,000 people abandoned their homes in New Mexico (Forbes 1994:174; cf. Gutiérrez 1991:107). Among the refugees were 317 Christian Indians.

Although the Pueblo Rebellion was an indigenous uprising, the governor of New Mexico, Antonio de Otermín, reported that many *mestizos* and Tlaxcalans sided with the rebels (Forbes 1994:179, 181). In particular, many Tlaxcalans from Santa Fe conspired in the ambush and attack. They helped the Pueblos burn Santa Fe and force the colonists to retreat (Forbes 1973; Prince 1915:88). Governor Otermín also reported that many *mestizos* chose to remain among the Pueblo Indians.

The refugees were forced to march south and seek refuge in the colonial settlement of El Paso del Norte, founded in 1659 and located where Ciudad Juárez, El Paso, San Elizario, Ysleta, and Socorro are today (Metz 1994:10). The refugees gave life to the small colony, increasing the number of settlers and stabilizing the region. The royal crown granted the refugees permission to establish missions and ranches. Initially, most of the colonists established settlements in what is today Ciudad Juárez, while the mission communities were established on what is today the U.S. side of the border. Franciscans were in charge of the mission communities (Engelhardt 1929). The settlements located on the U.S. side came to constitute a zone within El Paso del Norte called El Paso Valley. In 1682 two mission communities called Ysleta and Socorro were established in El Paso Valley (Bowden 1971:129; Bronitsky 1987:153).[23] Senecú, an Indian pueblo, was also established at the same time along the present border of Ciudad Juárez and El Paso. Ysleta came to be inhabited by Tiwas, Senecú by Piros and Tompiros, and Socorro by Piros, Tanos, and Jemez (Bowden 1971). Socorro also contained a large number of *mestizos* who had married local Indians.

In 1681 the royal crown approved the construction of a presidio (a military administrative center) in El Paso del Norte as a means of assisting its colonists to fortify their settlements (White 1923:9). El Paso del Norte was also declared the new capital of New Mexico. Presidio del Paso del Norte was built a few miles south of El Paso in what is today Ciudad Juárez (Castañeda 1936:311). The presidio brought stability to the region, and the settlements soon prospered.

The Reconquest

Within a few years after the revolt, the Pueblo, Apache, and Navajo alliances began to dissolve. Many Pueblo Indians were angered when Popé, one of the Pueblo leaders of the rebellion, began to demand tribute from villages. Likewise, many Apache chiefs began to demand that they be given part of the valuables seized from the colonists, such as cattle, sheep, goats, and pigs. In 1691 the governor of New Mexico, Don Diego de Vargas, received news that the political union of the Indians of New Mexico was falling apart (Sánchez 1983:147).[24] This prompted Vargas to prepare a counterattack and begin negotiations with those chiefs who were prepared to switch alliances. The next year Luis Tupatú of Picuris, who was in favor of a Spanish reconquest, obtained support from many Picuri, Tano, and Tewa villages (Gutiérrez 1991; Hall 1989; Sánchez 1983; Weber 1992). Though a substantial number of Pueblo Indians preferred to have Spanish rather than Apache allies, the majority of them did not.

When Tupatú and his allies met with Vargas, they presented their demands: an end to the *encomienda* system, less scrutiny of ceremonial rights, and recognition of tribal property boundaries (Cutter 1986:44). Vargas conceded these points and agreed that the settlers would be ordered to establish small farms, rather than big estates requiring a large labor force. In this way the temptation to enslave Indians would be avoided. Vargas in turn demanded from Tupatú's people that they protect the settlers and allow the Catholic Church to reestablish missions in the Indian villages. Tupatú agreed to protect the settlers and to help Spain reconquer the region (Kessell 1989). The reconquest of New Mexico was launched in 1692, and a year later the Spanish military took over Santa Fe and most of New Mexico (ibid., 131). The Acoma, Zuni, and Hopi peoples, however, continued to resist for a few years longer. They were finally subdued when the chiefs of Zia, Pecos, and Santa Ana put an end to their rebellion (Lomawaima 1989). After the Spanish obtained control of New Mexico, the colonies were safe; anyone who resisted was condemned to a life of servitude or placed in prison.

The Growth of the Spanish Colonies

By 1804 New Mexico had approximately 35,750 to 40,000 inhabitants dispersed in colonial towns, missions, ranches, military settlements, and

Indian pueblos (Bautista Pino 1812::216).[25] The settlements in El Paso Valley were part of New Mexico until 1823 (Bowden 1971:157).[26] In the interior, three Spanish towns had been founded in Santa Fe, Santa Cruz, and Albuquerque (Carroll and Haggard 1942:50; Gutiérrez 1991:146), and over twenty-three Indian pueblos were under colonial control (Bautista Pino 1812:217).[27] Five of these Indian pueblos were largely populated by detribalized Indians and people of mixed Pueblo and Spanish descent (Archibald 1978:211; Carroll and Haggard 1942:27–28). In addition, most of these settlements contained missions.

In the southern region of New Mexico, in El Paso Valley, there were two additional mission communities in Socorro and Ysleta. By 1751 they had grown substantially and the residents had been given land grants to establish separate towns adjacent to the missions (Bowden 1971:41; Metz 1994:15). Ysleta and its adjoining mission continued to be solely populated by Indians, while the population of Socorro included many *genizaros* (detribalized Pueblo people of mixed Indian and colonial heritage) and *mestizos* (Bronitsky 1987). The Indian town of Senecú was also a lively community and came to be heavily populated by *mestizos*. By 1766 the population of these three communities is estimated to have grown to 5,000, with 2,000 being non-Indians (Metz 1994:16, 17).

In 1789 Presidio San Elizario was relocated to El Paso Valley from Porvenir, Mexico (Hendricks and Timmons 1998:15).[28] It was moved to the Socorro area to protect the residents of Socorro and Ysleta. There were other military headquarters in San Miguel del Vado and Taos, as well as a military jail in Santa Fe, an outpost in La Joya, and several cavalry detachments throughout New Mexico (Carroll and Haggard 1942:69–70; Hendricks and Timmons 1998:42, 44).[29]

San Elizario became one of the most important settlements in New Mexico as well as on the frontier because it was the resting place for travelers moving between Chihuahua and Santa Fe. It was also an important colonial-Indian trading center, founded in the same location as the abandoned Hacienda of Nuestra Señora de la Soledad de los Tiburcios.[30] The presidio consisted of outer walls, officer quarters, barracks, a chapel, stables, two defense towers, and several other buildings. A year after the presidio was founded, a presidial pueblo was constructed for the soldiers' families and other colonists. And a few years later seven Apache *rancherías* settled in the presidial pueblo, helping to stabilize the region by negotiating with other Apache groups to cease fighting. Among the allies were the families of Apache chiefs Barrio, Maya, and Maselchide. Throughout the Spanish period the settlements in San Elizario remained colonial strongholds in spite of the severe Apache attacks between 1792 and 1798 (Hendricks and Timmons 1998:31–37).

The People of New Mexico

Throughout New Mexico sexual relations between male colonists and female Tiwas and Tewas became quite common by the mid-1700s (Morfí 1977:2–28; see Gutiérrez 1991). Missionaries disapproved of these relations and attempted to enforce the Indian residency laws, prohibiting colonists from living in Indian towns or remaining there for prolonged periods (*Recopilación de leyes de los reynos de las Indias* 1774: Book 6, Title 3, Law 21). This was futile, however, because the governors did not enforce the residency laws in spite of protests by the church (Gutiérrez 1991; Morfí 1977). Often the children of mixed parentage became tribal outcasts and were forced to live among the colonists. If their parents did not provide for them, they were placed in missions or in homes where they worked as servants. These orphans, called *genizaros*, became detribalized Indians. In most cases they were treated as outcasts by Indians and as social inferiors by the colonists (see Hall 1989:96).

Because the *genizaros* eventually constituted a large impoverished population without tribal lands, the Catholic Church was morally forced to intervene on their behalf. The church petitioned the royal government to assist them by giving them farmland and the opportunity to establish their own villages. By the early 1800s they had received land; Santa Rosa de Abiquiú, Belén, Tomé, Ojo Caliente, Socorro, and San Miguel del Vado became known as *genizaro* settlements (Archibald 1978:211; Bustamante 1991:148; Cutter 1986:82; Gutiérrez 1991:305). Not all children of mixed parentage met the same fate as the *genizaros*. When Pueblo Indians married colonists, it was common for the families to live in the colonial settlements; the children were treated as part of the colonial population, rather than as outsiders (see Olmstead 1981). Historian Ramón Gutiérrez (1991:103) adds that after the seventeenth century most colonial settlements grew through local birth rates and a large number of the colonial residents were of Pueblo Indian descent. After that date few people from the interior of Mexico migrated to New Mexico.

The exact number of *genizaros* living in New Mexico during the Spanish era is uncertain because census enumerators generally did not classify them under a separate category. Census data from 1789 indicate that in New Mexico, including El Paso Valley, there were 10,664 Indians, 14,553 people who claimed to be Spanish, and 5,736 people of mixed ancestry (Cook and Borah 1974:214, 220). The size of the Spanish population, however, is dubious, as fair-complexioned *castizos* were often counted as Spaniards. Of the Indians, 1,667 lived among the colonists in the towns, villas, or ranches (Bustamante 1991:153).[31] The size of the *afromestizo* population is also uncertain, as local censuses often omitted the racial categories of the mixed population and counted them as part of the "gente de razón" (people of reason; see Chapter 6). Nonetheless, a census of Albuquerque in 1750 by Father Joseph Yrigoian offers a glimpse of the *afromestizo* population. Of the 196 families of Albuquerque, 43 were of partially African descent. Most of these families were composed solely of *afromestizos*, but in some cases the racial composition of the families was mixed (Olmstead 1981:73–89). Interestingly, Father Yrigoian was very careful to note the Black blood quantum of the *afromestizo* families. He found that 36 were *mulatto* (Spanish and Black), 3 *coyote* (Indian and *mulatto*), and 4 *lobo* (Indian and Black) (ibid.).

Within two centuries of Juan de Oñate's *entrada* into New Mexico thousands of Spanish missionaries, soldiers, government officials, businessmen, Indians, and farmers erected missions, towns, presidios, ranches, and outposts and converted other Indians into allies. Though the majority of the settlers were racially mixed, the royal government selected *criollos* and *peninsulares* as its ruling elite (Bustamante 1991; Gutiérrez 1991; Weber 1992). White governors and missionaries ruled the colony.

4

The Spanish Settlement of Texas and Arizona

During the late seventeenth century, Spain initiated its next colonization phase, identifying Texas and Arizona as the preferred sites (Polzer 1976:36–37; Weber 1992:154). The *entradas* were launched by the military and the church. Franciscan fathers were in charge of the missions in Texas, while the Jesuits founded the missions in Arizona (Engelhardt 1929:14; Polzer 1976:34; Weber 1992:95).[1] Before colonies could be established, however, Indian alliances had to be forged and places for future colonies identified.

Texas Colonial Settlements

The colonization of Texas began in 1690 when two missions were established in the northeast (Chipman 1992:88; Morfí 1935). Approximately twenty-nine missions were erected throughout the Spanish period (Chipman 1992:108–109, 148–149; cf. Weber 1992:150). Some lasted a few months, while others continue to serve a congregation today, such as Mission San José and Mission San Juan de Capistrano (see Photographs 5 to 8). The settlement of Texas was prompted by the threat of a French invasion (Bannon 1970:94). France's monarch, Louis XIV, disregarded Spain's claim to North America and failed to honor the 1493 papal bull giving Spain legal right over most of the New World (Hoffman 1973). By the seventeenth century most European countries disagreed with the papal bull and proposed that land in the New World belonged to the country that had military possession of it. To establish an official claim to East Texas and Louisiana, Louis XIV commissioned René Robert Cavelier de La Salle to establish colonies. In 1685 La Salle founded Fort Saint-Louis near Matagorda Bay, in East Texas (Chipman 1992:87). Although the colony failed

Photograph 5. Mission San José.
Courtesy of the San Antonio
Missions National Historical Park.
Photograph taken by author.

Photograph 6. Mission San Juan
de Capistrano and Aztec Dancers,
1996. Courtesy of the San Antonio
Missions National Historical Park.
Photograph taken by author.

Photograph 7. Mission San Juan de Capistrano and My Sons at the Soldiers' Quarters, 1996. Courtesy of the San Antonio Missions National Historical Park. Photograph taken by author.

Photograph 8. Mission San Juan de Capistrano: Altar. Courtesy of the San Antonio Missions National Historical Park. Photograph taken by author.

after most settlers met their deaths at the hands of Indians, France continued its crusade, concentrating its energies in northeastern Texas.

To avert a French invasion, the Spanish crown commissioned Captain Alonso de León to take a party of soldiers and missionaries into the northeast border area of Louisiana and Texas (Pertulla 1992). They were to establish two mission settlements among the Hasini Indians, a subdivision of the Caddo. Franciscan father Damién Mazanet was in charge of the colonies and was assisted by four friars (Newcomb 1986). On 20 March 1690 León departed from Monclavo, Coahuila, and led his party toward the northeast (Bannon 1970:102). His troops were ordered to remain there until the fathers were safely situated but to leave as soon as possible, to assure the Indians that the fathers came in peace. The fathers set camp in a Hasini village called Nabedaches and soon established two missions nearby. After a year the crown sent a troop of soldiers to replenish supplies, because giving gifts to the Indians was an effective way of befriending them (Weber 1992). Apparently the first two years were successful, and a large number of Indians came to visit the fathers. Relations began to deteriorate, however, when the military stopped coming to replenish supplies. As supplies dwindled, so did the interest of the Hasini converts. Compounding the fathers' problems was their inability to grow crops in arid soil (Newcomb 1986). They gradually became more dependent on the Indians and were unable to prove the worth of their farming technology. In New Mexico the *entradas* had been partially successful because the Spaniards had demonstrated to the Pueblo Indians the advantages of having allies with advanced agricultural technology (Engelhardt 1930). This process was not replicated in the northeast, and in 1694 the Hasini forced the missionaries to leave (Newcomb 1986:287).

Although the first *entrada* failed, neither the crown nor the Catholic Church abandoned the efforts to colonize Texas. New plans were drafted after the royal government learned that France had ceased its attempts to colonize the northeast. Now the colonization of Texas could proceed in an area closer to the northern colonies already founded in the present states of Coahuila and San Luis Potosí (Alessio Robles 1934; Frye 1996). Establishing colonies in close proximity to one another was better strategically. If a colony was under attack, troops could quickly be mobilized and a large counterattack could be mounted. In 1700 and 1703 three missions were established along the current Texas-Mexico border, near present-day Monclova (Newcomb 1986:36). Although these missions were part of the Texas-Coahuila mission program, the buildings were erected on what is today the Mexican side of the border. Fortunately for the fathers, the missions flourished and attracted a large neophyte population (Campbell 1977). Alliances were also established with a large number of Tejas and Coahuiltecan Indians living in *rancherías* located near the missions (Chipman 1992; Weber 1982).[2]

Throughout Texas and other parts of the Southwest many Indians lived in villages politically led by a chief or headman, in contrast to the theocratic government commonly practiced among the Pueblo Indians of New Mexico. These communities were called *rancherías*. In most cases *ranchería* Indians refused to move when they were invited to live in the missions, so their chiefs were asked to relocate their villages near the missions. Fathers expected the *ranchería* Indians to become Christians and to adopt Spanish customs in terms of dress style, to register their villages as ally settlements in a garrison or presidio, and to send members of the *rancherías* to the missions (Ezzell 1974; Polzer 1976). Because *ranchería* Indians were not economically dependent upon the Spanish and were not under daily surveillance as were the mission Indians, the fathers knew that their interethnic relations were fragile and that the Indians' way of life had to be respected. During periods of war, *ranchería* allies were also expected to form military auxiliaries and to assist the Spanish in fighting mutual enemies (Kessell 1989).

In turn the Christianized *ranchería* Indians expected a reciprocal relationship, with the soldiers protecting them from common enemies and the fathers giving them supplies (Engelhardt 1930). Through this relationship many *rancherías* officially became part of Spanish municipalities and legal subjects of the crown (see *Byrne v. Alas et al.*, 1888:525, 526; Weber 1982).

Civilian Colonies

In 1716 the first civilian colony was established in Texas (Castañeda 1936: 47–49). Once again plans were prompted by renewed French threats in the northeast (Weber 1992).[3] A successful French colony had been established in Natchitoches, along the present northeast Texas-Louisiana border. Making matters worse for Spain, France granted entrepreneurs willing to fund colonies permission to establish camps in the northern region of Texas (Castañeda 1936:22–24). This gave investors title to the land they controlled.

Spain determined that Texas must be settled to avert any further French *entradas*. It became necessary to start populating several regions with soldiers, civilians, Indians, and mission fathers. In preparation for the arrival of the colonists Spanish soldiers and missionaries were commissioned to explore Texas and to select sites for settlement. At this time most of these soldiers came from Coahuila, and a large number of them were from the Tlaxcalan towns of Saltillo and San Esteban (Hernández Xochitiotzin 1991; Meade de Angulo n.d.).

In mid-February 1716 Captain Domingo Ramón took approximately seventy-eight colonists into the northeast (Bannon 1970:112; Castañeda 1936:47). These settlers included nine priests, three lay brothers, dozens of colonists, and twenty-five soldiers. Many of the soldiers also brought their families. Among the colonists were *criollos, mestizos,* and *peninsulares.* Only seven of the colonists were Indian, and one was Black (Castañeda 1936:45–47). As the colonists migrated north, they stopped many times along their route to rest and to greet friendly Tejas Indians. The settlers finally arrived in the northeast on 26 June 1716 (Bannon 1970:114). They established a presidio five miles west of the Neches River and erected five missions nearby among various ethnic subdivisions of the Caddo Indians.[4] Although their initial journey succeeded, they soon experienced severe hardships when their gifts dwindled and they were no longer welcomed. Within two years the Caddo Indians became increasingly hostile and repeatedly attacked the settlers.

When the royal government in Mexico City received news of the problems, it became necessary to reassess the colonization project; if military assistance was not made available, it was only a matter of time before the Indians destroyed the settlements. Clearly, if the colonists needed help it was unrealistic to expect the military from Coahuila to dispatch a cavalry unit in a timely manner. It therefore became necessary to establish a second colony midway between the northeast and Coahuila. A temporary militia could be assembled there and dispatched while a larger cavalry group came from Coahuila (Bannon 1970). Upon hearing the news that a second colony was to be established, Father Antonio de San Buenaventura de Olivares, the head missionary of the Coahuila missions, took immediate action and petitioned the crown for the colony to be established in San Antonio and for all religious matters to be in his charge. In 1690

Father Olivares had sent Agustín de la Cruz, a Tlaxcalan neophyte, to explore present San Antonio and the current Texas-Coahuila border (Baga 1690:96). Upon his return, De la Cruz reported that the region was inhabited by peaceful village-dwelling Indians. Nearly two decades later Father Olivares visited the area and reported to the royal government that the Indians of San Marcos and San Antonio were well suited for mission life.

In 1718 Father Olivares's petition was approved by the royal crown. His plans were to erect a mission and a civilian settlement populated by Indians and governed by *peninsulares* (Weber 1992:163). These plans came to a temporary halt when Martín de Alarcón, the governor of Coahuila and Tejas, was appointed to recruit the settlers and establish a civilian colony. Although Father Olivares was commissioned to found the first mission in San Antonio, it was Alarcón who was appointed to control all secular matters in the colony. Their views on who should settle San Antonio clashed.

Alarcón, like Olivares, preferred to select Spaniards to settle San Antonio. This became an unrealistic goal, however, because Alarcón was only able to recruit a handful of Spaniards. Most of the people willing to take the journey into the frontier were people of color (Castañeda 1936:87). According to Alarcón, only *mulattos, lobos, coyotes,* and *mestizos* from Coahuila were prepared to risk their lives in exchange for land. Nonetheless, Olivares distrusted these colonists because he considered them half-breed savages and feared that if war broke out they would betray the Spanish. He believed that the colonists of color were not the best agents of Spanish acculturation since they still practiced Indian dances and traditions and could easily revert to their parents' lifestyle. Father Olivares several times attempted to delay the departure of the colony until a larger number of *peninsulares* could be recruited. Alarcón, unable and unwilling to fulfill the father's request, began the trek toward San Antonio after agreeing to return and recruit more *peninsulares.*

The colonists were divided into two companies. The first company departed from Mission San José, located along the current Texas-Coahuila border. It was composed of Father Olivares, two missionaries, twenty-five soldiers, and about five Indians raised by Olivares since childhood (Castañeda 1936:35). The second company, stationed in Saltillo, Coahuila, was composed of Alarcón and seventy-two settlers (Chipman 1992:117).[5] The settlers included many of the soldiers' families as well as a large number of artisans (de la Teja 1991). The two companies departed in early April and arrived in San Antonio several days apart. Father Olivares took a direct route to San Antonio and arrived on 1 May 1718 (Bannon 1970:117). On that day Father Olivares founded Mission San Antonio de Valero— the chapel that later became the Alamo. Alarcón arrived five days later, as he took a scouting route to explore the coast before proceeding to San Antonio.[6] Presidio de Béjar was formally founded upon his arrival, and the settlers clustered inside it. They were the first members of what later was destined to become the largest civilian settlement in Texas—Villa of San Fernando de Béjar,[7] later renamed San Antonio. At this time the settlers remained under military governance and could not establish a town council because people of color did not have the right to govern themselves (de la Teja 1991). The crown did not give them this privilege until a decade later, after a large colony of *peninsulares* arrived in San Antonio. Furthermore, these settlers were not awarded land grants and were only issued occupancy land rights (de la Teja 1991).

After the colonists settled in San Antonio, Father Olivares charged that the colonists of color were unacculturated and untrustworthy and therefore asked Alarcón to return immediately to recruit *peninsulares*. Alarcón ridiculed the father's request, responding that unlike Olivares, who had access to Spanish missionaries from the apostolic colleges, he could recruit no such Spaniards. In a letter dated 22 June 1718, Olivares derogatorily characterized the colonists of color as savage half-breeds who were less civilized than the Indians and asked the viceroy, the marqués de Valero, to force Alarcón to recruit other people:

> Such people are bad people, unfit to settle among gentiles, because their customs are depraved, and worse than those of the gentiles themselves. It is they who sow discontent and unrest among them and come to control the Indians to such an extent, that by means of insignificant gifts they make them do what they please. When it is to their interest, they help the Indians in their thefts and evil doings, and they attend their dances and *mitotes* just to get deer and buffalo skins from them. . . . It is with this sort of people, Your Excellency, that he wishes to settle the new site on the San Antonio and the Province of Tejas. (Father San Buenaventura de Olivares, in Castañeda 1936:87)

Although Father Olivares's request went unheeded, the crown did give him permission to send for additional Christian Indians from Tlaxcala and from the northern missions. They were to be used as models and beneficiaries of a Christian lifestyle (Bolton 1960:15; Castañeda 1936:73). Father Olivares also requested that Tlaxcalan masons and sculptors be transferred to San Antonio, as they were specialists in constructing mission buildings and designing iconographic religious art. Sculptors and masons from the Tlaxcalan town of San Esteban, Coahuila, were brought for the specific purpose of sculpting religious images on the mission buildings (Castañeda 1936:80). By 1720 San Antonio had a colonial population of 300 and several hundred mission Indians (Weber 1992:193).

The Northeast

While Olivares and Alarcón disputed over San Antonio, news arrived that the colonists of the northeast could no longer survive among the Indians and were prepared to abandon their post. Alarcón immediately departed for Presidio Nuestra Señora de los Dolores and later visited the missions, where he observed a pattern of disorder and despair. Most colonists were sick, their supplies depleted, their houses in disrepair, their fields destroyed by the Indians, and most of the missions empty, as the neophytes were better off on their own. Apparently, the local Indians and the French from Natchitoches had conspired to drive the colonists out. Alarcón assessed the damage and determined that it was necessary to retreat temporarily. He had to receive permission to do so, however. Matters got worse, and the colonists could no longer wait. While the viceroy assessed the petition, French soldiers attacked Mission San Miguel de los Adaes and forced everyone to flee. News of the attack reached the other northeast settlements. The settlers were warned that unless they abandoned their homes a French battalion of 100 soldiers was prepared to kill them. Father Antonio Margil, the head missionary of the northeastern missions, attempted to calm the settlers and temporarily convinced them to stay. He suggested that they congregate in Mission Concepción until the Spanish cavalry arrived. When the settlers arrived at Concepción, a sense of despair and panic prevailed. Many of the settlers, unwilling to wait for military aid, opted to withdraw immediately to San Antonio. Unable to assure the colonists of their safety, the fathers allowed them to leave. After accompanying the refugees to San Antonio, Fathers Margil and Espinosa returned to the northeast.

Although the crown allowed the settlers to leave, the recolonization of the northeast resumed in 1721 (Chipman 1992:121). The crown appointed José Azlor de Vera to launch a counterattack. Don José was officially known as the marqués de Aguayo. Two years earlier he had been appointed governor and captain-general of Texas and Coahuila. To fulfill his commission, Aguayo raised a force of 85 soldiers and 500 recruits to repopulate northeastern Texas (Castañeda 1936:122; Chipman 1992:120). It is uncertain what percentage of the colonists were people of color; Aguayo's reports did not provide a demographic description, indicating only that a large number of them were Indian, *mestizo,* and Black (Castañeda 1936:130). Although a census was not taken by Aguayo, Spanish census enumerators in 1777 reported that over 50 percent of the 130 families living in the northeast were people of color: 62 were classified as Spanish, 49 as partially Black, 13 as Indian, 5 as Black, and 1 as *mestizo* (Tjarks 1974:324–325).

Aguayo's forces departed from Monclavo, Coahuila, and arrived on the Neches River around mid-July 1721 (Bannon 1970:121). They were greeted by Father Espinosa and by the former mission Indians of the dismantled missions. Aguayo left a number of soldiers to reconstitute the Presidio of San Francisco (Weber 1992). After resting, he proceeded to the site where Mission San Miguel had previously stood, approximately twelve miles from Natchitoches. There he received a delegation of French soldiers who diplomatically asked him to place his colony somewhere else. Aguayo ignored the request and proceeded to establish Presidio de Nuestra Señora del Pilar de Los Adaes. He also assisted Father Margil to reconstitute Mission San Miguel, which was located near the presidio and renamed San Miguel de Los Adaes. To protect the settlements and to ward off further French attacks, Aguayo reinforced the presidio with a hundred soldiers and left artillery and six cannons behind. Twenty-eight of the soldiers were joined by their families, helping to populate and set claim to the northeast (Castañeda 1936:144). This region came to be known as Los Adaes. Before leaving the northeast, Aguayo reestablished six of the mission settlements and left two well-fortified presidios (Chipman 1992:123, 126).

Aguayo then moved south to fight further French intrusion and to solidify Spain's claim along the coast of Texas. After resting for the winter in San Antonio, he reassembled his troops and marched toward Matagorda Bay, where the French had built a fort. In 1722 his troops seized the fort and in its place founded Presidio Nuestra Señora de Loreto (Bannon 1970:121). Mission del Espíritu Santo de Zúñiga was also established nearby. Approximately ninety soldiers were left to protect these two settlements. After four years the settlements were moved inland near the Guadalupe River (Chipman 1992:127). The new location proved to be beneficial because it was accessible to a larger number of Christian *ranchería* Indians. The presidio was renamed Presidio Nuestra Señora de la Bahía del Espíritu Santo. The settlements remained small yet stable, and two decades later Mission Rosario was founded nearby. This region came to be known as La Bahía.[8]

The friars were able to develop a successful tutelage relation with hundreds of *ranchería* allies and establish a thriving cattle economy. In 1758 Mission Espíritu Santo alone owned 3,200 head of cattle, 1,600 hundred sheep, and 20 saddle horses (Castañeda 1939:23). Moreover, many Indians came to visit their relatives in the missions and were allowed to live there temporarily. In 1763 the missions had a total neophyte population of 312 and a colonial population of fifty families (Castañeda 1939:23, 25).[9] The colonists consisted of fifty soldiers, their nuclear families, and extended kin. Fourteen of the soldiers guarded the missions and lived on the grounds, while the rest of the colonial population lived in the presidio. Furthermore, 1777 census records indicate that the settlement in La Bahía was multiracial (Tjarks 1974:324). Approximately 53 percent of the settlers were registered as Spanish (N = 370), 27 percent as Indian (N = 185), 3 percent as *mestizo* (N = 24), and 17 percent as of partially Black descent (N = 117) (ibid.). As time passed, La Bahía's strategic location became increasingly important, and a third mission was built at present Refugio.[10] The Christian Indian population, however, continued to prefer to live in their villages rather than in the missions.

Success and Failures: Laredo and West Texas

Between 1747 and 1773 Spain expanded its colonization of its northeastern frontier (Beers 1979:97). Many missions and presidios were built in Texas and in a newly established territory called Nuevo Santander (Castañeda 1938). In 1749 Nuevo Santander was founded along the current border between southeastern Texas and the Mexican state of Tamaulipas.[11] Six thousand people were recruited to move there (Weber 1992:194), including seven hundred Tlaxcalan families (Bolton 1960:15; Simmons 1964:105). Although most of the colonists established their ranches in

Tamaulipas, the purpose of the Nuevo Santander colony was to populate the far northern frontier and to create an infrastructure to help protect colonial settlements in Texas.

Over twenty-three towns were established in Nuevo Santander. Laredo was founded in 1755 on what is today Texas soil and soon became a stable community (Alonzo 1998:34; Castañeda 1938). The Indians near Laredo were friendly and allowed missionaries to visit them. One of the *rancherías* became a mission *visita* called Visita San Agustín de Laredo, with about 500 Christian Indians (Castañeda 1938:161). A settlement called Dolores was established near Laredo by twenty-three families. Dolores remained a ranching community throughout its existence and did not grow into a town (Alonzo 1998:80). By the turn of the nineteenth century Laredo had over 718 residents, according to the census, including 321 Spaniards, 155 *mulattos*, 121 *mestizos*, and 111 Indians (Hinojosa 1983:124). The Visita of San Agustín had over 1,500 Indians (Alonzo 1998:54). Altogether, by that time Nuevo Santander had grown to over 20,000 settlers, with a sizable population residing on what is today the Texas side of the border (Weber 1992:195).

Unlike the flourishing communities in Nuevo Santander, the newly established settlements in West Texas failed. Spain began its colonization project in 1747 (Castañeda 1938:226). Spanish soldiers tried to enact treaties with the Lipan Apache, who controlled the region. The Lipan Apache first appeared in West Texas during the late 1600s, and by the mid-1700s hundreds more had arrived (Alonso 1995; Swanton 1984:323). If Spanish colonies were to be established in West Texas, it was necessary to befriend the Apache. Thus, the first Spanish *entrada* began with the founding of Mission Cíbola on the border between Texas and Chihuahua, at the conjunction of the Rio Grande and the Concho River near present-day Presidio, Texas (Castañeda 1938:226).[12] The mission was specifically founded for the Lipan Apache. The *entrada* failed; within a year the settlement was destroyed and the mission fathers and neophytes were killed.[13] The Spaniards once again attempted to colonize West Texas by establishing Presidio San Luis de Las Amarillas in 1757 and Mission Santa Cruz de San Sabá a year later, both located near the San Sabá River and present Menard (Beers 1979:96). The furnishings and supplies used for the San Sabá settlements came from the failed missions of San Marcos and Georgetown.[14] Both Texas missions had been built for the Apache.

Learning from the experience at Mission Cíbola, the Spanish had a new strategy: to populate West Texas solely with Indians. The plan was to place Indians in Apache territory on the theory that the Apache would not kill other Indians. In the northern states of Coahuila and San Luis Potosí, where similar *entradas* had been launched into hostile territory, sending Indian pioneers had apparently deflected the anger of the local Indians. Nine Tlaxcalan families and several fathers were sent to populate the mission at San Sabá (Castañeda 1938:394, 407). Although at first the settlements in San Sabá attracted many Lipan Apache families, and the presidio became a popular trading post, the life span of the mission was short. The Comanche and Lipan Apache did not want the colonial settlements and were angered that some Apache groups had befriended their enemies. The Comanche, like the Apache, saw the Spanish as intruders. Although most Comanches lived in North Texas, a few *rancherías* had moved to West Texas and more were advancing west (Chalfant 1991:5). Thus, when the San Sabá settlements were established hostile Indians raided the mission's livestock and in general made life miserable for the colonial residents (Chipman 1992; Corbin 1989). Within a year the mission was burned, and the survivors were forced to flee to San Antonio. Only the presidio was left standing.

The destruction of the mission led the royal government to reconsider its plans and temporarily cease the missionization of the Lipan Apache. In 1762, however, several Lipan Apache groups agreed to resume alliances and to be missionized (Castañeda 1939:42, 169). Two missions were established north of the Nueces River and forty leagues from present San Sabá in an area called El Cañón. The missions immediately attracted a neophyte population of over 700 Indians. In addition Chief Tacú and Chief El Chico, who controlled over 3,000 *ranchería* Indians, became allies of the Spanish (Castañeda 1938:398, 1939:108). Although these chiefs did not move their villages into the mission compounds, they actively became engaged in mission life. Once again, however, hard times befell the fathers as enemy Indian groups attacked El Cañón settlements and the presidio at San Sabá (Swanton 1984). This time the presidio was also destroyed. In 1767 all settlements in West Texas were destroyed (Bannon 1970:139).

In spite of the ongoing defeats the royal government ordered the colonization of West Texas to resume. It was painfully clear, however, that no settlements could be established near San Sabá and that another site had to be selected. In 1773 a new site south of San Sabá near the location of the failed mission of Cíbola was selected (Castañeda 1938:223–232). This region was called La Junta. Presidio del Norte at La Junta was built approximately three miles south of the city of Presidio and north of the Rio Grande (Beers 1979:97).[15] Finally, a permanent settlement had been established in Apache territory. Throughout its duration it remained a small and popular trading post.

The Canary Islanders and a Flexible *Casta* System

In 1731 fifty-five *peninsular* families came to San Antonio from the Canary Islands, enlarging the size of the White population. A few of these people later dispersed throughout Texas (Poyo 1991a:41). They were brought for the explicit purpose of governing the non-White population, as Spanish law prohibited non-Whites from holding positions on the town council. In Texas the royal government appointed the town council, called a *cabildo* (Haring 1963; Menchaca 1993; Poyo 1991b).

Canary Islanders were given special privileges because they were *peninsulares*. Besides being eligible for the *cabildo*, they qualified for the most prestigious occupations within the military and were accorded the title *hidalgo* (see Poyo 1991b; *Recopilación de leyes de los reynos de las Indias* 1774: Book 3, Title 10, Law 12). For example, ten Canary Islanders were given life appointments as councilmen, sheriff, notary, land commissioner, city attorney, and two magistrates who ruled on the legalities of community life (Poyo 1991a:42). Likewise, the Texas census of 1793 indicates that in San Antonio nearly 100 percent of the Canary Islanders were employed as professionals and farmers, while nearly 40 percent of the nonmission Indians and racially mixed peoples were employed as laborers and servants (Poyo 1991b:88, 93).

As *hidalgos*, the Canary Islanders were also eligible to receive land grants twice the size of those of other subjects and temporarily be exempt from paying taxes (see Castañeda 1936:296–301, 1938:90; Graham 1994). This land distribution policy adversely affected many *mestizos* who arrived to San Antonio after the Canary Islanders. Since the best land in San Antonio was owned by the missions, and the Canary Islanders were given most of the remaining irrigable land, the new immigrants received land without water and therefore were unable to become farmers (Poyo 1991b:89). Many worked as servants or field hands as a means of supporting themselves. The non-White settlers who arrived before the Canary Islanders were much better off, however, because they had obtained fertile land. They were not issued patents, but they did receive occupancy rights.

Although the racial caste system was transported to Texas, it was less rigid than in the interior. In Texas commoners of color could move out of their legal racial categories if they performed heroic acts for the state (Forbes 1966:245; *Recopilación de leyes de los reynos de las Indias* 1774: Book 7, Title 5, Laws 10 and 11). In the interior of Mexico such permission was uncommon and generally only accorded to wealthy individuals (see McAlister 1963; Seed 1988). The best known case of racial mobility in Texas is that of Antonio Gil Y'Barbo, a well-respected *mulatto* (Tjarks 1974:326). He was one of the settlers of Los Adaes and had established a successful ranch called El Lobanillo. In 1772, after a series of Indian attacks, the colonists from northeastern Texas were forced to flee to San Antonio (Poyo 1991b:97). While in San Antonio, Los Adaesanos elected Y'Barbo as their spokesperson (Castañeda 1939). After a year, Los Adaesanos became restless and asked to leave because they had been given farmland that was impossible to cultivate. Without land they were limited to selling their labor. After repeated petitions to leave San Antonio, Y'Barbo was given permission to establish a new colony and immediately began traveling throughout the northeast and the Gulf Coast. In 1774 he found several suitable places along the northeast coast near the villages of Caddo and Orcoquisac Indians (Poyo 1991b:97). The settlers spread along the coast and inland and founded the town of Bucareli (Block 1976, 1979; Castañeda 1936). The royal government rewarded Y'Barbo by appointing him captain and chief justice of the colonists. In spite of his racial lineage, Y'Barbo was later promoted to lieutenant governor and captain of the northeast (Tjarks 1974).

Historian Gerald Poyo (1991a) found in a study of the *casta* system in San Antonio that Y'Barbo's case was not unique: non-Whites could change their racial status and obtain the classification of *criollos* if they held a special skill. For example, census enumerators allowed individuals to change their racial classification. Poyo found it was common for *mestizo* and *afromestizo* craftsmen who were cobblers, blacksmiths, tanners, carpenters, or sculptors to move up in social standing. Many craftsmen who were identified in the 1770 census as *mestizos* or *afromestizos* (i.e., *coyotes, mulattos,* and *lobos*) were classified as *criollos* by the 1790s (Poyo 1991b:94, 95).

Poyo contends that the flexibility of Texas's racial order benefited the White population, since a large number of the people of color were financially secure ranchers. After the arrival of the Canary Islanders, the royal government was prepared to bring in more *peninsular* families. Plans were aborted, however, because local authorities reported that the Canary Islanders were dependent upon the other settlers (de la Teja 1991). Instead local authorities recommended that frontierspeople from towns in Coahuila, Zacatecas, Querétaro, Guanajuato, San Luis Potosí, Tula, and Jalpa be recruited (Tjarks 1974) because they were better suited to frontier life. This context led to improved interracial relations in San Antonio, because the Canary Islanders found life difficult and had to rely on their neighbors. Scholars attribute the prosperity of a larger number of the non-White settlers to the type of subsistence activities they engaged in (see Poyo and Hinojosa 1991). Many non-White settlers in San Antonio who established ranches which emphasized stock raising rather than farming were able to make handsome profits by selling hides and meat.

The Canary Islanders' inability to exploit the mission Indians also contributed to the racial leveling of the inhabitants of San Antonio. The fathers held tight control over the mission Indians and prohibited colonists from employing them. Without a free labor force the large land grants the *peninsulares* received were useless because they had insufficient numbers of employees to work their fields. Furthermore, since enslaving Blacks in Texas was also uncommon, most Canary Islanders did not have access to slave labor. The Spanish censuses in Texas indicate that between 1782 to 1821 the number of slaves never exceeded 37, the majority of them women (*Residents of Texas 1782–1836*). These labor conditions placed the Canary Islanders and other *peninsulares* at a disadvantage and generated the social ambiance for a flexible racial order, where non-White neighbors had to be treated diplomatically. Such flexible race relations were manifested in interracial marriages. In 1793 church records indicate that approximately 18 percent of the White population married non-Whites in San Antonio (N = 47 out of 257) and 28 percent (N = 26 out of 92) in the northeast (Tjarks 1974:331).

The Christian Indians

In San Antonio, La Bahía, and northeastern Texas there were thirteen active missions in 1763 with a neophyte population of over 2,354; each mission was also associated with one to three Christian *ranchería* villages (Castañeda 1939:14, 23, 40). The missions in San Antonio were the most successful. By 1768 there were over twenty-three Indian tribes affiliated with the five San Antonio missions (Castañeda 1939:6, 8). The Coahuiltecans were the most numerous, followed by the Jumanos and the Lipan Apaches (ibid., 6–14). Over 5,115 Christian *ranchería* Indians had been baptized in the San Antonio missions, and 1,246 were resident neophytes (ibid., 6, 8, 9, 14). Many of the *ranchería* Indians were second-generation Christians and had adopted some of the Spaniards' ways. They lived a sedentary life and had established farms and ranches (Castañeda 1936; John 1991; Morfí 1780; Weber 1982). Moreover, in the missions the Indians had adopted the town council form of government (Castañeda 1938:17).

The missions at La Bahía were also able to attract local Indians. Several Karankawa ethnic subdivisions were represented at the missions, including Cocos, Tamiques, and Xarananes (Castañeda 1938:187, 1939:40–44). Unlike the San Antonio missions, however, the missions at La Bahía never exceeded a membership of over 300 per mission and in the 1800s dwindled to a few families. La Bahía missions were poorly stocked, and when supplies dwindled people left. Many Indians would return only to visit the fathers or when goods were restocked. The fathers attributed the high attrition rate to the local terrain, which made agriculture difficult. They claimed that the main problem, however, was the royal government's failure to invest in this region because the Indians were peaceful and did not pose a threat.

A similar situation occurred in Laredo. The church petitioned the royal government for assistance to missionize the local *ranchería* Indians and asked for funds to establish a mission in Laredo, as several chiefs had agreed to relocate their villages there (Castañeda 1938:150, 172). The petition was rejected on the basis that there was plenty of room for neophytes at La Bahía and it was not necessary to give supplies to Indians who were peaceful. Although missions were not established, the Indians continued to attend church services at Laredo and to trade with the colonists (Castañeda 1938; Hinojosa 1983). Tejones and various ethnic subdivisions of the Coahuiltecan Indians, including the Nazos, Comecrudos, Pintos, and Narices visited Laredo.

The missions in the northeast were only able to attract a few families and basically failed. In 1765 King Charles III of Spain directly commissioned the marqués de Rubí, a royal inspector, to write a status report on the northern frontier colonies, including Texas (Hendricks and Timmons 1998:3). Rubí recommended that the northeast be abandoned because the Indians were unwilling to be missionized.

Rubí's Policy Recommendations

In 1768 Cayetano María Pignatelli Rubí Corbera y San Climent, commonly known as the marqués de Rubí, submitted a report entitled *Dictamen* on the status of the northern frontier and recommended that the northeast settlements in Texas be abandoned because the French no longer posed a military threat in that region (Hendricks and Timmons 1998:3). It was also wise to retreat temporarily from the northeast, which had become a battle zone. By the time of Rubí's visit thousands of Apaches and Comanches lived in Texas, competing for land inhabited by local Caddo groups and colonial settlers. Warfare between the colonists and the Apaches and Comanches often erupted in the west and north. Although the colonists had some Indian allies, they were outnumbered. Rubí recommended that the northeast missions be abandoned and the territory be left to the Comanches. The settlers and Indian allies would be relocated to San Antonio or La Bahía, where they could assist in the fortification of these stable communities. Through nuclear fortification a gradual expansion from the center into the periphery would be possible. A similar plan had succeeded two centuries earlier in the Gran Chichimeca when the colonists concentrated their energies on the fortification of Zacatecas and then gradually moved outward.

Rubí further recommended that, instead of colonizing the north, funds be spent in southwestern Texas near Presidio del Norte at La Junta to create another heavily fortified zone such as San Antonio. This area would serve as a resting place for settlers traveling from San Antonio to El Paso or Santa Fe. The idea was to create a line of missions from La Bahía to other parts of the Southwest (Castañeda 1939:253). A single cordon of presidios situated forty leagues (a hundred miles) apart could halt any invasion (Hendricks and Timmons 1998). Rubí proposed as part of the presidial plan that Laredo be further developed and converted into a military center. If the crown invested in this large peaceful Indian population, it could be converted to a powerful military force to use against hostile Indians.

Rubí also offered a very unpopular opinion that was heatedly rejected by the missionaries. He recommended that Spain terminate all Lipan Apache alliances (Castañeda 1939:256–258). Rubí charged that the Lipan Apache allies were treacherous and unreliable, a liability rather than an asset. He also proposed ending all alliances for strategic reasons; he envisioned that the Comanche would massacre the Apache if the Spanish did not intervene. If this occurred the number of troublesome Indians would decline, and the colonists could concentrate their energies on subduing the Comanche. The Catholic Church disagreed, as many Apaches had joined the San Antonio missions and lived in peace. Likewise, Presidio del Norte at La Junta had a large Lipan Apache ally population (Castañeda 1938:223–232). To the Catholic Church Rubí's plan to abandon the Lipan Apaches was a disgrace and an insult to the advances the fathers had made.

The royal government chose to implement only part of Rubí's recommendations regarding Texas. It continued its alliance with Apache groups, but agreed to evacuate the northeast. In 1772, after several Indian raids, the southward exodus began (Poyo 1991b:97).[16] Rubí's recommendations were only temporarily implemented, however. As previously mentioned, within a year of moving to San Antonio, Los Adaesanos found life unbearable and returned to the northeast. Antonio Gil Y'Barbo led 347 Los Adaesanos to the northeast and left nineteen *afromestizo* families behind (Castañeda 1939:317; Tjarks 1974:320, 323). Within a few years Los Adaesanos were attacked by Comanches and forced to move once again. Though this was a tragic event, their new homeland was much safer, because the local Indians left them alone. In 1779 they finally established a permanent colony and called it Nacogdoches (Chipman 1992:206; see Photograph 9).[17] It became Mexico's northeasternmost frontier settlement.

The Racially Diverse People of Texas

By the late eighteenth century the settlers of Texas were concentrated in four regions: Nacogdoches, San Antonio, La Bahía, and Nuevo Santan-

Photograph 9. Spanish Plaza, Nacogdoches, Built in 1779. Courtesy of the Texas State Historical Commission. Photograph taken by author.

der. Censuses taken between 1780 to 1798 indicate that the nonmission settlements in these regions were multiracial (Poyo 1991b; Tjarks 1974). The majority of the settlers were classified as Spaniards and *afromestizos*, while Indians and *mestizos* constituted the smallest percentages. For example, in San Antonio (excluding the mission communities) 61 percent of the residents in 1780 were registered as Spaniards (N = 885), 25 percent as *afromestizos* (*mulattos, lobos,* or *coyotes*) (N = 361), 6 percent as Indians (N = 85), and 3.5 percent as *mestizos* (N = 51) (Tjarks 1974:324–325).[18] Furthermore, though the largest number of residents were registered as Spaniards, the majority of the heads of household were *afromestizo*. About eighty-six of the families reported that the male head of household was an *afromestizo* (ibid., 328). That same year in La Bahía the census reported a similar demographic composition. In the nonmission settlements 63 percent (N = 340) reported that they were Spaniards, 34 percent *afromestizos* (*mulattos, lobos,* or *coyotes*) (N = 183), and 4 percent *mestizo* (N = 21) (ibid., 324–325). Furthermore, the census identified 52 percent of the heads of households as *afromestizos* (ibid., 328). A similar pattern emerged in Laredo. The 1789 census reported that 45 percent were Spanish (N = 321), 22 percent *afromestizo* (N = 155), 17 percent *mestizo*

(N = 121), and 16 percent Indian (N = 111) (Hinojosa 1983:124). In 1793 in Nacogdoches 24 percent were Spaniards (N = 109), 28 percent *afromestizo* (*mulatto, lobo,* or *coyote*) (N = 130) 2 percent Black (N = 10), 26 percent *mestizo* (N = 117), and 6 percent Indian (N = 29) (Tjarks 1974:324–325).[19]

The interior of Texas failed to attract a large number of settlers and only grew to a colonial population of 4,000 by 1803 (Weber 1992:299). Most people who moved to the far northern frontier chose to settle in Nuevo Santander, which later became the Mexican side of the border. Historians David Weber (1992:195) and Donald Chipman (1992:163) attribute Texas's failure to attract a large colonial population to two main factors. First, the ongoing Apache and Comanche raids in the west and northeast made Texas an undesirable place to live. Second, when new settlers arrived in San Antonio and La Bahía the best land was reserved for the Christian Indians and what was left over was parceled out to *peninsulares* (Jackson 1986). Exacerbating this land tenure practice was the refusal of the royal crown to issue titles to newcomers and to allocate land to the children of the settlers. Most newcomers had to enter the labor market because they could not become farmers or ranchers.

Though most people did not want to settle in what today is the interior of Texas, other parts of the area continued to grow. El Paso Valley, which was part of the territory of New Mexico during the Spanish period, attracted a large colonial and mission Indian population and by 1790 had over 3,140 colonists (Weber 1992:195) and 2,000 Christian Indians (Metz 1994:17). By 1819 Laredo had grown to 1,418 (Hinojosa 1983:123). The interior of Texas was part of the colonial and cultural infrastructure of the northern frontier and was closely linked to Nuevo Santander, which had grown to 56,937 by 1810 (Alonzo 1998:40). In these areas the royal crown continued to grant people title to land and to accommodate the growth of the native population (see Chapter 7 for a discussion of the land tenure system in the Southwest). In addition to the colonists, there was a sizable Christian Indian population that was part of colonial society.

The Founding of Arizona

Arizona's colonization is radically different from the pattern in the rest of the southwestern territories settled by Spain. Arizona's desert regions, its extremely hot climate, and the danger posed by the Apache were deterrents to building large colonial settlements. In other territories the first colonists were brought by a person commissioned by the viceroy, but in Arizona the migratory movements were composed of extended family units who generally followed kinsmen stationed as soldiers or officers in the frontier (Engstrand 1992). Arizona was the least populated of the Spanish territories in the Southwest. Its colonial population primarily grew through the conversion of local people into Christian Indians. During the Spanish period, the Indians living in the missions or presidios became acculturated, and their children followed a similar cultural path. Many of the colonists were second-generation acculturated Indians, rather than Spanish or *mestizo* immigrants.

Arizona's colonization history is intertwined with the founding of northern Sonora, Mexico, which was colonized under the same seventeenth-century program (Spicer 1981). This entire region was known as Pimería Alta. In 1692 the first mission buildings were erected in northern Sonora, rather than in Arizona (Spicer 1981:123). Overall, approximately twenty-four missions were founded by the Jesuits in Arizona and northern Sonora (Kessell 1976:7, 10; Polzer 1976:36–37). Most of the missions only lasted a few years.

During the first years of the conquest of northern Sonora, missions were built near Indian *rancherías* that did not pose a threat to the missionaries. Meanwhile, in Arizona friars visited Indian villages near present Tucson, but did not erect any buildings (Polzer 1976:37).[20] Though the visits were infrequent, these early *entradas* into Arizona were planned and supervised by the Sonoran Rectorate of Nuestra Señora de Los Dolores. At this time Spanish-Indian relations were peaceful in both regions (Bolton 1960; Spicer 1981).

In the early 1720s, however, when colonists arrived in large numbers and settled near the missions of northern Sonora, relations turned hostile. Conflicts arose over land disputes, as the Christian *ranchería* Indians inhabited the best land along the rivers and the Sonoran settlers were unwilling to abide by preestablished territorial boundaries. Upon seeing the mission fathers' inability to convince the settlers to respect their land, the Indians turned on them and refused to be their allies. The Christian Indians burned several missions, ousted the colonists, and for over a decade suspended most communication with the church.

Relations resumed in Pimería Alta when missionaries regained the trust of some Opata and Upper Pima groups in 1732 (Kessell 1976:2). These initial alliances were prompted by the fear that many Indians had

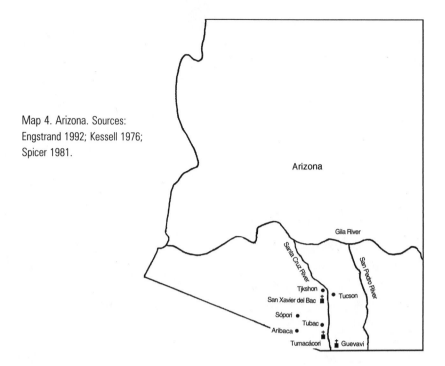

Map 4. Arizona. Sources:
Engstrand 1992; Kessell 1976;
Spicer 1981.

Arizona

Gila River

Santa Cruz River

San Pedro River

Tjkshon ●
San Xavier del Bac 🛉   ● Tucson

Sópori ●
Tubac ●
Aribaca ●
Tumacácori 🛉   🛉 Guevavi

of the Apache (Smith 1962b). At that time hundreds of Apaches descended into Arizona and Sonora and began to occupy territory already claimed by other Indians. The Opata and Pima, to protect their land, resumed their alliances in return for military assistance. Spaniards took advantage of the intertribal conflict and used this as an opportunity to recolonize Pimería Alta. This time, however, the church and royal government shifted the colonization project to southern Arizona.

The mission system in Arizona finally gained a foothold in 1732 (Kessell 1976:2; Spicer 1981:122), when the missions of San Xavier del Bac and San Miguel de Guevavi and the mission *visita* of Tumacácori were established (see Map 4). Parish buildings were erected in San Xavier and Guevavi.[21] Although a parish was not built in Tumacácori at this time, it received regular visits from the fathers, masses were offered, and new converts were baptized. From these mission settlements the fathers were able to reach more Indians living in nearby communities. Eventually about ten mission *visitas* were founded in the Santa Cruz and San Pedro valleys of southern Arizona (Kessell 1976:7).[22] The Upper Pima became the largest Indian group to be missionized.[23]

The Spanish Settlement of Texas and Arizona 119

While the first missions were being erected in Arizona, a series of Indian revolts once again erupted in northern Sonora. Hundreds of Christian Indians rebelled against the illegal kidnapping of their kinfolk. The mission fathers tried to intervene, but were unable to stop the kidnappings. The revolts led to the temporary collapse of the northern Sonora missions, leaving only the missions in Arizona standing. Unlike the Indian conflicts of northern Sonora, relations between the Christian Indians and the Spanish in Arizona remained peaceful and generated the ambiance to permit a modest expansion of the mission system.

The Arrival of the Colonial Settlers in Arizona

The first colonists to settle in Arizona arrived in groups of extended families following kinsmen stationed as soldiers or officers on the frontier. The northward move began in the 1720s, when the Indian rebellions in northern Sonora forced people to find new homes (Mattison 1946:276). They settled on the current Sonora-Arizona border and established farms above Guevavi, where a large Christian *ranchería* was located. Some years later silver mines were discovered in southern Arizona, prompting more Sonoran settlers to move north. Several mining camps were established near the newly built missions at Guevavi and San Xavier del Bac. To protect the families from Apache attacks, a presidio was established southeast of Mission Guevavi, on the Mexican side of the present Arizona border in 1741 (Engstrand 1992:121). Eight families moved to the presidio that year, and later a number of them moved further north. They dispersed themselves throughout Arizona's Santa Cruz and San Pedro valleys and began establishing mining camps and ranches. A few years later more settlers moved to Arizona and settled in Mission Guevavi and in the Santa Cruz Valley, where the *visitas* of Aribaca and Sópori had been established (Mattison 1946:277). In 1753 Presidio Tubac was founded to protect the growing population (Engstrand 1992:134; Kessell 1976:2). Its superior fortification attracted many frontier families as well as several Christian Indian families.[24] Within a few years Presidio Tubac became a lively community with over 500 colonists in residence and the social focal point of the ranching families (Mattison 1946:283). Captain Juan Bautista de Anza was the commander of the presidio and was put in charge of 120 soldiers and their families (Dobyns 1962:10).

By 1762 Tubac had become the main colonial center, and its inhabitants constituted one-third of the 1,500 colonists in Arizona (Mattison 1946:277). When the royal crown sent the marqués de Rubí to inspect the status of the Spanish settlements, however, he observed that Tubac could easily be destroyed by a large-scale Apache raid and advised that its population be moved near Tjkshon, the largest allied *ranchería*. Tjkshon was inhabited by over 400 Upper Pima Indians and was surrounded by numerous Christian *rancherías* (Dobyns 1962:11). It was impossible for hostile Indians to penetrate this zone. Tjkshon was well fortified and had a massive wall surrounding its church and adobe buildings (Dobyns 1962).[25]

Rubí's recommendations were implemented a few years later after Captain Hugo O'Conor arrived to supervise the move and determine the future of Tubac. In 1775 he resettled the colonists across the river from Tjkshon and founded Presidio Tucson (Dobyns 1976:58). Tjkshon and the presidio became the foundation of present-day Tucson and the center of the colonial population. By 1797 Presidio Tucson had over 297 colonists in residence (Dobyns 1962:28). Although a new presidio was established, Tubac was not abandoned. Several Indian soldiers and their families remained behind, forming a small community of acculturated Indians.

Residential Patterns

In the presidios most colonists were given small plots of land to build houses and grow gardens. Those colonists who moved to the missions were also given small plots of land adjacent to the Indians' fields (see Engstrand 1992). Although settlers were given land to subsist on, only elites such as officers, their families, or affluent subjects were issued property deeds. To obtain a deed people had to prove that they had funds to make structural improvements (construct a house, cultivate the land, or build stables or other types of buildings) and that the land grant would be permanently inhabited. A petitioner had to present a claim outlining how the grant would be subdivided into several parcels and submit a map indicating where houses, ranches, farms, or mining camps would be constructed.

During the Spanish period, only four land grants were issued (see Mattison 1946).[26] Three of the grants were awarded to colonists and one allocated to a community of acculturated Indians from Tumacácori. The land grants were enormous and were inhabited by the extended kin of the petitioners. The first land grant was awarded to the Otero family in 1789 (ibid.,

282). The Otero land grant was subdivided into four farming lots (*suertes*), each consisting of approximately three leagues (total 13,314 acres); in addition approximately one-eighth of a league (800 acres) was reserved to build the main family ranch and house (ibid.; Engstrand 1992:243).[27] The second land grant was issued in 1807 to a community of Tumacácori Indians. They were awarded over 52,000 acres (Mattison 1946:291–294; see Mattison 1967). The third land grant, called La Canoa, was issued to the Ortiz brothers in 1821 (Mattison 1946:294–297). This land grant was situated five leagues from Tubac and was subdivided into four cattle ranching lots (*sitios*), totaling 46,696 acres. The fourth land grant, called San José de Sonoita, was issued to the Herrera brothers that same year (ibid., 298–299). This land grant was the original site of the abandoned mission *visita* of Sonoita. It consisted of nearly two square leagues totaling approximately 8,874 acres, subdivided into two lots (*sitios*) to establish cattle ranches. Although only four land grants were issued, many families were permitted to establish permanent ranches in southern Arizona, in Aribaca, Santa Cruz, Sonoita, San Rafael de la Sanja, San Bernardino, and several other places in the San Pedro Valley (ibid., 286).[28]

Blurred Racial Categories among the Colonists

In Arizona the officers' families formed the upper class, while the soldiers' families were the commoners (Dobyns 1976; Engstrand 1992). The officers and their families claimed to be White, while the commoners were clearly people of color. Although the officers most likely were White, there were few *peninsulares* among them. Iris Engstrand's study *Arizona hispánica* (1992) illustrates this point. According to Engstrand, presidial records indicate that most officers were *criollos* and were part of second- or third-generation military families from Sonora, Sinaloa, or Coahuila. Engstrand also found that most of the *peninsulares* in Arizona were missionaries. Although she identified documents indicating that the officers were *criollo,* she found few records to verify the race of their relatives. This vagueness is partly due to the scarcity of racial data in Arizona's colonial censuses and marriage records.[29] Racial terms were usually used only in military and mission roll documents. Missionaries and military officers, who were often responsible for preparing the census reports on the civilian population, preferred to use cultural rather than racial terms. The label "gente de razón" was often used in reference to non-Indians (Collins 1970; Dobyns 1976:65, 137–139).

Moreover, Engstrand found that baptismal records frequently did not include the entire family racial history in an effort to hide the true racial identity of a child. For example, when a child's father was a Spaniard, the race of the mother was omitted and the child was classified as *criollo* (Engstrand 1992:160). In most census records, except for the mission Indians, missionaries preferred to classify their parishioners as *vecinos* or *peones* in order to avoid indicating their actual racial identity (ibid., 254–255). *Vecino* was a social class and not a racial category, referring to the landed elite, whereas *peón* denoted a foot soldier and his family (see Gutiérrez 1991:82). Ramon Gutiérrez also concludes that missionaries preferred to emphasize common cultural attributes rather than distinguishing people by race, since the categories of *mestizo* and Indian carried a social stigma. The only racial categories that are certain are those used to classify the military personnel and the mission Indians. Officers were classified as Spaniard, while soldiers were counted as Indian, *mestizo*, and *afromestizo* (Dobyns 1962:23–27, 1976:153, 171–173).

The families of the officers claimed that they were of pure Spanish descent and primarily intermarried among themselves (Dobyns 1976). For example, elite marriage networks included the de Anza, Elías González, Vildosola, Díaz del Carpio, Otero, Robles, Carrillo, and Aro y Aguirre families (Engstrand 1992:160, 274–276). Moreover, these families lived in relative luxury. Their homes were well furnished, their children were schooled by tutors, and they imported clothes from Europe or from the interior of Mexico. Unlike the elites, soldiers and Christian Indian families lived in modest adobe homes, with beds, stools, and tables serving as their sole furniture. They also dressed modestly (ibid., 159–161). Although social class differences distinguished the colonists, they remained a closely knit community and socialized during weddings, birthdays, funerals, and most everyday life events.

Among the commoners, intermarriage between soldiers and Indian women was an accepted practice and was encouraged by the royal crown. The Royal Order of 1790 gave soldiers incentives to marry local indigenous women (Mattison 1946:281–282). A soldier who married an Indian woman was given four square leagues of land, which was a tremendous amount of land for a commoner.[30] The order was designed to attract males to Arizona and encourage them to become permanent residents. In this way, Arizona's population would increase and the culture of the soldiers would be diffused to their wives and kin.

Throughout Arizona's Spanish period eleven colonial villas were founded (Kessell 1976:138, 311). Because of Apache attacks, however, most villas were abandoned after a few months and the colonists forced to move to the presidios, missions, or *visitas* (Smith 1962a). By the end of the Spanish period the colonial population was concentrated in Tucson, Tubac, and the missions of Tumacácori and San Xavier del Bac, as well as dispersed on the ranches. During the early nineteenth century, the colonial population ranged from 1,800 to 2,291 (Dobyns 1962:29; Kessell 1976:246). This estimate included the colonists who were not mission neophytes or residents of Christian *rancherías*.

Christian Indians

In the late eighteenth century the size of the Christian Indian population grew, and so did the demand for missions (Kessell 1976: Chapter 3). Although many *ranchería* Indians were willing to become neophytes, the royal government was reluctant to establish new missions because of the threat that the Apaches posed outside the fortified zones.[31] Establishing new missions would be a financial disaster if they came under attack. As the size of the Christian Indian population expanded, some *visitas* were structurally improved to accommodate new converts and took on the character of mission pueblos: adobe homes were built, and some pueblos even had modest parishes. A priest was not in residence but visited the Indians regularly. The fathers selected a spokesperson to govern the mission pueblos. If the pueblo was composed of one *ranchería*, the chief became the spokesperson; if it was composed of more than one *ranchería*, one of the chiefs was selected. The spokesperson was officially granted the title of *gobernador* and acted in the capacity of a mayor. The fathers also encouraged the *gobernadores* to reorganize their tribal governments into town councils (Ezzell 1974:121–127). The *gobernadores* were encouraged to select two assistants, called *alcaldes*.

Five of the *visitas* became mission pueblos, including Tjkshon, Sonoita, Calabazas, La Purísima, and Tumacácori (Engstrand 1992:177; Kessell 1976:311).[32] Most were located within a short distance of the missions or presidios. It was common for secularized Indians or *ranchería* allies to reside in the mission pueblos, while space in the missions was reserved for recent converts (Kessell 1976:788–789). The missions and mission pueblos were inhabited throughout the Spanish period and only temporarily abandoned during Apache attacks, except for the mission at Guevavi, which was dismantled after a series of sustained Apache attacks during the late 1760s (Engstrand 1992:122; Kessell 1976:57). Soon Tumacácori was elevated to a mission and took its place.

Mission settlements were usually inhabited only by Indians. The church preferred to separate the neophytes as a means of avoiding the problems that had arisen in Sonora, where the colonists enslaved Indians and generated the conditions for revolts. Only when colonial settlements were under attack were colonists allowed to seek temporary refuge in the mission settlements. By 1774 the mission communities contained 168 colonists and 2,018 Christian Indians (Kessell 1976:88).

The largest number of missionized Indians were Opatas, Upper Pimas, and Papagos (Dobyns 1962; Ezzell 1974; Spicer 1981). Many of these Indians assimilated into Spanish society by moving into the mission pueblos and adopting some of the ways of the colonists. In one case several Indian groups chose to replicate the Spanish township pattern. After having lived in the missions, several secularized Opata and Upper Pima families established a town that was independent of the colonists and the church. In 1807 they received a land grant from the royal crown and called their community Tumacácori (Mattison 1967:72). They established ranches and farms on 52,000 acres (Mattison 1946:291–294), while reserving 6,770 acres to establish civic buildings (see Kessell 1976:207–212; Mattison 1967:72).[33]

Indians also chose to become part of Spanish society by relocating their *rancherías* near the missions or presidios (Collins 1970; Doyle 1989; Kessell 1976; Polzer 1976). Often they did so because of their fear of the Apache, as in the case of hundreds of *ranchería* Indians who moved near Presidio Tucson (Dobyns 1962). A census taken in 1825 by Lieutenant Mariano de Urrea indicates that approximately 9,200 Indian allies were dispersed in ten *rancherías* near Tucson and scattered nearby in the Santa Cruz Valley (Kessell 1976:264). Other Indians chose not to move, yet became allies of the Spanish. Many Pima, Papago, and Yuma Indians who lived west of the Santa Cruz Valley and along the present border of Sonora and Arizona formed military alliances of convenience (Ezzell 1974). They were farmers and sought the aid of their colonial neighbors during harvest season. Likewise, throughout the Spanish period the colonists sought the military assistance of their Indian allies. For example, the early 1760s, the mid-1770s, and 1781 were periods of intense Spanish-Apache conflict (Dobyns 1962:20, 40, 82; Engstrand 1992:197–198, 228). Because the Apaches were so successful in their raiding, the colonial settlements were confined to the San Pedro and Santa Cruz valleys.

Although the fathers were able to Christianize many Indians, the Navajo and most Apaches resisted.[34] The Navajo distanced themselves in the far north, while most Apaches remained feared enemies.

5

The Settlement of California
and the Twilight of the Spanish Period

In this chapter I examine the expansion of the Spanish Empire into California and identify the indigenous groups who were incorporated within the mission system. In unfolding this history, I illustrate the racial diversity of the colonial population and show that while the church and royal government were entrenching their imperial power in the Southwest, the masses and *criollo* elite in the interior of Mexico revolted against Spain's racial order. The changing ideological stance on race culminated in the 1821 Mexican War of Independence and threatened the royal government's projects in the Southwest (Weber 1992:30). Of utmost significance was the racial equality legislation passed by the new government, specifically designed to make Indians acculturated citizens.

Setting Claim to Alta California

Alta California was the last territory of the Southwest to be colonized by Spain. Its colonization was prompted by the fear of a foreign invasion by Russia and England (Weber 1992). England was pushing its westward expansion from Canada to the Pacific, and Russia was moving down the northwest coast from Alaska. If one of these countries took over Alta California, it could threaten the stability of New Mexico, because English or Russian colonies would lie closer to New Mexico than the well-fortified cities in the outskirts of Mexico City. It was only a matter of time before the threat was executed, as Alta California's coast had not been colonized and several countries were aware of its value. Many areas along the coastline were inhabited by sea otters, and any country that colonized Alta California could easily develop a sea otter pelt industry. The pelts fetched high prices on the international market, particularly in

China, where they were a valued commodity (Takaki 1990). When news arrived in 1768 that Russia had begun to establish colonies along Alta California's coast, Charles III, the monarch of Spain, promptly initiated its colonization (Bannon 1970:153). The king awoke to the necessity of occupying Alta California or forfeiting control of it. José de Gálvez, a special emissary of the monarch, was ordered to take immediate action. Gálvez ordered the invasion to be launched from Baja California, the peninsula adjacent to Alta California. Nearly a century earlier, missions and presidios had been established in Baja California and many Indians Christianized. Beginning the colonization from the peninsula would facilitate the transfer of supplies and mission neophytes.[1]

Gálvez initiated his plan by personally traveling to the peninsula and soliciting the aid of Father Junípero Serra, the padre-presidente of the Baja California missions. Gálvez also enlisted the assistance of Gaspar de Portolá, the governor of Baja California, and Mexican-born Captain Fernando Rivera y Moncada, the commander of Presidio Loreto. Gálvez had two ships built in the port of San Blas during his visit and later had the ships loaded with supplies. In preparation for the expedition people were recruited and commissioned to form two land parties and three sea companies. To reach Alta California, Gálvez envisioned that the commanders of the expeditions were to be guided by the maps drafted by Sebastián Vizcáino. In 1602 Vizcáino sailed along Alta California's coast and reached the Bay of Monterey in present northern California (Engelhardt 1929:53). He described it as a magnificent harbor where a large colony could easily sustain itself. Vizcáino also identified other possible colonial sites where the terrain was pleasant and inhabited by sedentary Indians. After studying Vizcáino's maps and reports Gálvez selected the Bay of Monterey and present San Diego as the first regions to be colonized. Although Gálvez was confident that the maps were reliable and could safely guide the captains along various sea routes, he was uncertain about how the land parties would reach Alta California, since the lower peninsula had not been explored inland beyond the head of the Gulf of California (Bannon 1970). Gálvez knew that a dangerous journey awaited the land parties.

Nonetheless, plans were set. Gálvez ordered the ships to leave the port first, followed shortly afterward by the land parties. Once the ships arrived, the captains were to wait for the land parties at San Diego. After the colonists were reunited, the second phase of the journey would begin. Captain Portolá and a group of soldiers would continue on foot until they reached the Bay of Monterey, the proposed capital of Alta California. In Monterey a third ship, the *San José*, would be waiting for the men.

On 10 January 1769 Gálvez's plans became a reality (Engelhardt 1929: 378) when the first ship, the *San Carlos*, cleared La Paz harbor. It was commanded by Vicente Vila and carried a total of sixty-two men (Chapman 1930:221). Twenty-eight of the men were Catalan soldiers under the supervision of Lieutenant Pedro Fages, a *peninsular* (Bancroft 1964:733). The racial background of the other men is uncertain. We know only that two of the other soldiers were blacksmiths and one a baker and that the ship also carried a chaplain and a physician (Bannon 1970:155). The second ship, the *San Antonio*, carried a crew of twenty-six men and two Franciscans. The ship was commanded by Juan Pérez; only the fathers and the captain are definitely known to have been *peninsulares.* The ship left La Paz harbor on 15 February 1769. The third ship, the *San José*, set sail on 16 June 1770, but was lost at sea; the men it carried never reached California (ibid.).

After fifty-four days at sea, the *San Antonio* finally arrived at San Diego on 11 April (Bannon 1970:155). The *San Carlos* reached the harbor at San Diego on 29 April, after 111 days at sea. Most of its men were deathly ill with scurvy. It had sailed through ocean storms and had been unexpectedly delayed. Worst of all, the ship had become lost at sea when its pilot misread Vizcáino's map and passed San Diego.

Meanwhile the land expedition was divided into two companies. The first company was under the command of Captain Fernando Rivera y Moncada, with Fray Juan Crespi serving as chaplain and historian. It left on 24 March 1769 from camp Velicatá, thirty miles beyond Santa María, the northernmost of the Jesuit missions (Bannon 1970:155; Weber 1992:243). Twenty-five soldiers, three muleteers, and forty-two Christian Indians accompanied Captain Rivera y Moncada (Chapman 1930:222). In total there were about seventy-two colonists; the majority of them were Indians from the missions and Christian *rancherías* of Baja California (see Engelhardt 1929:381–383).[2] The second party, commanded by Governor Gaspar de Portolá, started from Loreto on 15 May 1769, following the trail previously blazed by Jesuit missionaries to the mouth of the Gulf of California (Engelhardt 1929:401) and the path marks left behind by Captain Rivera y Moncada. Portolá's party consisted of Father Serra, Sergeant José de Ortega, ten soldiers, two servants, and forty-four Indian colonists (Chapman 1930:222). A large number of the Indians were orphaned children from the Baja missions. Portolá's company included a total of fifty-nine people, the majority of whom were Indian.

Captain Rivera y Moncada's party arrived in San Diego on 14 May with only a small number of casualties (Bannon 1970:157). Several Indians had died on the road. Four hundred cattle also survived the journey (Chapman 1930:224). Upon arriving in San Diego, the captain found a disastrous situation. Twenty-four of the soldiers on board the *San Carlos* had died (Chapman 1930:221); eight soldiers on the *San Antonio* had met a similar fate, and most of the men were deathly ill with scurvy (Bannon 1970:157).[3] Rivera y Moncada now faced the dual responsibility of tending to the ill and preparing a military defense against some Yuma Indians who were displeased with their arrival.[4]

Nearly a month and a half later, on 1 July, Portolá and Father Serra finally arrived at San Diego (Bannon 1970:157). They had been detained when many of the children fell deathly ill along the way. Several died, and the company dwindled from fifty-nine to twenty-seven (Chapman 1930:222). In spite of the problems faced by the second land party, on 3 July Father Serra raised a cross on what was later called Presidio Hill, formally establishing the mission system of Alta California (Bannon 1970: 157) (see Photograph 10). One hundred and fifty survivors were left to continue the colonization of California (Chapman 1930:224).

Within a few days of reaching San Diego, Portolá decided to move on and search for the Bay of Monterey. Leaving behind Serra and a group of others to take care of the sick, he took a company of men and proceeded north. He also dispatched Captain Juan Pérez on board the *San Antonio* to return to the lower peninsula to obtain supplies rather than following Portolá by sea. Portolá was unaware that the third ship, the *San José*, which was supposed to be waiting for them in Monterey, had been lost at sea. Continuing with Gálvez's plan, Portolá moved up the coast and drafted maps of the terrain. He identified villages where friendly Indians lived and possible sites for future settlements. He noted that the friendliest *ranchería* peoples were from present San Juan Capistrano, Buenaventura, Gaviota, Carpinteria, Santa Bárbara, Santa María, Santa Cruz, Pájaro (Watsonville), and Las Pulgas (Engelhardt 1930). In these places the colonists were greeted by Indians and given food. Portolá also observed that from Buenaventura to Santa María the Chumash Indians were among the friendliest people he encountered.

In early October Portolá reached the Bay of Monterey but did not rec-

Photograph 10. Reenactment of the Settlement at Presidio Hill, with Beds and Tents Used by the Colonists, 15 June 1996. San Diego, California. Photograph taken by author.

ognize it and continued to search for his destination point (Engelhardt 1930:54–60). Unable to find the bay and confronted by Indians unwilling to share their food, Portolá had to decide whether to continue without provisions or return without fulfilling his commission. He decided to march onward—until he realized he was lost. His party had reached Half Moon Bay, which was beyond Monterey according to Vizcáino's map. Before Portolá ordered his men to return, he sent Father Crespi and a group of men under Sergeant Ortega's command to scout the surrounding region. On this part of the journey Ortega's company reached the Bay of San Francisco. They returned with news of their discovery and excitedly reported that a great harbor, a mission, and colony could easily be established there. Though Portolá knew his men had made an important discovery, he remained disappointed that he had failed to reach the Bay of Monterey. He ordered his men to march back to San Diego. On their way back they were attacked by Indians at San Bruno but managed to flee. They continued to move south; as they approached Santa Bárbara (in central California) the Indians helped them and gave them food to complete their journey.

While Portolá was exploring northern California, the *San Antonio* reached San Lucas in Baja California. When the viceroy, Antonio María Bucareli y Ursúa, learned from the ship's captain, Juan Pérez, about the critical situation in San Diego and was informed that Portolá's men would be waiting for a ship at Monterey, he immediately ordered the *San Antonio* to be loaded with supplies. He directed Juan Pérez to sail directly to Monterey because he feared that Portolá's men would die if supplies did not reach them immediately. The viceroy was aware that the *San José* was lost at sea and would never reach Monterey. The *San Antonio* was not to stop in San Diego, although supplies and medicine were needed by the colonists. On his way to Monterey Pérez was forced to land in the Santa Barbara Channels to refill his water supplies. While the *San Antonio* was anchored, a group of Chumash Indians greeted Pérez and informed him that Portolá's party had already returned south (Engelhardt 1930:89–91). Pérez immediately raced back to San Diego, where he was greeted by a cheering and hungry crowd, who quickly unloaded the cargo of supplies and medicine. The colonists no longer had to rely on the local Yuma Indians, who were not pleased that strangers had set foot upon their land.

Once the health of the soldiers improved, Portolá organized a second expedition to find the Bay of Monterey. Father Crespi and a group of men accompanied Portolá by land. This time a sea company was to follow the path blazed on foot. Father Serra also joined the expedition and set sail on board the *San Antonio,* once again under the command of Captain Pérez. In late March 1770 Portolá finally reached the Bay of Monterey (Bannon 1970:158). He had previously misread the land marking left by Vizcáino and mistakenly called it the "Bay of Pines." On May 31 the *San Antonio,* with Serra on board, anchored in the bay (ibid.). Two days later royal possession of northern California was formalized when mass was officiated and the region colonized in the name of Jesus Christ and King Charles III. A mission and the presidio of San Carlos Borroméo were subsequently erected there. After the colony was established at Monterey, Portolá's commission was completed, and he departed to fulfill other exploratory journeys for the royal government.

Establishing a Land Route through the Yuma Crossing

After missions and presidios were built in San Diego and Monterey, Father Serra founded five additional missions by 1774 (Weber 1992:247). Two years later the colonial population (excluding the mission Indians) was estimated to have reached around 475 (Chapman 1930:274, 299, 303, 307). Viceroy Bucareli and subsequent viceroys sent adequate supplies to ensure the prosperity of the Alta California settlements. Tools, seeds, and livestock were sent to the missions in an effort to help the fathers develop a self-sustaining agricultural and ranching economy. By the early 1800s most of the missions produced sufficient livestock and crops to sell their surplus at market (see Mason 1986). During Bucareli's term as viceroy, plans to increase the size of the colonial population were also executed. Bucareli commissioned Juan Bautista de Anza, the commanding officer of the Arizona colonies, to establish a land route from Sonora to Alta California, connecting California to the interior of Mexico. The proposed route would cross the coastal deserts of Sonora, pass through southwestern Arizona, and end in Alta California at the mission in San Gabriel. If Anza was successful, Vizcaíno's sea route could be avoided. It had become a dangerous route, forcing ships to sail against prevailing winds and often deviate from course, endangering the life and cargo of those on board. Besides avoiding the perils of maritime travel, it was also more expedient to establish an alternate land route; the supplies from the missions in Baja California were depleted, and they could no longer continue provisioning the colonies. It had become necessary to obtain supplies from the interior of Mexico, where they were plentiful. A direct land route had to be established, however, because at that time transporting products from the interior was an extremely arduous journey. Before supplies reached San Diego they generally had to be transported through the deserts of Sinaloa and Sonora, taken to the Sonoran coastline, and there loaded onto ships going to Baja California. From the peninsula the goods had to reach San Diego by sea or land.

Plans to establish a land route connecting the interior to Alta California were also motivated by a period of relative calm between the Spanish and Indians along the Arizona-Sonora border and by the political alliances between Juan Bautista de Anza and Chief Palma. Palma, a powerful Yuma chief, was in control of several *rancherías* along the border of southwestern Arizona, California, and Sonora. He controlled a large region near the Yuma Crossing, a long stretch of land inhabited by Yuma and Pima groups who did not want Spaniards near their territories. He was also influential in the political affairs of his neighbors. Anza and Palma's relations had previously been solidified when the chief dressed in Spanish clothing and traveled to Mexico City to meet Viceroy Bucareli. In return for his loyalty Bucareli had promised to build missions for his people. Maintaining this alliance was important to the growth of the frontier settlements because Palma's warriors could assure the colonists passage through the Yuma Crossing. Without Palma's help it was nearly impossible to move supplies and children through the area (see Bolton 1966; Engstrand 1992).[5]

In addition, Anza was confident that he could fulfill Bucareli's plans since Father Francisco Garcés had completed a trek on horseback alone from Mission San Xavier del Bac in Arizona, through the desert country of the Lower Colorado River, and into the outskirts of California (Engelhardt 1930:157; Weber 1992:251). Anza and Bucareli concluded that if Garcés could travel alone from Arizona into California a well-equipped military force could definitely blaze a similar trail.

On 4 January 1774 Anza and a company of soldiers departed from Tubac, where preparations for the journey had begun (Weber 1992:251). Anza was able to recruit Father Garcés and Sebastián Tarabal, an Indian who had traveled on foot from Mission San Gabriel to Altar, Sonora. Both Garcés and Tarabal acted as guides. Tarabal and his wife had previously traveled this route with a third companion. The three were runaway neophytes from Mission San Gabriel in Alta California (Hurtado 1988). Tarabal and his wife were part of the neophyte population that had left Mission San Gertrudis in Baja California and joined Serra and Portolá on their journey to San Diego. When Tarabal and his wife arrived in San Diego, Portolá chose them to march with him on to Monterey. After Portolá left California, they were placed in Mission San Gabriel. Sadness and possibly homesickness drove them to desertion. On the way to their old homes, Tarabal's companions starved and perished on the road. Tarabal did not stop; he traveled past the Colorado River into Arizona then south into Sonora. While in Sonora he encountered a troop of soldiers and was taken to Presidio Tubac, where Anza was commander. Tarabal conveyed his account to the soldiers of Tubac. The hardships he had experienced evoked consternation in the ranks; yet though this account was frightening he had proven to the soldiers that a troop of well-provisioned soldiers need not fear crossing the desert since he had crossed it without provisions. Tarabal therefore was chosen by Anza to act as his second guide (Engelhardt 1930:158).

Besides Garcés and Tarabal, Father Juan Díaz, twenty male volunteers from Tubac, eight Indians, one Pima translator, and one soldier from Alta California accompanied Anza, some thirty-four people in all (Chapman 1930:299). The party was well supplied and prepared for a long journey, with 35 packs of provisions, 65 head of cattle for food, and 140 horses. Nearly two and a half months later the company arrived at Mission San Gabriel. Their trip proved that a land party could travel from Sonora to Alta California. A land route connecting Alta California to the interior of Mexico and to other parts of the Southwest had finally been established. Having fulfilled his commission, Anza traveled to Mexico City to await further orders from Bucareli.[6] Meanwhile, the party in Alta California dispersed; some remained in California, while others returned to Tubac with news that the Yuma Crossing could be passed (Engelhardt 1930:159).

The Colonies of Captain Fernando Rivera y Moncada and Captain Juan Bautista de Anza

While Anza was in Mexico, Captain Fernando Rivera y Moncada was in Sinaloa recruiting civilians. Bucareli had commissioned the captain to take a land party to Alta California, following the same trail he had previously blazed. This colony would include the first group of non-Indian women and children. Rivera y Moncada recruited approximately six families and several single males (Chapman 1930:302). Seven women and their children preceded the land party by sea on board the *Santiago*, under the command of the well-known maritime captain Juan Pérez (Castañeda 1993:73–74; Weber 1992:248, 450). Rivera y Moncada personally took charge of the land division. He escorted several families from Sinaloa to the peninsula, where they rested in camp Velicatá. Because the party was exhausted and the supplies were nearly depleted, the captain marched ahead to Monterey to obtain supplies to complete the journey. During his absence, the party members became anxious and decided not to wait any further. They left Velicatá and continued their trek, arriving in San Diego on 26 September 1774 (Chapman 1930:303). At San Diego they were reunited with those who had traveled by sea.

Once this party composed primarily of women and children arrived, it was possible to produce a *castizo* population in Alta California. Though the women were not Spaniards, they were light complexioned; historians have considered them the first non-Indian women to arrive in Alta California (Castañeda 1993:73; Chapman 1930:303). Historian Charles Chapman comments that women who were nearly White were now available for a limited number of soldiers:

> Thus did the first real settlers come to Alta California, since for the first time white women set foot in the province. Though their whiteness of skin was undoubtedly tinged with Indian red, they were suitable wives for a limited number of soldiery and by their children were able to contribute yet more to the permanence of the colony. (Chapman 1930:303)

David J. Weber also comments on the significance of these women, who gave the colony stability:

> The arrival of Rivera y Moncada's party in 1774 raised the non-Indian population of New California to about 183 and helped to make it more secure. Rivera y Moncada had traveled by way of Baja California with some 51 soldiers from Sinaloa, including some of the first Hispanic women and children to come to California. (Weber 1992:248)

After resting in San Diego, the colony members dispersed; some followed Captain Rivera y Moncada to Monterey, where they were anxiously awaited.

A month after Rivera y Moncada's settlers arrived, disputes ensued between Father Serra and the captain over the future growth of Alta California. Rivera y Moncada had been promoted to comandante-general of Alta California and was given the authority to move forward with his vision of Alta California. In particular, his influence had increased after the arrival of the women. Rivera y Moncada disagreed with Serra's proposal that the colonization of Alta California should focus on the Christianization of the Indians and the establishment of mission communities among peaceful Indians. Serra argued in favor of building missions among the Indians from San Fernando to San Luis Obispo. In particular, he wanted to Christianize the Chumash Indians, who were peaceful and demonstrated interest in being missionized (Engelhardt 1930:163). Rivera y Moncada, however, preferred to explore new sites to the north in the direction of San Francisco. Unlike Father Serra, he was not concerned at this time with building missions among Indians who were already peaceful. Instead he planned to fortify the surrounding regions near Monterey, where Indian groups were hostile and the land was fertile. His main concern was to solidify Spain's claim over northern California. Although the two men disagreed, they compromised and agreed that a mission in San Juan Capistrano was a priority. To Serra's displeasure the missions among the Chumash of the present counties of Ventura, Santa Barbara, and Santa Maria would have to wait (Hoover, Rensch, and Rensch 1966).

In 1775 Juan Bautista de Anza was once again commissioned to bring people to colonize northern California (Bannon 1970:162), following the same route previously blazed by Anza. Tarabal and Lieutenant José Joaquín Moraga were to assist Anza. Moraga had been one of the members of the Serra-Portolá expedition and the officer placed in charge of the colonists who planned to settle in San Francisco. Anza began the trek in Horcasitas, Sinaloa, where most of the colonists were recruited. They then stopped in Tubac, where they enlisted sixty-three settlers. In total 240 people were registered in the Anza expedition, accompanied by nearly 1,000 animals (Bannon 1970:162; Chapman 1930:304–308). The majority of the colonists were poor *mestizos* seeking to improve their standard of living (Chapman 1930:304; Engstrand 1992:192). Less than one-third were classified as Spaniards (Weber 1992:327). Historian Jack Forbes (1966:236) found that eight of the soldiers and their families were *afromestizos*. Twenty-nine of the people in the party were women, the majority of them being wives of the soldiers stationed in Alta California. Other members of the party included the soldiers' relatives, three officers, one purveyor, three missionaries, thirty-eight soldiers, twenty muleteers, three herders, four servants, and three Indian interpreters (Chapman 1930:304–308).

On their way to Alta California several women gave birth. Though the colonists encountered hostile Indians in the Yuma Crossing, Chief Palma's warriors protected them and secured their passage. The colony reached Mission San Gabriel in early January 1776 (Weber 1992:253).[7] Many of the families decided to continue their trek and follow Anza and Moraga to Monterey. When they arrived in Monterey, a few moved on and helped to found Presidio San Francisco. Later some of these families once again dispersed and joined other families to found the first township in Alta California in 1777, the present city of San José (Weber 1992:258, 259). Indeed the Anza party was dispersed throughout California.

Broken Promises: Revenge at the Yuma Crossing

The next colonists arrived in Alta California in 1781 (Chapman 1930:337–338).[8] This time Rivera y Moncada was commissioned to lead forty-odd families plus several soldiers. They were recruited to populate two new settlements in Los Angeles and Santa Bárbara. The families came from Sonora and Sinaloa, and a large number of them were *afromestizo* (Engelhardt 1930:704). Unfortunately, one of the divisions of the colony met a tragic fate when it was attacked at the Yuma Crossing (Weber 1992:259). At the time of the journey Rivera y Moncada was unaware that the Yuma Indians had destroyed two colonies on the southern border of Arizona and California. Mission Purísima Concepción and the mission pueblo of San Pedro y San Pablo (near present Yuma) had been attacked, leaving over one hundred dead colonists. Apparently, the Yuma revolts were spurred by interethnic conflict dating back a few years. The first major sign of conflict had begun in 1775, when the Indians of Mission San Diego de Alcalá destroyed the mission (Bolton 1966; Engelhardt 1930). They protested against the invasion of their lands and the forcible seizure of many of their women. Although the revolt was crushed by the military forces of Anza and Rivera y Moncada, and the mission rebuilt on top of a well-fortified hill, the Indians continued to harbor ill feelings (see Photograph 11).

The revolts at Mission Purísima Concepción and San Pedro y San Pablo erupted after a series of disputes over territorial boundaries. The Indians evidently resented the colonists' constant demands for food and supplies and in particular the encroachment upon their farmland. The colonists were also bad neighbors, because they allowed their cattle to wander and graze on the Indians' fields. When the Indians complained, their concerns were ignored. The Yuma thus chose to settle their differences in their own way and responded by killing their hostile neighbors. Similar ill feelings were harbored by other Yuma groups, and a widespread rebellion broke out as Rivera y Moncada was passing through the Yuma Crossing.

Exacerbating matters was the anger the royal government had aroused in Chief Palma. He decided to join the rebellion after the royal government failed to fulfill its promises and did not build his missions (Engstrand 1992). Palma felt betrayed and took revenge. Since he had agreed to protect the colonists, he was told of the dates when Rivera y Moncada's group would pass through the Yuma Crossing. He was also told that the

Photograph 11. Mission San Diego de Alcalá, San Diego, California. Courtesy of Monsignor Thomas Prendergast. Photograph taken by author.

colonists would not be well protected, because Rivera y Moncada had divided the party into two divisions. Only one group would pass through the Yuma Crossing, while the second would avoid this route and walk along Baja California. Thus, Palma conspired to ambush them and told his tribal allies when the party was to pass through the Yuma Crossing (Chapman 1930:338). When the colonists entered the trap, most were massacred, including Rivera y Moncada. Only a few women and children survived, but were taken captive. Meanwhile, the second division blazed through the peninsula and reached their destination safely. Twelve of the original families in this division survived, the majority of whom were *afromestizos* (Engelhardt 1930:375, 704). Once in California the colonists dispersed. Most of the group settled in Los Angeles and became the founding families of the city, while others moved onward and helped to found Presidio Santa Bárbara as well as settling in other parts of California (Forbes 1966).

Los Angeles was founded in 1781 and became California's second township (Weber 1992:259). The founders of Los Angeles consisted of eleven families, including twenty-two adults and twenty-two children; twenty-six were *afromestizo*, eleven Indian, five *mestizo*, and two Spanish.[9]

After Rivera y Moncada's death, the Spanish military quickly suppressed the rebellion and rescued the captive women and children. Within a few months relations resumed with Yuma groups who pledged not to fight any longer. The royal government, however, distrusted the Yuma; the new viceroy, Martín de Mayora, declared all travel through the Yuma Crossing to be extremely dangerous. He temporarily discouraged travel from the interior of Mexico to Alta California and suspended all royally sponsored journeys. Under viceregal orders people who chose to come to Alta California were allowed to do so only at their own risk and were expected to fund their own journey.

Colonists and adventurers continued to migrate to California on their own means. By 1793 the non-Indian colonial population is estimated to have grown to around 1,066 (Aguirre Beltrán 1946:230).[10] Of the colonists 435 were classified as *criollos*, 418 as *castas* of various racial mixtures, 183 as *mulattos*, and 30 as *peninsulares* (ibid.); 24 of the *peninsulares* were clergy. Although the colonial population was relatively small, the missions attracted Indians and the neophyte population grew; 7,428 Indians resided in the missions in 1790 (Bancroft, in Bowman 1958:148).[11]

California Mission Indians

Overall twenty-one missions were founded in California, and the mission system lasted until 1834 (Merriam 1955:188; Weber 1982:48). Mission records indicate that throughout the duration of the mission system nearly half a million Indians were baptized in California (Bowman 1958:145–148). These records, however, do not include the baptism registries of all the Christianized *ranchería* Indians, as it was a common practice for the friars to visit these settlements, baptize groups of Indians, and not register their names in mission documents (Cook 1976; Engelhardt 1930). The first Indian baptism in California took place on 22 July 1769, when Father Crespi baptized a dying Indian girl in northwest San Diego County (Bowman 1958:145), and the first Indian baptism in a mission was on 20 December 1769 in Monterey (Bowman 1958:146). The neophyte mission population was relatively small between 1769 to 1774, numbering under 800 (Bowman 1958:148).[12] This was a period when the mission fathers were beginning to befriend the Indians.

Although San Diego was the site where the missionization of the Indians began, the friars at first found it difficult to convert them. Apparently, problems began when soldiers attacked a nearby *ranchería*, stole food, and raped Indian women. News of the tragedy spread among the local Indian *rancherías* and caused many to stay away from the colonists (Chapman 1930; Weber 1992). In spite of the setbacks, by 1777 the mission fathers had befriended hundreds of *ranchería* Indians and established eight missions with their assistance (Bowman 1958:146). Many Indians chose to live in the mission buildings once they were constructed, and the size of the neophyte population increased to 1,985 (ibid.). The neophyte population increased to over 6,189 within ten years and steadily continued to rise, reaching over 20,269 in 1817 (Bowman 1958:148). Between 1804 and 1829 the neophyte population remained stable at an annual residential rate of approximately 20,000 (Bowman 1958:148).

The mission fathers were also very successful in converting *ranchería* Indians. Sherburne F. Cook (1976) found in a demographic study of the Indians of California that mission records indicate that the entire coast of California was under colonial control by 1834. Outside of the missions, over 64,500 Christian Indians were dispersed among the settlers or resided in Christian *rancherías* (Cook 1976:42–43). The most successful missions flourished in southern and south-central California, from the present cities of San Diego to Lompoc (Costello and Hornbeck 1989; Engelhardt 1930; Weber 1982). These missions were inhabited by Chumash, Yumas, and a small number of Indians from four Shoshonean tribal subdivisions, including the Luiseño, Juaneño, Gabrieliño, and Fernandeño. Besides the neophyte population, the fathers of the southern California missions of San Fernando, San Gabriel, San Juan Capistrano, San Luis Rey, and San Diego were also able to Christianize 183 groups of *ranchería* Indians (Cook 1976:41; see Photographs 12 to 17). Christianized *ranchería* Indians chose to be allies of the mission fathers, but preferred to live in their villages.

The Chumash, who lived in an area from present-day Ventura to San Luis Obispo (south-central region), eventually became the most widely Christianized Indians of California (Castillo 1989; Menchaca 1995; Thompkins 1967; Triem 1985). They were the ethnic group most widely represented in the missions (Cook 1976:25–26), and over 200 Chumash

Photograph 12. Mission San Luis Rey. Courtesy of the Franciscan Friars of Mission San Luis Rey. Photograph taken by author.

Photograph 13. Mission San Luis Rey: Remains of the Soldiers' Sleeping Quarters. Courtesy of the Franciscan Friars of Mission San Luis Rey. Photograph taken by author.

rancherías established alliances with the Spanish (Merriam 1955:188–225).[13] Of these *rancherías,* 38 had developed close relations with the mission fathers by 1771 and 107 were in constant contact (Cook 1976:35). Eighty-five percent of the Chumash had migrated to the missions by 1803 (Larson, Johnson, and Michaelsen 1994:264), and six missions were specifically built for them (Hoover, Rensch, and Rensch 1966; see Photographs 18 to 22).[14]

The tribal structure of the Chumash facilitated their conversion (John-

Photograph 14. Mission San Luis Rey: Luiseño Women's Weaving Room. Courtesy of the Franciscan Friars of Mission San Luis Rey. Photograph taken by author.

Photograph 15. Mission San Luis Rey: The Candle Manufacturing Room. Courtesy of the Franciscan Friars of Mission San Luis Rey. Photograph taken by author.

Photograph 16. Mission San Luis Rey: Luiseño Metates and Grinding Stones. Courtesy of the Franciscan Friars of Mission San Luis Rey. Photograph taken by author.

son 1989). From the outskirts of the cities of San Fernando (Los Angeles County) to San Luis Obispo, the Chumash practiced a triblet political system, where each local chief controlled at least three *rancherías*. When a chief was Christianized, the members of his *rancherías* were pressured to convert. An alternate explanation for the massive conversion rate of the Chumash has also been advanced. According to anthropologists Daniel Larson, John Johnson, and Joel Michaelsen (1994), between 1786 and 1803 climatic changes caused by the ocean storm El Niño devastated the region

Photograph 17. Mission San Juan Capistrano: Courtyard. San Juan Capistrano, California. Courtesy of Mission San Juan Capistrano. Photograph taken by author.

inhabited by the Chumash. They propose that El Niño struck California a few years before the Spanish invasion and subsequently created high climatic variability, several years of ongoing droughts, and significantly elevated sea surface temperatures. This was a difficult period of high subsistence risk for the Indians of central and southern California, especially for those who depended on a maritime lifestyle. It was also a difficult period for the inland Chumash because the roots and flora they depended on were practically destroyed. When the Spanish arrived, the Chumash welcomed the agricultural skills introduced by the missionaries (Engelhardt 1930). For the Indians a closer relationship with the church meant that they would obtain the agricultural technology they needed to improve their subsistence base.

The missions in northern California were not as successful in their conversion efforts. The northern missions were located from the present cities of San Luis Obispo to San Rafael and were inhabited by Costanoan, Salinan, and Miwok Indians (Swanton 1984).[15] Though most missions in these areas were not filled to capacity and their success rates varied, Missions San José de Guadalupe (located in the present city of Frémont), San Luis Obispo de Tolosa, San Francisco de Asís, and Santa Clara de Asís be-

Photograph 18. San Buenaventura Mission. Courtesy of Pastor Patrick O'Brien. Photograph taken by author.

came thriving communities (Cook 1976; Hutchinson 1969), filled to capacity. Mission fathers blamed the failure of many of the other northern California missions on the Indians' work ethics. The friars alleged that unlike the civilized Indians of southern California, the Costanoans and Miwoks, who constituted the majority of the neophytes, were lazy and left clandestinely after obtaining what they wanted from the fathers (Hurtado 1988).

A second explanation for the failure of the missions stresses the roles played by the colonists and the church. Allegedly many Indians in northern California were coerced into moving to the missions. They often entered the missions in fear of being placed in servitude by the colonists and thus saw the missions as the lesser evil (Guest 1978; Sánchez 1986). At other times the Indians were forced to remain in the missions when they had only planned to stay there for a short while (Castillo 1989; Hoover 1989; Hornbeck 1989). It was common for Indians to move to the missions when they were sick. Once Indians entered the missions, however, mission rules required that they remain there until the fathers secularized them. They were not allowed to leave at will or without permission. Furthermore, many Indians also sought to leave the missions because they were discontent with the life they were pressured to assume. The

Photograph 19. Mission Santa Bárbara. Courtesy of Santa Bárbara Mission Archive-Library. Photograph taken by author.

Photograph 20. Mission Santa Bárbara: Courtyard. Courtesy of Santa Bárbara Mission Archive-Library. Photograph taken by author.

Photograph 21. Mission Santa Bárbara: Entry Corridor. Courtesy of Santa Bárbara Mission Archive-Library. Photograph taken by author.

Photograph 22. Mission Santa Bárbara: Main Kitchen. Courtesy of Santa Bárbara Mission Archive-Library. Photograph taken by author.

fathers wanted the Indians to become farmers, a lifestyle many did not want. Indians often left because they preferred to hunt for food.

Although the Costanoans and Miwoks were not ideal mission converts, by 1805 thousands of Indians had been baptized in the northern California missions (Bowman 1958:148; Cook 1976:23–25). Thirty-nine *rancherías* converted and were associated with the northern California missions (Engelhardt 1930:643).

Spanish Towns and *Ranchos*

In 1777, as previously noted, the first Spanish town was founded in San José, California (Weber 1992:259). Two other towns and four presidial towns were then established along the coast. Officially only San José, Santa Cruz, and Los Angeles were founded as towns. When the colonists arrived, however, many preferred to live near the presidios, which thus took on a township structure (see Photograph 23).[16] The presidios were

Photograph 23. Avila Adobe in Olvera Street, Los Angeles, California, Built in 1818. Courtesy El Pueblo de Los Angeles Historical Monument.

located in San Diego, San Francisco, Santa Bárbara, and Monterey. This presidial township ambiance was created as the soldiers' families, as well as other colonists, established ranches adjacent to the presidios.[17] They became the focal social point for the colonists, as festivities were held in presidial compounds and Sunday services were officiated in the presidial chapels (see Photographs 24 to 27).

To keep the settlers in California the Spanish crown gave them ranch land. The grants, however, differed in size, and most settlers were not given property deeds. There were three types of land grants in California: mission, *rancho del rey*, and private property (see Garrison 1935; Rush 1965). The mission lands were used to raise the subsistence products needed by the neophytes as well as to establish for-profit cattle ranches (Engelhardt 1930). Cattle raised at the missions were sold at market, and the profits were reinvested in the missions. Once the Indians were Christianized and were acculturated in the lifestyle of the Spanish, they were secularized, and a plot of mission land was partitioned for their use. Indians were not issued property deeds (Guest 1978). Throughout the Spanish period disputes over mission property often erupted between the fathers and the colonists. The colonists felt it was unfair that the missions pos-

Photograph 24. Santa Bárbara Presidio, Founded in 1782. Courtesy of the Santa Barbara Trust for Historic Preservation. Photograph taken by author.

Photograph 25. Santa Bárbara Presidio: Comandante's Office. Courtesy of the Santa Barbara Trust for Historic Preservation. Photograph taken by author.

Photograph 26. Santa Bárbara Presidio: Oven. Courtesy of the Santa Barbara Trust for Historic Preservation. Photograph taken by author.

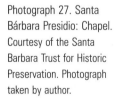

Photograph 27. Santa Bárbara Presidio: Chapel. Courtesy of the Santa Barbara Trust for Historic Preservation. Photograph taken by author.

sessed the best land in California and that it was reserved for the Indians (Mason 1986).

Over time, the governors in California attempted to convince the viceroy to reconfigure the boundaries of the missions and award part of the land to the colonists. The friars protested, saying that the colonists merely wanted the mission land because it had been improved. The colonists allegedly wanted to take possession of the land because structures, roads, orchards, farms, and irrigation systems had already been built. In three cases disputes over land arose when Governor Pedro Fages reduced the acreage of the missions and redistributed it among his military officers. In two of these cases the mission fathers of San Gabriel fought back when part of the mission land was redistricted and awarded to Don José María Verdugo and Don Manuel Nieto (Garrison 1935:9–11, 86). The dispute centered on Mission San Gabriel's cattle-grazing property. Verdugo and Nieto insisted that the land was vacant and did not belong to the church. Nieto's claim was immediately dismissed when the fathers were able to convince Governor Fages that the land indeed was being put to use. Verdugo's claim was validated by the governor, but the fathers appealed directly to the royal government in Mexico City and forced Fages to rescind his decision. Verdugo's claim was reduced in size. A similar incident occurred in Mission San Fernando. Francisco Reyes's land grant was reduced when the fathers protested that his claim overlapped with mission property (Garrison 1935:12, 86).

The second type of land grant was called a *rancho del rey*, and its owner was the king of Spain. Its function was to set aside land to sustain the military in California. In this type of land grant soldiers raised cattle and some crops for personal use as well as to sell at market. The governors of California also had the authority to carve plots out of the *ranchos del rey* that could be awarded to the settlers and Indians. Though people were given property at the discretion of the governors, the king retained title to the land. The land grants ranged in size from small house plots with attached gardens to massive grants of thousands of acres. Under Spanish law each head of a household was eligible to receive four square leagues of arable land. The problem with this arrangement was that the land grantees did not own the land they occupied. During the Spanish period, only military officers were given legal title to the land that was carved out of the *ranchos del rey*. These private-property grants constituted the third type of land grants issued in California.

The individuals who received private land grants during the Spanish period were distinguished officers or were members of the founding families of Alta California (Garrison 1935:1–37). Officers, however, were only given land grants if they had performed heroic acts during battle or had explored important regions such as San Francisco Bay. All land grantees were obliged to make structural improvements, and if they wished to retain ownership their property had to be continuously inhabited. Of the Spanish land grantees, only two individuals were not soldiers or officers in the companies of Portolá or Rivera y Moncada. Don Luis Peralta and Don Ygnacio Alviso came to California as children during the Juan Bautista de Anza expedition. These two men were awarded large land grants for suppressing Indian revolts and acting as Indian brokers (cf. Bancroft 1964:I-Q 773, A-E 695; Garrison 1935:19, 49). Both men held various military appointments throughout their lifetimes and when they retired became active members of the local government assemblies.

The first three private land grants were located in southern California and covered enormous amounts of land. The first land grant was issued in 1784 to Corporal José María Verdugo (Garrison 1935:9). The grant was located near Los Angeles and covered 36,403 acres (Rush 1965:1). That same year Governor Fages issued two other land grants. The grant to Manuel Nieto covered a total of 45,000 acres (Garrison 1935:11; Rush 1965:1). It contained the land where the cities of Long Beach, Downy, and Riviera were later built. The other land grant was awarded to Don José Domínguez and covered 43,119 acres (Garrison 1935:11), from San Pedro to Los Angeles. Overall, some thirty-four *ranchos* were founded during the Spanish period, located from the present cities of Long Beach to San Francisco.[18] In southern California the ranches were located in the Los Angeles District, Long Beach, San Fernando, Ventura, Santa Barbara, San Pedro, and Santa Ana (Garrison 1935). In northern California the ranches were primarily located in the Monterey District and a few other places, including two in San Francisco, one in Santa Clara, and two in the present cities of Redwood City, Belmont, and Menlo Park. Since many of these ranches consisted of thousands of acres and were owned by high-level military officers, it was common for the owners to hire poor colonists to farm their property and to raise sheep and cattle. Indians who were landless or village outcasts were also hired to do the same tasks (Mason 1986; Menchaca 1995; Sánchez 1986).

Moreover, some colonists chose to establish ranches on land inhabited by Indians (Menchaca 1995). In these cases, unscrupulous colonists knowingly took possession of land belonging to peaceful Indians under the rationale that only they could properly cultivate the land. This was a blatant disregard of the Fundo Legal property laws, which protected land inhabited by peaceful and Christian Indians (see Borah 1983:136). Under the Fundo Legal, Indians owned the land they inhabited unless the crown amended this right. The Indians were often unaware that their land had been granted to military officers, because they were not disturbed by the colonists, and therefore were unable to challenge the claims. In other cases, Spanish officers and land administrators stole the Indians' land by blatantly breaking the law. For example, all of the northern California private land grants were founded on the original sites of peaceful Indian rancherías (Garrison 1935:17, 19, 145). In southern California overlapping land claims were not a serious problem during the Spanish period because the fathers were successful in protecting the land of their Indian allies. In one case, however, the mission fathers failed. In 1780 Spanish settlers in San Diego (present Old Town) turned on their Yuma allies and usurped a large part of their land (Carrico 1987; Hutchinson 1969; see Photographs 28 to 30). The rationale used by the *ayuntamiento* (town council) was that the Yumas needed to be placed on farms located near the colonists, allegedly to accelerate their acculturation. This was a highly suspect rationale, given that this land was coveted by the colonists.

Of course, not all Indians of California lost their land in this manner. During the Spanish period, the royal government enforced the Indian property laws because it was one of the best approaches to maintain peaceful Indian relations (Cutter 1986; see also Borah 1983). The Fundo Legal, which protected the land of Christian Indians, was successfully invoked by the fathers to protect mission and *ranchería* property. In areas where Spaniards held high-level military positions and their families resided in the Southwest, however, the governors ignored the royal orders (Spicer 1981). Small farmers also attempted to dispossess the Indians of their land by appealing to the governor or to the members of the *ayuntamientos* who could influence the governor. Such commoners were unsuccessful (Cutter 1986, 1995). It was more important to the governors of California to enforce the property laws as a means of maintaining peace with the Indians and the church than to side with the settlers who were poor people of color and politically powerless.

Photograph 28. Old Town, San Diego. Courtesy California State Parks. Photograph taken by author.

Photograph 29. Old Town, San Diego: Estudillo House. Courtesy California State Parks. Photograph taken by author.

Photograph 30. San Diego: Presidio Hill Cannon. Collection of the San Diego Historical Society. Photograph taken by author.

Racial Boundaries

In the first decades following California's settlement the racial order in Mexico underwent political shifts, largely in response to the growing political unrest among the non-White population. Scholars estimate that by the late 1700s over 77 percent of the population in Mexico was Indian or racially mixed (Aguirre Beltrán 1946:213, 221, 225, 237; Cope 1994:121; Meyer and Sherman 1995:218, cf. 271). Although in California as in other parts of the Southwest the racial order was flexible and non-Whites were allowed to enter most occupations, in the interior of Mexico it was not, and most people were dissatisfied with the legal and economic privileges enjoyed by *peninsulares*. Thus, when California was being settled non-Whites began to challenge Mexico's racial order. Ironically, this adversely affected the growth of California and other colonies in the Southwest, because the funding of the towns, presidios, and missions was largely dependent on the personal funds of the royal family.

In the interior the privileges enjoyed by the *peninsulares* were in clear contrast to the opportunities open to *criollos* and the masses. For example, while *peninsulares* monopolized all high-level positions within the royal and ecclesiastical governments, *criollos* were only able to obtain the highest positions within the military or colleges. By the close of the eighteenth century 227 of a total of 361 officers in the regular regiments were *criollos*, and in the militia they held 338 commissions of 624 officer positions (Meyer and Sherman 1995:275). Likewise, in the universities and colleges most professors were *criollos* (Haring 1963:215). The Catholic Church also discriminated against its *criollo* parishioners. They were excluded from serving as bishops; by 1808 only one *criollo* had been granted such an honor (Haring 1963:195; Miller 1985:180). Furthermore, in the private sector the royal government placed pressure upon the commercial houses, which controlled the importation and exportation of commodities, to reserve high-level administrative positions solely for *peninsulares* (Haring 1963:196). This angered the *criollos*, because the commercial houses paid the best wages in Mexico and offered their administrators funding opportunities to establish firms (e.g., the tanning industry, textiles, dyes) and to trade their commodities through the commercial houses. The only types of industries open to *criollos* within the private sector were in mining and agriculture. Even in these domains, however, *criollos* were restricted: they were not allowed to trade freely and were subject to high taxes.

By 1774 the royal government was aware that most people in Mexico were dissatisfied with its racial order (Haring 1963:320). It nonetheless chose to retain the occupational restrictions and only attempted to placate part of its *criollo* elite by giving merchants special privileges. In 1774 the crown permitted merchants in Mexico to trade directly with merchants from other New World Spanish colonies, thus allowing Mexican *criollos* to get rid of *peninsular* administrators who acted as middlemen and retained a large percentage of the trading profits. This did not pacify *criollo* merchants, however, and the crown was forced to pass more radical reforms. In 1790 it abolished the Casa de Contratación, which for 287 years had tightly controlled shipping and commerce, giving only *peninsulares* the opportunity to accumulate great fortunes (Meyer and Sherman 1995:254). The crown also lowered some commerce taxes and revised its custom duties.

Overall, these royal reforms stimulated the economic prosperity of its *criollo* elite. A new class of merchants arose who had smaller sums of money to invest but were content with the profits they were making. Ironically, this eventually enabled the *criollo* elite to challenge the commercial monopolies. With increased profits to reinvest many *criollos* began to replace *peninsulares* in the domestic markets and established themselves as the most powerful merchants in the towns (Haring 1963: 322). Though the *peninsulares* controlled international trade, the *criollos* became economic rivals, who gradually accumulated massive fortunes and ousted *peninsulares* from many local markets. The commercial reforms invigorated the economy in Mexico, and more money remained in the domestic market. This changeover led to increased prosperity. For the masses, more wage labor was available; for the church, an improved commerce translated into higher tithes. Although the commercial reforms led to increased prosperity, they did not pacify the *criollos* or the masses. For *criollos*, the prosperity they experienced only led to increasing discontent. They considered their subjection to the crown more and more a liability rather than an asset, as *peninsulares* continued to monopolize power in Mexico and remained the crown's privileged subjects.

The social and economic position of the *mestizos* of the interior had somewhat improved by the turn of the nineteenth century, partly due to labor shortages and the crown's attempt to pacify them. In the late 1700s, when the crafts guild experienced a labor shortage, *mestizos* were gradually recruited to fill that void (Cope 1994:102; McAlister 1963:362). Only *mestizos* whose fathers were Spaniards were given such a privilege, however. Though many *mestizos* entered the crafts guilds, their occupational mobility was limited since they could only work as apprentices and were prohibited from becoming journeymen. To alleviate the tensions at the crafts guilds, the royal crown chose to lift some of its occupational restrictions and began to employ *mestizos* in low-level government positions (Haring 1963:253). This improved the opportunities available to the *mestizos*, but did not assure their loyalty to the crown.

To pacify the *mestizos* and *afromestizos* the royal crown allowed the children of some racially mixed marriages legally to obtain a *criollo* racial label. The children of *peninsulares* who were born in legitimate marriages were to be classified as *criollo* whether or not a parent was *mestizo* or *afromestizo*. The decree was called "Limpieza de Sangre" (cleansing of one's blood) and was issued on 15 October 1805 (Aguirre Beltrán 1946:253). Aguirre Beltrán (1946:250) claims the passage of this decree was necessary because most people in Mexico were racially mixed and the church, without the consent of the government, had already institutionalized this practice. The government was aware of this and had to conform to the social norms of the period. Historian Patricia Seed (1988:209–220) adds that not only were racial boundaries becoming blurred among Mexico City's elite, but by 1774 intermarriage between *peninsulares* and racially mixed people had also become acceptable. This form of intermarriage generally only occurred among *peninsular* families who were aristocratic but had lost their fortunes. To maintain their social status such families preferred their daughters to marry individuals who were wealthy and racially mixed, rather than *peninsulares* without fortunes.

In the case of free *afromestizos*, although life for the wealthy improved, the racial boundaries remained in place for the majority of the commoners who lived in the interior of Mexico. *Afromestizos*, like Indians, were not allowed to enter the crafts guilds. For *afromestizos*, the only economic opportunities available were occupations in the military. Between 1762 to 1810, when Spain perceived Great Britain as a threat to its hold over the colonies in North America, the crown authorized improvements in the training of its military and ordered a professional standing army to be recruited (Meyer and Sherman 1995:257). One-third of the army was to be made up of professional soldiers. The availability of jobs in the military allowed a large number of *afromestizos* to become year-round soldiers and improve their family's economic standing (McAlister 1963:368).

In the case of the Indians of the interior, the only change in the racial order was the availability of wage labor. By the late 1700s Indians could enter most occupations except the crafts guilds (Meyer and Sherman 1995:274). Before then they were limited to working as farm hands and servants. Wages, however, were terribly low, providing only the barest necessities, and many were tied to a peonage system. Exacerbating matters, Indians still bore the obligation of paying tribute to the crown, unlike other subjects.[19] The easiest way of fulfilling this obligation was to remain in the *haciendas* or Indian pueblos where labor was organized to raise the tribute taxes.[20]

Liberal Racial Legislation and Mexican Independence

Toward the latter part of the Spanish period the royal crown realized that the commercial reforms it had passed were insufficient and began to legislate more laws to improve the civil rights of the masses. Spain's motives were not altruistic. In the early 1800s, as a result of international wars with France, the United States, and England, Spain experienced tremendous financial problems (Lafaye 1974; Meyer and Sherman 1995). France attempted to invade Spain; the United States encroached upon Louisiana; and England challenged Spain's control of parts of South America (Hall 1989). Moreover, at this time Spain's colonial subjects in Mexico began to protest against unfair taxation and discriminatory racial laws favoring *peninsulares* (Weber 1982). In essence, Spain's hold over Mexico, including the Southwest, was in jeopardy.

In 1808 Spain's control of Mexico was further threatened when Napoleon Bonaparte's forces invaded Spain and kidnapped the country's monarch (Miller 1985). In the absence of Spain's legitimate monarch, power fell to the Cortes, the Spanish parliament. The Cortes was composed of liberal thinkers, including representatives from Mexico, who passed legislation reforming the autocratic government into a constitutional monarchy (Hall and Weber 1984). Several groundbreaking laws were specifically designed for the overseas colonies in efforts to avert revolutionary movements. Indians and *mestizos* were the target of the reforms, because they constituted the majority population. By 1810, out of a total population of a little over 6 million, close to 3,676,281 were Indian and 1,328,707 were *castas* (*mestizos* and *afromestizos*) of various racial mixtures (Aguirre Beltrán 1946:236; Meyer and Sherman 1995:271). Together these racial groups constituted 84 percent of Mexico's population. The aim of the reforms was to make Indians and *mestizos* loyal subjects by accelerating the Indians' assimilation and opening economic opportunities for both peoples. To implement these desired objectives, the Cortes abolished the "racial caste system" and gave Indians, *mestizos,* and free *afromestizos* many of the legal rights of Whites. Although the Cortes indeed passed liberal racial legislation, it chose not to free the 10,000 Black slaves residing in Mexico (Aguirre Beltrán 1946:236–237).

The first reforms were aimed at Indians. On 25 September 1810 Indians were released from paying tribute to the crown and to the local government (Borah 1983:395).[21] They were to be taxed in the same manner as other subjects. On 9 February 1811 the royal crown decreed that Indians were permitted to raise any crop they chose, to enter any profession, and to transact business with whomever they wanted (Borah 1983:396; Hutchinson 1969:10). In sum, all economic and occupational restrictions were lifted. The 1811 decree also abolished racial restrictions in the craft guilds and was directed to all non-Whites, excluding Black slaves. Prior to that date, only *peninsulares* and *criollos* had been allowed to be master craftsmen, while *mestizos* were restricted to being journeymen or unskilled laborers (Chance and Taylor 1977; McAlister 1963). Indians and *afromestizos,* of course, had been barred from the craft guilds. Outside of the frontier zones, lifting the racial restrictions in the guilds was of utmost importance to non-Whites. For them, the guilds were the main method of advancing economically or improving their social standing (Cope 1994; Seed 1982).

Finally, to the utmost surprise of the masses, the Cortes abolished most racial restrictions when it passed the 1812 Law of Cádiz, proclaiming under the law that Indians, mixed-bloods, *criollos,* and *peninsulares* were equal (Barreiro 1832:271, 280–281; Hutchinson 1969:80; Menchaca 1993:586). Before then, non-Whites could only obtain the legal rights of White subjects if they performed heroic acts during time of war (*Recopilación de leyes de los reynos de las Indias* 1774: Book 7, Title 5, Laws 10 and 11) or if they bought *cédulas* giving them the legal status of Whites (since 1795; Forbes 1966:245; McAlister 1963:369). On 13 September 1813 the

Spanish Cortes passed a landmark reform aimed at improving the economic and political status of the Indians (Hutchinson 1969:85). Missions more than ten years old were to be secularized and the land distributed among Christian Indians (Engelhardt 1929).

In the Southwest the reforms of the Cortes primarily served to improve the community social standing of the non-White population. They had minimal economic impact on individuals since many of the racial reforms were already in practice (Cutter 1995). On the southwestern frontier, by tradition, the racial restrictions had been less rigid than in the interior of Mexico. The Spanish crown had never enforced the craft-guild racial restrictions (Bancroft 1964; de la Teja 1991; Persons 1958; and Tjarks 1974). Non-Whites, including Indians, were able to enter any profession (e.g., tanner, blacksmith, carpenter, mason, printer, or artist). Although the reforms had little impact in the economic domain in the Southwest, in the political and social spheres the reforms allowed non-Whites to improve their standing. Prior to the reforms, non-Whites were prohibited from participating in the local government and were barred from positions as generals of garrisons or presidios (Haring 1963; *Recopilación de leyes de los reynos de las Indias* 1774: Book 3, Title 10, Law 12). After the reforms non-Whites could run for local offices and be eligible for high-level appointments within the government and the Catholic Church.

The church responded with caution to the reforms directed toward the missions, refusing to terminate its hold over its neophytes and to relinquish title to mission lands (Engelhardt 1929). Most likely this was a wise decision, for in 1814 the Spanish monarch returned to the throne and brought the reform movement to a halt. In 1820, however, the Spanish crown was forced to reinstitute the reforms to avert independence movements (Hall and Weber 1984:7). At this time the church was confronted with the probability of the secularization of the missions, as the liberal reformers of the period considered the mission system to be paternalistic and an obstruction to the Indians' attainment of equality under the law (Hutchinson 1969).

In 1821 the Spanish crown was unable to prevent revolutionary action, and Mexico obtained its independence from Spain. The new Mexican republic immediately passed new reforms and instituted unprecedented legislation in the area of racial policy. The 1812 philosophy of the Law of Cádiz was reinstated (Hall and Weber 1984). Whites, Indians, *mestizos,* and free *afromestizos* were declared citizens of Mexico. The new

Mexican republic went even further than the Cortes, introducing the legal infrastructure to dismantle slavery (Aguirre Beltrán 1946:236–237; Schwartz 1975:7–8). Furthermore, the difference between the new republic's proclamation and Spain's previous legislation was that the new racial policy was to be enforced with deliberate speed. This meant that Indians were to be assimilated and incorporated as practicing citizens, even if they refused. Thus, philosophical racial problems soon arose within the new republic. The main question was how the Indians would be dealt with if they refused to become part of the republic. In the Southwest this dilemma was very serious, for unlike the situation in the interior, where most indigenous tribes had been acculturated or had ceased warring against the state, on the northern frontier the Apache, Navajo, Comanche, and Shoshone controlled nearly one-third of the territory and considered themselves separate nations (Weber 1982).

6

Liberal Racial Legislation during the Mexican Period, 1821–1848

In this chapter I examine how the people of the Southwest were affected by the racial legislation passed in Mexico following the Mexican War of Independence. After independence Spain's racial order was dismantled, and socioeconomic policies were adopted to redress the effects of the *casta* system. Racial distinctions became increasingly blurred during the Mexican period, and people in the Southwest were often referred to in government and church documents in cultural rather than racial terms. The label *gente de razón* replaced the hierarchical racial categories used to distinguish the people of the Southwest.

During the Mexican period, the racial legislation ended *de jure* discrimination in theory, but in practice it did not dismantle all forms of racial stratification, in particular in the area of land policy. The question of who became a Mexican citizen in the Southwest is a central issue in understanding the trajectory of Mexican American racial history. My narrative opens with a brief glimpse of the racial legislation passed by the federal government following Mexican independence.

Mexico's Liberal Racial Legislation

The Spanish crown lost control of Mexico in 1821, after the Mexican War for Independence, and a new republic was born (Weber 1982:16). The transfer of power resulted in immediate political and territorial changes throughout Mexico, including the Southwest. The victorious rebels issued the Plan de Iguala, a provisional constitution to govern the people, and reaffirmed the liberal racial philosophy of the 1812 Law of Cádiz. Under the Plan de Iguala race could no longer be legally used to prevent Indians, *mestizos*, and free *afromestizos* from exercising the citizenship rights enjoyed by Whites. Though the plan did not eradicate slavery, it set

161

the foundation for the removal of all forms of legal racial discrimination. The drafting of additional racial legislation was temporarily interrupted, however, because within months of independence economic and political conflicts arose that had to be addressed immediately. Most importantly, the debate about whether Mexico should become a federal republic or a constitutional monarchy took center stage (Meyer and Sherman 1995).

Sadly, this was not the worst problem faced by the Mexican people. The war of independence had disastrous effects on the national economy. During the war, fields were destroyed and agricultural production declined, leaving the country in a crisis. There was insufficient food to feed the masses. In the mining industry production practically came to a halt, as many workers had left the mines to join the war and machinery had been damaged. This produced a financial strain, because the mining industry had been one of Mexico's strongest assets, generating employment for a large segment of the population (Haring 1963). In 1821 the mining industry reported a loss of over 20 million pesos (Meyer and Sherman 1995:304). Mexico also experienced an economic drain when Spanish elites left the country, taking their assets; worst of all, the Spanish crown left the Mexican government bankrupt, with a debt of over 76 million pesos (Meyer and Sherman 1995:307, 319).

In spite of these enormous problems, on 27 November 1823 the Mexican people elected congressional representatives and began the process of ratifying a constitution as well as settling their differences on the political structure of the country (Meyer and Sherman 1995: 313). On 4 October 1824 the Constitution of 1824 was adopted, and congress reorganized Mexico into a federal republic composed of nineteen states and four territories (Meyer and Sherman 1995:314). Texas was declared to be part of the state of Coahuila y Tejas, California and New Mexico remained territories, and Arizona became a province of the state of Sonora (Officer 1987).[1] In addition, two regions which are part of Texas today went through territorial boundary shifts. El Paso Valley was separated from New Mexico and incorporated as part of the state of Chihuahua (Metz 1994:21), and Laredo as well as the rest of Nuevo Santander became part of the newly organized state of Tamaulipas (Hinojosa 1983:38).

In the area of racial legislation, the spirit of the Law of Cádiz was reaffirmed and all people in Mexico excluding slaves became citizens (Weber 1982:22). Though many congressmen favored emancipating slaves immediately, others argued that if the 10,000 slaves left in bondage were set free this would cause an economic crisis in Veracruz and Acapulco, where most slaves were concentrated (see Bugbee 1898).[2] Instead of abolishing slavery, a more liberal slave code was issued to improve their lives and to give slave owners time to prepare for emancipation. Under the constitution all forms of the slave trade, including purchasing and selling slaves in Mexico, were prohibited. The constitution also decreed that any slave introduced into Mexico by way of purchase or trade would immediately be emancipated. The most important change was the proclamation that slave children born in Mexico would be set free at age fourteen. After serving ten additional years, adults in bondage would likewise be set free (see Bugbee 1898:394–398, 401).

Racial legislation affecting the missions was also drafted.[3] Congressmen overwhelmingly voted in favor of dismantling the mission system, concurring that it obstructed the conversion of the Indians into citizens (Weber 1982). Missions more than ten years old were to be immediately converted into parishes, while other missions were given until 1842 or whenever the federal government deemed it appropriate (Kessell 1976:301–304). Exemptions were given to recently established missions and to those with a large number of first-generation neophytes, who were in danger of returning to their previous lifestyle if secularized. The Indians already prepared for secularization were to be converted into farmers or ranchers, and their profits would be taxed (Engelhardt 1913:108, 124–185).[4] Each secularized family was to receive a plot of mission property. The federal government envisioned that Indians would favor becoming commercial farmers and in this way would become integrated within Mexico's monetary economy (Menchaca 1993; Padilla 1979). Federal officers assumed in theory that if Indians were granted full political rights they would choose to acculturate and thus would become tax-paying Mexican citizens. Each territory or state was allowed to develop the particular procedures to secularize the Indians as long as the constitution was upheld.

Anglo-American Immigration: Mexico's Strategy to Pacify the Non-Christian Indians

Northern Mexico, including the Southwest, experienced the same legislative changes after independence as the interior did. Indians, *mestizos*, free *afromestizos*, and Whites were given citizenship and were accorded full political rights.[5] The slave code reforms, however, had little effect in the Southwest because enslaving Blacks was uncommon there. Most *afromestizos* had migrated to the Southwest as free people (Schwartz 1975). Furthermore, the new racial laws had limited effects on the majority of the non-Christian Indians because they were unaware of or unconcerned with the national political changes. The new government therefore had to address this problem and somehow convince the non-Christian Indians to become members of the new republic. This transformation had to be accomplished without incurring new debts, because the federal government was bankrupt (Lafaye 1974).

A military invasion to force non-Christian Indians to conform was also out of the question because it could not be financed. The Mexican government's finances were in such disrepair that immediately after independence the missions were ordered to support the military at no cost (Engelhardt 1913:186). With the exception of Santa Fe and San Elizario, most presidios were left with few soldiers or were converted to centers under civilian military control (Hendricks and Timmons 1998:52–60). Mexican citizens were required to take full responsibility for their military defense and were expected to form civilian militia units. Many citizens were issued military titles and authorized to command the civilian militia. The townspeople were also responsible for suppressing Indian raids. The federal government was aware that this restructuring placed the civilians at a disadvantage and that it had to offer them some type of assistance in controlling hostile Indians. The government chose to liberalize its immigration policies and for the first time allow immigrants from the United States to settle in the Southwest, with the rationale that more settlers were needed to pacify the unconquered Indians. The first immigration policies were drafted under the provisional government set up after the Plan de Iguala. The Azcárate Commission, which was authorized to address the military problems in the area, recommended that citizens from the United States be recruited to settle in the Southwest (Weber 1982:161–162). The commission's immigration reforms were later reaffirmed under the Constitution of 1824.

The immigration reforms were well received in Texas because Mexicans needed assistance to fight the Comanches and Apaches who dominated nearly half of the area. With dwindling military support from the government, Mexican Tejanos welcomed any help. In 1822 Anglo Americans began migrating to the Southwest, and most chose Texas as their destination (Weber 1982:164). The price of attracting them, however, posed a moral dilemma for Mexico, as many Anglo Americans settling in Texas owned slaves (Schwartz 1975). Many of the congressmen detested the federal government's actions; once the Constitution of 1824 had been passed, they drafted a series of congressional bills to enforce the emancipation clauses and thereby restrict the growth of slavery in the Southwest. Texas was the particular target of the congressional bills. Abolitionist congressmen argued that allowing Anglo Americans to introduce slaves into Texas was illegal and went against the spirit of the Constitution of 1824. Congressional opponents, however, successfully argued that the constitution was not violated, since slaves in Texas had been purchased on United States soil and most had been transported before the constitution was ratified (Bugbee 1898:394, 407). Though proslavery congressmen won their case, they knew it was a temporary victory, because bringing slaves into any part of Mexico did violate the spirit of the constitution. Nevertheless, the victory of the proslavery activists gave Texas enough time to allow slavery to flourish.

Mexican abolitionists were angered and shifted to state-level politics. In 1827 they won a major battle when the legislators of the state of Coahuila and Texas enacted a state slave code that nearly dismantled slavery (Bugbee 1898:407). Anglo Americans had little say in this matter since abolitionists dominated state government. Under Article 13 of the 1827 state constitution, all persons born in Texas were declared free people and any slave brought into Texas was to be emancipated after six months (ibid.). While most slave owners ignored the law, others found ways of complying without releasing their slaves. In particular, slave owners who held positions within the state or local governments were pressured to comply or at least appear to do so. In general, public officials alleged that they had emancipated their slaves but had been forced to place them under a lifelong peonage contract because they did not have the ability to support themselves financially (Bugbee 1898:409–412). Emancipated slaves were obliged to work without wages in return for food and shelter. The peonage argument was developed by James Brown Austin and successfully used in false compliance with the law. James was one of the political leaders of the immigrants and the younger brother of the first Anglo American contracted by the Mexican government to bring immigrants, Stephen F. Austin (see Chapter 7).

In 1829 proslavery advocates were finally defeated when President Vicente Guerrero, a person of African descent, issued Mexico's Emancipation Proclamation (Appiah and Gates 1999:882–883; Meyer and Sherman 1995:320; Weber 1982:176).[6] There was to be no exception to the law, and all former slaves were declared Mexican citizens. The following year Texas was given a direct order to comply or expect federal military intervention. Slave owners resisted and instead actively became engaged in secession movements. Before discussing this chapter in history, however, I must examine the unfolding of other federal racial legislation.

Racial and Cultural Border Zones: Changing Racial Labels

Throughout Mexico changing attitudes toward race were exemplified in the federal government's demographic record-keeping. After independence the government suspended the collection of statistical racial enumerations in government documents on the grounds that this practice had been used to distinguish the races and hence used for discriminatory purposes. Allegedly such records were no longer necessary because most people, with the exception of slaves, had been declared citizens with equal rights and obligations. Though this practice certainly exemplified the nation's liberalism, in the Southwest it obscured a close record of how race relations evolved; when land reforms were later implemented, it made it nearly impossible to determine whether *afromestizos* were treated in the same manner as the rest of the citizenry. The policies instituted by the Mexican government were influenced by record-keeping projects during the last years of the Spanish period.

By the early 1800s church, government, and census reports frequently used cultural labels to refer to the inhabitants of Mexico rather than identifying people of color by their stigmatized racial categories, the most popular term being *gente de razón* (Bautista Pino 1812; Engstrand 1992; Gutiérrez 1991; Haas 1995; Ríos-Bustamante 1986; Weber 1982, 1992). The regional practice of enumerating Mexico's population solely on the basis of cultural characteristics rather than race began in Guadalajara in 1760 and appears to have been a liberal measure (Cook and Borah 1974:183). The archbishop of Guadalajara allowed parish priests, who were responsible for conducting the regional censuses, to omit racial categories. This practice then spread to other parts of the northern frontier and to Oaxaca and Puebla (Cook and Borah 1974:187–207). Many parish priests, however, continued to maintain racial records in baptismal and marriage registries, but did not give this information to the national census enumerators. Sherburne F. Cook and Woodrow Borah (1974) conclude in their widely acclaimed historical demographic study *Essays in Population History: Mexico and the Caribbean* that the Catholic Church encouraged the omission of most racial categories from census records for two primary purposes: (1) most of the population was so thoroughly mixed that the racial classifications were no longer appropriate, and (2) the parish priests took a political stance against the government's discriminatory use of the data.

By 1810, during Mexico's preindependent revolutionary period, regional censuses omitting most racial distinctions had become common (Cook and Borah 1974:188). *Gente de razón* became the most frequently used term to count people who were White, racially mixed people, and also Indians who were detribalized. Cook and Borah propose that the category *gente de razón* was not restrictive and allowed many cultural indices to accommodate the heterogeneity of the colonial population. Individuals were counted as part of the *gente de razón* because they practiced Spanish-Mexican traditions, they were Catholics, and they recognized only the sovereignty of the government of Spain.

Though *gente de razón* became a widely used and inclusive label, the Indian category did not completely fall out of use. This category was restrictive and fundamentally focused on politics and culture. Cook and Borah (1974:188) found that to be enumerated as an Indian an individual must (1) be of homogeneous descent, (2) retain the aboriginal culture, (3) speak the aboriginal language, and (4) be a member of a tribe or an Indian corporate community who recognized two sovereignties, the tribe and the royal government. This enumeration, of course, applied only to the peaceful Indians of Mexico. Nomadic Indians were not included as part of the national nineteenth-century censuses.

This form of enumeration was replicated throughout the Southwest (Ríos-Bustamante 1986; Weber 1992). Historian Ramón Gutiérrez comments on how it was practiced in New Mexico during the early 1800s:

Beginning in 1800 the proportion of racial status labels declined both in absolute terms and in relation to civic status, nationality, and "no mentions." . . . The intermediate hues of race, so important between 1760 and 1799, had begun to disappear from the records by 1800. (Gutiérrez 1991:193)

Though Gutiérrez found in a review of government and church records that cultural labels were used to identify the colonists, the Indian category remained operative, as it did in other parts of Mexico. Cultural labels were used in reference to the colonists and their descendants, while the Indian racial category continued to be used for those people who practiced Indian traditions and lived in Indian communities.

Historian Iris Engstrand (1992:159–161) found a similar method of enumerating the population in a review of early 1800s Arizona censuses. The priests who conducted the regional censuses continued to count the mission and Christian *ranchería* Indians apart from the settlers, yet refused to identify the race of the settlers. This was done to hide the fact that many of the settlers were actually detribalized second-generation Arizona Indians. The most common terms used by the priests were *vecinos* and *gente de razón.* Engstrand comments on this practice:

> . . . the entire system of racial classification was quite arbitrary, and it became more arbitrary toward the closure of the Spanish period. The father of the mission of Tubutuma, Francisco Iturralde, did not even try to leave any information on the origin of the inhabitants in his region, as he classified them by the term "gente de razón," arguing that he had no other information. The census of Tumacácori [1796] prepared by Father Gutiérrez offers similar vague data as that of the anterior. He includes 29 "vecinos," the majority of them being peones and ranch hands. (Engstrand 1992:254; my translation)[7]

Though most racial classifications at the regional level were out of use during the last years of Spanish rule, the royal crown continued to demand a national racial count. It commissioned professional enumerators to maintain a close record of race. After the Mexican War of Independence, however, the federal government ordered the recording of race to cease in all government documents (Cook and Borah 1974:187; Gutiérrez 1991:194). Distinguishing people as Indian and non-Indian was also prohibited in most cases. Exceptions, however, were granted in areas where the Catholic Church served a large number of recently Christianized Indians, such as in the northern and southern border areas of Mexico.

This was done to determine the size of the Indian population residing in the missions and to determine if the Catholic Church was converting new populations.[8]

After independence, maintaining a count of the Christian Indian population in the Southwest continued to serve an important function and became a political vehicle to justify delaying the closure of the missions. Under the Mexican Constitution of 1824, missions more than ten years old had been issued secularization orders, and only recently established missions were given exemptions (Engelhardt 1913:108, Kessell 1976:301–304). Thus, it was important for the Catholic Church to demonstrate the utility of the missions in preparing neophytes to become Mexican citizens. With this intent, many missions maintained a record of their neophyte populations, in particular in California and Arizona. Both territories also counted the number of Indians living in Christian *rancherías* since this demonstrated the important role missionaries played in acculturating Indians. Although this practice of distinguishing neophytes and Christian *ranchería* Indians from others continued in some areas, however, similar identification of the *afromestizo* population ceased. *Afromestizos* were counted as part of the *gente de razón*.

Demographics during the Mexican Period

In some regions the practice of lumping together the racially mixed populations, Whites, and the acculturated Indians obscured a close accounting of the impact the racial reforms had in the Southwest. The demographic data that we have primarily describe the location of the settlements and their numerical sizes. This accounting practice also made it nearly impossible to determine the racial background of those colonists who settled in the Southwest after independence. A case in point: in 1834 the federal government organized a colony of settlers to migrate to California. Only information on their occupations and skills was noted, and their racial backgrounds were omitted. Apparently 239 settlers arrived from Mexico, many of them with professional skills (Weber 1982: 185–186). Among them were teachers, lawyers, doctors, carpenters, distillers, tailors, and shoemakers. Only 20 percent of the colonists were farmers (Hutchinson 1969). Though the omission of race after independence obscures matters, demographic data on the Indian population of Arizona and Alta California are available, indicating that in these two territories the majority of the citizens were acculturated Indians. The available data also indicate that the colonial settlements continued to grow.

In Alta California the people categorized as *gente de razón* are estimated to have totaled 3,200 in 1821 (Chapman 1930:385; cf. Weber 1992: 265),[9] dispersed in the towns, presidios, and ranches. They were a notably smaller population than the 21,000 neophyte Indians (Bowman 1958:146; Costello and Hornbeck 1989:313). The neophyte Indians resided in the missions but on occasion were given permission to return to their *rancherías* to visit relatives (Engelhardt 1930:285). Mission records indicate that in 1834 there were 64,500 Christian *ranchería* Indians (Cook 1976:42–43). Most of these Indians lived along Alta California's coast in villages and colonial towns. The last census distinguishing the *afromestizo* population from other people was the census of 1793, which indicates that at least 22 percent of the population was *afromestizo* (Aguirre Beltrán 1946:230). After independence, however, we are uncertain whether more *afromestizos* migrated to California or whether the blood quantum of the *afromestizo* population was further diluted through intermarriage.

A genealogical study of prominent *afromestizo* families of nineteenth-century California by Jack Forbes (1966) sheds light on this issue. Forbes found that by the Mexican period several prominent *afromestizo* families were only one-eighth to one-fourth Black. The original pioneers of Alta California had been *mulattos* (one-half Black), but over time their descendants married people of other races and the Black blood quantum was further reduced. For example, many members of the distinguished Pico extended family were *afromestizos*. They were dispersed in what today are the counties of Santa Barbara, Ventura, and San Luis Obispo and were part of the wealthiest ranching families of Alta California. The best-known member of the Pico family was Pío Pico, who served as governor of California (Forbes 1968:13–15; Rush 1965:116). Pío Pico's grandparents migrated to California during the late 1700s (Forbes 1966:244; see also Chapter 7). His grandmother was a *mulatta* married to a *mestizo* or *criollo*. Pico's grandparents' children married *criollos*, Indians, *afromestizos*, and *mestizos*. Thus, the Pico family was racially mixed, and their Black blood quantums differed. Pico was one-eighth Black. Other well-known Mexican *afromestizos* with similar backgrounds were Tiburcio Tapia, a mayor and judge of Los Angeles, and Lieutenant Colonel Manuel Victoria, one-term governor of California and distinguished military officer (Bancroft 1964:R-Z 762; Forbes 1966:66; Pitt 1970).

In Arizona, as in California, the neophyte and Christian *ranchería* Indians outnumbered the *gente de razón*. In 1820 there were 2,291 *gente de razón*, concentrated in Tucson and Tubac and also scattered throughout the ranches and mission settlements (Kessell 1976:246). Although the neophyte population in 1820 was also relatively small, numbering only 1,127, the Christian *ranchería* Indians constituted a sizable population (Kessell 1976:246). A federal census in 1825 found that 9,200 Indians lived near Tucson and were politically organized under the command of ten justices of the peace, the term used for an Indian political leader (Kessell 1976:264). Most of the Indians were Upper Pimas, with a few Papagos and Cocomaricopas scattered among them.[10] Unfortunately, a similar census of other Christian *ranchería* Indians living near the missions was not conducted, so we do not know the population sizes of these groups. In 1843, however, missionaries reported that Christian *rancherías* were located near Missions Tumacácori and San Xavier del Bac (Engstrand 1992:273). It is uncertain how many *afromestizos* lived in Arizona during the Spanish and Mexican periods because a comprehensive record of their population size was not kept. Engstrand (1992:215, 216) found that only in Tucson did government reports identify *afromestizos*.

In New Mexico the regional censuses did not distinguish the population by race (see Carroll and Haggard 1942). After independence, the first regional census was taken in 1827 by Colonel Don Antonio Narvona, military commandant of New Mexico (Carroll and Haggard 1942:88, 89). He reported that 43,433 citizens were dispersed in the capital of Santa Fe, villas, ranches, colonial towns, and Indian pueblos. By this time Ysleta, Socorro, and the presidio at San Elizario were no longer counted as part of New Mexico; in 1823 they had become part of Chihuahua (Bowden 1971:157). Though neither Narvona nor other census enumerators distinguished people on the basis of race, an estimate of the size of the Christian Indian population is available, based on a census count of the people who lived in the Indian pueblos.[11] For example, Carroll and Haggard (1942:89) estimate on the basis of New Mexico's census of 1840 that out of a total of 55,403 New Mexican citizens there were 10,566 Christian Indians living apart from the colonists. Though these authors recognize that their estimate may be low because many Indians lived in the colonial settlements and were counted as part of the *gente de razón*, the available data at least indicate the size of the Indian population residing in the Indian pueblos.

Ramón Gutiérrez (1991:198) proposes that in New Mexico by the early

1800s the descendants of *afromestizos* had interbred with the Indian and European-origin population so that their former distinctiveness was no longer apparent. This view is supported by Don Pedro Bautista Pino, New Mexico's representative to the 1812 Cortes at Cádiz and author of various reports on New Mexico. Bautista Pino alleged that in 1812 New Mexico no longer had Black residents (Bautista Pino 1812:243). Historian Adrian Bustamante disagrees with Bautista Pino and Gutiérrez, arguing that although there were few Black people, the 1790 census of New Mexico and Mexican documents clearly indicate that there were people of Black descent living in New Mexico toward the end of the Spanish period. For example, the 1790 census indicates that *afromestizos* were dispersed in seventy-six settlements, with most residing in Santa Fe (Bustamante 1991:156). Seventy-nine families had a head of household who was identified as *afromestizo* (*mulatto* or *coyote*) (ibid., 150–153). Gutiérrez (1991:196) acknowledges that Spanish documents in New Mexico often used the word *mulatto* or *pardo*, but he argues that these terms simply meant that an individual was of mixed Spanish-Indian ancestry. Bustamante (1991:161) disagrees and asks why the words would be used differently than in the interior of Mexico, where they clearly referred to a person who was Black or of partially Black ancestry. Gutiérrez and Bustamante agree, however, that during the Mexican period the terms *pardo* and *mulatto* were gradually replaced by the national ethnic identifier *mexicano* and that cultural rather than racial terms were used in reference to the non-Indian population.

After independence the population of Texas was enumerated without using racial distinctions (Alonzo 1998).[12] By the 1820s most mission Indians had been secularized and were part of the *gente de razón* (Hinojosa 1991:72–73). Only the Indians at Missions Espíritu Santo and Rosario had not been secularized. By 1830, however, the last mission Indians had been secularized, and most of them moved to other settlements in Texas (Weber 1982:56). Five years later, the Mexican population of Texas is estimated to have grown to 7,800 (Meyer and Sherman 1995:336).[13] This estimate does not include the populations from El Paso Valley and Laredo, which at that time were both part of other territories.[14] It also does not include the Christian Indians living outside of the colonial settlements or the Anglo-American immigrants, who were enumerated separately. Government reports estimate that by 1834 the Anglo-American population had outgrown the Mexican population and reached over 30,000 (Meyer and Sherman 1995:336; Schwartz 1975:27). There is no estimate of the Christian Indians living in *rancherías*. Because racial classifications were not used during the Mexican period, we do not know the actual size of the *afromestizo* population in Texas. An estimate of the size of the Black slave population brought by Anglo-American immigrants is available, however. By 1836 over 5,000 Black slaves had been transported to Texas from the United States (Richardson, Wallace, and Anderson 1970:160).

Indian Acculturation and Mexican Citizenship

Throughout the Spanish and Mexican periods the Catholic Church and colonial governments attempted to Christianize the Indians of the Southwest and incorporate them as part of the state. After independence, Indian allies were granted Mexican citizenship and expected to acculturate (Menchaca 1993). Indians were expected to change their lifestyle by adopting new traditions and practices and shedding old ones; in cases where the culture of the Indians was practical, they were encouraged to recombine the old and the new to produce bicultural innovations. Essentially acculturation was a process through which Indians became functional in the language of their conquerors, replicated many of their daily life practices, and were knowledgeable about their norms. My analysis of Indian acculturation during the Mexican period in the areas of political structure, material culture, religion, language, and education is based on a synthesis of the writings of historians and anthropologists. The goal of this discussion is to outline the group behavioral changes that occurred among the Indians who became incorporated as Mexican citizens. I am not implying that they all followed a common acculturation pattern. It has been well documented by scholars that individuals in any acculturation process do not follow the same degree of cultural change, because some individuals accommodate while others choose to resist.

I concur with Pierre Bourdieu (1992) that acculturation is dependent upon how one internalizes externality. Individuals form different types of relations with people and are affected by formal institutions in diverse ways (e.g., government, school, church). The experiences people undergo with representatives of such institutions in turn influence how they internalize their views of life, government, religion, and school. These experiences also have an effect on individuals' sentiments about their cultural group as well as their opinions of the way of life of the dominant cultural group in power. Overall, acculturation is a highly individual process that is internalized based upon one's life experiences. As part of this individual process, however, the role of the family is significant. As Milton Gordon (1964) notes, the family unit has a strong impact on how the individual internalizes externality. Gordon posits that family members generally only acquire basic cultural knowledge when they first come into contact with the ethnic group that dominates them. Not until the second generation do family members acquire the correct social comportment expected of them by the dominant cultural group. It is also important to note that the community in which a family and individual reside influences familial and individual acculturation.

Pierre Bourdieu (1992) and Ronald Cohen (1978) assert that when individuals live among people who share their same ancestry group pressures are placed upon the family and individual to interpret externality in a similar manner, thus maintaining a parallel progression in the level of their community's acculturation. Although the community plays a significant role, Bourdieu asserts that in the end it is the social relations that the individual forms which exert the strongest force in determining whether a person accommodates, resists, or passively accepts the social pressures to change. Although I concur with Bourdieu, I must add that those who are socially dominated acknowledge that it is necessary to be operational in the culture of the dominant group if one is to pursue a life of happiness or succeed economically (Barth 1969; Despres 1975). I must also note that when individuals acculturate this does not mean that they shed their ancestral culture (Keefe and Padilla 1987; Menchaca 1989). Individuals can acculturate and at the same time retain the knowledge and practices of their ancestors. This process has been called biculturalism and ethnic retention and is not considered to be in conflict with acculturation. Thus, my analysis of the Indians' acculturation is based upon writings that record group behavior and not necessarily the private lives or political views of individuals.

Christian Indian Acculturation

The same groups who were colonized by Spain remained allies of the Mexican state, and their acculturation continued to occur at an individual, family, or village level. Only in El Paso Valley and in La Junta in Texas were a large number of Apaches converted during the Mexican period (Beers 1979; Castañeda 1938; Hendricks and Timmons 1998). In New Mexico the *genizaro* population also increased during the Mexican period (Archibald 1978:211; Bustamante 1991:148). Because members of this population were clearly bicultural, they were ostracized by the Indians and the colonists alike. The Pueblo Indians did not give *genizaros* tribal membership, and the colonists treated them as outsiders and troublemakers. By independence these marginalized indigenous people had formed their own towns and were concentrated in the five pueblos of Belén, Santa Rosa de Abiquiú, Ojo Caliente, Tomé, and San Miguel del Vado (Gutiérrez 1991:305).

Political perception was one of the main cultural areas in which Indian allies underwent change, as they had to pledge allegiance to Spain or to the Republic of Mexico. As part of this political enfranchisement they were expected to modify their tribal government by adopting a political structure handed down from Spain (Carroll and Haggard 1942; Doyle 1989; Engstrand 1992; Officer 1987; Polzer 1976). Under the town assembly structure the chief became the *alcalde* (who functioned as mayor or justice of the peace) and selected at least two *regiadores* (town assembly members) (Ezzell 1974). The duties of these officials ranged from organizing social activities to ensuring that the orders of the colonial government and church were enforced. Indians from Christian *rancherías* as well as the Pueblo Indians of New Mexico had greater flexibility to choose to follow this form of government or ignore it altogether. Because they were not under daily military supervision, it was up to them to modify their tribal structure.[15]

In contrast to the political flexibility enjoyed by the Pueblo and Christian *ranchería* Indians, the mission Indians were closely supervised and had to organize town assemblies (Engelhardt 1986; Grant 1978b). In their case it was common to merge indigenous political forms of government with the one imposed upon them. Essentially, a bicultural political structure emerged. In missions that were inhabited by one tribe or *ranchería*, their chief was appointed to the position of *alcalde* (Engelhardt 1930). The *regiadores* were appointed from among the neophytes. In missions where the neophytes came from different tribes and their chiefs also lived among them, the *alcalde* and *regiadores* were elected or appointed by the fathers.

After Mexican independence, the political structures of Christian Indians living in *rancherías* and the Pueblo Indians of New Mexico were not affected. If they had organized town assemblies, that form of government continued. When the missions were secularized, however, the Indian political structures were dismantled. Because Christian Indians were given citizenship, they were to participate in the town assemblies organized by the colonists. In theory, no political distinctions were to be made between them and the colonists. In practice, as the next chapter illustrates, the colonists overwhelmingly controlled the Indians by monopolizing all governmental committees.

Indians also experienced cultural changes in their daily lives, including the way they dressed, the tools they used, and how they cooked their food (Monroy 1990). Women and men were expected to be fully clothed (Bolton 1921; Engelhardt 1929; Monroy 1990). Indians who did not practice farming were also encouraged to plant beans, peas, lentils, and cereals rather than to depend upon roots (Hoover 1989). They obtained spades, hoes, and other tools from the colonists (Ezzell 1974). After the introduction of cattle by Spain, Indians were encouraged to raise cattle as a source of protein. Cooking utensils made from metal were also a welcome innovation. Indians were encouraged to modify the shape of the ceramics and baskets they manufactured, however, rather than to abandon this technology. On the contrary, the colonists adopted the Indians' ceramic technology and modified it by using Spanish glazes and firing techniques. Guns, lances, and horses were also introduced, not only by the Spanish, but through trade with the English, French, or Americans (Powell 1952). This gave Indians rapid mobility and overall made warfare more dangerous.

The tenets of Catholicism were also introduced to the Christian Indians. Neophytes and first-generation Christian Indians often practiced nepantlism, a form of religious syncretism, merging indigenous and Catholic ontological views (Anzaldúa 1986; Engelhardt 1929). Although indigenous religious tenets were replaced by Christian doctrines in succeeding generations, they were not completely abandoned. Jacques Lafaye (1974) argues that the analysis of indigenous religion must be understood through a private vs. public dichotomy. In public Indians accommodated in an effort to please the fathers, yet in private veneration of indigenous deities persisted. This analysis is supported by the fact that indigenous religions survive to this date (Horcasitas 1992). Through catechism the fathers taught Indians the basic tenets of Christianity and concurrently attacked the validity of their indigenous religious beliefs.

Though the missionaries' ministering styles varied and some refused to allow religious syncretism, it was common for liberal missionaries to ease the transition from one belief system to another by teaching the Indians to associate their deities with the Catholic saints, Jesus Christ, and the Virgin Mary (Gutiérrez 1991).

Religion also influenced Indians linguistically and frequently became the vehicle for bilingualism. To facilitate interethnic communication the Catholic Church instructed missionaries to learn the Indians' languages (Engelhardt 1929). Although interpreters were often used, it was necessary for the friars to become bilingual if they were to evangelize the Indians successfully (Polzer 1976; Spicer 1981). When the friars were not bilingual, catechism lessons were interpreted. The eventual goal of the friars, however, was to convert the Indians to become Spanish speakers (Monroy 1990).

The length of time that Indians needed to internalize Catholic beliefs and learn Spanish was highly dependent upon their place of residence. Mission Indians were under daily supervision; from Monday to Saturday they were required to attend mass in the morning before beginning their work and to study their catechism lessons before eating supper (Bannon 1970; Engelhardt 1929). On Sundays and during religious holidays they also attended mass. In contrast to this daily routine the Indians from the Christian *rancherías* and the Pueblo Indians of New Mexico did not experience similar pressures and had greater freedom to internalize or reject the teachings. The frequency of the missionaries' visits also varied, depending on the proximity of the *rancherías* to the missions. In California, Texas, and New Mexico it was common for the *rancherías* and Indian pueblos to be adjacent to the missions or to be within a few hours' ride (Merriam 1955; Poyo and Hinojosa 1991; Prince 1915). In contrast, the Yuma *rancherías* in the area of the Gila and the Santa Cruz rivers in Arizona were far from the missions, and the fathers were only able to visit the Indians three to four times a year (Kessell 1976).

Formal schooling in the Southwest was uncommon; yet in places where schools were available Indians were allowed to attend, and schooling was used as a vehicle of acculturation (Menchaca 1999).[16] Schooling policies during the Mexican period were inherited from Spain and were applied to Indians and colonists alike. Usually the children of the colonists and Indians only learned to read and write if their parents were literate or if they were taught by missionaries (Sánchez 1976). High-level

Spanish officers were the only ones able to educate their children in the interior of Mexico, a form of private education unavailable to the commoners or most Indians.

Texas was the first territory in the Southwest to establish a formal school that employed a professional teacher to develop a curriculum and to instruct students on a regular basis. Founded in San Antonio in 1746, the first formal school was a private Catholic school limited to children whose parents were able to pay tuition (Berger 1947:41). It primarily served the needs of the *peninsular* elite. After 1782 the church ordered the missionaries throughout the Southwest to increase the secular education of the Indians in the fields of agriculture, horticulture, mechanical arts, and stock raising (Engelhardt 1930:401). In essence the function of the missions was not to be solely religious, but rather to prepare the Indians to become ranchers and to enter occupations needed to improve the stability of the colonies. Every mission was to offer classes in agriculture and in other industrial occupations.

In 1793 a royal decree ordered local governments in the Southwest to establish public schools (Engelhardt 1930:490). This was part of the crown's liberal philosophy of improving the cultural lifestyle of the colonies by schooling the children of the settlers and the Christianized Indians. Under this decree, school attendance was to be compulsory and the schools were to be funded through taxes levied by local government and through private donations. Indian children were allowed to attend public schools but were not allowed to speak their native languages. If Indian students could not speak Spanish, they had to be taught to speak it, because all instruction was to be in that language. The royal decree was ambitious for its time and difficult to implement. Only Texas and California enforced the decree and began formal education.

After 1793 a few schools were established in Texas in the garrisons and missions as well as one additional private school in San Antonio (Berger 1947:42).[17] The application of the royal decree of 1793 was especially successful in California, as Governor Diego de Borica enthusiastically prepared plans to establish schools in all major settlements (Berger 1947). Although professional teachers were not hired, officers who were literate and willing to act as teachers were relieved from military duties. Within two years of the decree the government in California had established five public schools—four schools in the presidial towns of Santa Bárbara, San Diego, Monterey, and San Francisco and one in the civilian township of San José. In 1817 a sixth school was opened in Los Angeles (Weiss 1978:117).

Public education got underway in New Mexico after 1813 and was made available to the colonists, Indians, and *genizaros* (Barreiro 1832: 291). Unlike the situation in California and Texas, however, where students were allowed to attend public schools irrespective of their parents' ability to pay teachers' salaries, only the children whose parents contributed to the teacher's stipend were allowed to attend school. The royal decree of 1793 was apparently ignored by the local government until a direct order was issued. On 26 January 1813 the royal government ordered that public education must be made available in New Mexico (Barreiro 1832:290–292). New Mexico's governor was also ordered to establish plans for offering some form of higher education in Santa Fe, the capital.

Following this decree, New Mexico established six schools (see Menchaca 1999). The date of their founding is uncertain; however, an 1832 report by government inspector Antonio Barreiro entitled *Ojeada sobre Nuevo México, que da una idea* (A Glimpse of New Mexico, Which Gives Us an Idea) tells us that the schools were established during the Spanish period and that they remained in operation during the Mexican period (Barreiro 1832). According to Barreiro, the schools were founded after 1813 in the towns of Santa Fe, Albuquerque, and Cañada and in the Indian-*genizaro* towns of Belén, San Miguel del Vado, and Taos.

Public schools were not available in Arizona during the Spanish and Mexican periods, and few children were schooled by missionaries. The missionaries, who traditionally played important roles in the schooling of children in other regions, were preoccupied with their multiple duties as farmers, medical aides, and religious representatives. Their missionary work required that they travel hundreds of miles to reach their Christian *rancherías*, which left little time to teach children. Arizona settlers contemplated opening two public schools in Tucson, however, after the visit of friar Juan Baptista de Cevallos. In 1814 the crown assigned Cevallos, the commissionary prefect, to inspect Arizona settlements (Dobyns 1976:48–49). He found no schools in Arizona and immediately ordered the settlers to hire two teachers to establish schools in Tucson and in Mission San Xavier del Bac. Neither Cevallos nor the settlers acquired the necessary funds to establish the schools.

After Mexican independence, under the Constitution of 1824, Mexico's Congress ruled that the federal government would promote public education by assisting the states and territories in developing educational policies (see Larroyo 1946).[18] In California the public schools established during the Spanish period continued to function during the Mexican period. The missions also continued to school children. After secularization orders were issued in 1834, to assist the badly funded yet energetic educational system in California the Mexican government commissioned twenty teachers to open schools (Hutchinson 1969:266). They arrived at San Diego as part of the Padres-Hijares Colony, which brought 239 colonists. Upon their arrival the teachers replaced the lay instructors in the schools at Monterey, Los Angeles, and Santa Bárbara and in several of the secularized mission settlements. The educational system in New Mexico did not expand during the Mexican period; the only improvement was in the availability of textbooks (Tyler 1974). Father Martínez, the teacher at Taos, obtained a printing press and wrote, printed, and distributed textbooks throughout New Mexico (ibid.). After independence, most schools in Texas temporarily closed, but were reinstated in 1828 (Berger 1947). Only one private school in San Antonio remained open during this period. When public schools were reopened, they were established in San Antonio, La Bahía, and Nacogdoches.

Though schooling in the Southwest was badly financed and limited to those students who resided in a few areas, schooling was not restricted solely to the colonists. Furthermore, education served an important acculturation function: Indians were instructed in Spanish and were forced to become bilingual if they chose to be educated.

In sum, by the Mexican period Christian Indians and their ancestors had experienced diverse forms of acculturation. They had not all experienced the same degrees of acculturation, however. Some had more contact with the colonists, and these relationships served to familiarize them with the culture of those in power. In particular, those children who attended formal schools became highly acculturated. Pablo Tac, a Luiseño, serves as an example (see Haas 1995). Tac was schooled by missionaries at San Luis Rey, California. At age eleven he was taken to Rome to begin his studies in Latin, rhetoric, humanities, and philosophy. While in Rome Tac wrote a manuscript on his native language, leaving a treatise on Luiseño grammar. Unfortunately, he died at age twenty and was not able to write other books. Though his case was uncommon, thousands of Christian Indians did acculturate and became citizens of Mexico after independence. Most non-Christian Indians, however, remained outside the Mexican government's political domain, as the new government was unable to conquer the vast majority of the nomadic and *ranchería* Indians (Weber 1982). In particular, vanquishing the largest tribes in the Southwest became nearly impossible; most Apaches, Navajos, Comanches, and Shoshones remained independent (John 1975; Kessell 1976; Kutsche 1979).

Land: The Reorganization of the Mexican Settlements

In 1824 the federal government instituted laws to reorganize the land grant system in the Southwest and to privatize mission lands (Engstrand 1978:329). The goals were to redistribute land among the colonists and to transform Indians into land-owning farmers (Mason 1986; Ríos-Bustamante 1986). This was part of the federal government's social policies to eradicate the effects of the *casta* system. Ironically, the liberalism of the new government was accompanied by cruel and unrealistic policies toward the Indians of the Southwest (Menchaca 1995). Under the 1824 General Law of Colonization, Mexican citizens, including Christian Indians, were to be given patent to the land they inhabited, cultivated, and used for pasture (see Hall and Weber 1984). In addition, all vacant lands were eligible for distribution (Articles 2 and 9 in the 1824 General Colonization Law, cited in *Laws of Texas, Vol. 1*, p. 99). Indians and other people planning to found a new town were also given four additional leagues (17,752 acres) to erect its public buildings (Engstrand 1991; Robinson 1948).[19] Although the colonization law was designed to help Christian Indians acquire the lifestyle of Mexicans by making them property owners like the rest of the citizens of the Southwest, it unfortunately resulted in distributing a large part of the property belonging to the Christian Indians among the colonists (Engelhardt 1929, 1930).

The Colonization Law of 1824 was fundamentally flawed with respect to the rights of the Christian Indians because the federal government reinstated the Property Law of 1813, which declared that all vacant lands were to be made available for redistribution (Hall and Weber 1984:9). The 1813 law legally dispossessed the nomadic Indians of their hunting grounds, for unless they were allies of the state their land could be declared vacant and sold or granted (Sánchez 1986). It also made the unused land of the Christian Indians available for redistribution, unless it was clearly demarcated for a township or was privatized into family parcels (Kessell 1976). Likewise the Property Law of 1813 targeted the uninhabited Spanish land grants for redistribution. In general, a major aim of the federal government's land policy in the Southwest was to redistribute property among all Mexican citizens and not to privilege any racial group, as Spain had done for centuries (Leonard 1943). The Spanish crown had previously given massive land grants to its favorite subjects, who were mostly *peninsulares,* and reserved land for mission Indians and the Pueblo Indians of New Mexico. After independence, since all people were declared equal citizens, no one was to have greater rights to land. The colonists welcomed the reforms, yet many Indians did not share their sentiments. In particular, a large number of Pueblo communities of New Mexico protested the land reforms. They knew they had to be exempt from federal policy if they were to retain their ancestral lands.

Furthermore, under Article 2 of the 1824 General Colonization Law the federal government created a new economic incentive to attract immigrants and citizens from the interior of Mexico to the Southwest (Engstrand 1978:329). Heads of households would be allowed to claim a maximum of eleven square leagues (48,818 acres). This included one square league of irrigable land, four of nonirrigable land, and six for grazing. Only *empresarios* (individuals commissioned to bring colonists or immigrants) would be allowed to exceed the eleven-square-league limit. In essence, these generous land grants offered to the new settlers were a federal strategy to increase the population size of the Southwest (Weber 1982). In this way, the colonial population would grow and there would be more people to pacify and conquer the Apache, Navajo, Comanche, and Shoshone.

Privatizing Claims

Under the 1824 General Colonization Law, the federal government decreed that residents in the Southwest were the owners of the land they possessed as long as there was no overlapping claim and the occupant was not an enemy of Mexico (Haas 1995; Hall 1989; Ross 1974; Rush 1965). The federal government ordered each state and territory of the Southwest to develop the particular procedures to be followed to issue titles to Mexican citizens. It appointed administrators to investigate, survey, settle land disputes, and confirm land grant titles. Missionaries were included in the validation process: they were to notify the Christian Indians of the land reforms and assist them to do an appropriate survey of their lands and complete the claim process (Menchaca 1995; see *McMullen v. Hodge and Others*, 1849; Ross 1974). The federal government also gave governors the right to organize and preside over the land commissions which would review the claims (Hall and Weber 1984).

Tragically, in its haste to privatize land the federal government committed a mistake of enormous proportions by allowing governors to issue patents (Engstrand 1991:39, 1978:329). Though most governors were honest, in California a few became land speculators and primarily granted land to their relatives and friends. Corrupt governors did not discriminate against the Indians or colonists: they seized the property of anyone who was in their way. By 1836 the federal government had realized that this policy was flawed and rescinded it (Mattison 1946:287). After that date only appointed federal officials had the power to issue final patents. Unfortunately, in Arizona and California the reform came too late, as a considerable amount of land had been seized by the governors.

Other problems soon developed. Most colonists and Indians failed to survey their land properly and to complete the application process as recommended by the federal government. Under the Spanish land tenure system, not possessing a patent had not been a problem; and as long as a person's claim remained unchallenged there was little incentive to obtain a patent during the Mexican period because the process was time consuming and expensive. To file a claim it was common for people to have to travel hundreds of miles to meet the appropriate officials. The applicants then had to pay fees, prove that Christian Indians did not own the land, and pay for a survey; after this exhausting process was completed, they could finally obtain a patent.

A case in point is the experience of José Joaquín Ortega, one of the first land-grant owners of what today constitutes Santa Paula (Menchaca 1995). He was the grandson of José Francisco Ortega, one of the officers in the Portolá and Serra expedition.[20] In 1834 José Joaquín Ortega obtained title to more than half of Santa Paula, in Ventura County (California Land Case No. 550, 1853:44). To receive patent he had his grant properly surveyed and improved the land by establishing Potrero de Santa Paula (a ranch). After unsuccessful attempts to cultivate crops, Ortega moved to San Diego and received a second grant. Between 1834 and 1839 several Mexican and Chumash families migrated to Santa Paula and settled on Ortega's property (see Menchaca 1995). Ortega allowed them to become his tenants since a large part of his land remained uncultivated. In 1839

Photograph 31. Lopez Adobe, near Ojai, California, Built circa 1830. Courtesy of the Ventura County Museum of History and Art.

Photograph 32. Rancho Camulos Adobe, Piru, California, Built circa 1839. Courtesy of the Ventura County Museum of History and Art.

Photograph 33. Rancho Camulos Chapel, Piru, California, 1839. Courtesy of the Ventura County Museum of History and Art.

Manuel Jimeno Casarin became aware of Ortega's situation (ibid., 6). He was California's secretary of state and the federal official commissioned to certify and compile a registry of all valid land claims in California. Jimeno Casarin subsequently filed a petition to dissolve Ortega's title over the *potrero* on the basis that the land was abandoned. Ortega attempted to retain title, but when it became clear that he was about to lose the grant he requested that the families living on his property be issued patent. This ordeal led Ortega to travel from San Diego to Santa Bárbara twice, to meet with Jimeno Casarin, the governor, and the land commission officials and to offer testimony to a court reporter. Furthermore, since Ortega asked that the claim be transferred to his tenants, they also had to accompany Ortega and offer testimony.

In the end, Ortega and the families lost the claim and needlessly spent time and money, as Jimeno Casarin chose to apply for the grant himself. The point of this account is that colonists and Christian *ranchería* Indians in the Southwest often lived great distances from the places where they had to file their claims. Thus, as long as a claim remained unchallenged there was little incentive to travel hundreds of miles and lose time from ranching and farming activities (see Photographs 31 to 33).

Unfortunately for the colonists and Christian Indians alike, they were unaware that the federal government's land reforms were indeed prudent, since radical changes were soon to take place. The Mexican government's effort to recruit United States citizens was successful. In 1822 the mass arrival of Anglo-American immigrants began (Weber 1982:164), first in Texas and then in California.

In the beginning the federal government considered its immigration policy to be a brilliant strategy, as the increased number of settlers facilitated the pacification of the hostile Indians (Smith 1962a, 1962b). By the mid-1830s, however, the Mexican government regretted its immigration policy, because it proved to be disastrous (Menchaca 1993; Weber 1982). It became the gateway for the arrival of a population who did not share the new republic's ideals or racial philosophy.

7

Land, Race, and War, 1821–1848

This chapter examines the aftermath of the land reorganization laws instituted in the Southwest following Mexican independence. Under the 1824 General Colonization Law the federal government decreed that all heads of households in the Southwest who were citizens of or immigrants to Mexico were eligible to claim land (cited in *Laws of Texas, Vol. 1*, pp. 97–98; Engstrand 1978:329). This legislation differed from previous Spanish decrees, as people were to be given patent to the land they claimed and not solely occupancy rights. Moreover, no racial group was to be favored in the amount of land received.

The aim of the Law of 1824 was to undo the effects of the Spanish land grant system, which had overwhelmingly favored Whites and military officers. Though many commoners obtained property deeds and many Indian villages evolved into Mexican towns, the federal government's color-blind legislation did not work as expected. People struggled for land, and some individuals were better equipped to validate their claims. In New Mexico the Pueblo Indians had to launch several legal battles to defend their tribal lands because the territorial government alleged that the size of their population did not merit the amount of land Spain had reserved for them. In Arizona and California military chiefs and the governor's kinfolk took possession of the best lands. And in Texas the federal government had not envisioned that its color-blind property legislation would lead to the overwhelming concentration of land in the hands of Anglo-American immigrants. Even worse events unfolded, as the United States government was also prepared to launch a war against Mexico as a means of expanding its southern border.

Land Reforms in New Mexico and the Pueblo Communities

When the racial *casta* system was dismantled in New Mexico after independence, people in theory were no longer to be privileged or disadvantaged on the basis of race. This threatened the Pueblo land reserves, as Spain's property agreements were nullified and the Pueblo Indians were to be treated in the same manner as other Mexican citizens. Prior to independence, the Pueblo Indians had a unique legal agreement: they could retain ownership of their tribal lands as long as they were at peace with Spain. The church did not hold title to their lands, as it did to the lands of other Christian Indians of the Southwest. When Spaniards came to New Mexico, the Pueblo Indians already lived in congregated villages; the church did not have to relocate them and create artificial communities as in other parts of the Southwest. Rather, the missionaries moved into their villages and established missions on the edges. The missions basically functioned as parishes with resident priests. David Weber (1982:57) summarizes this unique relationship and land tenure system:

> In New Mexico, Franciscans never had to entice Indians from scattered villages into artificial mission communities, or *congregaciones* as they did in California, Arizona, and Texas. The Pueblos already lived in tightly organized towns surrounded by communal lands. The Franciscans established missions on the edge of those communities but never controlled the fields and pastures, which continued to be worked by Pueblos who gave up only modest amounts of land and labor to support a resident priest. . . . Thus, in New Mexico the growing population of land-hungry *pobladores* had little to gain from secularizing the missions.

Because race could no longer be used as the basis of privilege or discrimination after independence, the unique Pueblo jural position was threatened. They possessed excess acreage that was deemed to be vacant by territorial authorities and was eligible for redistribution under Mexican law. This indeed was a problem, as the colonists and *genizaros* desperately needed land because Spain had failed to grant them land in proportion to their population growth. The colonists and *genizaros* welcomed the land reforms, whereas the Pueblo Indians saw them as a mockery of their newfound status as Mexican citizens.

At the time of independence there were about twenty Pueblo communities in New Mexico (Carroll and Haggard 1942:87; cf. Hall and Weber 1984:5), including Tesuque, Pecos, Cochité, Santo Domingo, Jemez, Zia, Santa Ana, Sandía, San Felipe, Ysleta, Laguna, Acoma, Zuñi, Santa Clara, San Ildefonso, Pojoaque, Nambé, San Juan, Taos, and Pecuris.[1] Land was owned communally, and tribal membership was necessary to retain property rights. Though each family had the right to a plot, land was not privatized; nor could it be sold without consent of the corporate group. The acreage of each pueblo differed and was based upon the borders delineated upon its conquest. Within each pueblo space was reserved for civic and ceremonial buildings, family houses, and family farming plots; communal lands were reserved for grazing, recreational activities, and future community growth.

Immediately upon the passage of the Law of 1824 many people applied for uncultivated Pueblo lands. The petitioners were not solely colonists: *genizaros* and detribalized Pueblo Indians also applied (Hall 1989; Tyler 1991). To institute the Law of 1824 a seven-member elected assembly was organized. The governor of New Mexico presided over the land assembly, which was called the *diputación*. The *diputación* reviewed all petitions and settled land disputes, which were then forwarded to the governor for final approval. In the first years of operation the assembly approved several petitions authorizing the redistribution of unused Pueblo lands (Hall 1989; Hall and Weber 1984). In response to the seizures Pueblo tribal councils presented a series of counterpetitions and lawsuits to the *diputación*.

The Pueblo Indians finally prevailed when the Pecos leaders protested and took their case to the federal government (Hall and Weber 1984:19–21). It was obviously futile for Pueblo groups to complain to New Mexican authorities. It was necessary to seek federal intervention and attempt to reach a neutral party. The Pecos complaint reached the federal Supreme Court in Mexico City and centered on the relationship between property and the rights of citizens. On 4 May 1829 Mariano Rodríguez, the Pecos spokesman, argued in front of the court that under the new republic the property of citizens was sacred and therefore Pueblo property should be treated in the same way (ibid., 20). He posited that since Indians possessed the same legal rights as the rest of the citizenry they had the right to own property and determine how it should be used. Rodríguez pointed out a contradiction in the enforcement of federal law: if the federal government had declared Indians citizens, why were they being treated as dependent wards and not allowed to participate in the enforcement of federal law?

Upon hearing the complaint, the federal Supreme Court judges asked New Mexico's *diputación* to rehear the case and reconsider similar cases that already had been reviewed. The following year the *diputación* re-heard the Pecos case and reversed its former decisions against the Pueblo Indians. The land board decreed that "since time immemorial the land in question was the property of the *naturales*" (ibid., 20). In 1836 the *diputación* continued to review cases but had to deliver its recommendations to federal officers for final approval (Mattison 1946:287). Throughout the Southwest the federal government began to oversee the governors' land-grant confirmation recommendations more closely. Though governors and land committees continued to exert considerable power in determining whose claims were validated, the federal government was now part of the process and could reverse decisions.

The Landless Commoners of New Mexico

Unlike the Pueblo Indians, the majority of the colonists, irrespective of their race, did not own farmland. Based on a 1796 census sample of 1,051 household heads in New Mexico, 40 percent (N = 420) did not own land (Gutiérrez 1991:321). In Santa Fe and Río Abajo, where the landed elite resided, this problem had led many landless peasants to enter a debt peon-age contract, as parents could not afford to feed all of their children. Many parents had to place their sons and daughters in the homes of those who were financially stable. In return for food and shelter paupers worked without receiving wages. Thus, the land reforms after independence were welcomed by many and had positive effects upon the colonists and *genizaros*. The peonage system quickly declined after land was distributed.

During the Mexican period, land grants were awarded to many people and the number of settlements grew. The government released thousands of acres previously owned by the crown as well as reissuing property that had not been developed. It is uncertain, however, how many private and communal land grants were issued after independence, as a master registry was never kept (Leonard 1943:74). During the Spanish period, it is estimated that approximately one hundred grants were issued, and close to half were awarded to individuals of financial means

(Engstrand 1978:330; Gutiérrez 1991:325). Only sixty-one were communal land grants (Engstrand 1978:330; Leonard 1943:74).

Thus, after independence, to remedy the land shortage problems quickly, the *diputación* issued approximately thirty communal land grants and an undetermined number of private land grants (Engstrand 1978:330; Leonard 1943:74). The rationale for awarding communal grants was that the land could be quickly distributed at the village or town level by the local judge or by a town assembly in communities of over 2,000.[2] A land grant was to be subdivided among the families of each community, and part of the land was to be reserved for future community growth. Most community land grants included farming plots, house lots, and communal property for recreation, farming, dumping, and pasturing. The colonists and *genizaros* were dispersed throughout approximately nine million acres (Engstrand 1978:330; Morrow 1923:25).[3] A census report by Governor Manuel Armijo in 1840 illustrates the growth and dispersal of the settlements of New Mexico after the reforms were instituted. Whereas in 1827 people were concentrated in around twenty Indian pueblos and eleven colonial communities (cities, towns, and villages), Armijo found that by 1840 people had dispersed themselves into fifty-nine additional settlements (Carroll and Haggard 1942:88, 91–93). The community sizes ranged from settlements called *lugares* (places), generally composed of a nucleus of families living in ranches adjacent to one another, to larger settlements that had begun as family ranching zones and evolved into villages. Examples include Arroyo Hondo, which split from Taos when forty-three families separated and established a village (Tyler 1991), and San Miguel del Vado, which splintered into ten villages (Leonard 1943:83).

Land Reforms in Arizona

In Arizona the implementation of the land reforms failed because the federal government was more concerned with the survival of the colonies than with distributing land. If the Apaches in Arizona could not be pacified, there was no point in issuing deeds to ranches that could not be occupied. Because most Arizona ranches were sporadically attacked, leading to their ongoing abandonment, a pattern of retreat and reconquest created a lifestyle where land was temporarily occupied, abandoned, and reclaimed by others. When the colonists were able to reconquer their homes, the ranches were often repopulated by new families. As a result of this problem, few people petitioned to receive deeds and the government failed to secularize and distribute property among the Indians. It was mainly the elite who filed land patents, as they could hold on to their property by funding military auxiliaries to protect their ranches.

Throughout the Mexican period Presidio Tucson and its adjacent Indian pueblo, Tjkshon, remained well fortified and became military retreat zones for colonists and Christian Indians when under attack. The mission community at San Xavier del Bac was also highly fortified. The first major Apache attack during the Mexican period occurred in 1823, forcing most ranches in Arizona to be abandoned temporarily (see Kessell 1976:261–264). People were forced to retreat to the fortified zones. Presidio Tubac was nearly destroyed at this time. After a series of battles, the Apaches retreated and people returned to their ranches. Peaceful relations ensued until the early 1830s (Kessell 1976:263; Officer 1987:146–147). Once again the Apaches launched a series of attacks and forced the settlers to retreat. This time the anger of the Apaches was centered on the Christian *ranchería* settlements. The *visitas* at Aribaca and Sópori were destroyed and most of the Indians murdered. The survivors were forced to seek refuge in the fortified zones (Mattison 1946). Two of the mission pueblos were also devastated. Calabazas was destroyed and thereafter permanently abandoned (Kessell 1976:280). Guevavi's inhabitants were also nearly annihilated; many Christian Indian families held on, however, and continued fighting the Apaches. They suffered devastating losses, and Guevavi was left without a community hub. The pueblo changed into a scattered ranching zone. Though Presidio Tubac and Pueblo Tumacácori were also attacked, many Christian Indians hung on and launched counterattacks (ibid., 280, 283). During this period, both settlements lost the vast majority of their population to Tucson.

In the mid-1830s the Apache raids ceased; a period of tranquillity followed, allowing some individuals to rebuild (Officer 1987:130–137). In particular, many residents returned to Tumacácori and Tubac. Presidio Tubac once again had enough residents to form a town and in 1838 was officially reorganized into a township (Mattison 1946:283). Most of its inhabitants were Mexicans of Pima and Apache descent (Officer 1987:17, 171, 193, 215). Although the Apaches left the colonial settlements alone and only launched sporadic attacks throughout the 1840s, the Christian pueblos ceased to grow; most settlers remained near the fortified sites at

Tucson, Tubac, and Mission San Xavier del Bac (Officer 1987). The failure of the colonists to spread throughout southern Arizona was largely due to their military vulnerability. Like other parts of the Southwest, Arizona had its troops radically reduced after independence, and the colonists were mandated to organize civilian militia units (Weber 1982). The army at Tucson was inadequate and had to rely on civilian armies organized by regional political chiefs. Wealthy men who had the influence to organize and fund military detachments were issued military titles. The best-known political chiefs were part of the Elías González family, which was dispersed throughout Sonora and Arizona and was part of the landed elite. Rafael, Ignacio, and Simón Elías González were the most influential political chiefs in Arizona and Sonora (Kessell 1976; Officer 1987). They were given the authority to command presidial soldiers in the regions under attack. Their military influence, however, came from being able to fund the equipment needed by the troops. In Arizona they were able to launch effective counterattacks against the Apaches and give the colonies stability.

The military achievements of the Elías González family were recognized by the federal government and were handsomely rewarded. During the Mexican period, the federal government only approved twelve grants, and six of these were issued to the Elías González family. Between 1828 and 1843 they were given land grants in Babocómari, San Rafael, Los Boquillos, San Pedro, Agua Prieta, and Los Nogales (Mattison 1946:309, 313–322). The land grants were massive. Babocómari was the largest land grant, consisting of 128,000 acres, and Los Nogales the smallest, only about 38,000 acres (ibid., 310, 314). Lieutenant Ignacio Pérez, another influential political chief and relative of the Elías González family, was also rewarded by the federal government and issued a land grant (Dobyns 1976). Pérez established Rancho San Bernardo. The rest of the grants issued to Arizona residents were awarded to five citizens from Tubac and Tucson (Engstrand 1992). In turn, these people partitioned their land grants into smaller ranches and house lots for the use of their extended families. Overall, within the twelve Mexican land grants approximately ninety-eight ranches were established by the extended families of the grantees (see Mattison 1946).[4] Since the race of the families was not recorded, it is uncertain if these citizens were White, *afromestizo*, Indian, or *mestizo*. We only know that the Elías González and Pérez families were identified as *criollos* in Spanish censuses (Engstrand 1992).

Irrespective of race, most inhabitants in Arizona did not file land patents. Moreover, in the 1840s many residents were unable to file land claims because the small communities that grew outside of the fortified zones in Babocómari, San Pedro,[5] Ciénega de Heredia, Rancho Cuitaca, and the mines of Candelaria (Kessell 1976:311) were on property owned by the political chiefs (see Mattison 1946).

We also know that the secularization of the Indians and parceling of mission lands did not take place. Outside of the Spanish land grant issued to the Tumacácori Indians, deeds were not issued to other Christian Indians (see Chapter 4). Instead the church became discouraged with the lack of support from the federal government, and in 1842 the last missionaries left Arizona (Kessell 1976:297). No one was left to secularize and parcel out mission land. Mission San Xavier del Bac was later converted into a parish, while Mission Tumacácori gradually fell into disrepair. A few Indian families remained within the mission compounds at San Xavier del Bac but were not officially granted land. By the late 1840s Arizona had ceased to grow. Without financial support from the federal government, the existing infrastructure deteriorated and the inhabitants were left on their own means. In the end the land reforms had little effect in stabilizing the colony or hastening the acculturation of the Indians. A few became landed elites, while the majority continued their struggle to survive. The safety zones were inhabited by colonists and acculturated Indians.

Land Reforms in Texas: Ending Racial Privilege

After Mexican independence, most of the residents of Texas were in dire need of land reforms. In the late 1700s the Spanish crown had ceased to allocate new parcels of land in San Antonio and La Bahía (Poyo 1991b:89). People were not issued land grants, and families were seldom allowed to occupy additional land to accommodate the growth of their families. Altogether only around forty-six Spanish grants were issued in San Antonio and La Bahía (Jackson 1986:239, 407); most grantees were *peninsulares* (Poyo 1991b). Although new land grants were not issued there, people who moved to the northeast were given land or at least given occupancy rights to as much land as they needed. During the late 1700s, some fifty-two land grants were awarded to residents of Nacogdoches and surrounding settlements (Jackson 1986:441; Texas General Land Office, file "Guide to

Spanish and Mexican Titles in Texas"; hereafter cited as TGLO-SMTT). These families had their grants confirmed under a royal proclamation issued in 1792 (Jackson 1986:441). Occupancy rights were also issued to *afromestizos* from Nacogdoches after they founded ranches in Liberty and Orange counties (Block 1976:12).[6]

Excluding the northeastern area, where settlers were needed, most people in Texas suffered the devastating consequences of a land system that privileged *peninsulares*. Thus, after the first Mexican constitution was passed and general procedures were established to allocate land in the Southwest, the state government of Coahuila and Texas quickly moved to interpret federal law. Under the State of Coahuila and Texas Law of Colonization of 1825 each head of a household was eligible to receive a private grant (cited in *Laws of Texas, Vol. 1*, pp. 99–106). A color-blind process was instituted, and no racial preferences were extended. Land was to be distributed to all who were eligible, deeds were to be issued to those who already occupied land, and stipulations to allot land to immigrants were also included. The Law of 1825 did not apply to South Texas and El Paso Valley, which at that time were under the jurisdiction of the states of Chihuahua and Tamaulipas.

Though the state legislators of Coahuila and Texas carefully drafted a plan, their color-blind policies had unintended results. Within a few years of Mexico's independence Anglo Americans immigrated to Texas in large numbers and soon constituted the majority population. Since by law they had the right to receive the same amount of land as Mexican citizens, they were issued most of the land grants. They spread throughout Texas, populated regions outside of the boundaries of the former Spanish colonies, and began separatist movements as they saw themselves outnumbering Mexicans. In 1836 Anglo-American settlers favored secession, and their actions culminated in the Texas War of Independence (Weber 1982:251).

The Coahuila and Texas Colonization Law of 1825

Under federal and state law Mexican citizens and immigrants in Texas were eligible to file land claims. Indians were included as part of the eligible population (1825 State of Coahuila and Texas Law of Colonization, Article 19, cited in *Laws of Texas, Vol. 1*, p. 102). The Law of 1825 specifically delineated the appropriate land distribution procedures to be followed in Texas. Under Article 11 of the Law of 1825 a person who did not possess property was eligible to lay claim to one square league of irrigable land (4,438 acres). Soldiers were given first choice, followed by citizens and immigrants (ibid., Article 10, p. 100). Only *empresarios* and individuals with large families were exempt from the one-league limit. Federal law prohibited laying claim to land that was already inhabited, unless deemed necessary by state officials (General Law of Colonization 1824, Articles 2 and 9, cited in *Laws of Texas, Vol. 1*, pp. 97–98). If such action was taken, the state had to compensate the occupants. People already in possession of property became the legal owners as long as they had not fought against Mexico during the war of independence (Jackson 1986:540).

The state government instituted additional stipulations to give people land if the general allotment was insufficient and drafted a plan to make land available as the population of Texas increased in numbers. Based on Article 11 of the Law of 1825, if a family was large and could not sustain itself on the one-square-league allotment the acreage could be increased by recommendation of the town council (1825 State of Coahuila and Texas Law of Colonization, Articles 11 and 17, cited in *Laws of Texas, Vol. 1*, p. 101). Furthermore, under Article 14 a family that owned cattle was to receive one additional league for grazing (ibid., Article 14, p. 101). State officials also made provisions for the future growth of communities. Under Articles 15 and 16 a bachelor who married and a bachelor living independently could obtain one league (ibid., Article 16, p. 101).[7]

Immigrants were subject to the same policies as citizens, the only difference being that a petition could not be approved if a citizen filed an overlapping claim (ibid., Article 10, p. 100). The Law of 1825 also stipulated under Article 19 that Indians who had migrated to Texas after Mexican independence and were not native to Texas would be treated as immigrants and bound by the property laws applied to immigrants. In order to receive the property rights of immigrants, however, Indians had to lead a sedentary lifestyle. Article 19 stipulated:

> The Indians of all the tribes on the confines of the States, as also those of the wandering tribes in it . . . if thus induced by kindness and confidence any of them should be desirous . . . to establish themselves in any of the settlements which may be formed, they shall be admitted, and obtain the same quantity of land as the

settlers mentioned in Articles 14 and 15, the natives being always preferred to the Indians coming from a foreign country. (1825 Law of Colonization of the State of Coahuila and Texas, Article 19, cited in *Laws of Texas, Vol. 1*, p. 102)

Indians who were immigrants were also entitled to receive additional land to establish a township.

Once the Law of 1825 was drafted, thousands of people recertified their Spanish grants and others obtained new land claims. Not everyone followed this procedure, and many people failed to file a petition.

The Mexicans Who Obtained Deeds

Based on Spanish and Mexican land grant records in the Texas General Land Office, it is clear that thousands of people certified their claims. These records only reflect the size of the population that was eligible to present a petition during U.S. occupation (after 1836), however, and not the number of people who owned land in Texas after Mexican independence. After Texas seceded from Mexico, new property laws were passed by the Republic of Texas, and many people were not eligible to recertify their claims (see Chapter 8). Indians and Blacks were part of the population whose deeds were nullified (see Constitution of the Republic of Texas, 1836, Article 6, Sec. 10, cited in the *Laws of Texas, Vol. 2*, pp. 1079–1080). Thus, the description here is based only on the land grant petitions that were reviewed and archived by the Texas General Land Office. To supplement this incomplete history, however, two case studies of the mission Indians serve as an example of the numerous property deeds that were nullified and excluded from the land grant registry.

The Texas General Land Office identifies a total of 779 land petitions filed by Mexican citizens (TGLO-SMTT). This figure does not include claims submitted by Anglo Americans. The petitions were for property in San Antonio, Nacogdoches, and La Bahía. In addition to these records, the land office has a few deeds issued by the Mexican government to groups of secularized Indians. These deeds were turned over by the Mexican government but were never used to validate a claim. In one case in 1824, José Antonio de Saucedo, the provincial political chief, obtained approval from the governor of Coahuila and Texas to award fourteen Mexican families land grants from San Antonio's Mission Espada (Texas Gen-

eral Land Office, archives, File 121:45, "Espada Mission Land Records").
These petitioners were Christian Indians who already held title to secularized mission property but were asking for additional acreage. Saucedo
issued the families deeds and registered their surveys. He also obtained
the signatures of over twenty-eight witnesses who testified that the petitions did not overlap with any person's property.[8] Many of the witnesses
were neighbors of the claimants.

We also know that on 4 April 1830 Ramón Músquiz, the political chief
of the department of Béxar (San Antonio), who was in charge of distributing secularized lands, wrote a letter to José María Viesca, governor of Coahuila and Texas, acknowledging receipt of the governor's order to issue
deeds to the Indians of Missions Espíritu Santo and Refugio (Texas General Land Office, file "Guide to Department of Bexar/Texas Records,"
p. 27). That year both missions had been secularized (Weber 1982:56). On
18 May 1830 José Miguel Aldrete, mayor of La Bahía, wrote to Ramón
Músquiz that the land had been parceled as ordered (Texas General Land
Office, file "Guide to Department of Bexar/Texas Records," p. 27).

Land Grants Issued to Anglo Americans

The most comprehensive land records retained by the Texas General
Land Office are based on the Mexican land grants awarded to immigrants
and naturalized Mexican citizens. Approximately 3,420 land grant applications were submitted by immigrants and naturalized citizens (TGLO-
SMTT). Most of these petitioners were Anglo Americans. The first group
of immigrants arrived under the *empresario* contract issued to Stephen
Austin in 1822 (Weber 1982:164). The 300 colonists settled near the Brazos
River, approximately sixty miles west of present Houston, and then dispersed. They covered an immense territory ranging from the Gulf of
Mexico in the south to near Dallas in the north. Austin subsequently
brought three other colonies, totaling 900 families. He was rewarded
quite well for his efforts. The Mexican government gave Austin a total of
239,628.38 acres (TGLO-SMTT:7–9). In return for the government's gen-
erosity, Austin became a political broker and a close friend of many Mexican officials. He proved his loyalty by becoming a naturalized citizen and
encouraging others to follow his example. Twenty-three other *empresarios* also brought immigrants. None of them, however, were so generously

rewarded. Only one of these *empresarios* brought Mexican citizens; the rest of the settlers came from the United States.

In 1825 the Mexican government continued to award land grants to Anglo-American settlers, yet it became concerned with *empresario* Hayden Edwards's attitude toward Mexicans in Nacogdoches (Castañeda 1950:206). Edwards and his brothers posted notices warning Mexicans that they had to present their property deeds to Edwards or their land would be subject to redistribution. Failure to comply would result in the loss of their land. The parcels would be confiscated and granted or sold to the first bidder. Edwards believed he had the right to issue such an order because he had been given a contract by the Mexican government to bring 800 families to Nacogdoches and process their land applications. Mexican authorities immediately informed him that he was mistaken and ordered him to stop. After a series of confrontations with Mexican authorities, Edwards felt betrayed and believed himself a victim of personal hatred. On 16 December 1826 Edwards, his brothers, and approximately thirty settlers issued a proclamation of independence and declared they had founded the Republic of Fredonia (ibid., 210). Stephen Austin, upon hearing of the disturbance, dispatched a militia of 250 men to Nacogdoches to end the revolt and support the Mexican troops. Green DeWitt, another *empresario,* and many other Anglo Americans supported the Mexican authorities and sent letters to the governor of Coahuila and Texas disassociating themselves from Edwards.

Without support, Edwards fled from Mexico, and the revolt ended. This event, however, became a clear message to the Mexican government that storms were brewing in Texas. Afterward the federal government continued to receive complaints from state authorities on the worsening conditions of race relations in the area. It became necessary for the federal government to dispatch General Manuel Mier y Terán to investigate the outcome of the Law of 1825 and to issue recommendations on immigration. In 1829 Mier y Terán drafted an alarming report (Meyer and Sherman 1995:320). He concluded that Anglo Americans preferred to isolate themselves from Mexicans and that most refused to be naturalized. Furthermore, the slave reforms passed by the State of Coahuila and Texas were ignored (Bugbee 1898; Schwartz 1975). Ironically, to the distress of the immigrants, the general's report was published the same year that Mexico's first *afromestizo* president, Vicente Guerrero, issued the

Photograph 34. Adolphus Sterne House, Nacogdoches, Texas: Meeting Place for Texas Independence Revolutionaries. Courtesy of the Texas Historical Commission. Photograph taken by author.

nation's emancipation proclamation and abolished slavery (Appiah and Gates 1999; Meyer and Sherman 1995:320). For Texan slave owners, this certainly was a perilous time, as they were about to lose their labor force.

A few months later, on 6 April 1830, the administration of the newly appointed president Anastasio Bustamante issued a series of reforms ordering Texas to comply with the emancipation proclamation as well as other orders perceived by the immigrants to be unfair punishments (Castañeda 1950:243–244, 252; Meyer and Sherman 1995:337). First, the Mexican government rescinded its property tax law, which had exempted recent immigrants from paying taxes (i.e., immigrants residing in Texas for less than ten years).[9] It also increased the tariffs on all goods entering Mexico from the United States, which ultimately resulted in higher prices. Finally, it prohibited further immigration to Texas from the United States. Anglo Americans were allowed to immigrate to other parts of Mexico, but not to Texas. Instead of coercing immigrants into compliance, the reforms angered them, and a spirit of revolt spread like wildfire throughout the Anglo-American colonies (see Photograph 34).

The Mexican government became increasingly alarmed when United States citizens did not cease immigrating to Texas. Mexican officials could not do anything to stop the flow of illegal immigrants, as people were pouring in by the thousands. By 1834 the Anglo-American population had increased to over 30,000, far surpassing the Mexican population (Weber 1982:177). Soon Mexicans found themselves surrounded by hostile colonists who viewed them as foreigners and intruders.

Stephen Austin and other colonists loyal to the Mexican government were unable to avert revolution. Austin at first attempted to dissuade his compatriots from revolting by pushing the agenda to make Texas a state independent from Coahuila. This was considered a partial solution because the Anglo-American majority, through the electoral process, would be able to dominate state government and in this way legislate laws favorable to themselves. Austin's attempt failed, however, when federal authorities rejected his proposal and had him arrested. To the immigrants this was the last straw. On 7 November 1835 Anglo Americans who favored independence convinced the majority of their compatriots to join them and declared war against Mexico (Weber 1982:242). After a series of battles, the Anglo-American majority defeated the Mexican army. The war ended on 21 April 1836, and Texas became a separate Republic with the right to nullify Mexico's property laws (Metz 1994:24).

Land Reforms in El Paso Valley and South Texas

After Mexican independence, El Paso Valley and present South Texas came under federal land reforms. At this time these regions were culturally linked to Texas's cultural infrastructure, yet remained juridically separated. El Paso Valley was separated from New Mexico's political jurisdiction and joined to the state of Chihuahua. And South Texas, the territory south of the Nueces River to the Rio Grande, was united with Nuevo Santander and other territories in the state of Tamaulipas. In El Paso Valley the 1825 Chihuahua Colonization Law was passed to stipulate the procedures to distribute land (Bowden 1971:1), whereas in Tamaulipas, including South Texas, the state government passed the Tamaulipas Colonization Law of 1826 (Texas General Land Office 1988:1).

In the case of South Texas, by the time of independence most land had been granted and a ranching economy had been established (Alonzo 1998; Jackson 1986). During the Spanish period, approximately 227 private land grants were issued in South Texas (Texas General Land Office 1988). People were issued private rather than communal land grants as a result of a political struggle that occurred in 1766 between José de Escandón and the founding colonists of Nuevo Santander (Alonzo 1998:36). José de Escandón, the *empresario* of Nuevo Santander, instituted a communal land grant system to distribute land. The colonists protested, perceiving this to be a ploy to benefit those settlers arriving after Nuevo Santander was stabilized. As was the common practice throughout the Southwest, *criollos* and *peninsular* families generally arrived after a colony was fortified and Indian insurrections were under control. In 1766 the colonists, supported by the Catholic Church, sent a complaint to Mexico City, accusing Escandón of unfair land practices (ibid., 36). The crown responded by sending a royal commissioner, who supported the colonists and ordered that they be awarded private grants. This set a pattern wherein the residents of Nuevo Santander were issued private land grants.[10] During the Mexican period, under Tamaulipas's colonization law, an additional 137 private land grants were issued in what today is South Texas (Texas General Land Office 1988). A large number of them were awarded to the descendants of the founders of Laredo. Altogether during the Spanish and Mexican periods approximately 364 land grants were issued in South Texas.

During the Spanish period, a large amount of land in El Paso Valley was also issued to the first group of colonists who settled the region. The allocation of land in El Paso Valley began in 1751, when the royal government awarded the mission Indians of Ysleta, Socorro, and Senecú three communal grants to erect towns and ranches (Bowden 1971:129, 140–151). The Senecú grant was located on the border between the cities of El Paso and Ciudad Juárez.[11] In 1790 a fourth communal grant was issued to the settlers from the presidial town of San Elizario (ibid., 156). Hundreds of settlers moved from Chihuahua to San Elizario after irrigable land was made available near Socorro and Ysleta. In addition to the communal grants, one private land grant was issued during the Spanish period. In 1692 Fray Joaquín de Hinojosa received a grant consisting of three parcels (ibid., 165) in Ysleta, Socorro, and Senecú (U.S. side). He obtained the grant from Governor Diego de Vargas after demanding that the Indians be given private land grants. Father Hinojosa believed that if Indians were to be converted into tax-paying subjects they must own their ranches, make their own decisions, and enjoy the profits of their labor. He thought that only the church profited from collective farming. The governor refused to comply, but to pacify Father Hinojosa instead gave him a grant where he could launch three experiments.

During the Mexican period, the communities in El Paso Valley continued to prosper and all Spanish land grants were recertified. At this time the valley consisted of Ysleta, Socorro, San Elizario, part of Senecú, and the north side of El Paso del Norte (north of the Rio Grande), which was situated where the city of El Paso is today. Because El Paso del Norte covered a large region and was sparsely populated, the Mexican government attempted to increase its population by awarding land to new settlers (Bowden 1971). Once land became available, El Paso del Norte grew tremendously; by 1824 it had over 2,000 residents (Hendricks and Timmons 1998:49). Though thousands of new settlers moved to El Paso del Norte, few settled north of the Rio Grande. Between 1823 to 1847 only nine grants were allocated north of the Rio Grande (Bowden 1971). Seven private grants were issued to residents of El Paso and one communal grant to thirty families who settled north of El Paso and founded what later became the town of Canutillo, Texas (ibid., 94). In addition to these grants the Mexican government awarded a communal grant to several families from Ysleta (ibid., 140).

Land Reforms in California

In California the 1824 General Colonization Law was not well received by many of the colonial families. Their complaints centered on the advantages indigenous peoples were given and the policies delineating the rights of new settlers (Haas 1995; Hutchinson 1969). Political leaders, including Guadalupe Mariano Vallejo and Pío Pico, argued that Mexican pioneers should be given the same rights to mission lands that the indigenous people had. Under the Law of 1824 people who were in possession of land became its legal owners, which automatically made the Indians who resided in and near the missions the owners of the highly coveted mission lands. The colonists claimed that as descendants of the founders of California they should be privileged in the allocation of land because their parents and grandparents had colonized and stabilized California, whereas recently Christianized Indians, immigrants, and incoming Mexican colonists had not contributed anything to the colony. The colonists also disputed the large allotments all newcomers were eligible to receive.

To interpret federal law a colonization law was finally passed in California in 1833 (Hutchinson 1969:244). In the meantime the governors held full authority to interpret federal land reforms, recertify grants, issue deeds to occupied land, and award new grants. During the term of Governor José Figueroa, California's Colonization Law of 1833 went into effect (ibid.).[12] It was based on the recommendations of previous committees on colonization but was substantially revised by the governor, who chose to protect the Indians' mission land rights. To the displeasure of the colonists, Figueroa followed federal mandates: all heads of household were eligible to obtain equal proportions of land, as dictated by federal policy (see Chapter 6). Families who already held deeds or were in possession of property were eligible to retain that property. If such people occupied a parcel smaller than the federal allocation, they could petition for more land. Setting claim to new parcels, however, was dependent upon a priority system. The allocation of mission and vacant land was to be assigned: first, to Indian families in those territories; second, to military officers residing in California; third, to residents of the territories who did not own land or owned less land than federal law allotted; fourth, to recently arrived Mexican families; fifth, to foreign families who migrated on their own; sixth, to the families brought by *empresarios*; and seventh, to former convicts wishing to reside in California (ibid., 166–171, 239).

On 9 August 1834 Figueroa issued a direct order to commence the land distribution process as mandated by the Law of 1833 (see Hutchinson 1969:255–259).[13] He ordered ten of the missions to be immediately secularized and converted into towns. Each town was to be given land to erect the community's civic buildings (ibid., 255–259). He also stipulated that mission Indians who were heads of households and all mission Indians over the age of twenty-one were to receive a town lot. This grant was in addition to the farmland they had received. Secularized mission communities were also to be given half of the livestock belonging to the local mission. When this stage in the land reforms was completed, others could petition for mission land.

Mariano Guadalupe Vallejo became one of the most outspoken critics. He argued that all Mexicans associated with the missions and not just Indians should have first priority in filing a mission claim. Vallejo suggested that the Law of 1833 be amended.[14] He argued that an *ejido* system should be established and that all of the families associated with the missions should be allowed to file a claim for mission property (Hutchinson 1969). Those eligible would include mission Indians, their relatives, and Mexican colonists associated with the missions. To maintain mission lands in the hands of the original grantee families, people would be prohibited from selling mission property and would have to pass the patent to family members. His logic rested on the premise that only those people who built the missions should be able to profit from them and that Indians who lived near the missions but were recent converts should not receive mission lands merely because they were Indian. Ironically, though by law Indians who lived in the vicinity of a mission had a greater claim to land, in practice Vallejo's views were shared by many, and his vision eventually became a reality. A loophole in federal law allowed the colonists to circumvent Figueroa's reforms, because the governor and Congress had the right to modify cases (Constitutive Acts of the Mexican Federation 1824, Article 49, Secs. 17 and 24, reprinted in *Laws of Texas, Vol. 1*, p. 79; Mattison 1946).

Mexican Indian Land Grants

In California most people did not file land claims; consequently the information we have on the Mexican land reforms is incomplete. The available data are based upon those who filed claims, such as the immigrants and the new settlers who had to file claims to obtain land, Spanish grantees with massive grants who needed to recertify their claims to obtain exemptions from the federal limit, elites who received special grants from the governors, grantees who occupied land where it was scarce and obtained patent to avoid overlapping claims, and Indians who completed the certification process. Information is also available from mission records and from the registry compiled by Manuel Jimeno Casarin, the official commissioned by the federal government to compile a registry of all deeds (Menchaca 1995:6). His commission, however, was interrupted in 1846, when war erupted between Mexico and the United States. He did not complete a master list because he did not retrieve many of the documents left in the possession of the former governors' families or in the archives of the Catholic Church (Ross 1974). Likewise, he did not visit all of the secularized missions and did not note how many towns had been established by the Indians. Fortunately, missionaries retained copies of deeds and wrote local histories of some of the Indian towns that did not survive past the mid-nineteenth century.

In the case of the ranches established by the Christian Indians, most families failed to file patents. Indians obtained patents in forty-one identifiable cases, however, and twenty-nine of these were carved out of mission lands (Cowan 1977:35, 37; Engstrand 1991:42; Garrison 1935:142–146; Haas 1995:39, 54; Jackson 1903:140–145; Robinson 1948:42, 61, 71, 72; Rush 1965:29–31, 90, 93–98). The ranches founded on mission lands included Guajome, San Felipe, San Vicente y Barona, Escorpión, Moserate, El Encino, Encino, Temacula, Coches, and twenty ranches established in the common land grant of San Jacinto near Mission San Luis Rey (*Byrne v. Alas et al.*, 1888; see Cowan 1977:34, 89, 184; Engstrand 1991:42; Garrison 1935:146; Robinson 1948:71; Rush 1965:58, 59). Only Coches was located in northern California; the rest were spread from San Diego to San Luis Obispo.

Ranches with patents located outside of the mission lands ranged from Santa Bárbara (in central California) to Suisún (in northern California). The ranches in Santa Bárbara and San Luis Obispo included Huerta de Cuatí, Jamacha, Buena Vista, Chorro, Zaca, and Alamo Pintado (Cowan 1977:14, 20, 27, 31, 69; Engstrand 1991:42; Robinson 1948:71; Rush 1965: 10). Those spread throughout northern California included Cañada de Huerra, Yokaya, Olompalí, Nicasio, Ulistac, and Suisún (Cowan 1977:28, 39, 52, 103, 106; Engstrand 1991:42; Garrison 1935:141–149; Jackson 1903: 122, 140–145; Robinson 1948:71; *United States v. Ritchie*, 1854).[15]

Besides owning ranches, Christian Indians also established at least twenty-three villages and towns. In most of these cases, however, the communities did not obtain township charters; nor did the town councils obtain a civic grant. These communities were founded by mission and *ranchería* Indians throughout California. The five communities located in northern California were Sonoma Pueblo, Cosumnes, San Juan Bautista, San Juan de Castro, and Carmelo (Robinson 1948:42, 72). Only Cosumnes and San Juan de Castro held patents. In San Luis Obispo County in central California four thriving Indian towns with patents were built upon the secularized lands of missions San Luis Obispo and San Miguel: San Luis Obispo, Nacimiento, Estrella, and Gallina (Cowan 1977:35, 37, 50). The mission fathers followed the appropriate secularization procedures and wisely counseled their Indian parishioners to file township incorporation patents. In Santa Barbara County in central California the Indians of Santa Inés established the Pueblo of Zanja Cota. It did not receive a township patent, however (Engelhardt 1986). Thirteen Indian towns were established in southern California: San Pascual, Las Flores, San Dieguito, Janal, Los Tularitos, Sabobá, Pueblo San Jacinto, Peñasquitos, Tecate, San Juan Capistrano, San Juan de Argüello, Santa Ysabel, and San Jacinto. Of these only San Juan Capistrano, San Pascual, Santa Ysabel, and Las Flores obtained patents (Haas 1995:39, 54, 60; Jackson 1903:122; Robinson 1948:72). Las Flores, however, lost its patent within a few years; in 1841 Governor Juan Bautista Alvarado regranted it to his brother-in-law Pío Pico and Andrés Pico (Rush 1965:94).

The question as to why most Christian Indians failed to file land patents cannot be answered with certainty, because the reasons vary. Two cases of Christian Indian communities shed light on this problem, however. The case of Chief Francisco Solano's *ranchería* offers a glimpse as to why some Indians obtained a patent, while the case of the mission Indians of Santa Inés is a contrasting example of the obstacles faced by Indians in completing this procedure. In 1834 Chief Solano, from present Sonoma County, obtained patent for the land inhabited by his tribe, the Suisún people (Robinson 1948:64). He was given patent to 18,000 acres and assured by Mariano Guadalupe Vallejo that no one would be issued an overlapping claim (*United States v. Ritchie*, 1854:535, 536). Vallejo was commanding general of northern California's military detachments and civilian militia. He advised Chief Solano, who was a military ally, to file a patent. Because Solano petitioned for a private land grant rather than a communal grant, he became the sole owner of the land occupied by his tribe. Solano remained an important military ally of Vallejo throughout the Mexican period, as his warriors helped to patrol the colonies established by Anglo-American immigrants near the mission at San Rafael and at Sutter's Fort in present Sacramento (Hutchinson 1969).

Unlike Solano, the Indians from Mission Santa Inés did not receive any assistance from the government. On the contrary, government officials made life miserable for the missionaries and Indians. Mission Santa Inés included Chumash Indians from the present cities of Ventura, Santa Barbara, and Santa Inés. The mission was founded in 1804 and was exempt from federal secularization orders because these Chumash people were not considered to be prepared for secular life (Engelhardt 1986:11). In 1836 the state government ordered an inventory of mission property (ibid., 42). It was valued at $50,962.62, and this impressive figure immediately came to the attention of the governor. Indeed Santa Inés was one of the territorial government's most valuable assets (ibid., 42). After the review Governor Mariano Chico ordered the mission Indians to be secularized, the mission converted to a parish, and its belongings placed under the control of a civilian board. Within a few months of the order, mission furnishings began to disappear. After a series of administrative battles between the fathers and the civilian board, the mission's belongings were no longer stolen, and life at the mission proceeded as usual. Many Indians continued living in the mission, and Zanja Cota, the mission pueblo, was left undisturbed. A small pueblo had grown outside of the mission compounds to accommodate the families who preferred to live outside of the mission yet remain in close proximity to their relatives.

In 1842 the next governor, José Manuel Micheltorena, received many complaints from the president of the missions of California, asking him to visit Santa Inés and review the civil board's policies, because the colonists were obstructing the fathers' acculturation projects and many Indians were leaving Santa Inés (Engelhardt 1986:49). After his visit Micheltorena disbanded the board and returned the administration of the mission to the church. Furthermore, after reviewing the assets of the mission and evaluating the fathers' plans for the future growth of Santa Inés, he approved the construction of a seminary college and a private school. Santa Inés was an ideal location to found a center of higher learning. Indians were to be educated for free, while others were to be charged a hefty fee of 350 pesos. To ensure the fathers that the college would never come under the administration of the local government, Micheltorena gave the Catholic Church the land where the schools were to be built. In this way the schools would remain private and independent. He also gave the fathers a personal stipend and promised an annual donation of 500 pesos (ibid., 54). Oddly, while the governor issued a land grant to the church, he did not issue land grants to the local Indians; nor did the fathers request such an action.

A few years later, Pío Pico was appointed governor of California. In 1845 he sent his brother Andrés to assess the financial stability of Mission Santa Inés (ibid., 60). While Andrés Pico was at Santa Inés, most of the mission's cattle and stock were stolen. Taking this loss into consideration, he concluded that without this asset the mission was financially unsound. He did not make any decision on the schools, but the fathers knew that without the mission's cattle and stock the schools would not survive. Pico believed that the many people who lived in the mission would be unable to remain there unless mission property was sold. He therefore recommended that the mission's orchards and dormitories be leased in order to raise money to maintain the grounds and pay stipends to the fathers. Funds were also needed if the fathers wanted to feed the Indians who were dependent on the mission. Pío Pico followed his brother's recommendation, and this time the fathers had no legal recourse because under the Law of 1837 the federal government gave governors the right to sell mission property when funds were needed by the state (Kessell 1976:302).

Pío Pico clearly abused federal law, however, because governors only had the power to sell or lease mission property valued under 500 pesos. Without holding an auction or soliciting a bid, he leased the mission lands to his nephew José Covarrúbias and to his close friend Joaquín Carrillo. Within a year Pío Pico sold most of the mission land to the lessees for 7,000 pesos (Engelhardt 1986:66). Only the mission pueblo and its surrounding gardens were left unsold. Pico failed to issue the Indians a patent for their pueblo. Sadly, a close examination of these two case studies indicates that the enforcement of Mexican property law pertaining to Indians was highly subjective and dependent upon the Indian groups' political power. Chief Solano's people served an extremely important military function, while the Indians of Santa Inés were an impediment to the economic prosperity of the governor's nephew and friend.

Grants Awarded to Mexican Colonists and Immigrants

As in the case of the Christian Indians, it is uncertain how many parcels were occupied by Mexican colonists, because many people did not file land claims. Archival records of the California Land Commission indicate that at least 813 claimants owned land (Bowman 1958:105; Engstrand 1991:44). About 30 of these grants were issued during the Spanish period and the rest awarded by the Mexican government.[16] These land commission records, though extremely informative, are incomplete because they only reflect the number of people who filed land petitions after California became part of the United States and not the number of people who obtained patents during the Mexican period. Clearly, the size of the population in California indicates that few families submitted petitions during U.S. occupation. In 1846 there were over 7,000 *gente de razón*, 1,300 immigrants, and over 64,000 Christian Indians (Cook 1976:42; Lagum 1987:23).

Though California Land Commission archives are incomplete, they are very useful in identifying the size of the land grants. The grants certified by the Mexican government ranged from modest parcels measuring 0.25 acre to massive land grants of over 100,000 acres (Ayers 1886). The average grant was 22,190 acres or less (Cowan 1977:5). The smallest land grants, called *solares* (house lots), were usually located in mission communities where land was scarce. The largest land grant was Rancho Santa Margarita y Las Flores (San Diego County), with 133,440.78 acres (Ayers 1886:2). The original patent was issued to Pío Pico. Though the grants varied in size, only four exceeded the federal limit of 48,818 acres (Ayers 1886; see Chapter 6). These grants were issued to Guadalupe Mariano Vallejo, Andrés Castillero, Pío Pico, and one partitioned between José Antonio Aguirre and Ignacio del Valle (Cowan 1977:60, 92, 93, 101). All of these men held high-level positions in the Mexican government, serving as governor, military general, and state secretary of administration.

There were many other large land grants, although they did not exceed the federal limit. These grants were also issued to influential people associated with the government, including both Mexicans and immigrants. For example, of the twenty-two grants reaching the federal limit, nineteen were awarded to government officials and to the governors' friends, relatives, and colleagues.[17]

Because of massive corruption, federal law limited the power of governors to issue patents after 1836 (Mattison 1946:287), but they retained control of the recommendation and petition certification process (Engelhardt 1986). They also had the power to sell vacant mission land when the state needed funds. Both of these powers allowed governors to allocate land at will. Thus, during Governor Juan Bautista Alvarado's tenure (1836–1842) he issued grants to his close friends Carlos Carrillo, José Antonio Castro, José de la Guerra, and Francisco Rico (Bancroft 1964:A-E 743, 751, F-G 768, R-Z 695; Cowan 1977:140–141).[18] Alvarado also recommended to federal officials that his uncle Mariano Guadalupe Vallejo and his brother-in-law Pío Pico receive grants similar in size (Rush 1965).[19]

During Governor Manuel Micheltorena's tenure (1842–1845), a similar pattern is apparent; however, he chose to favor his administrators, rather than family members. Rafael Sánchez was his personal secretary, Antonio María Osío his accountant, and Andrés Castillero was in charge of his administrative affairs (Bancroft 1964:I-Q 711, 761, A-E 749; Cowan 1977:140–141).[20] Micheltorena also rewarded his close friend Joseph Limantour, a French immigrant who transacted many business deals with

Mexican elites (Bancroft 1964:I-Q 714; Cowan 1977: 119). During Pío Pico's second term in office (1845–1846), he obtained approval for grants to his relatives, including his brothers Andrés and José J. Pico and his brother-in-law John Forster. He also obtained approval for the grants given to his friends such as Antonio María Suñol and his wife, María Dolores Bernal (Bancroft 1964:I-Q 776, R-Z 777, 738; Cowan 1977:141), and to William Workman, an Englishman who was a close political ally and established a bank in Los Angeles (Bancroft 1964:R-Z 744, 781; Cowan 1977:51, 77).

Most immigrants, like most Mexicans, did not receive large grants. On the contrary, most of their grants were issued in Indian country, outside of the coastal area. Only immigrants who were business associates or relatives of Pío Pico were issued grants in southern and northern California, where property was of higher value (Cowan 1977:140–141). Immigrants were welcomed in California as long as they settled in uncolonized areas. Most immigrants came from the United States and were used to expand the frontier of California toward the north into present Shasta, Tehama, Folsom, Glen, and Tehama counties and toward the northeast into Butte, Yuba, Sutter, Sacramento, and San Joaquín. Sixty-eight of the eighty-nine grants issued to immigrants (76 percent) were in northern California (ibid., 115–123). In southern and central California, where land was in high demand, only twenty-one grants were issued to immigrants. Ten of these grants were located in San Luis Obispo and Santa Bárbara (central), and eleven others in Los Angeles and San Diego (south).

Nearly half of the grants in southern and central California were issued between 1845 and 1846, when international relations between Mexico and the United States were tense and war was inevitable. At this time, Governor Pío Pico began awarding grants and selling mission property to business associates, friends, and relatives without following federal procedures (Haas 1995; Rush 1965).

Pío Pico, Mission Lands, and the Mexican American War

Political corruption began in the gubernatorial tenure of Pío Pico between 1831 and 1833, when he granted large parcels of land to his family and relatives (Cowan 1977:143). At this time Pico was acting governor.[21] Corruption did not cease at that point, because in 1834 Pío Pico married Doña María Ignacia Alvarado, sister of Juan Bautista Alvarado, governor of California from 1836 to 1842 (ibid., 143; Garrison 1935:36). The collusion between these two men continued, and grants were overwhelmingly awarded to their relatives and friends. Most disastrous, however, were the land speculation deals of 1845–1846, when Pico, once again governor, sold thousands of acres of mission lands. In several cases he sold entire mission communities. Eight of the total of twenty-one missions were sold during Pico's tenure. In three other cases Pico gave the mission property to friends (Cowan 1977:141; Garrison 1935:34).

Pico began selling mission land without federal authority when international boundary disputes erupted between the United States and Mexico in 1845 and the Mexican government prepared itself for an invasion (Weber 1982:67, 274). After the United States government annexed Texas, boundary disputes began. The U.S. Congress claimed that the border lay below South Texas on the Rio Grande, while Mexico charged that the Nueces River, a few miles south of San Antonio, was the boundary.

In the meantime, Pío Pico began to liquidate state assets by selling mission property, including land, buildings, livestock, and furnishings. He validated this action under the Law of 1837, which gave governors the power to sell mission property if the state was in financial distress (Engelhardt 1986:73; Kessell 1976:302). He did not follow legal procedures, however, and sold property assessed at over 500 pesos as well as failing to hold a public auction or investigate if a claim was pending. Worst of all, Indians were not given the opportunity to file a claim or place a bid as required by law. For example, over 35,000 acres of mission land in Santa Bárbara were sold to Richard Den for 7,500 pesos (Cowan 1977:84,91). In Ventura José Arnaz, a Spanish immigrant, was sold over 60,000 acres of Mission San Buenaventura for 12,000 pesos (ibid., 74). All the mission lands of La Purísima in present Lompoc were sold to banker John Temple for only 1,100 pesos (ibid., 65). Pico's brother-in-law John Forster, who by 1846 owned most of the San Juan Capistrano region, bought the remaining mission lands for 710 pesos (ibid., 82, 98). Eugelio Celís purchased 57,694 acres of San Fernando Rey mission land inhabited by Indians for 14,000 pesos (ibid., 76). Josefa and Feliciano Soberares purchased 8,900 acres of land belonging to Mission Soledad for only 800 pesos (ibid., 99). Andrés Pico and former governor Alvarado bought all of the mission land in San José for 12,000 pesos (ibid., 80). Antonio María Pico and Antonio María Suñol together bought most of the land belonging to the mission of San Rafael, in northern California (ibid., 87). And in Santa Inés the mission property was sold to José María Covarrúbias and Joaquín Carrillo (Engelhardt 1986:66). Covarrúbias, however, never paid Pico any money.

In assessing Pío Pico's actions Hubert Howe Bancroft argues that he has been unjustly villainized by historians (Bancroft 1964:I-Q 778). Bancroft knew Pico and obtained his life history in interviews conducted in 1878 (ibid.). Excluding the land grant for Rancho Jamul (San Diego County), his actions in California's land reforms purportedly have been exaggerated since he did have the authority to favor people. Bancroft adds that Pico's motives are much more complicated than generally considered. Unfortunately, he does not elaborate upon this point and instead comments that historians have chosen to ignore Pico's role as a statesman and influential architect of modern civic government in California. Bancroft is probably referring to Pico's popularity as governor and as a critic of federal reforms which discriminated against the common person. From 1836 to 1846 an addendum to the constitution stated that a citizen must have an annual income of 100 pesos to vote and hold public office (Weber 1982:34). Though this restriction was later deleted and generally ignored, Pico gained popularity by opposing it.

Nonetheless, Pico's actions cannot be justified; he and Andrés rustled herds of cattle belonging to secularized Indians not once but three times. The Indians from Las Flores, Santa Inés, and the mission community of San Luis Rey lost their entire herds (Engelhardt 1986:59). In San Luis Rey alone, the stock amounted to over 10,000 cattle, 15,000 sheep, and 2,000 horses (Garrison 1935:34; Rush 1965:94). Furthermore, when Pico and his brother obtained title to Rancho Jamul and Santa Margarita y Las Flores they evicted the Indians who protested and converted the ones who remained behind into ranch hands.

Robert Cowan (1977) to some degree concurs with Bancroft in his classic study on California's Spanish and Mexican land grants. Cowan argues that Pico's behavior may be explained in part by his very large extended family, with over 400 family members and relatives (Bancroft 1964:I-Q 776–779). Pico had 15 legitimate sons and daughters, 116 grandchildren, and 97 great-grandchildren (Cowan 1977:9, 10). All of these people were eligible to obtain land grants under Mexican law. Cowan's argument can be strengthened if we interject race and remember that Pico and part of his extended kin were *afromestizos* who were not awarded land by Spain.

Pío Pico was the grandson of Santiago Pico, a *mestizo* or *criollo* who was married to María Eustaquia López, a *mulatta* (Forbes 1966:244–245).

Santiago and his family arrived in California around 1790 and initially settled in Los Angeles (Bancroft 1964:778). Santiago had children with more than one woman; only José María, Pío Pico's father, was registered as his legitimate son.[22] José María was one-fourth Black, and his half-brothers were White and *mestizo* (Bancroft 1964; Forbes 1966; cf. Garrison 1935). Though Santiago's illegitimate sons obtained land grants in 1795, José María did not and was unable to leave an inheritance to Pico and his brothers and sisters.[23] Why Pío Pico's father did not obtain a land grant and his uncles did is unclear. This practice was consistent with Spain's racially discriminatory land policies, however, and may partly explain Pico's land-grabbing behavior.

Though it is difficult to justify Pío Pico's actions by any means, we might ask who actually profited from his transactions. Property laws changed after the United States government won the Mexican American War of 1846 to 1848. Within days of the war's end, the U.S. government nullified most of Pico's transactions and awarded these lands to Anglo-American homesteaders. Furthermore, the outcome of Pico's actions becomes more complicated if we consider the role of race in the land grant process, since in the aftermath of the Mexican American War property law was altered and became highly dependent on racial policy. Mexicans holding property deeds in most cases, unless they were *mestizo* or White, did not have a very good chance of retaining their ranches and remaining in their homes. Worst of all, under United States law, as during the Spanish period, race once again determined whether a person enjoyed basic civil rights.

8

The Treaty of Guadalupe Hidalgo and the Racialization of the Mexican Population

In 1848 the United States and Mexico signed the Treaty of Guadalupe Hidalgo, ending the Mexican American War (Menchaca 1993:584). The United States government stipulated in the treaty that Mexicans who lived within the newly annexed territory of the Southwest would be "incorporated into the Union of the United States" with the "enjoyment of all the rights of citizens" (*Nine Statutes at Large and Treaties of the United States of America, 1845-1851*, Article 9, p. 930). The treaty thus promised to protect the political rights of the conquered population. Tragically, within a year of the treaty's ratification, the United States government violated these citizenship equality statements and began a process of racialization that categorized most Mexicans as inferiors in all domains of life. I define this process of racialization as the use of the legal system to confer privilege upon Whites and to discriminate against people of color. Under this legal process Mexicans who were White were accorded the full legal rights of United States citizens, while most *mestizos*, Christianized Indians, and *afromestizos* were accorded inferior legal rights.

The violation of the Treaty of Guadalupe Hidalgo was yet another stage in the legacy of discrimination that had been part of Mexico's colonial history. It was part of the drama of empire rooted in power and the role of "the Other" that had been played out under Spanish rule. When the United States government violated the treaty, the Mexican people of the U.S. Southwest found themselves cast in a racialized role that reenacted the processes of categorization, repression, and domination that characterized the racialization of Mexicans under Spanish rule. The victory experienced by people of color after Mexican independence was short-lived, for the U.S. government breached the treaty and established a racial order that again provided Mexicans of color inferior civil rights.

The Treaty of Guadalupe Hidalgo

Through annexation, conquest, and purchase, the United States government acquired Mexico's northern frontier between 1845 and 1854 (Weber
1982:xv).[1] Mexico began to lose its hold over the Southwest when Anglo-
American immigrants won the Texas War of Independence and separated
from Mexico in 1836 (ibid.). Matters worsened after the United States
annexed Texas in 1845 and continued to pursue the conquest of other
parts of the Southwest (Menchaca 1999:19). The following year the United
States declared war against Mexico, charging that Mexican troops had
invaded U.S. territory by crossing the Rio Grande. The dispute centered
over where the Texas-Mexico border had been set after Texas obtained its
independence. Mexico claimed that the border lay on the Nueces River
and did not include South Texas, while the United States charged it was
further south along the Rio Grande. The U.S. government declared war,
and the Mexican-American War began on 11 May 1846 (Weber 1982:274).
Within a year and a half, the professional and well-equipped U.S. military defeated Mexico and easily vanquished the civilian Mexican militia.
Before the war, due to financial troubles, the Mexican government had
withdrawn most of its military troops from the outposts and garrisons in
the Southwest, leaving its citizens to defend themselves (Castañeda 1950;
Weber 1982). The citizens had been required to take full responsibility for
their military defense and were expected to form civilian militia units.
Therefore, the badly armed civilians quickly fell into the hands of the
U.S. military during the Mexican American War (Spicer 1981). Although
Mexico did send troops to aid its civilians, their numbers were insuffi-
cient to fend off a foreign invasion.

The four border states of California, Arizona, New Mexico, and Texas
were acquired by the United States. Mexico also lost parts of its northern frontier that today include Nevada, Utah, parts of Colorado, and
small sections of Oklahoma, Kansas, and Wyoming; these areas contained no Mexican settlements and remained under the control of indigenous peoples (Weber 1982). Only southern Arizona did not fall into U.S.
hands at this time. The Treaty of Guadalupe Hidalgo ended the war. It was
executed on 2 February 1848 in the city of Guadalupe Hidalgo, Mexico,
and ratified and exchanged at Querétaro, Mexico, on 30 May 1848 (*Nine
Statutes at Large and Treaties of the United States of America, 1845–1851,*
p. 922; Tate 1969:2). It stipulated the political rights of the inhabitants

of the ceded territories, set the U.S.-Mexico border, and included several binational agreements on economic relations.

Unfortunately, within a year the United States violated the treaty with respect to the citizenship articles and refused to extend Mexicans full political rights on the basis that the majority population was not White (Menchaca 1993). Instead the U.S. government began the process of racializing the Mexican population and ascribing them different legal rights on the basis of race. Mexicans who were White were given full citizenship, while *mestizos*, Christianized Indians, and *afromestizos* came under different racial laws. At the time of the ratification of the treaty, U.S. racial laws conferred full political rights only upon free Whites (i.e., individuals who were not indentured servants or criminals), while Blacks and Indians could be indentured or enslaved in most states. People of mixed European and Indian ancestry could not be enslaved, but they could be barred from voting, practicing law, or becoming naturalized citizens, and in many states the selection of their marriage partners was restricted (Konvitz 1946; May 1929; Menchaca 1993). Thus, Mexico's liberal racial laws were nullified after the Mexican American War, and Mexicans entered a new racial order similar to that practiced by Spain.

The United States chose to violate Treaty Articles 8 and 9, which incorporated all Mexicans as U.S. citizens. Article 8 stated that the United States agreed to extend citizenship to all Mexican citizens who remained in the ceded territories. If these persons did not want citizenship, they had to so indicate within one year; otherwise, they would automatically become U.S. citizens (cited in Tate 1969). Under Article 9 the United States further agreed that Mexicans who chose to become U.S. citizens would have all the attendant rights. Article 9 stipulated that "Mexicans who, in the territories aforesaid, shall not preserve the character of citizens of the Mexican Republic . . . shall be incorporated into the Union of the United States, and be admitted at the proper time . . . to the enjoyment of all the rights of citizens of the United States" (cited in Tate 1969:20).

Almost immediately, the United States government abandoned its federal responsibilities to its new citizens. Within a year of the treaty, the U.S. Congress gave the legislators of the ceded territories and states the right to determine the Mexicans' citizenship status (Dale 1951:7; Menchaca 1993:587). At this time the states had the power to determine citizenship eligibility requirements, a power given to them by the Constitution of the United States (U.S. Constitution, Article 4, Sec. 2, cited in Hyman and Wiecek 1982:517–531). This move had a severe impact on Mexicans because the state legislators chose not to give most people of color the legal rights enjoyed by White citizens.

Racialization: Indians Denied U.S. Citizenship

After U.S. occupation, Congress racialized the Indians of the Southwest and determined that they were distinct from Mexicans (Bowden 1971:144; Minter 1993:35–36), although it did recognize that some Christian Indian communities deserved part of the rights extended to Mexicans. Indians who were peaceful and lived in towns or villages would be visited by an agent of the Bureau of Indian Affairs (BIA) to determine if they should be extended legal privileges (Dale 1951; see Minter 1993; and *Nine Statutes at Large and Treaties of the United States of America, 1845–1851,* Chap. 106, p. 383; Chap. 82, p. 519; Chap. 14, p. 587).

Each agent, before making a final report, was expected to consult an ethnologist. To determine whether a Mexican community was actually Indian, the agent would investigate whether it was governed by a tribal council. Communities that had retained a tribal government would be classified as Indian, but would be exempt from the federal laws applied to nomadic Indians. Instead, such communities would be governed by the specific legislation drafted by their respective state or territorial governments. They would immediately come under federal law, however, if they joined political forces with nomadic Indians, as would any Indian who became a vagrant (Heizer and Almquist 1977; Jackson 1903; Lamar 1966). Individuals who lived outside of an Indian community but were culturally identifiable as Indian would also be governed by the laws passed by their state or territorial governments (Minter 1993; *Suñol v. Hepburn,* 1850; see *United States v. Sandoval,* 1913). Each state or territory would have to determine if these ethnically identifiably detribalized Indians were part of the population declared citizens of Mexico under the Plan de Iguala and the Mexican Constitution of 1824 and, if so, decide if they were to be protected by the Treaty of Guadalupe Hidalgo.

Nomadic Indians, however, fell under federal jurisdiction, and uniform policies were enacted. They would not be extended any of the political rights enjoyed by the Indians conquered by Mexico. In 1849 the U.S.

Congress gave the War Department management over the nomadic Indians of the Southwest and ordered it to relocate them onto reservations (Dale 1951:7). If they refused they would be punished (Forbes 1982; Takaki 1990). Specifically, they came under U.S. congressional legislation outlined under the Indian Intercourse Act of 1834 (*Four United States Statutes at Large 1789-1845*, Chap. 161, pp. 729-735). The act was based upon previous congressional acts relating to Indian affairs. In Section 1 of the act Congress delineated the boundaries of the areas where Indians were to reside and indicated the locations of future reservations. Section 12 gave the president the authority to extinguish Indian rights over land they claimed and to relocate them forcibly. And in Section 19 Congress gave the president the authority to send the military into Indian country: (1) to maintain the boundaries set forth to contain the Indians, (2) to protect White settlements, and (3) to punish Indians.

Furthermore, Section 29 of the Act of 1834 adopted several inhumane provisions of the Indian Intercourse Act of 1802 (*Two United States Statutes at Large, 1789-1845*, Chap. 13, pp. 139-146). The purpose of these provisions was to maintain the Indians on the reservations and to sentence them to death if they chose to flee. Section 14 of the Act of 1802, which gave U.S. courts the right to arrest and press criminal charges against people leaving the reservation, and Section 19 of the same act, which prohibited Indians from traveling on roads that connected Indian and White settlements, were reinstated. If Indians broke these provisions, Section 15 of the Act of 1802 gave judicial courts the right to sentence them to death:

> And be it further enacted, That the superior courts in each of the said territorial districts, and the circuit courts, and other courts of the United States . . . are hereby invested with full power and authority to hear and determine all crimes, offenses and misdemeanors against this act . . . and in all cases where the punishment shall be death, it shall be lawful for the governor of either the territorial districts where the offended shall be apprehended . . . to issue a commission of oyer and terminer to the superior judges of such district, who shall have full power and authority to hear and determine all such capital cases. (*Two United States Statutes at Large 1789-1845*, Chap. 13, Sec. 15, p. 144)

In effect, the Indian Intercourse Act of 1834 was designed to contain nomadic Indians on the reservations at all cost, through severe punishment and even death sentences (Dale 1951; Forbes 1982; Takaki 1990).

Thus, after the Southwest became part of the United States the War Department pursued a removal campaign against the nomadic Indians (Jackson 1903; Larson 1968; Spicer 1981). Fortunately, the Christian Indians acquired from Mexico were spared such a disastrous fate, because they had demonstrated their civility by remaining at peace with Spain, Mexico, and the United States. Through these legal mandates Indians were categorized and racialized apart from other Mexican groups.

Citizenship and Racialization: California

In California the state constitution of 1849 granted only Whites full citizenship and gave only U.S. males and White Mexican males the right of suffrage; Indians, *mestizos,* and people of Black descent were ineligible to vote and were gradually stripped of most political rights (California Constitution, 1849, Article 2, Sec. 1, p. 4). California joined the union as a free state and prohibited slavery. Mexican citizens who were *afromestizo* and free Blacks who had immigrated to California from other parts of the United States were allowed to settle and were not placed in bondage or deported (California Constitution, 1849, Article 1, Sec. 1, p. 3; Heizer and Almquist 1977).[2] Christian Indians also retained their freedom of movement, but it became necessary for the state legislature and the courts to clarify their political status, as clear stipulations were needed to distinguish them from the nomadic Indians and the *mestizos.*

To determine whether the Christian Indians acquired from Mexico merited any constitutional rights, the California Supreme Court ruled in 1850 in *Suñol v. Hepburn* that emancipated Indians did obtain citizenship under the Plan de Iguala and the Mexican Constitution of 1824. The judges ruled that Mexican citizenship had not granted them any constitutional rights, however, because emancipated Indians had been given the same constitutional status as lunatics, children, women, and other people dependent upon the state (*Suñol v. Hepburn,* 1850:279). Under this interpretation of the Plan de Iguala, the judges reasoned that the Christian Indians acquired from Mexico had never had, and should not be given, any U.S. constitutional rights.

After the state constitution was drafted, California legislators also had to clarify the blood quantum Mexicans needed to have in order to receive the legal rights of Whites. Likewise, it was necessary to determine when a person should be categorized as a *mestizo* or *mulatto*, since it was a well-known fact that most Mexicans were of Indian descent. In 1849 a person with one-half or more Indian blood was considered non-White and a person one-eighth or more Black a *mulatto* (California Statutes, 1850, Chap. 99, Sec. 14, p. 230; Chap. 142, Sec. 306, p. 455, cited in *Perez v. Sharp*, 1948:719; Goodrich 1926:93). In 1851 the blood quantum for being White became more restrictive, as people of one-fourth Indian descent were considered non-White (California Statutes, 1851, Sec. 394, p. 114).

These laws remained in operation into the twentieth century and were often used during the 1800s to deny people of color citizenship (see *Perez v. Sharp*, 1948). A case in point: in 1870 Pablo De La Guerra, a distinguished citizen of Santa Bárbara and one of the delegates to the first constitutional convention of California (Ross Browne 1850), was prosecuted by the state of California for attempting to exercise the rights of a White citizen (*People v. Pablo De La Guerra*, 1870). He was also a land-grant heir, part of the founding families of California, and after U.S. occupation served as a district judge and state senator (Bancroft 1964:F-G 769). De La Guerra was a person of predominantly Spanish ancestry, yet there was an uncertainty in his blood line. On his father's side, he descended from a distinguished Spanish family (ibid.). De La Guerra's father had migrated to Mexico from Spain around 1798 and later married Antonia Carrillo, who was also part of a distinguished family. Though the Carrillos were one of California's founding families, their genealogy did not derive from Spain; possibly they were *mestizos* rather than *criollos*. Doña Maria's father, José Raimundo Carrillo, was a native of Loreto (Baja California) whose parentage was uncertain (Bancroft 1964:A-E 746; Garrison 1935). He arrived in California as a soldier and a member of the first land expedition. At first Pablo De La Guerra enjoyed the privileges of a White citizen; however, in 1870 the state of California attempted to strip him of this status and treat him as a person of color (*People v. Pablo De La Guerra*, 1870). De La Guerra, a man of wealth, fought for his right to be classified as White.

In the California Supreme Court hearing, the attorneys for the state argued that Pablo De La Guerra was not a U.S. citizen because the Treaty of Guadalupe Hidalgo had never had the power to make citizens of Mexicans or Indians and because he was not White. In his defense, De La Guerra argued that he was White and was therefore exempt from California's racial laws. The court records indicate that De La Guerra testified that he "was born at Santa Barbara in 1819, and has ever since resided at that place and is admitted to have been a White male citizen of Mexico" (*People v. Pablo De La Guerra*, 1870:339).

Although the state supreme court ruled in favor of De La Guerra, concluding that he was White and therefore not subject to Indian jurisdiction laws, it passed a convoluted decision that upheld California's right to limit citizenship on the basis of race. The court ruled that although De La Guerra was entitled to the full rights of citizenship, non-White Mexicans were not entitled to the same rights. It stated that the government had the power to limit the political privileges for certain types of Mexicans. The court's concluding statement affirmed California's right to discriminate against Mexicans of Indian descent:

> The elective franchise is denied to certain persons who had been entitled to its exercise under the laws of Mexico. The possession of all political rights is not essential to citizenship. When Congress admitted California as a State, the constituent members of the State, in their aggregate capacity, became vested with the sovereign powers of government, "according to the principles of the Constitution." They then had the right to prescribe the qualifications of electors, and it is no violation of the treaty that these qualifications were such as to exclude some of the inhabitants from certain political rights. (*People v. Pablo De La Guerra*, 1870:343–344)

De La Guerra triumphed and escaped the one-fourth Indian blood classification.[3]

By the 1880s elites like De La Guerra continued to enjoy financial security but had lost all political influence (Pitt 1970:273). Throughout California Mexicans no longer were appointed to judicial positions, and it was rare for a Mexican to be elected to office at the local level.

Afromestizos and the Nomadic Indians of California

People of Black descent in California were accorded civil rights similar to those of *mestizos*. Indeed, for those days this policy was outright radical, as slavery was prohibited in California and people of Black descent were allowed to remain in the state and own property (Heizer and Almquist 1977). Though Mexicans who were *afromestizo* and U.S. Blacks who had immigrated to California were treated better in comparison to the treatment that Blacks received in other states, they were racialized and came under the laws extended to free U.S. Blacks (e.g., they were prohibited from marrying Whites, from testifying in court against Whites, and from entering certain professions) (California Statutes, 1850, Chap. 140, p. 424, cited in *Perez v. Sharp*, 1948:719; Larson 1968).

The issue of placing Black people in bondage was discussed during the first constitutional convention of 1849, but was defeated; several Anglo-American delegates were abolitionists and offered convincing arguments on why California had to enter as a free state (Ross Browne 1850). Among the abolitionists were eight Mexican delegates. Antonio María Pico was the most outspoken on this issue and heatedly argued that slavery should not be permitted in California. He was Pío Pico's uncle, but as discussed earlier he was not part of the family branch which was racially mixed. Unlike Pío Pico, he is described as a White person (Garrison 1935).

The Indian groups who had not been conquered by the Mexican government came under the governance of the War Department after the Treaty of Guadalupe Hidalgo was ratified. They were classified as nomadic Indians and declared enemies of the state. To address the specific problem posed by the nomadic Indians of California, the U.S. Congress commissioned the War Department to clear hundreds of thousands of acres of their homeland in preparation for the arrival of Anglo-American settlers (Dale 1951; Takaki 1990). This resulted in the massive reduction of the Indian population from 310,000 in 1850 to 50,000 in 1855 (Cook 1976:44, 199; Hurtado 1988:2, 125–168). Sadly, only a few nomadic Indian tribes were spared their lives, and most who survived were Christian Indians.

Citizenship and Racialization: New Mexico

In New Mexico the Mexican constitutional delegates who were in the majority at the first territorial assembly resisted the racialization of the conquered population. From 1850 to the mid-1870s, a period when the Mexican *mestizos* retained considerable negotiating power, relatively liberal legislation was passed in New Mexico (Larson 1968). New Mexico's first territorial constitution was drafted on 15 May 1850 and was entitled the Organic Act of New Mexico. Twenty delegates were present at the constitutional convention: eleven Mexicans and nine Anglo Americans (ibid., 18). Father Antonio José Martínez, a schoolteacher of Taos and the author of New Mexico's first textbook, became the president of the constitutional delegates. The Organic Act conferred full rights of citizenship upon free Whites and those citizens of Mexico who had become citizens of the United States as a result of the Treaty of Guadalupe Hidalgo (First Legislative Assembly 1851:20). Within days, confusion arose over two issues. Were the Pueblo Indians part of the conquered Mexican population that had obtained U.S. citizenship under the Treaty of Guadalupe Hidalgo? If so, did they thereby acquire the right of suffrage? A month after the constitution was drafted, the Cochiti Indians (part of the Pueblo Indians) sent a delegation to Santa Fe, where it met with government officials to discuss the Cochitis' citizenship status (Larson 1968). The Cochitis were assured that they counted as part of the conquered Mexican population and were therefore eligible to vote, which they did in New Mexico's first territorial election. Father Martínez was instrumental in this decision, as he advised several Indian groups to assert their rights.

On 5 September 1853, however, the U.S. Congress rescinded the Pueblo Indians' voting rights (Larson 1968:82). In defense of the Indians' political rights, New Mexico's legislators attempted to bypass Congress's hostile response by giving Pueblo Indians full citizenship rights at the county and township levels (Deavenport 1856:142). New Mexico's courts also prohibited federal Indian agents from relocating any Pueblo Indian onto a reservation. The courts proposed that because the Pueblo Indians had adopted the Spanish culture and the Mexican township system, they had the right to obtain special privileges not extended to other Indian groups.

In *United States v. Lucero* (1869), for example, the New Mexico Supreme Court prohibited homesteaders from settling in Pueblo territory. The main purpose of the ruling was to ensure that the Pueblo Indians would not be converted into landless paupers and thus come under the jurisdiction of the Indian Intercourse Act of 1834. Allegedly the Pueblo Indians had become a Mexicanized Indian race that had adopted the culture, names, and traditions of their Mexican neighbors. Therefore, they deserved special privileges because generations of Spanish cultural indoctrination had uplifted them. The court offered the following opinion on the Pueblo Indians' citizenship and political rights:

> At the date of the treaty of Guadalupe Hidalgo the Indian race, in the Spanish sense of the term, were as much and fully citizens of

the republic of Mexico as Europeans. . . . This court . . . does not consider it proper to assent to the withdrawal of eight thousand citizens of New Mexico . . . and consign their liberty and property to a system of laws and trade made for wandering savages and administered by the agents of the Indian department. . . . The pueblo Indians of New Mexico are not within the provisions of the intercourse act [sic] of 1834. . . . In the absence of law or decision on the subject, are we not at liberty to conclude from these facts that the laws, the decision of the courts, and the acquiescence of the people, all recognized the pueblo Indians as citizens, as "Mexicans"? We do so conclude. (*United States v. Lucero*, 1869:422, 432, 441, 456)

In short, the court decided that the Cochitis and other Pueblo Indians were part of the conquered Mexican people, who—though the federal government denied them U.S. citizenship—were entitled to receive some rights under the Treaty of Guadalupe Hidalgo.

The liberal New Mexico Supreme Court ruling and territorial laws were short-lived. In 1876 the U.S. Supreme Court ruled the Pueblo Indians did not obtain any political rights under the Treaty of Guadalupe Hidalgo (Davis and Mechem 1915; *United States v. Joseph*, 1876). Federal judges stipulated that the Pueblo Indians were not Mexican, as they were part of the U.S. tribes under the jurisdiction of Congress. The dissolution of the Pueblo Indians' citizenship rights coincided with the growth of the Anglo-American population. In the late 1870s the Anglo-American population gradually increased; by 1880 it had become the majority, numbering over 90,000 (Lamar 1966:475). And with population growth came political power.

The political status of the population of Black descent following the Mexican American War was tragic. Under the Organic Act of 1850, citizenship was extended to all former citizens of Mexico. That year, however, U.S. Congress refused to recognize that Mexico had "ever" extended citizenship to Blacks (Lamar 1966:19). The U.S. Congress also ruled that Blacks could not become citizens anyway since Hispanos had to pledge allegiance to the new government to become citizens and under the new system of law Blacks did not have this privilege. Thus, since Blacks were not allowed to take the oath of citizenship, the Organic Act could not apply to them. Although Congress refused to confer U.S. citizenship upon Blacks, it did uphold the antislavery position passed by New Mexico's delegates in the first constitutional assembly (Larson 1968:33–34, 312). The delegates appended a statement to the Organic Act entitled *To the People of N. Mexico* in which they openly expressed hostility toward slavery. This document contained the declaration of rights of the inhabitants of New Mexico. Here the legislators stated:

> Slavery in New Mexico is naturally impracticable, and can never, in reality, exist here; wherever it has existed it has proved a curse and a blight to the State upon which it has been inflicted—a moral social and political evil . . . we have unanimously agreed to reject it—if forever. (cited in Larson 1968:33–34)

As the slavery debate continued throughout the United States, congressmen from Texas and other proslavery states pressured New Mexico legislators to change their position on slavery. New Mexico's representatives to Congress were issued a warning—unless New Mexico supported slavery, proslavery legislators would vote against New Mexico's becoming a state. New Mexico citizens were also warned that Washington would withhold all favors until their legislators passed a slave code. In 1856 Miguel A. Otero, the territorial congressional delegate, finally succumbed to the pressure and offered a compromise (Larson 1968:64). New Mexico would not become a slave state, yet it would prohibit Blacks from living in the territory. Blacks would be allowed to continue to live in New Mexico for no more than thirty days. Unfortunately, this is how New Mexico's legislators confronted the racial problem imposed upon them by Congress.

Citizenship and Racialization: Arizona

After the Mexican American War, Mexico only ceded part of Arizona; the southern region where the colonial settlements had been established remained under Mexican rule (Spicer 1981). Only northern and central Arizona came under U.S. occupation and was temporarily governed by the laws of New Mexico. Within a few years after the war the U.S. government became interested in purchasing southern Arizona. One of the main motives was the information contained in a military report identifying the Mexican settlements as excellent locations to establish garrisons from which a successful campaign against the Apaches could be launched (Officer 1987). The second motive was the possibility of constructing a railroad route through the Mexican towns, former missions, and military centers. At that time, a railroad connecting northern Arizona to other parts of the United States could not be built because the Apaches posed a dangerous threat to the workers. The officers reported that, although the Mexican settlements were in disrepair, Mexico had pacified the area and there were many Mexicans and Indians prepared to fight the Apaches (ibid., 276).

On 30 December 1853 Mexico agreed to sell southern Arizona; six months later the transaction was completed when the U.S. Congress ratified the purchase (Tate 1969:33). On 30 June 1854 the Gadsden Treaty was enacted to protect the political rights of the Mexican population remaining in the territory (Officer 1987:391). The treaty also established the boundary between Arizona-Sonora and resolved several international economic issues. The Gadsden Treaty was based on several provisions contained in the Treaty of Guadalupe Hidalgo. Article 5 of the Gadsden Treaty stipulated that Articles 8 and 9 of the Treaty of Guadalupe Hidalgo would be extended to southern Arizona. Mexicans would be given the right to become U.S. citizens, and their property rights would be protected. Article 5 of the Gadsden Purchase Treaty stipulated: "All the provisions of the eight and ninth . . . articles of the Treaty of Guadalupe Hidalgo, shall apply to the territory ceded by the Mexican republic" (cited in Tate 1969:39).

After annexation, Arizona was temporarily governed by the laws of New Mexico, but in 1863 the United States government gave it separate territorial status (Menchaca 1993:589). Once it was independent, Arizona's legislators decided to rescind the citizenship clauses passed by New Mexico and instead draft their new constitution based upon the California model. Members of the first territorial convention of Arizona included twenty-seven Anglo Americans and three Mexicans (Wagoner 1970:41). Under Arizona's territorial constitution only White males and White Mexican males were incorporated as citizens with full attendant rights (Organic Act of Arizona 1863, revised 1864, Chap. 24, Sec. 6, cited in Hoyt 1877:226). No specific legislation was drafted to determine who qualified as a White Mexican male. During the late nineteenth century, however, only White males were allowed to practice law (Menchaca 1993: 593), and between 1864 to 1909 no Mexican acted as district judge (Wagoner 1970:504). Arizona delegates chose to enter the union as a nonslave state, and Blacks were allowed to remain in the territory (Organic Act of

Arizona, Bill of Rights, Sec. 3 and Article 20, cited in Hoyt 1877:16, 26). This liberal policy applied to very few people; U.S. census enumerators counted no Blacks in Arizona in 1860 and only twenty-six ten years later (U.S. Census 1872:20).

The Christian Indians were allowed at first to remain in their homes, and specific policies were not enacted (Officer 1987). On the contrary, they were recruited by the military to fight the Apaches and Navajos who resisted forced relocation onto the reservations. In 1873, however, when Anglo Americans began migrating in large numbers, the massive relocation of peaceful and hostile Indians began (Dale 1951:100–101, 115; Lamar 1966:187). Except for some Apache groups who eluded capture, most Indians in Arizona were rounded up and placed on reservations. Relocation was allegedly necessary for the protection of both the Indians and Whites. Many Whites did not respect the rights of the Indians and regarded them as deadly enemies, to be slaughtered without regard for sex and age, while many Indians, in particular the Apaches, were used to a nomadic lifestyle and were unwilling to change. It is uncertain how many Christian Indians were placed on reservations at this time. During the nearly twenty years since Arizona had become part of the United States, Christian Indians had been left alone and given the opportunity to assume a Mexican public identity (Officer 1987; Spicer 1981). Thus, in Arizona the racialization of the Mexican population resulted in the incorporation of Whites as citizens with full political rights, whereas others were ascribed inferior legal rights.

Citizenship and Racialization: Texas

In Texas the racialization of the Mexican population began in 1836, immediately after the Texas War of Independence, and continued after the rest of the Southwest was annexed to the United States. The 1836 Constitution of the Republic of Texas extended the rights of citizenship to free Whites and to Mexicans who were not Black or Indian (Constitution of the Republic of Texas, 1836, Secs. 7, 9, and 10, in *Laws of Texas, Vol. 1*, p. 1079). When Texas was annexed to the United States (1845), these citizenship clauses were upheld (Weber 1982:272). The U.S. government passed additional stipulations liberalizing policy toward Indians, however, while becoming more restrictive toward Mexican immigrants. To acquire the right of citizenship Mexicans had to have resided in Texas prior to 1845 (Texas Constitution of 1845, Article 3, Sec. 1. pp. 5–6; Padilla 1979); any person migrating after that date who was not White was ineligible for naturalization and thus was prevented from becoming a qualified elector (see Menchaca 1993). At that time only Whites were allowed to apply for naturalization (Naturalization Act of 1790, Chap. 3, Sec. 1; Naturalization Act of 1802, Chap. 28, Stat. 1).

Under the Constitution of 1845 detribalized Indians who owned property and paid taxes became eligible to vote (Minter 1993; Texas Constitution of 1845, Article 3, Sec. 1, pp. 5–6). They could acquire this right only if they had relinquished all tribal affiliations and had somehow obtained property. Though this ruling was very liberal (no other state had extended such privilege to Indians), it affected few people because after Texas's independence Indians lost all their grant lands. In 1849, when the Texas State Supreme Court passed *McMullen v. Hodge and Others*, Christian Indians theoretically became eligible to become U.S. citizens, as the legal infrastructure to allow them to claim mission lands was finally passed (Menchaca 1993; Paschal 1874:1364–1366). Under this ruling Indians could claim mission lands if they could prove that they had adopted Mexican culture (Menchaca 1999; see Paschal 1874:1364). To receive such special consideration Indians must prove that they and their ancestors: (1) held no tribal affiliation, (2) had been Spanish subjects or practicing Mexican citizens (e.g., voted, ran for office, practiced the holy Catholic sacraments), (3) spoke Spanish, and (4) (if they were former mission Indians) had passed a two-year secularization probationary period where they were observed to have practiced Mexican traditions (*McMullen v. Hodge and Others*, 1849:43, 46–47, 82–83, 85–86). Indeed this was a liberal ruling; but, sadly, the Texas General Land Office has no records of Christian Indians having been issued land grants in Texas. *McMullen v. Hodge and Others* came too late: the mission lands had already been appropriated by others, and this legal infrastructure could not be used by Indians choosing to become U.S. citizens.

Citizenship Denied to Tribal Indians and Blacks in Texas

Though detribalized Indians received some political rights under U.S. law, such opportunities were not extended to tribal Indians. By the early 1860s most nomadic Indians had been exterminated, and those who survived were placed on reservations or were driven into Mexico (Newcomb

1986:357–360). The Apaches and Karankawas were pushed into Mexico, and the Comanches and Wichitas were placed on Oklahoma reservations (Alonso 1995; Chalfant 1991; Weber 1982). Most of the Caddo Indians were exterminated; those who survived either migrated toward Mexico or moved to reservations outside of Texas.

Only two Indian communities with tribal governments were allowed to remain in Texas, although they were not included among the Indians who could apply for U.S. citizenship. These peoples were the Tiwa of Ysleta in El Paso Valley and the Alabama-Coushatta of northeastern Texas. The area where the Ysleta Indians lived became Texas territory in 1850, two years after the Mexican American War, when the U.S. government acquired El Paso Valley and gave this region to Texas (Metz 1994:33). These two Indian peoples were not driven out because agents of the Bureau of Indian affairs and influential Anglo-American citizens recommended to the state legislature that they not be removed (Bowden 1971; Minter 1993). BIA agents advocated that the people of Ysleta be left alone because in tradition and customs they were Mexican (Fewkes 1902; Stallings 1932). The agents did not recommend they be given citizenship, however, because they refused to relinquish their tribal government. The Alabama-Coushatta had lived in Texas since 1804 and had established several communities under Mexican rule (Minter 1993:50). They had petitioned for Mexican land grants, but did not receive patents because the Texas War of Independence broke out and interrupted the process. Under the Republic of Texas they were removed from their homes, but were not forced to leave Texas. Finally, in 1846, they enacted a treaty with the U.S. government and were subsequently rounded up and placed on two reservations within the state (ibid., 4).

In the case of people of Black descent, Texas was not very kind. Most decisions pertaining to *afromestizos* who were Mexican citizens and to Blacks who had immigrated to Texas from the United States were made after Texas's independence and were later ratified by the U.S. government upon annexation. Texas endorsed the practice of slavery as a Republic and later joined the Union as a slave state. The size of the slave population grew enormously, from 2,000 in 1830 to 58,161 in 1850 and to the astounding size of 182,566 by 1860 (Schwartz 1975:27; U.S. Census 1854:160; U.S. Census 1864:486). After independence, people of Black descent were not recognized as part of the Mexican population, who had the right to become citizens of the new Republic (Constitution of the Republic of Texas,

Article 6, Sec. 10, cited in *Laws of Texas, Vol. 2*, p. 1079). Exacerbating matters, on 5 February 1840 the Senate and House of Representatives of the Republic of Texas gave people of Black descent the dubious choice of remaining in Texas and becoming slaves or being deported to Mexico if they wished to remain free (see Schoen 1937b:267). The 1840 act was consistent with the proslavery position adopted in Texas (Schwartz 1975).

Free Blacks, including former Mexican citizens, immediately fought against their deportation and mobilized by asking their White friends and business partners to appeal the act. Legislators received numerous petitions from influential Texans asking Congress to make exemptions for free Black families of good character. Those who lobbied in behalf of free Blacks proposed that hundreds of Black families were racially mixed and for generations had lived prudent and enterprising lives. The most effective lobbying effort was launched by wealthy cattleman Aaron Ashworth, who had become a prosperous rancher during Mexican rule and had fought on the side of the Republic during Texas's war for independence. Aaron and his family were less than one-fourth Black, and many of the family men were married to White women (Block 1976; Williams 1998). Taking into consideration Aaron Ashworth's loyalty, the Texas Congress developed the legal infrastructure to exempt some Blacks from deportation (Schoen 1937a). On 12 December 1840 it ruled that some Blacks would be exempt from deportation through the passage of special enabling acts. An "Act for the Relief of Certain Free Persons of Color," commonly referred to as the "Ashworth Law," became the first enabling act protecting free Black people from deportation (Act for the Relief of Certain Free Persons of Color, 12 December 1840, cited in *Laws of Texas Supplement, 1822–1897*, p. 549). For Blacks to be eligible for such consideration they had to prove that during Spanish and Mexican rule they had never been slaves (Schoen 1937b:277).

Although Ashworth's Law was certainly progressive, it did not suspend the Republic's deportation orders. On the contrary, the Texas Congress subsequently reduced the amount of time Blacks were given to prove they were free and gave anyone the right to question the status of a free Black person (Schoen 1937b:284–285). Black people had ten days to prove they were free, rather than the two-year period they had initially been given under the original act of deportation. If unable to obtain proof, such a person could be sold into slavery or required to leave Texas under penalty of law.

Though it is uncertain how many Blacks were deported or converted into slaves, we do know that Mexico took the threat seriously and responded by granting land to families who were deported from the United States (Schwartz 1975). We also know of one horrific case so massive in scope that it could not be hidden from public records. Ironically, the account concerns the Ashworth family, the individuals for whom the legislature made the "special exemption law."

The Ashworth family arrived in Texas between 1831 and 1834 (Block 1976:94). The patriarchs of the family were Aaron, William, Joshua, and Abner. Racially some of the family members were at most "quadroons" or one-fourth Black. All of the brothers were married to White women, or at least their wives appeared to be White. The family settled in *empresario* Lorenzo de Zavala's colony, near the outskirts of an Orcoquisac Indian village, in present-day Madison in Jefferson County. The Ashworths were part of a group of immigrant Black families joining Zavala's colony. One of the brothers, Aaron Ashworth, became a successful cattleman and the wealthiest person in the county (Jackson 1986:607). He owned large tracts of land on which he grazed over 3,000 cattle. His cattle and property alone were worth over thirty thousand dollars. His other relatives were also economically successful. After Texas became a Republic, Aaron and his relatives were exempt from the deportation orders. Unfortunately, several years later many of his White neighbors were not as liberal or sympathetic as the Texas Congress had been.

One tragic day, on 15 May 1856, the good fortune of the Ashworth family was cruelly reversed (Block 1979:11). Samuel Ashworth, a nephew of Aaron, became embroiled in a fistfight with William Blake, a White man. Witnesses accused Samuel of using abusive language against Blake, which was against the law. In those days Blacks in Texas were not allowed to insult White folks. Samuel was immediately arrested, taken to jail, fined, and given thirty lashes (Block 1979). News of the event spread and agitated many White people. Samuel's neighbors began talking and concurred that the Ashworth clan were a bunch of arrogant troublemakers. A mob of White folks decided to take action. That night a meeting was called for White people from Jefferson and Orange counties. They met outside the jail where Samuel had been detained. In the meantime, one of Samuel's cousins had helped him break out of jail. Samuel fled to the hills and sought shelter among some Indians. When the angry mob had everything ready to lynch Samuel, they entered the jail and found an empty cell. Frustrated at the perceived social injustice, they decided to seek revenge by forcing all Black people from Orange and Jefferson counties to leave. That night White men went into the homes of Black people and ordered them to leave within twenty-four hours or suffer repercussions (ibid.). Taking the threat seriously, Black people assembled as much property as they could carry in their wagons and within a few hours organized several caravans. Some took a northern route toward Louisiana, while others journeyed south in the direction of the U.S.-Mexican border.

A few months later Samuel Ashworth, accompanied by Indians, boldly resurfaced in Madison. Oddly, no one attempted to lynch or arrest Samuel for his alleged crimes or for the added charge that he had possibly killed a deputy (Block 1979). Samuel found no family members and returned to the hills, where he had started a new life among the Choctaw Indians. Two other members of the Ashworth family also returned to Madison, only to find that White folks were living in their homes and had appropriated their cattle (Jackson 1986). Not much is known about the further welfare of the Ashworth family, except that Samuel stayed among the Indians and during the U.S. Civil War resurfaced as a Union soldier. William Ashworth, who had been a wealthy man, returned to Jefferson County and was not enslaved, but was reduced to being a day laborer for those people who at one time had been his neighbors. It is uncertain why he returned to lead a destitute life.

Now I ponder: was this an isolated incident? Probably not; it was merely a major event that could not be hidden. We know that Ashworth's Law did not protect those it was designed to help. We are certain that wealth did not protect the Ashworths; on the contrary, their prosperity became a source of envy and resentment. We are also certain that Blacks in Texas, like the Ashworths, lost their Mexican land grants.

U.S. Congressional Land Policies and Racialization in the Southwest

Article 8 of the Treaty of Guadalupe Hidalgo was designed to protect the property belonging to Mexicans in New Mexico, California, Arizona, and parts of Texas:

> Mexicans now established in territories previously belonging to Mexico, and which remain for the future within the limits of the United States, shall be free to continue where they now reside . . .

retaining the property which they possess in the said territories . . . property of every kind, now belonging to Mexicans not established there, shall be inviolably respected. The present owners, the heirs of these, and all Mexicans who may hereafter acquire said property by contract shall enjoy with respect to it guarantees equally ample as if the same belonged to citizens of the United States. (Treaty of Guadalupe Hidalgo, Article 8, in *Nine U.S. Statutes at Large and Treaties of the United States of America, 1845-1851*, pp. 929-930)

Unfortunately, though the treaty guaranteed the property rights of all Mexicans, the new sovereign power chose to violate its agreement. The U.S. Congress held the power to interpret Article 8 and chose to deny Mexican Indians U.S. citizenship. Under this interpretation, Congress had the power to draft land policy for Mexican Indians because it had obtained this authority under the Northwest Ordinance of 1787, and this right was later expanded in subsequent Indian Intercourse Acts and Federal Supreme Court rulings (*Johnson v. McIntosh*, 1823; Minter 1993; *United States v. Rogers*, 1846). Under the Northwest Ordinance, Congress had ruled that Indians did not own the land they inhabited and extinguished all their property rights. Congress, however, took on responsibility to ensure that Indians lived on reservations or had a place to live. On reservations it had the option to give Indians a patent or sole occupancy rights. Thus, after the Mexican American War, Congress held full authority to validate or extinguish all land grant agreements that Spain and Mexico had made with Mexican Indians, including the mission Indians.

In the area of land policy *mestizos* and people of Black descent were also affected by racially prejudicial federal and state policies. Each state and territory passed different types of property laws, which affected people of color in diverse ways. Likewise, state and territorial legislatures had the freedom to interpret federal property laws according to their political views. The racialized category of Mexicans highly influenced whether people could validate their claims and whether they could enjoy the benefits of other state or territorial property laws.

Congress did pass one land act that affected all people of color in a similar way. Under the Homestead Act of 1862 Congress allowed homesteaders throughout the United States to claim 162 acres of public lands (*Twelve Statutes at Large, Treaties, and Proclamations of the United States of America, 1859-1863*, Chap. 75, pp. 392-39). In the Southwest there was plenty of land available, because vast tracts of land had not been colonized by Mexicans and property inhabited by Indians was declared public and eligible for distribution. Congress required the petitioner to be a citizen of the United States or an immigrant eligible for naturalization, however. This stipulation, though appearing to be "race neutral," was not and disqualified a large number of Mexicans. In California and Arizona the Homestead Act discriminated against native-born Mexicans, since both states restricted citizenship to Whites. At the national level only free White immigrants were eligible to become citizens in those days, so many Mexican immigrants of color were disqualified (Naturalization Act of 1790, Chap. 3, Sec. 1; Naturalization Act of 1795, Chap. 20, Stat. 2, Sec. 1; Naturalization Act of 1802, Chap. 28, Stat. 1).[4] Sadly, all racial restrictions prohibiting non-White Mexicans from obtaining citizenship were not removed until 1898 (see Chapter 9; In re Rodriguez, 1897; U.S. v. Wong Kim Ark, 1898).

In 1878 Seymour D. Thompson asserted in his classic study *A Treatise on Homestead and Exemption Laws* that when Congress drafted the Homestead Act of 1862 it only envisioned Whites as its beneficiaries. Its intent was to create and preserve a free White citizenry, independent from landlords:

> Accordingly we find that the benefits of most of the exemption laws of those states were limited to free white persons. Under such a statute, defining the person entitled to the benefit of the homestead exemption as "a free White citizen of this state," it was presumed in the absence of countervailing proof, that the person claiming the exemption was a person of this description. (Thompson 1878:83)

Thompson did qualify his critique and argued that in 1878 a few legal theorists like himself were in the process of developing arguments to extend the Homestead Act to non-Whites. Later, historians Douglas Monroy (1990) and Herbert Brayer (1949), among others, concurred with Thompson and added that the Homestead Act was largely developed to populate the Southwest with White settlers. The intent of the act was not to allot land to the native populations. The Homestead Act of 1862 remained in effect until 1889 (*Twenty-five Statutes at Large, Treaties, and Proclamations of the United States of America, 1887–1889*, Chap. 381, Sec. 1, p. 854).

People of Black descent were discriminated against by other land policies besides the Homestead Act. Their racialized category also nullified their opportunity to claim land in New Mexico and Texas. These accounts are discussed in the next section, which examines how Mexicans fared in the land-grant confirmation process of each state and territory. For now I must qualify my critique by acknowledging that in some cases the U.S. Congress and state legislatures passed special enabling acts to exempt people from the country's property laws. The exemptions clearly reflect the liberal racial views held by some representatives and state legislators. In many cases, officials and judges argued in favor of allowing all Mexicans to keep their homes.

Furthermore, based on U.S. property records, it is clear that many Mexicans had their land grants confirmed, indicating that Congress upheld the Treaty of Guadalupe Hidalgo in many cases. That is, a person had the opportunity to validate a claim as long as s/he was considered to be part of the people protected by the treaty and was able to complete all congressional stipulations. Under congressional orders all eligible claimants were to present to the regional land surveyor's office a petition accompanied by corroborating evidence (see Bowden 1971; Van Ness 1976). A deed was the best method of proving ownership. If a deed was lost, ownership could be proven by presenting a survey approved by a Mexican official or by submitting a certified copy of the deed and proving it was on file in a Mexican or Spanish government land office. A claimant was also responsible for proving that the land had been continuously occupied by the grantees, heirs, or tenants; otherwise the grant would be considered abandoned. Only land vacated as a result of Indian raids did not have to be continuously occupied. As part of the petition, the claimant also had to submit a current survey conducted by an authorized U.S. surveyor and to fulfill the specific requirements of each state and territory. Once all requirements were met, the regional land office assessed the petition and offered a recommendation. The report was submitted to the General Land Surveyor Office, which in turn prepared another report to Congress. Congress then approved or rejected the petitions.

If a petition did not reach Congress because it was rejected by the regional office, a claimant could appeal to the judicial branch of government and possibly have to follow the case until it reached the U.S. Supreme Court. Mexicans who could complete this procedure were assured a patent. By 1891 thousands of cases were still pending, so Congress established the Court of Private Land Claims. Claimants were to take their petitions or appeals directly to the court. Any land grant not confirmed became the property of the federal government (Van Ness and Van Ness 1980).

Texas: Unfair Land Policies Affecting Blacks and Indians

In Texas the confirmation of the Spanish and Mexican land grants began in 1836 under the Constitution of the Republic of Texas and proceeded after the Mexican American War. During the Republic, Article 6 of the constitution decreed that all persons residing in Texas on the day of the declaration of independence were entitled to the land they occupied and would be granted property if they did not possess any. This decree, however, exempted Indians and Black people. Article 6 stipulated:

> All persons (Africans, the descendants of Africans, and Indians excepted) who were residing in Texas on the day of declaration of Independence, shall be considered citizens of the republic, and entitled to all privileges of such. All citizens now living in Texas, who have not received their portion of land, in like manner as colonists, shall be entitled to their land. (Constitution of the Republic of Texas, 1836, Article 6, Sec. 6, cited in *Laws of Texas, Vol. 2*, p. 1079)

After the decree was issued, an "Act to Establish a Land Office for the Republic of Texas" was passed in 1838 (Act of 1838, Sec. 21, cited in *Laws of Texas, Vol. 1*, p. 1276). Its purpose was to confirm or reject the land claims issued under Spanish and Mexican rule. It was in the congressmen's best interest to develop an infrastructure to validate the Mexican land grants that they and other Anglo Americans had received quickly and with deliberate speed. To confirm a land grant, a person needed to have a deed or a survey or to have had the claim registered by the Mexican government. The Texas General Land Office reviewed the claims pertaining to the internal provinces, a term used for those regions obtaining independence in 1836. The final decision was rendered by the Republic's congressmen. Landless people could claim public land as long as they were not Black or Indian.

After the United States annexed Texas and replaced the Republic's congressional structure with a state legislature, special commissions were established by the legislature to review new claims (Bowden 1971). This became a very important task, because in 1850 the U.S. Congress gave Texas jurisdiction over El Paso Valley and present South Texas (Metz 1994:33). The state legislature was given full authority to interpret Article 8 of the Treaty of Guadalupe Hidalgo. Legislators did not need congressional approval for any decision pertaining to property. When the Republic of Texas joined the Union, the U.S. Congress gave the Texas legislature control over public land and the confirmation of land grants acquired after the Mexican American War—a unique privilege not extended to the other southwestern states and territories. Congress only retained authority over federal land reserves used for national defense. To verify a Spanish or Mexican grant in Texas, people followed a procedure similar to the practice prior to annexation.

Though the application procedure throughout Texas's history appears to have been fair, for many Mexicans of color it was an ordeal, particularly in the case of Black people and Indians. After the Republic of Texas nullified the land grants belonging to Blacks, later verification of claims under U.S. occupation was a moot point because Blacks had already been dispossessed of their land. Only nine Black men are known to have received an exemption, and this occurred during the Republic (if others did validate their claims, they were not identifiably Black). The men were Emmanuel J. Hardin, Robert Thompson, James Richardson, Samuel McMullen, John T. Weber, Greenborg Logan, Levi Jones, Samuel Hardin, and Hendrick Arnold (Texas General Land Office, file "Afro-Americans in Austin's Colony"). Apparently, all of these men were part of Stephen Austin's colony and obtained their grants under Mexico's 1824 General Colonization Law. They were issued deeds as a reward for their military services during the Texas War of Independence. With the exception of Greenborg Logan, who was a successful Mexican immigrant, very little is known about the men.

Logan immigrated to Texas in 1831 and settled in present Brazoria County, in the region known as "Chocolate Bayou" (ibid.).[5] This area was part of one of Stephen Austin's colonies. Though Austin was very generous in allowing Blacks to join his colonies, he only gave them one-quarter of the land traditionally allocated to other settlers. During the Texas War of Independence, Logan fought on the side of the rebels, only to find afterward that his land rights were rescinded. On his behalf, twenty-three prominent Anglo-Texans petitioned Congress to exempt him from the Republic's property law. On 21 June 1838 his petition was endorsed. His Mexican land grant, however, was not reinstated; instead he was issued a

"Donation Certificate" (a special homestead) for 640 acres and a bounty grant for 320 acres (a land grant for military service). His new grants were located in present Brower and Callahan counties. Indeed, Logan was compensated quite well for his participation during the war of independence.

Besides the Black men who fought on the side of the rebels, there is one other account of a Black person owning property after independence. William Goyen did not retain his Mexican land grant, yet he was able to protect the land he had purchased. Goyen was a Mexican citizen who moved to Texas during the Spanish period; upon Mexican independence he was part of the population declared a citizen. The Goyen case illustrates that a Black person who had not been deported after independence and had purchased property had a better opportunity to keep it. Of course, the property owner had to have the means to have the case litigated. William Goyen was a successful businessman who settled in Nacogdoches in 1820 (*New Handbook of Texas History* 1996:296). He was a free Black immigrant from Moore County, North Carolina. Goyen became an important citizen of Nacogdoches. He acted as a conciliator in local lawsuits and during Mexican rule was appointed as agent of Indian affairs. Goyen was also a successful blacksmith, wagon maker, and businessman. He often traveled to Louisiana to trade merchandise. During Mexican rule, he married Patty Sibley, a White settler.

After Texas obtained independence, Goyen was unable to confirm his grant, yet he was able to validate the property he had purchased four miles west of Nacogdoches. This site came to be known as Goyen's Hill. There he built a large two-floor mansion and expanded his business to include a sawmill and gristmill. His remarkable success infuriated many White neighbors. Despite their continuous efforts to take Goyen's Hill, they lost all court battles. To protect his rights, Goyen employed the best attorneys in Nacogdoches, including Thomas J. Rusk and Charles S. Taylor. He retained his property on the basis that it had been purchased.[6] In those days Blacks and detribalized Indians could own property if they had bought it. Goyen died on 20 June 1856 and was buried at Aylitos Creek. His case illustrates that wealthy Black people did have a chance to retain their property if they had influential friends and the money to litigate a costly case. Even then, however, not all wealthy Black people kept their property. We must remember the Ashworth incident, when Black people in Orange and Jefferson counties were forced to leave Texas (Block 1979; Jackson 1986). The wealth and influence of the Ashworth family was insufficient to control the anger of a White mob determined to dispossess Black people of the property that they deemed rightly belonged to them.

Most Indians, like Black people, lost their homes and property after Texas's independence. As previously noted, Indians in Texas who had not been under the governance of Mexico were chased out or exterminated; if they tried to remain in Texas, they were rounded up and placed on federal Indian reservations in Oklahoma (Chalfant 1991; Newcomb 1986). Only detribalized Indians were allowed to live among Mexicans and White people as well as in two tribal Indian communities. After Texas's annexation, the state supreme court theoretically developed the legal infrastructure for Indians to claim mission lands under *McMullen v. Hodge and Others* in 1849, but the ruling did not benefit any Indian. It was a moot point, because mission lands were already occupied. The Texas General Land Office has no record of any private land claim being awarded to Christian Indians, including the fourteen families from Mission Espada who had held Mexican deeds (see Chapter 7; TGLO-SMTT; Texas General Land Office 1988).[7]

Though Indians lost their land after Texas's independence, partial exceptions were made in the case of two federally recognized Indian communities, the Tiwa of Ysleta and the Alabama-Coushatta. As noted, because both peoples were recognized to be peaceful they were spared their lives and allowed to remain in Texas. During Texan rule, the Alabama-Coushatta were not removed as a result of Sam Houston's appeals to Congress (Minter 1993). Houston argued that the Alabama-Coushatta had proven to be law-abiding people by complying with the laws of Spain and Mexico. They also had shown their loyalty to the Republic by assisting the military to capture hostile Indians. In 1865 the Texas legislature finally gave them a 263-acre reservation, and they became the only tribe in Texas given such a privilege (ibid., 5). Prior to that date they were shifted from one place to another; wherever they were relocated, they were soon forced to leave.

The Tiwa Indians of Ysleta were the second group to be given some property. Their land tenure history helps to explain why they received a partial exemption (Metz 1994:33). Ysleta is located ten miles outside the city limits of present El Paso, and the residents have retained a tribal government to this day. Under Spanish rule the people of Ysleta received a land grant of approximately 4,000 acres to establish a town consisting of civic buildings, house lots, and a communal zone designated for small family gardens (Bowden 1971:141). Under Mexican rule the grant was confirmed and additional acreage was awarded to several families, where they established a communal ranch. In total the Tiwa of Ysleta owned over 17,712 acres (Metz 1994:14–15). After the Mexican American War, the U.S. federal government categorized the people of Ysleta as an Indian community and rescinded their land grant rights (Bowden 1971:171–175). They were allowed to remain in their homes, however. In 1850 the federal government gave the Texas legislature jurisdiction over Ysleta (Metz 1994:33). Four years later the legislature offered the opinion that the people of Ysleta were a bicultural people deserving some of the privileges extended to Mexicans and confirmed one of their grants. The township grant was confirmed, yet the land grant to the communal ranch was rejected.[8] In the transaction over 11,000 acres were lost, which later were granted to the trustees of the Pacific Railway Company and to other prominent Anglo Americans with close connections to the legislature (Bowden 1971).

In 1871 Ysleta was incorporated as a town by the Texas legislature and its status as an Indian community dissolved (Minter 1993:25). The residents of Ysleta could not vote against the incorporation because as Indians they did not have the right to vote. The federal government could not intervene because it did not have jurisdiction over Texas. When Ysleta became a town, property boundaries were redrawn; anyone wishing to live there had the right to settle and claim land. Sadly, the Texas legislature did not set a limit on how much land one person could claim. It also did not require people who owned land in Ysleta to live there. Within months, most of Ysleta fell into the hands of a few Anglo Americans. Though the people of Ysleta lost most of their land, its members held on and retained a cohesive community. Within a few decades they were able to gain federal support to be reincorporated as an Indian town.

Ysleta is a prime example of how the racialization process affected bicultural Mexicans who were classified as Indian. Without the protection of the Treaty of Guadalupe Hidalgo, their chances to keep their land were minimal. If they had been granted citizenship, like other communities in El Paso Valley, they would have had a better opportunity to defend their land or at least to profit from holding a perfect land title. For example, the people of Socorro shared a similar bicultural Mexican-Indian heritage. They were of partial Piro, Tano, and Jemez descent. Like the people of Ysleta, they obtained a Spanish land grant and later became secularized

Indians (Bowden 1971:151–154; Metz 1994). Unlike the people of Ysleta, they were classified as Mexican citizens by the Bureau of Indian Affairs. In 1858 the Texas legislature upheld the Treaty of Guadalupe Hidalgo and confirmed Socorro's land grants (Bowden 1971). Thus, the people of Socorro, by not being categorized as Indians, fared better under U.S. occupation. Like other Mexicans throughout Texas, however, many people in Socorro eventually lost their property. After assessing the financial problems of litigating their cases, many Mexicans chose to sell their land grants, rather than pursue cases which they could potentially lose. They did at least profit financially from holding perfect land titles.

Land Rights in Texas for Those Declared Mexican

Mexicans fared well in the land confirmation process in comparison with people categorized as Black and Indian. Mexicans submitted 1,157 claims for review (Bowden 1971; Texas General Land Office 1988; TGLO-SMTT). Of these claims, 896 (77.4 percent) were confirmed and 261 (22.5 percent) were rejected or withdrawn by the applicants. The acceptance rate is comparatively lower than for Anglo Americans, yet it remains impressively high. Out of 3,420 claims submitted by Anglo Americans, 2,932 were confirmed, an acceptance rate of 85.7 percent (TGLO-SMTT). In addition to these grants, Mexicans and Anglo Americans acquired land through other means. During Texas's stage as a Republic, congressmen confirmed the town charters of five towns established during the Spanish and Mexican periods. San Felipe (Austin), Liberty, San Patricio, Victoria, and San Antonio were recertified as towns (TGLO-SMTT; Act of 4 December 1837, cited in *Lewis v. San Antonio*, 1851:289–291). Each town was given title to the vacant and unappropriated land within its boundaries. The town government held title in trust for the inhabitants. Because land was entrusted to the local officials, however, they had the power to retain or redraw new boundaries dividing house lots. Only if residents previously had been issued title to a lot was their property outside the legal jurisdiction of the town assembly. Many disputes between residents and town assemblies soon followed and had to be settled in the courts (see *Lewis v. San Antonio*, 1851:288).

After Texas was annexed to the United States, the town charters of Laredo, Ysleta, Socorro, and San Elizario were recertified and many residents were allowed to keep their house lots (Bowden 1971; "An Act to

Quiet the Land Titles in the Towns of Socorro, Ysleta, and San Elizario," 2 April 1889, Chap. 16, cited in the *Laws of Texas Supplement, 1822–1897*, pp. 1371–1372; Texas General Land Office 1988). To this date a study has not been conducted on the ethnic breakdown of the subdivision of the town lots. We are uncertain whether all Mexicans were treated the same and whether Blacks and detribalized Indians were also given town lots. This is an important issue because in San Elizario during Mexican rule over 1,200 Apaches became Mexican citizens (Hendricks and Timmons 1998:50–59).

Moreover, a regional breakdown of the land grants indicates that Mexicans fared differently depending on where they lived in Texas. The petitions submitted by Mexicans in South Texas were confirmed at the astonishing rate of 89.2 percent, since 364 claims were submitted and 325 confirmed (Texas General Land Office 1988). In contrast, Mexicans in El Paso Valley experienced the highest rejection rate: 8 applications out of 14 submitted (57 percent) were rejected (Bowden 1971; Metz 1994). Only a few petitions were submitted because most grants were communal and each petition represented a group of claimants. This extremely high rejection rate was uncommon in the rest of the state. The high rejection rate in El Paso Valley is related to the way the Texas legislature interpreted the Treaty of Guadalupe Hidalgo. Legislators agreed that the treaty would be respected; however, they also concurred that grants issued by Mexico between 1836 and 1847 were invalid. The legislators believed that following Texas independence El Paso Valley rightfully belonged to them (Bowden 1971). Fortunately, only private land grants were affected by the ruling, as the communal grants were issued prior to Texas independence.

In the internal provinces, the regions north of the Nueces River, 565 of the 779 Mexican land grants reviewed were confirmed and 214 rejected, a 72.5 percent validation rate (TGLO-SMTT). The regions with the highest rejection rates in the internal provinces were present Liberty, Jefferson, and Nacogdoches counties, areas with a history of being settled by Blacks. Paradoxically, it is astonishing that prominent residents of Nacogdoches such as former Mexican mayors and justices of the peace like Domingo Y'Barbo, José Y'Barbo, and José Caró did not receive land grants (Nacogdoches Archives, Boxes 2Q307, 2Q306, 2Q301, 2Q299, Center for American History collection; cf. TGLO-SMTT; Texas General Land Office 1988). They were native residents of Nacogdoches and had lived there before the U.S. occupation.

Furthermore, the Spanish and Mexican land grants on the northern border of Nacogdoches were void by a special act passed by the Republic's congressmen (Act of 9 January 1841, cited in *Laws of Texas, Vol. 2*, p. 641). The Act of 9 January 1841 eliminated peoples' land rights unless their appeal was reversed within a year after the act's passage.

Alan Minter (1993), former Texas assistant attorney general, concludes that the confirmation rate for Mexican grantees was quite high. He contends, however, that a bleaker picture emerges if we look at the total acreage rather than the number of grants. In total 17 million acres (10 million based on Spanish land grants and 7 million on Mexican land grants) were claimed by Mexicans and Anglo Americans (ibid., 36). All Spanish land grants were held by Mexicans, and most of these grants were rejected. Excluding South Texas, most Spanish land grants were converted to vacant or unappropriated land. Minter posits that a large part of the rejected acreage was also occupied by Indians, such as the people of Ysleta and the Alabama-Coushatta.

Minter's analysis is supported by an 1852 study conducted by the Mexican government's General Commission for U.S.-Mexico Relations, entitled "Agencia mexicana ante la comisión general de reclamaciones entre México y Los Estados Unidos—Reclamaciones mexicanas." Mexican officials found that 440 Mexicans had complained that their grant applications had been withdrawn or not allowed for submission and a few had been rejected (cited in Garza 1980:13).[9] The complaints came from throughout the state, with the highest number from Nacogdoches, Goliad, Liberty, Travis, Nueces, Starr, Cameron, and Reynosa counties. El Paso Valley was not surveyed in the study. Why so many people were not allowed to participate in or complete the land grant process is uncertain. We do not know if the Texas Land Office or the special land commissions reviewing the petitions asked people to withdraw their applications or if the grantees did so voluntarily.[10] We can only hypothesize that some of the complaints may have been related to the laws prohibiting Blacks and Indians from owning property. Another explanation may be the international border laws passed by the Republic. The Act of 9 January 1841 decreed all grants located within twenty leagues of the Republic's northern border void (*Laws of Texas, Vol. 2*, p. 641). This explanation is plausible but dubious, since many Anglo-American settlers obtained exemptions from this law. Though it is uncertain what actually happened after the Mexican government presented its complaint, many Mexicans did obtain patents, and there is no account of entire Mexican communities being uprooted and chased out of Texas as in the case of the Ashworth family and their neighbors.

On the contrary, after Texas was annexed by the U.S. government in 1853 the Texas State Supreme Court passed a ruling prohibiting anyone from treating Mexicans in the same way the Ashworth extended family was mistreated. Under *Cook v. Garza* (1853), the state supreme court justices ruled that only the U.S. government could deny Mexicans their property rights and that no person had the right to force Mexicans to vacate their homes. Once again we see a progressive position taken by Anglo Americans.

The Texas Supreme Court justices ruled that Cook and his friends acted illegally when they intimidated and forcibly evicted Mrs. de la Garza and her infant from their home. The problem began in 1853, in the town of Victoria, when William Cook and the Harper boys told Antonio de la Garza to abandon his ranch and turn over all of his belongings. Mr. de la Garza owned a ranch, a cow pen, and household furnishings. In court Cook alleged that de la Garza had agreed to do as he was told; therefore when he and the Harper boys entered the premises they were merely carrying out the oral agreement. De la Garza denied he had made such a ludicrous agreement. He did concede that Cook made several visits and without using violence told his family to leave the ranch. The court clerk descriptively transcribed the proceedings and noted: "It was in evidence that defendant Cook, in company with others, went to the house of the plaintiff, and asked him if he would give him possession; to which the plaintiff replied he would not" (*Cook v. Garza*, 1853:359).

Dissatisfied with the de la Garza family's response, Cook waited until the ranch was left unprotected. One night Mr. de la Garza took a trip. Cook and his friends immediately took advantage of the situation, trespassed onto the ranch, walked into the house, and began removing property. Mrs. de la Garza tried to stop them, but was physically and violently restrained. She was unable to fight back because she was trying to protect her infant son. The court reporter described the shameful scene:

> The defendant [Cook] . . . returned in the evening with the witness and the three Harpers. The plaintiff being absent, they requested his wife to go out of the house; which she refused to do. They then removed the furniture and effects, which were in the

house, into the yard. Cook and one of the Harpers then took hold of the plaintiff's wife, each taking her by an arm, and led her out of the house; she having an infant in her arms and resisting. They then pulled down one side and end of the house; they also pulled down the cattle pen and let out the cattle. The house and cow pen were of little value. The Harpers remained in possession for a time. . . . (Cook v. Garza, 1853:359–360)

When Antonio de la Garza returned to Victoria, he sought help from the local law authorities; together they forced the Harpers to vacate his house. The dispute entered the courts, reaching the Texas Supreme Court. The justices clearly ruled in favor of Antonio de la Garza and admonished Cook and the Harpers for their cowardly behavior toward Mrs. de la Garza. Cook asked for a retrial and a change of venue on the grounds that the justices were swayed by the Mexican community's outcry for vengeance. His request was denied. In sum, the de la Garza case is an important ruling; however, it is also a commentary on Mexican-Anglo relations in Texas. How frequent were events of this kind, and why was it necessary for the courts to admonish such behavior and warn White people to leave Mexicans alone? Indeed this ruling evokes a bleak picture of Texas regarding disputes over property. Sadly, this was not an isolated incident: in *Santa Paula Water Works et al. v. Julio Peralta* (1896) the California State Supreme Court had to issue a similar warning to Anglo Americans.

New Mexico, Land, and the Pueblo Indians

Land policies in New Mexico followed a similar allocation process as in Texas. Indians, Black people, and those classified as Mexican came under separate land policy confirmation processes. *Genizaros* were classified as Mexicans rather than Pueblo Indians, and their villages came under the property laws affecting Mexicans (see Brayer 1949; Leonard 1943).[11] In New Mexico Indians fared better in the land grant confirmation process than other Mexican groups. They were protected by a unique judicial interpretation of the Treaty of Guadalupe Hidalgo and by federal and state laws. Blacks fared the worst. They were prohibited from living in New Mexico; thus their property rights became a moot point (Larson 1968).

Mexicans also experienced devastating losses, as most did not possess private land grants and were unable to retain their farms. The best-case scenario was the experience of the Pueblo communities.

After the Mexican American War, the U.S. Congress did not break up the Pueblo villages and redistribute their lands. It instead commissioned the Bureau of Indian affairs to study their land tenure situation. In the meantime the New Mexico State Supreme Court offered an unprecedented opinion on Pueblo lands. In 1869, in *United States v. Lucero*, the justices ruled that Pueblo lands were protected by the Treaty of Guadalupe Hidalgo and prohibited homesteaders from filing claims. The court ruled that Indian wards were included as part of the population whose lands were protected by the Treaty of Guadalupe Hidalgo. This was an unusual opinion that was not replicated in any subsequent court ruling in the Southwest.

Pueblo lands were further protected by recommendations issued to U.S. Congress by the Bureau of Indian Affairs. Throughout the 1870s, the agents for New Mexico recommended against implementing the relocation policies contained in the Indian Intercourse Act of 1834 (Dale 1951:129–130). The bureau warned Congress that the Pueblo Indians were a civilized people; if placed on federal reservations they would join the 5,000 uncaptured Apaches roaming in New Mexico. It was advisable to leave the Pueblo communities alone and instead offer them federal protection as a means of avoiding Indian uprisings (Hall 1989). This was necessary to maintain territorial peace and thus generate the environment to attract Anglo-American colonists. Congress followed the recommendation of the BIA and treated Pueblo lands as "Indian Country"; though Congress reduced the amount of land, it protected the reserved land from homesteaders. The Pueblo Indians were not given title at this time, however. Sadly, such consideration was not extended to Apaches. Instead the War Department treated them as enemies of the state. By 1886 most Apaches had been killed, and those who survived sought refuge in Chihuahua, Mexico, or were removed from their homes and placed on reservations (Alonso 1995:132–144; Dale 1951:111, 116). Their former lands became open for homesteading or were converted into national forest reserves.

Apparently, the exceptional status given to the Pueblo Indians allowed them to remain on their land and thus ensured the growth of their communities. The BIA reported that for two generations following the Mexican American War the size of the Pueblo Indian population remained stable at approximately 40,000 (Dale 1951:58; Lamar 1966:92). Furthermore, because they were not restricted to the Indian villages, thousands chose to live in the Mexican towns as their ancestors had done for generations. In 1880 the Census Bureau reported that 9,772 Indians in New Mexico lived outside the Pueblo communities (U.S. Census 1882:379).

Though Pueblo lands came under congressional protection, a wealthy Anglo-American land speculator challenged federal law when he perceived his legal right to claim Indian lands to be thwarted by state and federal laws (Brayer 1949). Anthony Joseph was born in Taos, New Mexico, in 1846. He attended Webster College in Missouri and later returned to New Mexico, where he served in several local and territorial government posts, becoming a well-known politician, and was once elected to Congress. During his tenure as a politician, he became a land speculator (Brayer 1949). Joseph was a corporate real estate businessman speculating in the purchase of cheap property and reselling it for higher prices. His corporations advertised throughout the United States that cheap land was available in New Mexico. This news was used to attract thousands of settlers.

When Joseph challenged the Pueblo Indians' property rights and attempted to lay claim to a parcel of their land in 1874, he was fined by government agents and evicted from Pueblo lands. He refused to pay the fine, and the dispute was finally resolved in court. He lost the trial at the territorial level (*United States v. Joseph*, 1874) but appealed to the U.S. Supreme Court. In *United States v. Joseph* (1876) he argued that the Pueblo Indians had no legal right to land in New Mexico because they were not U.S. citizens. The justices ruled that although the Pueblo Indians were not U.S. citizens their land was protected from homesteaders. Disillusioned with the outcome of the case, Joseph pursued his real estate plans by purchasing a large percentage of the Mexican land grants in the Chama Valley and in the *genizaro* community of Ojo Caliente (Brayer 1949). Attempts to strip most Pueblo Indians of their land were futile, because by 1886 the U.S. Congress had given nineteen of the twenty Pueblo villages ownership (Dale 1951:120).[12]

New Mexicans, Communal Grants, and Documents

Federal interpretation of the communal land grant system had an adverse impact on the Mexican citizenry. After the Mexican American War, the U.S. Congress did not issue specific policies instructing Mexicans how they should validate their communal grants. People therefore assumed that as long as they held a deed or their land had been registered by the Mexican government the Treaty of Guadalupe Hidalgo protected their claim (Ebright 1980). Within a few years, Mexicans were alarmed when Congress announced that communal land grant patents did not necessarily constitute a valid claim. Only people whose names appeared in the original communal deed were recognized to hold a valid claim. Since most people in New Mexico did not have their names recorded, this meant that they needed to find alternate means of establishing ownership. Legal historian Malcolm Ebright (1980, 1991) and anthropologist John Van Ness (1976) propose that because communal ownership was an alien concept in U.S. law the government chose to treat communal lands as unappropriated public domain. The U.S. government claimed that Spain and Mexico had only given the grantees temporary occupation rights and had not issued all communal members ownership. Congress, therefore, had the right to evict most residents from public lands.

In 1854 the U.S. Congress established the Office of Surveyor General of New Mexico to investigate land grant claims and to offer recommendations to Congress (Rock 1976:55). The surveyor was to assess all claims meticulously and gather all possible documents that had been produced by Spain and Mexico. As part of the investigation he had to hold hearings, take testimony under oath, and collect and translate all documents. Congress allegedly instituted this very slow process because the communal grants were enormous and such a pace was necessary to investigate fraudulent claims.

Furthermore, before grantees could be issued title, the district and state courts had the responsibility of adjudicating overlapping claims and grantee disputes over titles. In 1855 *Pino v. Hatch* (cited in Rock 1976:56–59) became the first land grant case to reach the New Mexico Supreme Court and thus set the legal precedent followed in later decisions. Under *Pino v. Hatch* the justices reaffirmed Congress's position that only people who were mentioned in the communal deeds or registries had the right to file a claim. The court also ruled that land was to be subdivided only among those who could prove ownership. Legal historian Michael Rock (1976:57) succinctly summarizes the court's decision:

> ... the New Mexico Supreme Court has held that the interest the residents of a community land grant have in the common land of their grant vary [sic] according to the legal nature of the patentee. ... The patentee could be an unincorporated association, a New Mexico corporation, or an individual.

Under this ruling, however, the court did provide an escape clause giving people in unique cases the opportunity to prove ownership. If people could prove they or their ancestors were members of a corporation mentioned in a deed (for example, when a deed was issued to a business association, a family corporation, or a corporate political group), this could be used to establish proof of inclusion.

While the land grant process followed a snail's pace, many Anglo-American real estate investors arrived in New Mexico and took advantage of the situation. They correctly assessed the problem faced by the grantees—most people did not have funds to litigate a case or retrieve documents from Spain and Mexico. Investors such as Anthony Joseph and his corporate business partners proceeded to purchase grants from people that had a valid claim (Brayer 1949). Many farmers, distressed over their inability to obtain the needed documents, sold their portion of the grant rather than embarking upon a legal battle they would very likely lose. The investors gave the grantees a lump sum and in return obtained their interest in the grant. Often people negotiated the right to keep their house lots if their grant was confirmed. As part of the agreement, the grantees agreed to sell their grants at a low market value; in return for such a cheap price, the investors agreed not to sue the grantees if Congress rejected the claims. In pursuing a claim, investors had to pay for application fees, surveys, travel expenses, and the legal costs of arbitration until it reached Congress. Among the most active investors were English financier William Blackmore, politician Anthony Joseph, and land claim attorney Thomas Catron.

Between 1854 to 1870, 1,000 claims were submitted to the New Mexico surveyor general; 150 were recommended for confirmation, and only 71 were validated by Congress (Morrow 1923:25). Many of the successful claims were owned by investors. Though most grants were rejected on the basis that the claimant held only a communal land grant agreement, many private grants to individuals were also rejected under the suspicion that Mexican authorities had issued fraudulent documents (Ebright 1980:82). Sadly, neither the grantees nor their attorneys could dispute the decisions; only the government had access to the Spanish and Mexican archives, and it did not allow the grantees to review the documents. Usually, only wealthy individuals had the funds to search for corroborating documents in Spain or Mexico and thus challenge the government's claim (ibid., 79; Rock 1976:56).

The people of New Mexico were once again adversely affected when the U.S. Congress restructured its procedures to validate land grant claims and established the Court of Private Land Claims in 1891 (Van Ness and Van Ness 1980:10). The court, composed of five judges, chose to employ the Congressional Act of 1873, which limited all communal land grants to 17,712 acres, regardless of the actual size of the grant issued by Spain or Mexico (Brayer 1949:334). As a case in point, the *genizaro* town of San Miguel del Vado was reduced from over 400,000 acres to 5,024 (Leonard 1943:39). The claimants retained only their house lots. Between 1891 and 1904 the court reviewed over 300 claims affecting New Mexico, California, and Arizona involving 34,653,340 acres; 32,718,354 acres were rejected, or over 94 percent, and the land fell under congressional control (Ebright 1980:82; Van Ness and Van Ness 1980:10).[13] In New Mexico, at the closure of the court's commission, only 126 grants had been validated, making a total of 197 grants confirmed in the history of New Mexico (see Engstrand 1978:329; cf. Van Ness and Van Ness 1980:10). Only 12 of these New Mexican grants were communal.

The communal lands appropriated by Congress came under the administration of the Bureau of Land Management. Mexicans, however, were allowed to buy their farms back; if they were unable to purchase them, they could lease part of the property if it had not been sold to someone else (Ebright 1980). Land that was not bought back was subsequently sold, issued to homesteaders, or converted into national forests. Why Mexicans in New Mexico did not use the Homestead Act of 1862 to reclaim their grant land is uncertain. A study on this theme has not been conducted. Exacerbating the ordeal of this displacement, people also lost lots in the towns because most of them did not hold deeds. Though most towns were recertified under U.S. occupation, the government only confirmed the lots where the civic buildings stood (Rock 1976:56). Most people consequently lost their homes.

In many cases the people who did have their land confirmed eventually lost it by the turn of the century through failure to pay property taxes. For example, the successful claimants from Mora, Antón Chico, and La Joya obtained congressional approval only to lose their parcels for failing to pay taxes (Knowlton 1991; Leonard 1943). The irony in the government's action was that it had not required the families to pay taxes because their land rights were in question, yet once their titles were clear they were required to pay back taxes even if they had not been in control of their property.

The land displacement experienced by most Mexicans in New Mexico resulted in the conversion of small farmers into landless wage workers. By the late 1890s many found employment on the farms owned by Anglo Americans (Kutsche and Van Ness 1986). The newcomers had become the landed elite by purchasing land from real estate investors or acquiring it through congressional grants (Lamar 1966). Once the transfer of titles was complete, Anglo Americans established farms and offered employment to the now landless Mexican farmers. A new economic structure emerged in which the ruling class was predominantly White and Anglo American.

Land in Southern Arizona

In Arizona the racialization of the population into distinct racial groups does not appear to have had a profound impact on the division of land, because there were only a handful of people eligible to apply for grant confirmation. It did not matter whether a person was White or not, since most people did not have the opportunity to file a claim. Racialization did affect people's ability to claim land under the Homestead Act of 1862 (*Twelve Statutes at Large, Treaties, and Proclamations of the United States of America 1859–1863*, Chap. 75, Sec. 1, p. 392). The act disqualified people of color, because Arizona restricted citizenship to Whites (Menchaca 1993:589). The act also discriminated against immigrants of color, as in those days a person had to be White to become a naturalized citizen (Naturalization Act of 1790, Chap. 3, Sec. 1; Naturalization Act of 1795, Chap. 20, Stat. 2, Sec. 1; Naturalization Act of 1802, Chap. 28, Stat. 1).

The legal land restrictions placed upon Mexicans began in 1854 when the Gadsden Treaty was ratified (Tate 1969:43). Under Article 6 the United States government agreed to protect the land rights of the Mexican population; however, it only agreed to confirm tracts with legal titles. Article 6 clearly stipulated that occupancy was insufficient to claim ownership:

> No grants of land within the territory ceded . . . bearing date subsequent to the day—twenty-fifth of September . . . will be considered valid or be recognized by the United States, or will any grants made previously be respected or be considered as obligatory which have not been located and duly recorded in the archives of Mexico. (Gadsden Treaty, Article 6, cited in Tate 1969:40)

Article 6 effectively destroyed the land rights of most people in Arizona, except for a handful of elites who had acquired titles and surveyed their property (Mattison 1946). We do not know why the Mexican government accepted such an unjust provision and failed to include specific protectionist legislation in the Gadsden Treaty. What is certain is that Mexico abandoned its citizens and left them to negotiate their own futures, without creating legal policies that they could use to defend their homes and ranches.

After the purchase, the Mexican government acknowledged that Mexicans potentially could lose their homes if they were unable to fulfill treaty stipulations. In a half-hearted attempt to assist the Mexican population, Comandante Joaquín Comadurán was commissioned to certify and register property occupied by Mexican citizens. The registry would be archived in Mexico and a copy handed over to the United States government. The purpose of the registry was to create a legal document that could be used by Mexicans to support their land claims. Comadurán left Arizona in 1856, when all Mexican personnel were ordered to leave (Officer 1987:281–284). While in Tucson he certified surveys, registered sales transactions to generate deeds, and issued certificates of continuous occupancy when residents brought corroborating evidence, such as witnesses testifying that families had continuously occupied a tract. In any case, the Mexican government's attempt to help its citizens appears today to have been a mockery; it was at best a futile attempt since the registrations occurred after 25 September 1853, the date when land grants and certificates issued by Mexico became void (Tate 1969:40).

Anglo-American settlers began migrating to southern Arizona immediately after the treaty was signed. Most pioneers were businessmen prepared to purchase land grant titles that could withstand a land commission review. A few Anglo-American families arrived at this time, most settling in Tucson. A military camp was also established in Tubac. The soldiers' families eventually joined them, and within a few years Tubac became a lively Anglo-American settlement (Officer 1987). By 1870 thousands of Anglo Americans and European immigrants had arrived in Arizona; the state had nearly 10,000 residents, including the Mexican population (Lamar 1966:475; U.S. Census 1872:xvii).

To confirm the Spanish and Mexican land grants in Arizona, the U.S. Congress commissioned a surveyor general to investigate claims (Mattison 1946). In turn, local surveyors were hired to examine claims and arrive at decisions about both the extent and the validity of the purported grants. The surveyor general authored and submitted recommendations to the secretary of the interior, who prepared a report to Congress, where final decisions were rendered. Because Article 6 of the Gadsden Treaty stated that only land grants surveyed and issued title were eligible for consideration, the heirs of only fifteen of the sixteen grants issued by Spain and Mexico submitted petitions. The Tumacácori grant was not eligible for consideration because it had been issued to Indians and such grants were void (Mattison 1967; *Johnson v. McIntosh*, 1823). Within a few years the surveyor general rendered a favorable decision on thirteen cases and rejected two (Mattison 1946:290). Congress, however, delayed their confirmation for decades. By 1888 Congress had not confirmed a single grant. In the meantime, Anglo-American settlers arrived in large numbers and settled upon the grant lands (Officer 1987:293). This further delayed the confirmation process because grants could not be confirmed until all overlapping homestead claims were settled.

Due to congressional delays, thirteen of the grantee families sold their titles to Anglo-American investors. It was a wise decision, as the grants were enormous and the funds acquired from the transactions helped several families secure economic stability. Descendants of the Elías González family as well as the Otero, Robles, Carrillo, and Aro y Aguirre families negotiated successful contracts and were able to obtain sufficient funds to retain their elite status under U.S. occupation (Engstrand 1992: 275–276; cf. Mattison 1946). Congress finally rendered a decision on most of the grants by the turn of the twentieth century, after taking thirty-five to fifty years to resolve matters (Mattison 1946). Though the surveyor general approved thirteen grants, Congress confirmed only eight, containing

116,540 acres of the 837,680 acres under review (Mattison 1946:291; Officer 1987:293). It was a devastating economic loss for the investors, because two of the confirmed grants belonged to wealthy Mexican families.

Homesteaders also did quite well: when the Mexican grants were rejected, their overlapping claims could finally be approved by Congress. Moreover, eighty-one of the thousands of families who applied for land under the Homestead Act of 1862 were Mexican applicants (Soza 1994a: 13–14). Only thirty-one of them successfully completed all requirements and eventually obtained patents (ibid., 15–20). Why so few Mexicans obtained patents is uncertain.[14]

Though few Mexicans filed land claims, many families were able to retain their homes through other means. In 1862 Union army major David Ferguson registered the claims of 129 Mexican families from Tucson and several others living within a three-mile radius (Officer 1987:288). He also validated the claims of forty Anglo-American families who had recently settled in Tucson. The major did this to stop the ongoing violence between families disputing over property boundaries. This became the legal basis for families to take their claims to the surveyor general. Furthermore, in 1864, under the *Compiled Laws of the Territory of Arizona* (Chap. 47, Sec. 1, cited in Hoyt 1877:55), the territorial legislators ruled that settlements with a population of over 300 people would be incorporated as towns. Town boundaries would be settled by the state, and the responsibility for distributing house lots was entrusted to the local assemblies. Furthermore, in an unprecedented liberal stance congressmen decided in 1875 that Mexicans in Arizona who had become citizens under the Treaty of Guadalupe Hidalgo or the Gadsden Treaty and who were prohibited by U.S. property laws from obtaining patents to their town lots would be issued patents if they could prove continuous residence for twenty years (*Eighteen United States Statutes at Large 1873–1875*, Chap. 34, Sec. 1, p. 305). These were indeed liberal decisions, but once again it is uncertain how race and ethnicity affected the confirmation process, as a study on this theme has not been conducted.

Anthropologist James Officer (1987) suggests that it is likely that a large percentage of the Christian Indians faded into the Mexican population and obtained the political privileges of Mexican *mestizos*. For several generations after the Gadsden Purchase was ratified the military left the Christian Indians alone, so that they had the opportunity to assume a Mexican identity. Considering the politics of the period, Officer argues that it is likely that many Christian Indians passed as Mexican in public, in particular after the forced relocation policies began.

Historians Howard Lamar and Edward Dale offer corroborating arguments. Lamar (1966:187) states that by the mid-1870s, after the Apache no longer posed a major problem, the territorial government changed its policy toward all Indians. People who were identifiably Indian were placed on reservations by either force or inducement, and with few exceptions Indians were allowed to live among Anglo Americans and Mexicans. Dale (1951:117, 119) notes that only a few groups of Papagos and the Indians living near Mission San Xavier del Bac were allowed to live outside of the reservations. The 1890 census indicates that 28,469 Indians lived on reservations, while 1,512 lived among the colonists (U.S. Census 1894:41). Dale adds that to induce Indians to remain on the reservations, the government gradually gave them ownership of their lands; by 1887 most reservations were owned by Indians (Dale 1951:119). Such "generous" land policies were necessary because the non-Indian population had increased to 60,000 by 1890 and by popular opinion wanted them segregated (U.S. Census 1894:2). When Indians were placed on the reservations, their place of residence was fixed, and they were under the supervision of Indian agents and the military. Mexicans, however, did not have similar restrictions on their freedom of movement and often had the opportunity to keep their homes.

California, Land, and Indians

After the Mexican American War, Mexicans in California were racialized and placed in different legal categories in relation to property rights. Indians, with few exceptions, were allowed to keep their property, whereas Mexicans who were of White, *mestizo*, or Black descent were given the opportunity to file land petitions. Treating people of Black descent the same way as *mestizos* was a progressive ruling in accord with the anti-slavery position taken by California's state government (California Constitution of 1849, Article 1, Sec. 1, p. 3). *Mestizos* and people of Black descent were discriminated against under federal law, however, because the Homestead Act of 1862 required citizenship, and in California people of color were not granted such a privilege. In spite of these problems, the property laws in California were relatively liberal, and most people who were not Indians could keep their homes. The worst-case scenario was the situation of the California Indians.

During the first years of U.S. occupation, the Indian population of California continued to decline steadily and quickly. In 1849 the U.S. War Department received orders from Congress to place Indians on reservations or exterminate them if they refused (Dale 1951:7). By 1853 the military had only been able to place a few thousand Indians on reservations; thousands of White settlers began to descend upon California, resulting in the massive destruction of Indian villages (Hurtado 1988:143). In 1850 there had been around 310,000 Indians; by 1855 they had declined to 50,000 and by 1870 to 29,025 (Cook 1976:44, 199; U.S. Census 1872:21). Of the surviving Indians in 1870, census enumerators estimated that 13,500 remained uncaptured, 5,784 had been placed on reservations, and 7,241 were living peacefully among Anglo and Mexican colonists (U.S. Census 1872:21).

Historical demographer Sherburne F. Cook (1976) proposes that the reduction of the Indian population is no doubt primarily based on the extermination campaigns. He argues that the loss in population of the Christian Indians is also related to their integration into the Mexican community, however. Christian Indians were not required to live on reservations, but being an Indian was still very dangerous, particularly after a series of property laws left most identifiable Christians Indians homeless (Acuña 1972; Haas 1995; Monroy 1990; Pitt 1970).

Some of the most convincing arguments have been presented by legal historian Chauncey S. Goodrich and anthropologists Robert F. Heizer and Alan F. Almquist, who point to state legislation as prime evidence. They argue that after most of the Indians living among the settlers lost their homes, the legal infrastructure was created to convert them into indentured slaves. Under California's Act of 1850, commonly known as the Indentured Act, Indian vagrants and orphaned minors could be placed in indentured servitude (Goodrich 1926:93; see also Heizer and Almquist 1977:46–51). Indian paupers who committed any punishable offense could be placed in bondage. In 1860 the Indentured Act was amended: if an Anglo American lodged a complaint against the moral or public behavior of an Indian (that is, loitering, strolling, or begging) within twenty-four hours, that Indian could be placed in bondage and sold at auction (Goodrich 1926:94). Thus, the racialized category assigned to Christian Indians in California placed them in a legal position to become indentured servants—and this indeed was an incentive to assume a Mexican public identity. Many Indians probably did assume a Mexican identity, although it is difficult to determine how many did so. It is unlikely, however, that many nomadic Indians passed for Mexican, probably both because they had not acquired the cultural knowledge to hide their ethnicity and because they chose not to do so.

I certainly do not contend that most southwestern Indians passed for Mexican after U.S. occupation. Rather, I propose that many former mission and Christian *ranchería* Indians were pressured to change their public ethnic identity in order to avoid being killed, placed in bondage, reduced to paupers, or relocated to reservations. There was also a property incentive—Mexicans had the opportunity to submit land grant confirmation petitions, whereas Indians did not. Furthermore, acculturation may also be a factor in explaining why Christian Indians may have chosen a Mexican public identity in many cases. For centuries the Catholic Church and the governments of Spain and Mexico had pressured Indians to acculturate. This form of indigenous cultural erasure affected all Mexicans in the aftermath of the conquest, not only the mission and *ranchería* Indians (Borah 1983; Graham 1990). In the Southwest some Indians became acculturated as early as 1598, while others were undergoing this process in 1848. It is important to acknowledge that the mission program lasted close to 250 years; during that period, generations of mission and *ranchería* Indians underwent the same cultural pressures as did the Indians of the interior of Mexico. The policy of the governments of Spain and Mexico had been to transform the indigenous peoples into subjects and later citizens of the state with a common religion and national culture. Following the Mexican American War of 1846–1848, Christian Indians had accommodated to the culture of the colonists (in particular the culture prescribed and proscribed by the Catholic Church). After U.S. occupation, pressures to become "culturally Mexican" increased.

Cook (1976) concurs with this acculturation thesis and adds that in the case of the mission Indians their social networks contributed to furthering their Mexican acculturation. California mission records and interviews that Cook conducted with descendants of mission Indians in 1940 indicate that by 1848 most mission Indians were related to Mexican colonists and intermarriage was common. Cook notes that after the Mexican American War the relations between the mission Indians and the Mexicans were not severed, as most continued to live together.

Though the demographic question of how many mission and *ran-*

chería Indians chose to assume a Mexican public identity is beyond the scope of this book, the Epilogue elucidates this theme by providing auto/ ethnographic accounts of people who are of bicultural Mexican and Chumash ancestry, focusing on my affinal relatives from Santa Inés and Santa Bárbara. My husband Richard, our children, and his consanguineous relatives are part of the California Indian populations with roots in the missions, presidios, Christian *rancherías,* and colonial towns. After the Mexican American War, his ancestors took different paths. Some lived in the towns, others remained in the Indian villages, and others chose to be relocated to the reservations. Regardless of their choices, my husband's family networks were not ruptured, and they retain contact to this day. Currently, some identify as Chicanos, others as Mexicans, others as Americans, and many as Chumash. My point in presenting this case study is to illustrate that after the Mexican American War there were strong pressures and rewards for Christian Indians to assume the public identity of Mexican *mestizos.*

Land Displacement and the California Christian Indians

As previously discussed, under U.S. congressional orders and the U.S. Supreme Court ruling *Johnson v. McIntosh* (1823) Indian tribes did not own the property they inhabited unless they had purchased it or if a special agreement was extended to them by Congress. Though Christian Indians in California were not removed, their property rights were severely limited by state law.[15] Under *Suñol v. Hepburn* (1850) the California Supreme Court ruled that emancipated Indians (the legal term used for Christian Indians) could not retain title of the land grants given to them under Spanish or Mexican rule. The justices upheld federal opinion and addressed specific issues pertinent to Mexican Indians. The deeds of Christian Indians were nullified on the basis that they did not have the mental capacity to manage or develop property. Although the justices recognized that Christian Indians were among the peoples who acquired citizenship under Mexican rule, this status was interpreted to pertain merely to wardship.

This decision was unlike the New Mexico State Supreme Court ruling, where the justices offered a similar opinion on citizenship yet upheld the Pueblo Indians' property rights. In California the justices chose not to give Indians similar consideration, and the land commission implemented the orders. California land grant records indicate that fourteen Indians attempted to have their land grants confirmed; thirteen petitions were rejected and one confirmed (Cowan 1977). Only Lupe Iñigo, the wife of Robert Walkinshaw, a successful Anglo-American businessman, was issued an exemption (Ayers 1886:13; Cowan 1977:62). The land grant was confirmed in the name of Lupe and her spouse.[16]

Two years later the state legislature passed a more grievous assault against the Indians and converted most identifiable Christian Indians into landless paupers. The Preemptive Act of 1853 formally decreed that all Indian lands were public domain and were open for homesteading (Haas 1995:59). Land inhabited by the secularized Indians of the mission communities in San Antonio, San Carlos de Monterey, Santa Cruz, San Rafael, San Francisco de Asís, and San Francisco Solano immediately became available to homesteaders (Cowan 1977). Oddly, the U.S. Congress allowed state legislators to evict most Indians from their homes, although it was legally responsible for protecting Indian country against state legislation which could leave Indians homeless (*Johnson v. McIntosh*, 1823).[17] Congress merely responded by reserving some land in areas where the land was arid and inadequate to sustain farming communities. It also commissioned the military to prevent the relocated families from leaving the reservations (Hurtado 1988).[18] In 1853 Edward F. Beale, superintendent of Indian affairs in California, offered a scathing critique of Congress's failure to protect Indians under the Treaty of Guadalupe Hidalgo (Heizer and Almquist 1977:79). In his report to the commissioner of Indian affairs he provided ample documentation of the devastation caused by the Preemptive Act. Beale wrote of California Indians "who are reduced to despair—their country, and all support, taken away from them; no resting place, where they can be safe, death on one hand from starvation, and on the other by killing and hanging" (cited in Heizer and Almquist 1977:79).

Why was it necessary for the state legislature to dispossess Indians of their homes—and, more importantly, why did Congress fail to protect them? The answer lies in demographics. After all, these were the Gold Rush days in California: thousands of Anglo Americans and European immigrants were moving West. By 1849 nearly 100,000 settlers had migrated to California in search of gold and land, and these people needed permanent homes (Grodin, Massey, and Cunningham 1993:9). The Preemptive Act was necessary if Anglo-American homesteaders were to be accommodated, particularly because the Christian Indians were in possession of some of the best coastal lands in California.

Prior to the passage of the Preemptive Act Christian Indian communities had been identified by federal agents but had not been ordered to vacate their homes. On the contrary, Congress passed "An Act to Ascertain and Settle the Private Land Claims in the State of California," commonly known as the California Land Act of 1851 (*Nine Statutes at Large and Treaties of the United States of America, 1845–1851*, Chap. 41, Sec. 16, p. 634). The act reassured all Californians, including Christian Indians, that deeds were not necessary if occupied tracts were located in previously incorporated towns or villages.[19] As long as a town or village had a corporate body which was authorized by the community members to file a petition, Congress would confirm all plots and civic property. Under the Land Act of 1851 Congress did not add any stipulations excluding Christian Indians. Sadly, two years after the act was passed Congress shunned its federal responsibilities and did not rule California's Preemptive Act illegal when it clearly went against federal property law.

Although thousands of Indians were forced to abandon their homes, Christian Indians refused to move to reservations (Haas 1995; Hurtado 1988). Many moved to Los Angeles, where employment was available (Weiss 1978), while others resisted forced eviction and instead chose to rent homes near the villages of their birth. Christian Indians refused to abandon their communities in Sabobá, Temecula, Pala, San Pascual, in several neighborhoods in San Juan Capistrano, and in the villages of San Luis Obispo and Santa Inés (Bean and Shipek 1978; Engelhardt 1986; Grant 1978a; see Photograph 35).

Since Christian Indians became among the poorest people in California, they were forced to develop creative ways of supporting themselves financially. Allegedly, many former mission Indians were stealing, entering embezzlement schemes, and gambling (Grodin, Massey, and Cunningham 1993; Jackson 1903; Monroy 1990). They had produced an illegal underground economy that was a nuisance to others. Many Anglo Americans perceived this to be a problem and asked the state government to respond to their concerns. In 1865 the state government attempted to rescind the Christian Indians' freedom of movement and include them as part of the population that had to be placed on federal reservations (*People v. Juan Antonio*, 1865). The California Supreme Court acknowl-

Photograph 35. Mission Indians Who Refused to Disperse: General José Pachito and the Captains at a Meeting at Mission San Antonio de Pala, 1885. Courtesy of the University of Southern California, on behalf of the USC Library Department of Special Collections.

edged the state government's concern, but ruled against its removal recommendation. In *People v. Juan Antonio* (1865) the justices ruled that emancipated Indians were peaceful people and would be allowed to continue living outside the reservations.

In 1873 a federal Indian agent again offered the opinion that the Preemptive Act was a disaster and the federal government needed to address the problems produced by the state of California (Engstrand 1991:42–43; Haas 1995:59). John G. Ames reported that most Indian villages had been dismantled and that the Christian Indians were living in severe poverty. Some six years later, due to increasing public concern, the U.S. Congress was forced to address the plight of the California Indians. It once again earmarked land for reservations and in 1879 established a Mission Agency to address the particular problems of the mission Indians (Dale 1951:87). A few mission Indian families joined other tribal Indians and agreed to move to the reserved lands. All families were given wagons and plows to help them farm. California Indian agents, however, reported that most mission Indians refused to leave their communities because the reserved lands were nearly impossible to farm.

In 1881 Helen Hunt Jackson wrote *A Century of Dishonor: A Sketch of the United States Government's Dealings with Some of the Indian Tribes* (Dale 1951:91). This book and other ongoing articles on the mission Indians' poverty critiqued the legal procedures used to dispossess Indians of their land grants (Jackson 1903). In particular, Jackson damned Congress and asked people to demand that something be done in behalf of the mission Indians. Public opinion was aroused, and Congress finally responded by reserving fertile land near Los Angeles and San Diego as well as opening boarding schools for Indian children. Sadly, Congress made these reserves temporary and only gave families occupancy rights. People refused to move without being given deeds, Indian agents reported, because they knew very well that they would soon be forced to leave. It was better for them to continue living on their own and finding ways to become financially secure.

Though Congress refused to relinquish title to public lands, many Christian Indians fought back and attempted to keep their ranches by appealing to the courts, where they had received better treatment. In *Byrne v. Alas et al.* (1888) twenty Christian Indian families associated with Mission San Luis del Rey claimed the right to retain former mission lands on the basis that they were Mexican. The families included former mission Indians as well as Christian *ranchería* Indians. The California State Supreme Court ruled in their favor, arguing that the Treaty of Guadalupe Hidalgo protected their property rights because Mexico had made them citizens. It was an astonishing victory for the Christian Indians of California and a resounding reversal of *Suñol v. Hepburn* (1850) and the Land Act of 1851. Unfortunately, the following year the federal government intervened and overturned all cases with similar rulings (Goodrich 1926). In *Botiller v. Dominguez* (1889), the U.S. Supreme Court ruled that Spanish and Mexican land grantees could only have their grants confirmed if they had filed a claim under the California Land Act of 1851. This decision was immoral; at best, it was a hypocritical ruling since California laws had prohibited Indians from filing land claims.

Historian William W. Robinson (1948) proposes that although land grants held by Christian Indians were void some Indians probably did retain their ranches by claiming Mexican citizenship. This is plausible, since during the Mexican period the government did not record the race of the grantees. During the Anglo-American period, the grants of Indians who could convince others that they were Mexican could be confirmed.

Robinson suggests that a few of the confirmed grants held by Mexicans may have belonged to acculturated Mexican Indians. For example, he found that patent to Rancho Huerta de Cuatí in Los Angeles was granted to Victoria Reid. After investigating Reid's ethnicity, Robinson found that she was an Indian married to Hugo Reid, an Anglo American. Reid was presumed to be a *mestiza* and was given title to 128 acres (Ayers 1886:8; Cowan 1977:31).

By the turn of the twentieth century, Congress had refused to give most reservation Indians ownership of their communities. They lived on land owned or leased by the government. By 1903, 2,552 California Indians lived on twenty-seven reservations (Dale 1951:94), ranging in size from 280 acres to 38,600 acres. Less than fifteen reservation communities had been issued a patent.

Mexicans and Property in California

Any persons wishing to validate their land grant could do so, as long as they were not identifiably Indian. Mexicans and Anglo Americans submitted 813 petitions; 604 of these were confirmed (89 belonging to U.S. citizens or European immigrants, the rest to Mexican citizens), a 75 percent confirmation rate (Morrow 1923:144).[20] Of the grants reviewed, 190 were rejected and 19 were withdrawn (it is uncertain whether these petitions were rejected upon submission or whether the applicants withdrew them). In total the land grants confirmed by Congress contained 9 million acres (Morrow 1923:144).

In addition to the grants confirmed by Congress, Mexican and Anglo-American residents living within the boundaries of a town also had their house and ranch lots confirmed. The California Land Act of 1851 established the procedure to confirm town dwellings, even if a person did not hold a deed (*Nine Statutes at Large and Treaties of the United States of America, 1845–1851*, Chap. 41, Sec. 14, p. 634). Unlike the situation in New Mexico, where Congress refused to confirm town lots unless a person held a deed, in California U.S. congressmen did not issue a similar requirement. With the exception of Santa Cruz, and of course all the Indian towns and villages, the former Mexican township charters were confirmed. In most cases, however, the federal government took possession of a large part of the town's unused land and opened it for homesteading (Robinson 1948:41).

Though many Mexicans were able to retain their homes, hundreds lost a great deal of land when hundreds of thousands of Anglo Americans flooded California. By 1860, due to migration, the non-Indian population in California had grown to over 379,994 (U.S. Census 1864:34). These newcomers needed a place to live, and Congress developed the legal infrastructure to accommodate their needs by passing the Homestead Act of 1862. Settlers now had the right to claim vacant and public lands (*Twelve Statutes at Large, Treaties, and Proclamations of the United States of America, 1859–1863*, Chap. 75, Sec. 1, p. 392). As part of the act, Congress redefined vacant land as property that was not in use. If a homesteader could prove a Mexican grantee had abandoned his/her property or was not using part of it, Congress could extinguish the grantee's title (Morrow 1923). This became a serious problem for all grantees, as a large part of the ranch lands were used for pasture and not for farming (Acuña 1972; McWilliams 1968). Furthermore, because Congress had previously ruled under the Land Act of 1851 that it would not confirm any grant that had an overlapping claim, this policy delayed the confirmation process (*Nine Statutes at Large and Treaties of the United States of America, 1845–1851*, Chap. 41, Sec. 13, p. 633).

Under the Homestead Act of 1862 any person age twenty-one or over who was a U.S. citizen or was eligible to be naturalized and was in possession of a tract of land could file a homestead claim with the California Land Commission (*Twelve Statutes at Large, Treaties, and Proclamations of the United States of America, 1859–1863*, Chap. 75, Sec. 1, p. 392). This process, however, excluded all non-White people. Homesteaders who filed an overlapping claim could not be evicted unless the state or federal courts instructed them to leave. If a homesteader filed a claim that was challenged by a grantee, the dispute entered the courtroom. The grantee's litigation expenses increased if the case was not settled by a district court or when multiple overlapping claims were filed. The cost of litigation also increased if the case had to be appealed because the land commissioners had handed the homesteader a favorable decision. Under California's Land Act of 1851 grantees were responsible for paying all litigation costs if they challenged the commission's ruling (*Nine Statutes at Large and Treaties of the United States of America, 1845–1851*, Chap. 41, Sec. 10, p. 633). In such cases the grantee was often left bankrupt, even if the suit was eventually won. For example, former general Mariano Vallejo won cases at the district level, but because they were appealed to the

U.S. Supreme Court he had to pay for the litigation costs. These expenses eventually left Vallejo bankrupt (*United States v. Vallejo*, 1859; *United States v. Vallejo*, 1861a; *United States v. Vallejo*, 1861b). At Vallejo's death the only property he owned was the house he lived in (Bancroft 1964:R-Z 757–759).

Similar problems were experienced by former governor Pío Pico and his relatives. The titles of their enormous land grants were challenged by homesteaders, and several cases reached the U.S. Supreme Court (*United States v. Francisco Pico and Others*, 1859; *United States v. Andres Pico*, 1859; *Pico v. United States*, 1864). Pío Pico was reduced to being a town dweller with sufficient money to lead a life of leisure but no longer being part of California's elite (Bancroft 1964:I-Q 778). His brother Andrés, who became a political broker, did much better under U.S. occupation (Monroy 1990). In 1853 Andrés won a favorable decision against the land commission when the U.S. Supreme Court ruled that Rancho Santa Margarita y Las Flores was not vacant property (Rush 1965:93–100). The California Land Commission had tried to appropriate the ranch and allegedly convert it to a land reserve. Andrés questioned the commission's intent, because the property was sought by many San Diego real estate developers. He won by submitting a perfect title and surveys and proving that Indian tenants lived on the ranch. This favorable ruling left his property protected against future homestead claims. In 1862 Andrés sold the ranch to Pío Pico, who in turn sold half of the ranch to his brother-in-law, John Forster (ibid., 95). Homesteaders did not pose a legal problem for Forster.

The privileges that newcomers obtained under the Homestead Act also adversely affected Mexicans from San Francisco. Land was scarce in the downtown area, and only public land on the outskirts of the city was available for distribution. Needless to say, the U.S. Congress stepped in and developed the legal infrastructure to give land to the incoming settlers. A similar problem did not occur in other Mexican towns because after the Indians were evicted from their homes there was sufficient land to accommodate the new settlers. In San Francisco the redistribution of property began in 1852, when Anglo Americans began settling in the city (Robinson 1948:230). Many of the newcomers were families who had failed at farming or had not struck it rich in the gold mines of northern California. Instead they chose to settle in a city and work for a living.

In 1854 the California Land Commission recommended to Congress that San Francisco had enough residents to be incorporated as a city. It also suggested that the local assembly be allowed to submit recommendations for confirmation of grants, to subdivide tracts, to distribute new lots, and to survey all city tracts (ibid., 229–245). At this time San Francisco's Mexican population was in the majority and would have been the main beneficiaries of the land commission's recommendation. Though the local assembly was pleased with part of the decision, it disputed the redrawing of the city limits. The commissioners recommended that the city's Mexican land grant be reduced from sixteen square leagues to four. The confiscated property would then be distributed among the incoming homesteaders. The dispute immediately entered the courtrooms. It began at the district level and reached the U.S. Circuit Court.

While the suit was being litigated the Homestead Act was passed, and San Francisco was flooded by thousands of newcomers searching for permanent homes. Many came from the southern states in an attempt to escape the hardships of the U.S. Civil War and its aftermath. As San Francisco became crowded, people began fighting for prime lots. Often Mexicans found several families squatting in their yards and were unable to evict them, because it was against the law. Oddly, in 1866, after thousands of homesteaders had filed petitions for lots in San Francisco, Congress stepped in and rescinded the land commission's recommendation, approving the original sixteen-square-league petition submitted by the local assembly (Robinson 1948:231, 236). Prior to that date, Congress had refused to intervene. On the contrary, while Mexicans were in the majority it prevented the land commission from issuing patents to any city lot, even if the residents held a Mexican deed. Congress's reason for choosing to delay the confirmation process is blatantly clear. It was not ready to confirm the tracts when San Francisco was predominantly a Mexican city, when the homesteaders would not have had any right to set a claim. As long as a title was in question, the land was up for grabs. When San Francisco was finally issued a patent, everyone who was a resident was eligible to receive a tract of land. The city held title in trust for the residents and was responsible for redrawing boundaries.

Overlapping Claims and Ranching Elites: Different Scenarios

By 1879 Anglo Americans from throughout the United States had continued to settle in California and the non-Indian population had increased to over 865,000 (Grodin, Massey, and Cunningham 1993:9). In many cases

Photograph 36. Anglo-American Railroad Workers' Tent City, near Ventura, California, 1887. Courtesy of the Ventura County Museum of History and Art.

the newcomers settled on vacant land, only to find that they could not file a claim because it belonged to a Mexican or to an eastern capitalist who had purchased the grant (see Photograph 36). This often led to violence; when the homesteaders were in the majority, the landowners were vulnerable (Acuña 1972; McWilliams 1968). Homesteaders knew that there was power in numbers and that federal and state law protected them.

Two cases in Ventura County exemplify this point: the battles over the Sespe and Peralta ranches. On 24 March 1877 serious disputes over land erupted between the More family, the owners of Sespe Ranch, and a large crowd of homesteaders who had just arrived (Triem 1985:36). The Mores were part of an eastern capitalist family who arrived in Ventura County after the Mexican American War and purchased the land grant rights of local Mexican families. Upon their arrival in Ventura County, homesteaders found that the Mores and other wealthy investors had bought many of the Mexican land grants and that the land was now for sale rather than available for homesteading. The most violent encounter occurred between the homesteaders and the owners of Sespe Ranch. One night the homesteaders set fire to the Mores' barn; as Thomas More raced to rescue his animals, he was ambushed and shot to death (Stuart 1879). Although the More family had previously sold a large part of their Ventura County property to the incoming settlers, many others decided to take possession of Sespe Ranch. In response to the violence, the More family sold and gave away a large part of the ranch.

Rancho Peralta, adjacent to Sespe Ranch, was also the site of a violent takeover. The rancho was located in what is currently the northeast section of the city of Santa Paula, where I grew up. I have previously narrated this account in my book *Mexican Outsiders: A History of Marginalization and Discrimination in California*, where I offer a historical ethnography of race relations in Santa Paula (Menchaca 1995). Julio Peralta was a wealthy landowner who remained economically stable after the Mexican American War. He was the last Mexican in Santa Paula to keep his ranch; other Mexicans had lost their claims, and the Indians had been evicted from their villages by 1857 (*Davidson et al. v. United States Government*, 1857). When the U.S. government required Mexicans to settle their land claims, Peralta had sufficient resources to pay the costs of confirming his grant. Between 1869 and 1896 Peralta hired at least ten attorneys to defend his claims (Menchaca 1995:13–18). He originally tried to perfect his title by filing a petition with the California Land Commission. It was accepted on the basis of two points. First, Peralta held an indisputable and perfect land grant title. Second, he filed a claim under the Homestead Act of 1862 to strengthen his title. This gave him the right to own the ranch irrespective of whether or not his Mexican land grant was valid.

Unfortunately for Peralta, his victory was short-lived. In 1867 Santa Paula experienced a mass influx of Anglo-American migrants and several families settled near Peralta's ranch (Menchaca 1995:13). At first, his neighbors were friendly and accorded him respect as a prominent citizen of Ventura County. A few years later, however, Peralta's neighbors became annoyed with him. Soon they began terrorizing him and demanding that he leave Santa Paula. They also began to usurp and cultivate part of his land, in spite of his continuous protests (*Santa Paula Water Works et al. v. Julio Peralta*, 1893; *Santa Paula Water Works et al. v. Julio Peralta*, 1896). To frighten Peralta, his neighbors often shot at him and his hired hands. They also shot at his farm animals and killed several of them. When violence proved ineffective, the neighbors decided to challenge Peralta's land claim and thereby evict him legally. In 1893 the homesteaders filed an overlapping land dispute case in the Ventura County Superior Court, alleging that Peralta had sold them his ranch and later refused to move (*Santa Paula Water Works et al. v. Julio Peralta*, 1893). They testified that an oral agreement had been transacted with Peralta and to support their allegations presented as evidence a contract drawn and signed only by them. Peralta denied making any type of agreement and questioned the legality of the contract because he had not signed it. His statement was corroborated in that the contract submitted to the court by the homesteaders did not have his signature.

The homesteaders also argued that Peralta had never held legal title to the land because his grant was situated on mission property and thus was public domain. Peralta advanced documents proving that was not the case. Furthermore, he argued that the homesteaders' allegations were a moot point because under the Homestead Act of 1862 he was the legal owner. The superior court ruled that Peralta was the owner of the ranch but was obliged to share with others the water that ran through his property.

The dispute lasted for years, as the homesteaders ignored the court's decision and continued to inhabit the disputed property. In 1896 Peralta's neighbors appealed the superior court decision to the California Supreme Court (*Santa Paula Water Works et al. v. Julio Peralta, 1896*). W. H. Wilde and Orestes Orr, the attorneys representing Peralta's neighbors, argued that Peralta had no legal right to the ranch or to the water flowing through his property. To support their allegations, Wilde and Orr argued that Peralta was not a U.S. citizen because under immigration law he was not eligible to be naturalized or to own property. To contest the arguments advanced by the plaintiffs' attorneys, Peralta hired seven attorneys, Mr. Daly, Mr. Toland, Mr. Shepard, Mr. Eastin, Mr. Gottschalk, R. F. Del Valle, and J. L. Murphy. Their main counterarguments were that (1) the Ventura County Superior Court had previously ruled that Peralta was the legal owner of the land and (2) the state supreme court had ruled that Peralta was a United States citizen; therefore he was eligible to enjoy the full political rights of a citizen.

After listening to both sides, the state supreme court justices upheld the Ventura County Superior Court decision. Justice Britt, who wrote the opinion, also admonished the plaintiffs for their actions in this entire affair. He stated that no one in Santa Paula had the right to dispossess Peralta of his civil rights because they did not believe he was a citizen. Only the U.S. government had the right to investigate the citizenship status of individuals and determine if they had the right to own land. In closing, Justice Britt ordered that Peralta be allowed to resume his life on the ranch and ordered his neighbors to stop terrorizing him. Suffice it to say that although Peralta retained legal ownership of his property, he lost everything. The Ventura County sheriffs did not enforce the court

Photograph 37. Businessmen in Santa Paula, California, 1890s. Courtesy of the Ventura County Museum of History and Art.

order. Peralta's neighbors ignored the court ruling and used violence to chase him out of town (*Santa Paula Water Works et al. v. Julio Peralta 1893–1898*).[21] In any event, the homesteaders eventually became members of the prominent "founding families" of Santa Paula (see Photographs 37 and 38).

Though Peralta was chased out of town in Ventura County, a few Mexican elites were treated much better. The Oliva, del Valle, López, Ortega, de la Guerra, and Menchaca-Camarillo families kept their ranches and continued to prosper (Triem 1985:37–45). Moreover, the Menchaca-Camarillo family remained one of the wealthiest in Ventura County. They were not devastated by the war; on the contrary, they mixed well with local Anglo-American elites and established profitable business partnerships. Among their holdings were several ranches in the county, one of which specialized in raising fine Arabian and Morgan horses. In 1893 the Menchaca-Camarillo family had one of the largest estates in the county, with a Queen Anne–style home, a racetrack, and astonishing gardens (see Photograph 39). Though the Menchaca-Camarillos maintained their wealth into the twentieth century, the other ranching families were

Photograph 38. Interior of a Hardware Store in Santa Paula, California, 1880s. Courtesy of the Ventura County Museum of History and Art.

only able to maintain their elite status until the end of the nineteenth century (Menchaca 1995; Triem 1985:45). They were forced to sell their homes to pay their debts.

The Economic Decline of the Mexican Families

The devastating economic downturn of the Mexican community did not occur until the 1880s, when 70 percent of them were reduced to laborers (Haas 1995:69). This occurred in relation to two convergent events: the financial bankruptcy of the Mexican ranchers and increased migration to California, which produced an oversupply of labor. In the 1870s many Mexicans began selling their ranches after a series of droughts killed their livestock and ruined their fields (Haas 1995:64). Small farmers could not withstand the economic losses or the economic stress imposed upon them by the homesteaders who were treating Mexican ranch lands as public domain (Monroy 1990; Pitt 1970). Families like the Peraltas and Menchaca-Camarillos could withstand the economic pressures because

Photograph 39. Adolfo Menchaca-Camarillo Estate, Camarillo, California, 1893. Courtesy of the Ventura County Museum of History and Art.

they were financially secure, but the small-scale farmers were forced to sell their ranches before the homesteaders took their land by force.[22]

Exacerbating matters, a decade later employment became more competitive.[23] Between the 1860s and 1880s over 12 million immigrants entered the United States, and hundreds of thousands migrated to California—where land was plentiful (Feagin and Feagin 1999:77, 82, 135, 163). Employers took advantage of the situation by lowering wages and instituting a peonage system in the farms and a two-tier labor system in nonfarm occupations (Higham 1987; Reisler 1976; Takaki 1990). A large portion of the Mexican labor force became part of a peonage system in which farmers provided housing and food for their workers in lieu of wages (Almaguer 1979; Galarza 1964; Menchaca 1995). It was common to give farm employees only a few dollars a month.[24] In nonfarm employment, a segmented labor market emerged in which the best jobs were reserved for Whites. People of color were relegated to unskilled jobs paying the lowest wages (Gonzalez 1990; Menchaca 1995; Reisler 1976). Sadly, Mexicans could not join labor unions to protect themselves, because in those days they and other racial minorities in California and throughout the United States were prohibited from joining (Feagin and Feagin 1999; Takaki 1990). On the contrary, union leaders favored a two-tier labor system in order to restrict Mexicans and other minorities from competing for the higher-paying jobs.

This two-tier labor system continued into the twentieth century. A study conducted by the Dillingham Commission of the federal government found that by 1911 Mexicans were paid the lowest wages in the country in comparison to other ethnic groups. The commission concluded that on the average a Mexican farm worker was paid $1.42 per day, while members of other ethnic groups were paid at a minimum 50 cents more (Dillingham Commission, 1911, pp. 36–37, cited in Reisler 1976:19). The commission also found that in the railroad industry it was a common practice to pay Mexicans lower wages. For example, since 1908 the Southern Pacific Railroad had paid Greek labor $1.60 per day, Japanese $1.45, and Mexicans $1.25 (Dillingham Commission, 1911, pp. 13–19, cited in Reisler 1976:4). Once Mexicans lost the ranches, they also lost economic control of their lives and were forced to enter a labor system where people of color were discriminated against.

Concluding Thoughts

After the Mexican American War, the racial reforms enacted by Mexico were nullified and the conquered population embarked upon a new racial era in which they were distinguished on the basis of race and ascribed different legal positions. I have called this process racialization. Indians experienced heightened forms of racial discrimination because they were not protected by the Treaty of Guadalupe Hidalgo. The Pueblo Indians of New Mexico were the only Indians who were allowed to use the treaty in their self-defense.

Although Mexicans who were *mestizo* and White also experienced various forms of racial discrimination, the U.S. government allowed many of them to keep their homes and ranches, which protected them from the devastations experienced by most Indians. Indeed, having a place to live was a major advantage and became an incentive for Christian Indians to assume the public identity of a Mexican *mestizo.* Though the issue of land was an incentive, I do not presume that all Christian Indians took the path of *mestizaje.* My point is to argue that Christian Indians were well acquainted with Mexican traditions and practices and therefore had the ability to find ways out of their legal categories—if they chose to.

This narrative includes detailed accounts of the experiences of the Christian Indians, *mestizos,* and White Mexicans following the Mexican

American War, but my observations on the *afromestizos* have been limited. The federal government instituted a new racial project after the war and placed *afromestizos* under the legal mandates applied to U.S. Blacks. Theoretically, this made *afromestizos* part of the Black communities, and it is difficult to discern what happened in practice. Nonetheless, in my search to understand the history of the *afromestizos* I found countless sources in archives. I am convinced that this silenced history can be retrieved and am currently engaged in that task. For now, however, this endeavor is beyond the scope of my narrative. I do, however, want to add concluding comments and share my theoretical inquiries.

We know that in 1850 the U.S. Census counted 59,540 Black people residing in the Southwest (U.S. Census 1854: 160). Most of these people lived in Texas, and 58,161 of them were slaves. Free Blacks numbered 965 in California, 17 in New Mexico, and 397 in Texas (ibid.). In Arizona census enumerators did not identify any slave or free Black. Five years after the U.S. Civil War ended, in 1870, the size of the Black population of the Southwest had increased to 257,945 (U.S. Census 1872:20). Most of these people resided in Texas and were emancipated slaves. At that time California had a Black population of 4,272, New Mexico 172, and Arizona 26 (U.S. Census 1872:20).

My point in reviewing these demographic data is that following the Mexican American War a large number of Black slaves were transported to Texas and many free Blacks settled in California; these internal population movements obscure the history of the Mexican *afromestizos*. In Texas we are uncertain whether *afromestizos* became slaves, were deported, or continued to live among Mexicans. And in New Mexico we do not know whether they were deported or sought refuge in the Mexican or Indian towns. Likewise, since *afromestizos* in California obtained a legal position similar to that of *mestizos* it is uncertain whether they remained among Mexicans or mixed with U.S. Blacks. It is possible, however, that throughout the Southwest *afromestizos* sought refuge in the Mexican towns since they were after all Mexican and spoke Spanish rather than English (Forbes 1968:16, 1966:243–245). We must also not forget that *afromestizos* were racially mixed, and after the Mexican American War it was difficult to distinguish fair-complexioned *afromestizos* from darker Indians and *mestizos*. This certainly gave them an opportunity to pass for people of other races.

We also need to consider how *afromestizos* and other Mexican racial groups reacted to U.S. racial norms and were subsequently affected in the selection of marriage partners—especially since being Mexican and Black in the United States carried a double stigma. To complicate matters, perhaps the highly criticized observation made by Claude Lévi-Strauss (1982) in his classic book *Elementary Structures of Kinship* may be useful in evaluating this hypothetical quandary. According to Lévi-Strauss, regardless of a society's marriage taboos beautiful women are always sought after and lead men to break the marriage prohibitions of their families and communities. Keeping this thought in mind, and postmodernizing this structuralist analysis by changing the reference group from beautiful women to beautiful people, one can confidently presume that many people continued crossing racial boundaries.

This was quite possible, because after the Mexican American War U.S. marriage laws allowed *afromestizos* and most Mexicans to continue marrying each other—that is, as long as the Mexicans were not White. Following the war, Black people were permitted to marry Indians in California, Arizona, and Texas, but were prohibited from marrying Whites, including Mexicans placed in this legal category (California Stats., 1850, Chap. 140, p. 424, cited in *Perez v. Sharp*, 1948, p. 719; California Civil Code Sec. 69, cited in *Perez v. Sharp*, 1948, p. 712; *Penal Code of the State of Texas, Vol. 1,* Art. 492; Arizona CC 3837, cited in May 1929:47). Mexicans who were *mestizos* were permitted to marry Blacks in Texas, Arizona, and New Mexico, but not in California. California's antimiscegenation laws were very strict, and Mexicans who were one-half White could not marry Blacks (*Perez v. Sharp,* 1948). New Mexico did not have antimiscegenation laws (May 1929). Thus, excluding California, the marriage laws in the Southwest gave *afromestizos* the opportunity to continue marrying most Mexicans. The question, however, still remains: what community did *afromestizos* become part of?

Regardless, it is certain that *afromestizos* were among the founders of the first cities in the Southwest and that many Mexican Americans share that heritage. The myth that Black people never founded any major city in the United States should also be laid to rest, as it is clear that *afromestizos* were part of the population that founded Nacogdoches, San Antonio, Laredo, La Bahía, Albuquerque, Los Angeles, and Santa Barbara.

9

Racial Segregation and Liberal Policies Then and Now

In this historical narrative I have outlined the racial history of the Mexican Americans, identified and explored significant events influencing their racial heritage, and offered a critical analysis of the relations that evolved between Mexicans of different racial backgrounds. Under Spain's rule, Mexicans who were White enjoyed social and economic privileges not extended to Mexicans of color. However, as I have illustrated, due to a legacy of racial mixture under Spanish rule *mestizos* and *afromestizos* eventually shared some of the opportunities reserved for Whites. Following Mexican independence, both problems and progressive achievements transpired after Spain's racial order was dismantled. For Mexicans this period was short-lived, because the United States conquered the Southwest and reinstituted a racial order that gave people of color few civil rights. During the Anglo-American period, Mexicans who were White were extended the legal rights of U.S. citizens, while Mexicans of color experienced diverse forms of racial discrimination depending on their racial phenotype.

Before bringing my narrative to a close, I would like to examine the issue of when Mexicans in the United States were finally extended the political rights of U.S. citizens. After all, we know that today people of Mexican descent are no longer forbidden to become U.S. citizens on the basis of race. This discussion covers a liberal phase in United States racial history, between 1865 and 1898, when democratic philosophers enfranchised people of color and drafted legislation giving them the right to vote. Sadly, as we have seen in past decades, liberal reforms are often followed by a backlash. *De jure* segregation followed the enfranchisement of people of color, and Mexicans became part of the "colored" races who were not allowed legally to move freely among White people. Though restrictions on space and movement were already common practice, the novelty of legally sanctioned *de jure* segregation orders was that people of color no longer had the court system as a forum to object to segregation.[1]

Liberal Racial Legislation: The Thirteenth and Fourteenth Amendments

The legal foundation dismantling state and territorial laws preventing Mexicans from becoming United States citizens began in 1865 with the passage of the Thirteenth Amendment to the United States Constitution (Menchaca 1993:591). Though the amendment abolished slavery and involuntary servitude and was directed toward freeing Blacks, it became the foundation to improve the political status of Mexicans and other racial minority groups. Since Blacks had been emancipated, the question of whether they should be incorporated into the nation as voting citizens then arose. If Blacks were to be given such a right, the issue of whether all racial minorities should have the same rights had to be considered. The federal government determined that if racial minorities were to be allowed to vote, a federal law rescinding the states' right to prescribe citizenship requirements had to be enacted (Hyman and Wiecek 1982). The Fourteenth Amendment was passed in 1868 with the intention of legislating a uniform citizenship law and eliminating the states' rights to establish citizenship eligibility (U.S. Constitution, Amendment 14, Sec. 1, cited in Hyman and Wiecek 1982:517–531). Ironically, although the Fourteenth Amendment became the paramount law of the land and people born in the United States were granted full citizenship rights, including the right to vote, the amendment excluded the American Indians from its protection.

Throughout the late nineteenth century state governments prevented "American-born" racial minorities from exercising their citizenship rights under the Fourteenth Amendment (Kansas 1941). Anglo Americans argued that the spirit of the Fourteenth Amendment applied only to Blacks and Whites and that therefore Asians, American Indians, Mexicans, and "half-breeds" were not entitled to its protection. The account of Pablo De La Guerra illustrates the reluctance of government officials to extend Mexicans U.S. citizenship under the Fourteenth Amendment. As previously discussed, in 1870 Pablo De La Guerra was accused by the State of California of illegally acting as a U.S. citizen. In *People v. Pablo De La Guerra* (1870) attorneys for the state attempted to deny De La Guerra the political rights of a citizen by arguing that he was not part of the population who received citizenship under the Fourteenth Amendment. Though De La Guerra won the suit and was able to prove that his Indian lineage was too insignificant to rescind his classification as a White person, the state supreme court ruled that the Fourteenth Amendment did not apply to Mexicans who were clearly of Indian descent.

The government refused to grant Indians the right to obtain citizenship under the Fourteenth Amendment regardless of whether or not they adopted the lifestyle of Euro-Americans. A case in point is John Elk, an acculturated Indian who was denied that right in 1884. According to the U.S. Supreme Court in *Elk v. Wilkens,* Elk was technically a tribal Indian because his people had never enacted a treaty with the United States. Although Elk was a taxpayer, had terminated all relations with his reservation, and had served in the U.S. military, he was found unfit to claim citizenship. He was also denied the right to apply for naturalization, because Indians were ineligible: Indians could only become citizens by an act of Congress. With the *Elk v. Wilkens* ruling, the government made it clear that Indians were disqualified from applying for citizenship or naturalization. This law also applied to the Indians acquired from Mexico; the U.S. Supreme Court case *United States v. Sandoval,* though adjudicated nearly three decades later, illustrates that many Christian Indians were part of the populations included in the Elk decision.

In 1913 the U.S. Supreme Court upheld the Elk decision in *United States v. Sandoval.* Indians, including the Pueblo Indians of New Mexico, were not part of the populations who acquired citizenship under the Fourteenth Amendment. The Court ruled that only Congress had the power to determine which communities were Indian and when peoples ceased to be categorized as such (*U.S. v. Sandoval,* 1913:46). The Court added that Congress determined who was no longer an Indian by considering residence, family lineage, and cultural criteria and elaborated upon the standards used to classify communities as Indian: ". . . considering their Indian lineage, isolated and communal life, primitive customs and limited civilization, this assertion of guardianship over them cannot be said to be arbitrary but must be regarded as both authorized and controlling" (*U.S. v. Sandoval,* 1913:47).

Asian Americans, like Mexicans and Indians, were denied the right to claim citizenship under the Fourteenth Amendment because they were not White. An additional compelling argument was used against Asians. Paradoxically, government officials argued that American-born Asians who went on vacation to visit their parents' country of origin were to be legally considered immigrants when they returned (Konvitz 1946; *State of Nevada v. Ah Chew*, 1881). The rationale for this argument centered on the seditious ideology such a person supposedly acquired while abroad.

As large numbers of American racial minorities began to challenge the states' interpretations of the Fourteenth Amendment, their cases began to appear before the states' supreme courts. The U.S. Supreme Court was then pressured to offer a final and uniform decision on two citizenship questions. Were non-Black racial minorities who had been born in the United States citizens? And if they were, should they be entitled to full political rights? In 1898 the case of *United States v. Wong Kim Ark* reached the U.S. Supreme Court, and the racial questions were resolved.[2] The Supreme Court ruled that a child born in the United States acquired citizenship by virtue of the Fourteenth Amendment and that race and national origin could not be used to deny a person the right of citizenship. The Court also ruled that the Civil Rights Act of 1866 (Chap. 31, Secs. 1–6) guaranteed all persons born in the United States (and not subject to any foreign power), regardless of racial background, full and equal benefit of the laws enjoyed by White citizens.

Ironically, the Court exempted the majority of the American Indians, the rationale being that the spirit and language of the Fourteenth Amendment were based on the principles of the Civil Rights Act of 1866, which exempted most American Indians. Indians were allegedly exempt because they refused to relinquish their tribal government. Interestingly, the comments of Justice C. J. Fuller, who offered the dissenting opinion, evoke a glimpse of the opinions held by powerful men in those times. Justices Fuller and J. Harlan proposed that there was nothing wrong in denying certain races citizenship. Justice Fuller stated: "I am of opinion that the President and Senate by treaty, and the Congress by naturalization . . . have the power . . . to prescribe that all persons of a particular race, or their children, cannot become citizens" (*United States v. Wong Kim Ark*, 1898:732).

Following the *Wong Kim Ark* decision, Mexicans born in the United States were in theory guaranteed the full legal rights of citizenship. This ruling only applied to Mexicans born in the United States, however, because Mexican immigrants of color came under different racial laws. During the nineteenth century, many Mexican immigrants were denied the opportunity to become citizens because the naturalization laws of the period only applied to Whites (Menchaca 1993). This was damaging to the Mexican population as the era of Mexican migration began to unfold in the 1880s (Galarza 1964). Thousands of Mexicans were entering the United States in an attempt to reunite their families separated by the U.S.-Mexican border and to escape economic turmoil in Mexico. By 1890 there were over 77,853 Mexican immigrants in the United States, with the majority residing in Texas and California (U.S. Census 1894:cxxvi).[3]

During the late nineteenth century, as a result of economic problems in Mexico, Mexican migration steadily continued to increase (Acuña 1972). Because the Mexican government was unable to stimulate economic growth, there were insufficient jobs available in Mexico. The landed elite took advantage of the situation and continued to offer substandard wages because there was an oversupply of labor in Mexico. People working in agriculture did not receive a decent living wage (Galarza 1964). Exacerbating matters, in Mexico's northern region small-scale farmers experienced several periods of drought and were unable to produce enough crops to sustain their families. With such economic problems confronting thousands of Mexicans, many chose to leave and migrate north toward the United States.

These events converged with an economic boom in the Southwest. Buildings were being constructed, canals and roads were being built, industries were growing, and agriculture was thriving. In particular, the economy of California was growing as a result of the success of the agricultural sector and the evolution of the Mexican land grant system. By the 1880s, throughout California, eastern capitalists purchased most of the Mexican land grants and converted them into agricultural estates or what are commonly known as factories in the fields (Galarza 1964). Thousands of farm jobs became available in California and in other parts of the Southwest. The availability of jobs stimulated Mexican migration to the Southwest, whereas the lack of jobs in Mexico pushed people out. Unfortunately, though the U.S. government allowed Mexican immigrants to enter and work, it only allowed White immigrants to become naturalized U.S. citizens.

Dismantling Racist Naturalization Laws

In the nineteenth century Mexican immigrants who planned to participate in U.S. electoral politics and receive other political rights had to obtain citizenship by way of naturalization. For Mexicans and other racial minorities the process was arduous. Racial minorities did not have the right to apply for naturalization merely because they were immigrants (Hull 1985; Kansas 1941; Konvitz 1946). On the contrary, from 1790 to 1940 only "free white immigrants"—and after 1870 Black immigrants—were extended the privilege of naturalization (Naturalization Act of 1790, Chap. 3, Sec. 1; Naturalization Act of 1795, Chap. 20, Stat. 2, Sec. 1; Naturalization Act of 1802, Chap. 28, Stat. 1; Naturalization Rev. Stat. of 1870, Sec. 2169). If Mexican immigrants wanted to be naturalized, they had to prove that they were eligible to apply because they were White (Padilla 1979); they also had to prove that they were not Indian, because the naturalization eligibility requirements excluded Indians. In effect the naturalization process discouraged Mexican immigrants from asserting their indigenous heritage within the legal system.

It is difficult to determine how many Mexican immigrants were successful in obtaining naturalization and how many were turned down on the basis of race (Hull 1985). The case of In re Rodriguez (1897), however, delineates the type of rationale used by the naturalization board to exclude Mexican immigrants. In 1897 Ricardo Rodriguez, a citizen of Mexico, filed in the county court of Bexar County, Texas, his intention to become a citizen of the United States (In re Rodriguez, 1897:337). His application was denied on the ground that he was an Indian and therefore not eligible to apply for citizenship. Rodriguez appealed, and his case was heard by the San Antonio Circuit Court. In his defense, Rodriguez argued that although his ancestry was Indian he no longer practiced Indian traditions and knew nothing about that culture.

The naturalization board contested Rodriguez's right to apply for naturalization, arguing that the federal government did not extend this privilege to non-Whites other than Blacks. The board, represented by attorney A. J. Evans, asserted that although many Mexicans were White and qualified for naturalization, most Mexicans, like Rodriguez, were Indian and thus ineligible to be naturalized (Naturalization Rev. Stat. of 1870, Sec. 2169). Evans argued that Rodriguez was unmistakably Indian in appearance:

> I challenge the right of the applicant to become a citizen of the United States, on the ground that he is not a man or person entitled to be naturalized. . . . [The] applicant is a native-born person of

Mexico, 38 years old, and of pure Aztec or Indian race. . . . The population of Mexico comprises about six million Indians of unmixed blood, nearly one-half of whom are nomadic savage tribes, . . . about 5 million whites or creoles . . . and twenty-five thousand . . . mestizos, or half-breeds derived from the union of the whites and Indians. . . . Now it is clear . . . from the appearance of the applicant, that he is one of the 6,000,000 Indians of unmixed blood. . . . If an Indian, he cannot be naturalized. (*In re Rodriguez*, 1897:346–347)

Evans's colleagues, Floyd McGown and T. J. McMinn, presented supporting legal cases to contest Rodriguez's naturalization application. Offering several precedents in which racial minorities had been denied the privilege of naturalization, they argued that the federal government had made it very clear that only Blacks and Americans of pure European descent were eligible. McGown and McMinn stated that the precedent for denying Mexican immigrants the right to apply for naturalization had been set in 1878 by *In re Ah Yup*. In that case the circuit court of California had ruled that the Chinese were not White and therefore were ineligible to apply for citizenship. The attorneys argued that *In re Ah Yup* indisputably applied to Mexicans because everyone knew that Chinese, Mexicans, and Indians were Mongolians. That argument was their ethnological analysis.

The attorneys then stated that the decision to exclude "half-breed" immigrants from citizenship had also been upheld by the government in the case of *In re Camille* (1880), in which the circuit court of Oregon had ruled that "half-breed" Indians were not White and therefore not eligible for naturalization. Using *In re Camille* as their precedent, the attorneys for the board of naturalization argued that Mexican *mestizos* were disqualified from applying for naturalization because the court had ruled that a person must be at least three-quarters White to receive the privileges of a White citizen. They also appealed to a Utah Supreme Court decision on a Hawaiian immigrant (*In re Kanaka Nian*, 1889) as evidence that racial minorities who inhabited conquered territories were ineligible for naturalization. Employing unsubstantiated rhetoric, Evans and McGown asserted that inhabitants of ceded territories, such as Hawaii and the Mexican northwest, could not apply for naturalization. Because Kanaka Nian had been born in Hawaii and Rodriguez in Mexico, neither one was eligible.

The final case used to challenge Rodriguez's right to naturalization was the U.S. Supreme Court case *Elk v. Wilkens* (1884). The attorneys representing the board of naturalization argued that *Elk v. Wilkens* clearly indicated that the U.S. government had never intended to naturalize Indians, even those who were acculturated or had terminated their tribal relations. Therefore, they concluded Mexicans were ineligible because everyone knew that the true Mexican was an acculturated Indian. In sum, the attorneys for the board argued on the basis of race against extending Rodriguez the right to apply for naturalization. In supporting arguments they alleged that the Treaty of Guadalupe Hidalgo did not have naturalization powers, and they concluded by opining that acculturation did not transform an Indian into a White person.

The dissenting opinion was offered by T. M. Paschal in defense of Rodriguez. Paschal's opinion clearly supported Rodriguez, yet it had a racist tone and indicated an intolerant attitude toward cultural diversity. Paschal argued that Rodriguez was an undesirable candidate for naturalization and should be denied that right based on the fact that he was an Indian and an ignorant Mexican who was unable to read or write Spanish or English. Paschal asserted, however, that the federal laws of the land had to be upheld by the district courts and that Mexican immigrants had to be given the right to apply for citizenship. He argued that when the Treaty of Guadalupe Hidalgo was ratified the United States agreed to extend Mexican citizens the same political privileges enjoyed by Whites. Therefore, Paschal proposed, if the U.S. government had agreed to treat the Mexicans of the ceded territory as "White," then the same treatment had to be extended to Mexican immigrants, irrespective of race. Paschal concluded that although Rodriguez was an Indian, the racial precedents set by the *In re Ah Yup, In re Camille, In re Kanaka Nian,* and *Elk v. Wilkens* cases did not apply to Mexicans, for the U.S. government had agreed to extend them the privileges of Whites. Naturalizing Rodriguez, he argued, would not violate the racial clauses of the naturalization laws. To provide further evidence that Rodriguez was eligible, Paschal asked Rodriguez to testify in his own behalf and prove to the court that he no longer identified himself as Indian. The counsel's questions and Rodriguez's replies follow:

Q. Do you not believe that you belong to the original Aztec race in Mexico?

A. No, Sir.

Q. Where did your race come from? Spain?

A. No, Sir.

Q. Does you family claim any religion? What religion do they profess?

A. Catholic religion.

Paschal then said: "The supporting affidavits show upon their face that the applicant is attached to the principles of the constitution of the United States, and well disposed to the good order and happiness of the same" (*In re Rodriguez*, 1897:338). District Judge Maxey concurred with Paschal's defense. Maxey concluded that Rodriguez was eligible for naturalization based on international laws of territorial cession and on his having proven that he was no longer an Indian.

Interestingly, Elizabeth Hull (1985) argues that although a large number of Mexican immigrants were naturalized in the early twentieth century it was not until 1940 that the U.S. government changed the language of the naturalization laws and without a doubt conferred that privilege on Mexican Indians. According to Hull, it was only with passage of the Nationality Act of 1940 that the U.S. government formally allowed indigenous immigrants from the Western hemisphere to obtain naturalization rights and only with several revisions of the act that it allowed all "non-White immigrants" to obtain citizenship. Chinese were granted that privilege in 1943, Japanese in 1945, Filipinos and East Indians in 1946, and all others in 1952 (Hull 1985:19–22; Konvitz 1946:115).

De Jure Racial Segregation as a Response to Reverse Discrimination

In the aftermath of the Thirteenth and Fourteenth Amendments, when the legal foundations were set to forge a more equitable America where democracy could be shared by everyone in the republic, a backlash soon followed. Many government officials and White citizens who opposed the new liberal policies responded by demanding that limits be set upon the freedom of movement and civil rights extended to people of color. *De jure* segregation became the most appealing way to counterattack the gains made by racial minorities and liberal thinkers. In the late 1800s, when *de jure* segregation was enacted at the federal level, the question of whether or not the Mexican people came under the mandate of segregationist "Jim Crow" laws became salient. Because the federal government had failed to designate a racial category for Mexican people, their racial status in the courts remained ambiguous. The government acknowledged that most Mexicans were partly White, but because of their Indian ancestry it failed to classify them as Caucasian (Padilla 1979). Classifying them as Indian, since most were of that heritage, was politically problematic, however, because they did not practice a tribal government. There is evidence indicating that in the Southwest dark-complexioned Mexicans were segregated from Whites. In several judicial cases non-White people of Mexican origin were discriminated against by the U.S. legal system. To introduce this discussion, I will briefly review the first major segregationist cases to come before the U.S. Supreme Court, *Robinson and Wife v. Memphis and Charleston Railroad Company* (1883) and *Plessy v. Ferguson* (1896). These cases illustrate both the rationale for passing national segregationist laws and the rationale for including non-White Mexicans under those laws.

In 1883 the landmark segregationist ruling in *Robinson and Wife v. Memphis and Charleston Railroad Company* legally allowed the exclusion of racial minorities from hotels, restaurants, parks, public conveyances, and public amusement parks. This ruling also upheld the right of business owners to provide segregated services for racial minorities or to refuse them services. The arguments of subsequent segregationist laws were structured or supported by this Supreme Court decision, and they were not completely overturned until passage of the Civil Rights Act of 1964 (Salinas 1973).

The significance of the Robinson case was that it successfully overturned the liberal Civil Rights Act of 1875, which had prohibited discrimination on the basis of race, religion, and national origin. Sections 1 and 2 of the act were overturned because of their allegedly unconstitutional implications, for the Court concluded that they advocated reverse discrimination against Whites. The majority opinion was that allowing racial minorities to be in public places forced Whites to interact with them and thus violated the civil rights of White people. It also stated that excluding non-Whites from public places was not a violation of the Thirteenth and Fourteenth amendments because interacting with Whites was a privilege and not a right for racial minorities.

Thirteen years after the *Robinson* ruling, *Plessy v. Ferguson* (1896) was deliberated by the U.S. Supreme Court. This case became the most devastating segregationist ruling to date, as the Court legalized all forms of social segregation, including school segregation. The ruling also provided more specific language about who could legally be segregated. In *Plessy* the Supreme Court justices addressed the problem of racial classifications, ruling that for purposes of segregation every state had the right to determine who was White and who was non-White. It also gave each state the power to decide if any racial minority group should be segregated. That is, although the Court did not mandate that "all racial minorities" be segregated, it supported the states' rights to institute segregation if the state legislators so desired. The *Plessy* decision served to reinforce the Mexicans' inferior political status. During the era of *de jure* segregation, the indigenous heritage of Mexican-origin people linked them to the people of color, and dark-complexioned Mexicans could be racially segregated.

In Colorado and Texas, for example, people of Mexican origin were legally excluded from public facilities reserved for Whites. In *Lueras v. Town of Lafayette* (1937) and *Terrell Wells Swimming Pool v. Rodríguez* (1944), the courts concluded that Mexicans were not White and therefore were not entitled to use public facilities. Although the two Mexicans in these cases argued that they were of Spanish descent, their dark skin color indicated that they were racially mixed, and thus they lost the trials. Furthermore, in Texas a study conducted by the Inter-American Committee in 1943 found that over 117 towns in Texas practiced social segregation against Mexicans and most passed *de jure* segregation laws (Kibbe 1946:211–223). These social customs and laws ranged from Anglo Americans' prohibiting Mexicans from entering restaurants to demanding that they use separate facilities. Mexicans were forced to use separate bathrooms and drinking fountains and sit in separate sections of restaurants and theaters.

Social scientists Albert Camarillo (1984), Guadalupe Salinas (1973), and Gilbert Gonzalez (1990) report that similar civil rights injustices occurred in California and Arizona during the same period. Likewise, educational historian Rubén Donato and I have documented detailed case studies of social segregation in California. In Santa Paula city policies were used to maintain the Mexican and White students in separate schools, and violence was used by the Ku Klux Klan to intimidate Mexicans into accepting a segregated society (Menchaca 1995; see Photograph 40). For example, Mexicans were forced to live on the East Side of Santa Paula and only shop in stores on that side of town. Rubén Donato (1997) reported

Photograph 40. Ku Klux Klan Burning a Cross in Santa Paula, California, 1924. Courtesy of the Ventura County Museum of History and Art.

a similar situation in Brownfield, California, and found that educational segregation was the most blatant form of racial separation imposed by local policymakers.

School segregation cases serve as further illustration of racial discrimination against dark-complexioned Mexican-origin people. Although the rationales used to segregate Mexican students ranged from racial to social-deficit justifications (including language, intelligence quotients, and the "infectious diseases of Mexicans"), some legislators attempted to segregate Mexican students on the ground that most of them were non-White (Wollenberg 1974).

California provides the best examples of how the indigenous racial ancestry of the Mexican students was used to place them under the mandate of *de jure* segregation. During the 1920s and 1930s, government officials attempted to classify Mexican students as Indians; their intent was to pass a paramount state law that would give all school boards the unquestionable right to segregate Mexicans (Donato, Menchaca, and Valencia 1991:35). On 23 January 1927 State Attorney General U. S. Webb offered the opinion that Mexicans could be treated as Indians and therefore should be placed under *de jure* segregation (Hendrick 1977:56). At this time, however, a state law allowing Mexicans to be segregated under *Plessy v. Ferguson* could not be applied to all Mexicans because many were White. Nonetheless, in 1930 the attorney general again issued a similar opinion (Gonzalez 1990). According to Webb, Mexicans were Indians and therefore should not be treated as White: "It is well known that the greater portion of the population of Mexico are Indians and when such Indians migrate to the United States they are subject to the laws applicable generally to other Indians" (cited in Weinberg 1977:166). The opinion of the attorney general, however, once again failed to convince state legislators that most Mexicans were Indian.

In 1935 the California legislature finally passed legislation officially segregating certain Mexican students on the ground that they were Indian. Though the school code exempted Mexicans who were White, it clearly applied to Mexicans of Indian descent. Without explicitly mentioning Mexicans, the code prescribed that schools segregate Mexicans of Indian descent who were not American Indians:

> The governing board of the school district shall have power to establish separate schools for Indian children, excepting children of Indians who are wards of the United States government and children of all other Indians who are descendants of the original American Indians of the United States, and for children of Chinese, Japanese, or Mongolian parentage. (cited in Hendrick 1977:57)

The ambiguous school code made Mexican students the principal target of discrimination and released American Indians from mandated school segregation (Donato, Menchaca, and Valencia 1991; Gonzalez 1990). Dark-complexioned Mexican students could be classified as Indians, and the segregationist educational codes could be applied to them. California school boards now had the legal right to use race as a rationale to segregate certain Mexicans.

During the early 1930s, the two states with the largest concentrations of Mexicans practiced school segregation on a large scale. In Texas most schools teaching Mexican students were racially segregated by 1930 (Rangel and Alcala 1972:313–318). In California 85 percent of the Mexican students were in segregated schools or classrooms by 1931 (Hendrick 1977:90). The rationales for segregating Mexican students varied, however, as schools could not use race to segregate White Mexican students.

The case of *Independent School District v. Salvatierra* (1930) illustrates this point. In 1930 the Mexican community of Del Rio, Texas, won a partial victory when it proved in court that the Del Rio Independent School District had unlawfully segregated White Mexican students (Rangel and

Alcala 1972). The attorneys for the school board justified the segregation-ist actions by arguing that the Texas legislature, the U.S. Constitution, and federal statutes allowed government agencies to segregate Mexican students when it was necessary. They also argued that the district had primarily segregated non-White Mexican students. Judge Joseph Jones ruled that because half the Mexican population in Del Rio was Spanish and belonged to the White race, not all of the Mexican students were subject to the mandates of *de jure* segregation. The judge also ruled, however, that the Del Rio school board would not be asked to rescind its actions. First, the school board had not acted with malice when it segregated the Mexican students of Spanish descent. The judge proposed that this error resulted from the failure of the Texas courts to determine whether all Mexicans belonged to the same race. Second, because federal statutes on treaties had recently allowed government agencies to reverse treaty agreements, the school board had the right to segregate any Mexican student who did not speak English (*Independent School District v. Salvatierra*, 1930:794). The judge concluded that because a large number of the Mexican students were White it would be unjust to segregate Mexicans arbitrarily. White Mexican students, therefore, could be segregated only if they did not speak English.

Gilbert Gonzalez (1990) proposes that the Del Rio Independent School District case set the legal precedent cautioning school boards in the Southwest not to use race as the only justification for segregating Mexican students. After the Del Rio incident other rationales were often used to legitimate school segregation, but they were only smokescreens for racism. A case in point is *Roberto Alvarez v. Lemon Grove School District* (1931), in which a California school board used language as a justification for segregating Mexican students (see Alvarez 1986; Gonzalez 1990). In this case, however, the court ruled in favor of the Mexican community and ordered the desegregation of the Mexican students (Alvarez 1986), arguing that separate facilities for Mexican students were not conducive to their Americanization. Americanization symbolically meant the right to be acculturated into the Anglo-Saxon society (Gonzalez 1990).

Liberal Legislation: The End of *De Jure* Segregation

In 1947 the era of *de jure* segregation in the schools finally came to an end for the Mexican community of the Southwest. *Mendez v. Westmin-*

ster (1946, 1947) ended *de jure* segregation in California and provided the legal foundation for overturning the school segregation of Mexican students throughout the Southwest. In that case, Judge Paul J. McCormick ruled that the school board had segregated Mexicans on the basis of their "Latinized" appearance and had gerrymandered the school district in order to ensure that Mexican students would attend schools apart from Whites (Wollenberg 1974). He decided that neither *Plessy* nor the 1935 educational code of California applied to Mexican students because there was no federal law stipulating that all Mexicans were Indian (Gonzalez 1990). The judge also concluded that the segregation of Mexican students was illegal because the Fourteenth Amendment had guaranteed Mexicans equal rights in the United States. The Westminster school board appealed the ruling, but the U.S. Circuit Court of Appeals in San Francisco upheld the decision on 14 April 1947 (Gonzalez 1990).

Mendez was later used in Texas and Arizona to desegregate Mexican students (*Delgado v. Bastrop*, 1948, *Gonzales v. Sheely*, 1954, cited in Donato, Menchaca, and Valencia 1991:37–38). Educational segregation at the national level was finally overturned in 1954 when the U.S. Supreme Court ruled in *Brown v. the Board of Education of Topeka* (1954) that all forms of educational segregation were against the law. *Plessy v. Ferguson* (1896) was finally overturned in the area of education: school segregation was ruled to be unconstitutional under the Fourteenth Amendment because separate schools led to unequal education. Although schools were ordered to desegregate, many refused to do so. In the case of Mexican-origin students, at the national level, in 1968 nearly 50 percent of students in kindergarten to twelfth grade attended segregated schools (Donato, Menchaca, and Valencia 1991:28–29).

In 1961 the federal government acknowledged that racial minorities were socially segregated and discriminated against by majority group members (*Austin American-Statesman*, 26 March 1995, p. C-1). That year President John F. Kennedy issued an Executive Order creating the President's Committee on Equal Employment Opportunity, charged with recommending "affirmative steps" to achieve racial diversity in the labor force at all levels. Kennedy targeted the employment sector because it was common knowledge that racial minorities were underrepresented in many fields, often as a result of racial discrimination (Takaki 1990). By improving the employment opportunities of racial minorities, the adverse effects of racial segregation could be temporarily alleviated. All employers receiving federal funds were prohibited from discriminating in employment practices on the basis of race, creed, color, or national origin.

A few years later, the federal government recognized that it had not gone far enough in its efforts to eradicate racial discrimination. Merely ordering equal opportunity in some sectors of the labor market meant nothing unless there was a mechanism to ensure equal access. In 1964 the Civil Rights Act was passed, prohibiting discrimination on the basis of race, national origin, and religion. Under the act all forms of *de jure* segregation became illegal, as well as employment discrimination (Takaki 1994). An addendum to the act a year later prohibited gender discrimination. In the area of employment the act of 1964 gave people the right to turn to the courts if they were discriminated against. If employers were found guilty of discrimination, the courts could order firms to reinstate and compensate employees. If necessary, employers could also be fined by the courts.

In 1965 President Lyndon B. Johnson continued to institute liberal policies and issued an order requiring all agencies receiving federal contracts to take affirmative action against employment discrimination in all business operations, not just in fulfilling federal contracts (*Austin American-Statesman*, 26 March 1995, p. C-1). The order required "numerical goals and timetables" for improvement but did not mandate specific dates or quotas. Employers were required to recruit women and racial minorities by ensuring that such people would be included in the interview process. They were not required, however, to hire any specific person. The goal of affirmative action was to diversify the applicant pool and thereby give women and minorities the opportunity to compete (Jones 1981). In 1972 the U.S. Congress passed the Equal Employment Opportunity Act, allowing the Equal Employment Opportunity Commission to bring civil lawsuits against companies for discriminatory employment practices. The law was amended to allow the federal government to sue state and local governments. In essence the federal government instated the legal mechanisms to make equal opportunity accessible to racial minorities and women by pressuring employers to comply.

During this liberal phase, the U.S. Supreme Court finally prohibited the states from passing antimiscegenation marriage laws. In 1967 in *Loving v. Virginia* the justices ruled that the states had the power to "police" marriage contracts, but could no longer prohibit Whites from marrying people of different races. They concluded that it was a violation of the Fourteenth Amendment to prohibit a person from marrying freely (*Loving v. Virginia*, 1967:1011).

Though *Loving v. Virginia* was a national landmark decision, for Mexican-origin people antimiscegenation laws had been struck down nearly two decades earlier in the case of Andrea Perez, a Mexican woman who had been prohibited from marrying a Black man because the state of California included her as part of the legally defined White population. She refused to comply and took her case to the courts. In *Perez v. Sharp* (1948) the California Supreme Court ruled that it was against the law to prohibit Catholics who were White from marrying Blacks or any person on the basis of race. Specifically, the court ruled that prohibiting Catholics who were less than one-half Indian from marrying Blacks violated the Fourteenth Amendment. Andrea Perez was finally allowed to marry Sylvester Davis, a Black man. To prohibit her from doing so would have violated her constitutional right of religious freedom. *Perez v. Sharp* subsequently became the precedent case allowing Mexicans who were White to marry freely, and most important of all it became one of the main cases used to strike down antimiscegenation laws at the national level (Sickels 1972). The California ruling had set the precedent allowing marriage to be included as part of the rights guaranteed under the Fourteenth Amendment.

Accompanying this liberal decision were complementary congressional legislation and U.S. Supreme Court rulings improving the economic status of women. These rulings were very important because women of Mexican descent and other women of color were discriminated against by the double burden of discriminatory gender labor market practices. The Equal Pay Act was passed in 1963, requiring that men and women receive the same pay for the same labor performed (Cary and Peratis 1977:75). As a result of the Civil Rights Act of 1964 women obtained the right to take their gender discrimination cases to court. When their cases reached the federal courts, specific language was drafted prohibiting discrimination on the basis of a woman's body or because a woman was a mother.

In 1971 women won a series of federal cases litigated by the circuit courts and the U.S. Supreme Court. Under *Sprogis v. United Air Lines* (1971; Cary and Peratis 1977:56) employers could no longer institute discriminatory marriage policies that only applied to women. Before 1971 it was legal to prohibit women from marrying in certain professions, while excluding men from the same requirement. Most important of all, in *Rosenfeld v. Southern Pacific Company* (1971; Cary and Peratis 1977:55) companies were ordered to cease using height and weight requirements to prohibit women from entering management positions or from being promoted. Requiring certain "body shapes" that had nothing to do with fulfilling a job description was deemed illegal. Under *Phillips v. Martin Marietta Corporation* (1971; Cary and Peratis 1977:57) employers could no longer fire or refuse to promote a woman because she was the mother of young children. Finally, in 1978 the U.S. Congress passed the Pregnancy Discrimination Act, prohibiting employers from firing, not hiring, or discriminating against a woman because she was pregnant.

In sum, during the 1960s to 1970s the federal government attempted to protect racial minorities and women from different forms of discrimination. At this time gender and racial discrimination was not eradicated, but its legal infrastructure experienced a severe blow. Unfortunately, though many people in the United States favored the protectionist legislation directed toward women, they were not all in agreement with the federal positions taken on affirmative action and racial minorities. The political gains made by racial minorities came under attack.

The Charge of Reverse Discrimination

The same year that the U.S. Congress passed the Pregnancy Discrimination Act and warned employers not to discriminate against women, racial minorities lost ground when federal support began to erode. In 1978 *Regents of the University of California v. Bakke* evoked a bewildering replication of the same reverse discrimination sentiments expressed nearly a century earlier, including complaints against the Thirteenth and Fourteenth amendments (Takaki 1994:24).[4] Whites who perceived themselves to be harmed by the legal gains made by racial minorities cried out "reverse discrimination." The issue of "space" once again entered the court for deliberation, similar to the way in which it had been litigated during the segregationist ruling *Robinson and Wife v. Memphis and Charleston Railroad Company* (1883). In both *Bakke* and *Robinson* the persons who benefited from federal protection were upwardly mobile racial minorities who were accused of benefiting from reverse discrimination policies. In *Robinson and Wife* an upwardly mobile light-complexioned Black woman and her White husband sat in the railway's first-class section, reserved for Whites only. White passengers reacted by charging that these people were polluting their social space. In *Bakke* the question of space once again surfaced: the case dealt with the allegedly unconstitutional nature of reserving space in college admissions for racial minorities aspiring to become medical doctors. Interestingly, both cases dealt with White reactions against minorities who trespassed racially defined boundaries when they proactively attempted to enjoy the social privileges reserved for upwardly mobile Whites.

Regents of the University of California v. Bakke (1978) was the first major antiaffirmative action case to reach the U.S. Supreme Court (*Austin American-Statesman*, 26 March 1995, p. C-1). Allan Bakke, who is White, claimed the medical school's admission policy, which reserved 16 of 100 seats in each year's class for racial minorities, was reverse discrimination. The Supreme Court ruled that quotas were unconstitutional for educational purposes, but also ruled that it was not unconstitutional to pay "some attention" to race in deciding which students should be admitted.

Since *Bakke* the charge of "reverse discrimination" has been taken up by many Whites who profess that racial minorities have improved their social standing at their economic expense (see Valencia and Solorzano 1997). In response to the mobility experienced by some racial minorities, many conservative Whites joined local interest groups to undo the policies of the 1960s (Omi and Winant 1994:118–119). People sharing these views range from neoconservatives to individuals organized into "Far Right" movements.

Neoconservatives argue that the United States should become a "color blind society" because race does not matter any longer. They believe that the federal government should not be involved in employee hiring practices because affirmative action constitutes reverse discrimination; they are also against the government's participation in any form of school desegregation and propose that people should attend school with those who are similar to themselves (Valencia 1991). Instead, they promote the view that economic disparities between Whites and racial minorities are a result of the failure of racial minorities to value education and hard work (D'Sousa 1995). Neoconservatives profess that discrimination in the labor market is a myth—therefore they call for Congress to repeal the Civil Rights Act of 1964 (D'Sousa 1995).

Less sympathetic Far Right political activists share these views, but believe the root of all economic problems in the United States is racial desegregation. Their recommendation is to segregate racial minorities in neighborhoods or reservations and end immigration from Latin America, Asia, and Africa (see Valencia and Solorzano 1997; Omi and Winant 1994). To them, racial minorities are culturally and biologically inferior; when they marry or mix socially with Whites, they teach White people bad habits and contribute to the biological degeneration of the White race.

Though neoconservatives want to repeal the Civil Rights Act of 1964 and end all government intervention in school desegregation, they do not share the view that racial minorities should be resegregated in all domains of social life (D'Sousa 1995). I nonetheless wonder how this less antagonistic view on school desegregation can be justified when Mexican Americans and Blacks have yet to be desegregated. In 1988, 68 percent of Latinos (two-thirds of whom were Mexican-origin) and 63 percent of Blacks attended segregated K–12 schools (Orfield and Monfort 1992:3, 7). How can some people propose that there are no economic disparities between Whites and racial minorities when the 1990 U.S. Census reported that the median income of White families was $37,628, compared to $23,714 for Mexican Americans and $22,429 for Blacks (Feagin and Feagin 1999:98, 284, 310, 318) and $23,329 for American Indians (Feagin 1996:218; Feagin and Feagin 1999:224)? It is a paradox how measures to dismantle federal protectionist legislation are being called for when the federal government has not eradicated the vestiges of legally sanctioned school segregation. Is school desegregation not important in light of the fact that schooling has been identified as one of the main societal gatekeepers of economic success?

This is a bleak scenario of the present. History has taught me that this is merely a phase, however, and the battle to eradicate racial discrimination is ongoing. In writing this historical narrative, I have learned that under the governments of Spain, Mexico, and the United States there have been many White people who did not agree with their nation's racial laws and actively sought to institute liberal policies that were more racially equitable. Though I must end this racial history of the Mexican Americans at a bleak moment in time, the Epilogue about my relatives' personal racial history offers an upbeat note and a glimpse at how anthropological field methods can illuminate the way racial identity is conditioned by past experiences. These auto/ethnographic observations show that U.S. racial policies have strongly influenced the racial identities of some Mexican Americans and American Indians.

Epilogue

Auto/ethnographic Observations of Race and History

Auto/ethnography is a method that has been used in anthropology since the mid-1970s (Reed-Donahay 1997), combining autobiography or biography with ethnography. In a traditional ethnography an anthropologist interviews people, conducts observations, collects documents, and often reviews newspapers. When autobiography or biography is interjected in an ethnographic study, the field research becomes more personal and the anthropologist also becomes a subject of study. In writing the conclusion of this book I chose to use auto/ethnography as a means of continuing to personalize my narrative. As I stated in the Introduction, the racial history of the Mexican Americans is about "a people," but it is also about myself. While I have written an objective history, I recognize that I chose which historical scenes to stage in my drama. This is a subjective writing process that does not differ in the production of any type of historical text—all authors select the scenes they stage (Said 1979; White 1992). The use of auto/ethnography allows me to end my book with commentaries on the present and in this way to illuminate some dark shadows in history that can only be clarified by sharing personal stories.

I have chosen to focus on the history of my husband, Richard Valencia, because many stories of his relatives illustrate how California's mid-nineteenth-century racial policies unfolded and eventually had an impact on the federal government's classification of people of Chumash descent. Likewise, his family history shows how the government's racial categories influenced his relatives' racial identity. Some members of Richard's family have been classified by the Bureau of Indian Affairs as Native Americans, while others with a similar blood quantum are not classified as such.

Currently two of Richard's brothers and sisters consider themselves to be full-blooded Chumash, while the others believe they are racially mixed and share a similar blood quantum with most Mexicans—Indian and White. Of Richard's ten brothers and sisters only Betty Valencia-Cruz and Manuel Valencia consider themselves to be full-blooded Chumash. Based on my conversations with his family, it is my belief that the difference in their racial identification is largely because their mother married more than once. One of her husbands was a Chumash Indian, while the others were Mexicans of Chumash descent. In the interviews I held with my husband Richard, his sisters, Betty Valencia-Cruz and Martha Gonzalez, and his niece, Elena Gonzalez, as well as past conversations I have had with his relatives, I was told that their family was raised in a bicultural Mexican-Chumash environment. Family members heatedly disagree about whether the Chumash or Mexican culture predominated, however. They only concur on the fact that their community was racially segregated and their neighborhood was multicultural and multiracial: Mexican American, Chumash, and Black. As adults, however, four chose to identify as Chumash, while the rest preferred to identify as Mexican American. Only Betty and Manuel are officially registered on the BIA Native American registry.

Richard's family's racial history is based on oral narratives supplemented by anthropological and historical studies written about his relatives. I conducted the oral narratives in several visits during the mid-1990s and spent ten days with his family in 1999. During my last trip, I conducted several life-history interviews with Betty and Martha and also interviewed Elena, Martha's daughter. The setting is California, specifically the cities of Montecito, Santa Barbara, and Santa Inés. The main characters of my account are Evarista Romero, Richard's great-grandmother, and Rafael Solares, the great-grandfather of Raymond Gonzalez, who is Martha's husband, Elena's father, and Richard's brother-in-law. I have selected to focus on Evarista and Rafael because Evarista's account informs us why many Chumash *ranchería* people chose to fade into the Mexican community after the Mexican American War, while Rafael's account illustrates the experiences of many mission Indians who did not abandon their native customs and their tribal political identification.

Evarista Romero: Cultural Strategies of Self-Defense

Richard's great-grandmother Evarista Romero lived to be 103 years old (*Santa Barbara News Press*, 29 November 1959, p. 2). She lived in Montecito, California, her entire life and died in 1959. Montecito is a small city adjacent to Santa Barbara and today is an exclusive community where mansions are the most common residences. Its commercial zone caters to elites and is full of four-star restaurants and shopping centers where only affluent people can afford to shop. Evarista passed on to her descendants many stories about her Chumash ancestry, but also related to her kinfolk how it came about that many Chumash people became incorporated into the Mexican American community and faded as a distinct ethnic group. I collected Evarista's stories from Richard and his sisters Martha and Betty. They heard these historical narratives from Evarista and from Verónica Ruiz, who was their mother and Evarista's granddaughter. Betty was the most knowledgeable of the three and had newspaper clippings and old photographs to corroborate her account.

Evarista's parents were Chumash people from Santa Barbara. They moved to Montecito around the early 1800s. She told Richard and Betty the name of her parents' village, but they did not recall it. I believe, however, that her village was called Chalajuaj; according to anthropologist Clinton Hart Merriam (1955:197), this was the American Indian name for Montecito. The village was registered as part of the Christian *rancherías* of the Santa Bárbara Mission (ibid.). Interestingly, Evarista and her parents lived on the junction of Sheffield Drive and Ortega Hill, which has been identified as one of the oldest sites in Montecito (Hoover, Rensch, and Rensch 1966:421). After the Mexican American War, Chalajuaj was dismantled and evolved into several neighborhoods. The area where Evarista's family lived came to be known as Romero Canyon. After the war, for some reason, the members of the Romero clan were not forced to abandon their homes. They were not given title to their homes, however, and Pedro Masini became the legal owner of Romero Canyon (ibid.).

Evarista married her first cousin Amado Romero in 1877 and had thirteen children (*Santa Barbara News Press*, 29 November 1959, p. 2). Some of her children married Mexicans, others married Chumash people, and a few married Anglo Americans. Richard, Betty, and Martha do not know very much about Evarista's children. They only know about her daughter Felipa, their grandmother and Verónica's mother. Felipa died at an early age, and Verónica was raised by Evarista. They remember that Evarista's children were never registered by the BIA as Native Americans. Likewise, in the following two generations Felipa and Verónica chose not to register

Photograph 41. Some of the Last Full-Blooded Chumash Indians, Ventura, California, 1880s. Courtesy of the Ventura County Museum of History and Art.

their children. In those days, there was no incentive for Chumash people to be classified by BIA agents as Indian. On the contrary, there were dangerous risks, such as being removed and relocated to the reservations.

Apparently, Evarista's attitude toward the BIA was very common; anthropologists Phillip L. Walker and Travis Hudson propose that by 1880 most Chumash people escaped American prejudice by publicly passing as Mexican. The U.S. Census Bureau reported that in 1880 there were only 200 Chumash people in California (Walker and Hudson 1993:32; see Photograph 41). Although the Chumash population had certainly dwindled by the turn of the century, the census count was obviously inaccurate because there were several hundred Chumash in Santa Inés alone.

Richard's mother, Verónica Ruiz, possibly was not a full-blooded Chumash, but she was a full-blooded Indian. Her father was a Mexican from Santa Barbara. His family had resided there for many generations. Verónica's children do not know very much about their grandfather and only remember that he was a very dark Indian. They do not know anything about his lineage, other than his name. Verónica raised her family in the East Side of Santa Barbara. During the 1950s and 1960s, the East Side was racially segregated and only minorities lived there. Verónica raised her children biculturally, teaching them Mexican and Indian lifeways. They learned about their Chumash lineage, they were raised Catholic, they learned to appreciate Mexican music and Chumash dancing, their language was English, and their daily food was Mexican. Though their main staples were beans, tortillas, and rice, they also ate Indian fried bread and on special occasions "pelilis," a special type of fried bread that is sprinkled with sugar. Verónica also sang to her children a Chumash lullaby which they all remember and today sing to their children. Richard has taught the lullaby to our children, and they too have memorized the words: "Mimi, mimi, tata, lulu, lulu, rata."

Because only one of Verónica's husbands was Native American, only Betty and Manuel are today registered as Native Americans. Betty and Manuel's father was a BIA-registered Chumash Indian. Though only Betty and Manuel are officially Native Americans according to the BIA, two of Richard's other sisters married Chumash men whose families are also registered in the BIA rolls. Martha and Frances married two brothers from the Santa Inés Reservation, Raymond Gonzalez and Arnold Gonzalez. After their marriages Frances and Arnold lived on the reservation, while Martha and Raymond, who were also given reservation land, preferred to live somewhere else and instead purchased a home half a mile away. The rest of Richard's sisters and brothers married Mexican Americans and Anglo Americans.

The Gonzalez family history illustrates a different scenario, where people of Chumash descent refused to relinquish their tribal identity. This account is based on the oral narratives of Elena Gonzalez and Martha Gonzalez. I conducted this interview on 14 June 1999. Betty was present during the interview and often contributed to the analysis. The historical narratives are corroborated by anthropological studies on the Gonzalez ancestors.

Rafael Solares: The Last Antap Indian of Santa Inés

Raymond Gonzalez is the great-grandson of Rafael Solares. Rafael was the founder of the Santa Inés Reservation, one of the last Indian sacristans (caretakers) of the Santa Inés Mission and the last Antap Indian of Santa Inés. During Rafael's lifetime, he was studied, photographed, and interviewed by several anthropologists. Today his portrait stands in the entrance of the Santa Bárbara Mission Museum. The caption below his picture reads: "Rafael Solares the last surviving Antap. While serving as sacristan of Mission Santa Inés he continued to utilize native religious traditions along with Catholic ritual and practice, thereby helping to produce the distinctive lifestyle of the mission Indians" (Santa Bárbara Mission Museum, visited 15 June 1999).

Anthropologists describe the Antap as people belonging to a Native American religious cult dispersed throughout California (Walker and Hudson 1993). Elena, however, refers to the Antap as a political organization to which Rafael and her ancestors belonged. According to several anthropologists and Elena's family history, only high-ranking Chumash families belonged to the Antap organizations, including the chiefs' and shamans' families. Though the Antap members had great social prestige, they were obliged to perform many duties for their tribe: they had to learn their tribe's history, be able to perform magic and medicinal rituals, maintain knowledge of ritual language, and preserve the tribe's sacred songs, dances, and poetry (Walker and Hudson 1993:43). All tribal members were obliged to follow the proclamations of the head of the local Antap chapter.

Rafael Solares's memory has also been preserved by photographs commissioned by the Musée des Hommes of Paris. In 1878 Léon de Cessac photographed Rafael performing an Antap ritual (Grant 1978b: 514; see Photograph 42). Cessac also took other pictures that are less Orientalist in style and depict Rafael merely as a man (see Walker and Hudson 1993:10, 42). In 1900 Rafael and his family were once again visited by a researcher when anthropologist John Peabody Harrington was commissioned by the Smithsonian Institute to study the medicinal practices of the Chumash of Ventura, Santa Barbara, and Santa Inés (Walker and Hudson 1993). Elena informed me that several years later her grandmother was also visited by other anthropologists.

Rafael Solares was born in the Santa Inés Mission before the Mexican American War (see Photograph 43). He came from a line of Antap leaders and mission sacristans. After Santa Inés Mission was secularized in 1836, Rafael's family and other mission Indians continued to reside at the mission and in the adjacent mission pueblo (Engelhardt 1986:42). Though the Indians of Santa Inés were left undisturbed after secularization, the governor of California failed to give them legal patent to the mission lands. In 1855 the U.S. government dismantled their village and forced 450 people to vacate their homes (Engelhardt 1986:120). Many moved to

Photograph 42. Rafael Solares, Dressed in Antap Ritual Clothing. Photograph by Léon de Cessac, 1878. Courtesy of the Ventura County Museum of History and Art.

Santa Barbara and Los Angeles (Walker and Hudson 1993), while others like Rafael's family refused to leave Santa Inés. Those who remained behind obtained work on the local farms and ranches, now owned by Anglo Americans. By 1875 Santa Inés had evolved into a predominantly Anglo-American town (Engelhardt 1986:120). Few Mexicans lived there, and the Chumash had become the minority population. By then Rafael was an adult, and he took over the position of mission's sacristan. During the 1880s and 1890s, he was elected by the mission Indians to serve as *alcalde* (mayor) and *regiador* (town council member) of their community (ibid., 125–127; Walker and Hudson 1993:32). In 1913 Father Zephyrin Engelhardt met Rafael on a visit to Santa Inés and reported that he was the leader of the Spanish-speaking community and had organized the church choir (Engelhardt 1986:27). Engelhardt commented that he had a beau-

Photograph 43. Mission Santa Inés. Courtesy of the Capuchin Franciscans. Photograph taken by author.

tiful voice and was well versed in poetry and music. Rafael also organized other Christian festivities and was known for fusing Chumash and Catholic religious rituals.

By 1919 most mission Indians in Santa Inés had been reduced to severe poverty, and Bishop Francisco García appealed to the United States government to reserve land for the faithful families who had refused to abandon the mission (Engelhardt 1986:121). The government complied and that year established a reservation of 120 acres, the smallest reservation in the United States. Rafael became the first political leader of the Santa Inés Reservation tribal council. Anthropologists call these people chiefs, but Elena and Martha prefer to refer to them as chairpersons of the tribal councils. It is uncertain how many people initially moved onto the reservation because anthropologists disagree on this point. Campbell Grant (1978a:507) claims that 109 people founded the reservation, while Walker and Hudson (1993:33) claim that it began with 20 residents. In any case, Elena states that the Solares, Ortegas, and Mirandas were the principal families, and to this day the reservation is inhabited by their descendants. Over time, Rafael's male descendants served as chairpersons of their tribal council. The position, however, was passed among the male members of the reservation and was not passed down through a family lineage. Raymond served as tribal chairperson several times, and so did Elena's uncle Arnold.

Elena's Views on Race and Culture

When I asked Elena how she identified racially, in light of the fact that her mother Martha is perhaps not a full-blooded Chumash (i.e., she may also have been descended from another Indian group) and her grandmother on her father's side married a Mexican, Elena responded that culturally she identifies as Chumash, but racially without a doubt she is *mestiza* and a person of color. In Santa Inés she doubts whether there are more than a handful of people who are full-blooded Chumash. She added that most likely there are many full-blooded Indians, but they are mixed with other tribal peoples and with Mexican Indians. This may not be the case on other reservations, but because most people in Santa Inés married Mexican Americans most tribal members are mixed.

Though Elena considers most Chumash in Santa Inés to be racially mixed, she made it quite clear that people identify as Chumash. When I asked what made a person a Chumash Indian, Elena responded: "Well there are different types of Chumash people. There are people like Aunt Betty, who is a Chumash, but they are urban Indians and they do not belong to any tribal government, like we do." To Elena, participating in a tribal government is important because individuals are part of a formal community, which contributes to the survival of the tribe. She acknowledges, however, that there are many Chumash people who are urban Indians and have lost their tribal membership. In their cases, what makes them Chumash is the value they place on reproducing their culture and remaining knowledgeable of their history. Elena added that urban Indians do not have to fit the stereotypical image of Indians who attend powwows in order to prove that they are "real Indians—rather than wannabes." She believes that urban Indians must manifest their culture in some outward way, such as being familiar with their indigenous genealogy or being knowledgeable about their people's oral tradition.

According to Elena, when families lose their people's poems or stories, this indicates that they no longer value their American Indian culture, because they don't respect it enough to pass it down to the next generation.

Photograph 44. Gonzalez Family
Chumash Heirlooms. Photograph
taken by author.

For example, she pointed to her father's spiritual pole and stated that for many generations the men in her family have been making these poles (see Photographs 42 and 44). In Chumash culture, the pole is constructed because it is supposed to bring people good fortune and good health. It also serves as an ethnic marker of the value Chumash people place on their traditions. When I looked at the pole, I noticed that it is a replica of the spiritual pole that Léon de Cessac photographed in 1878, when Rafael Solares displayed his Antap regalia. It is also the same pole that Father Engelhardt described in his historical study of Santa Inés and derogatorily referred to as a cult superstition that had not protected Indians from disaster, disease, and bad fortune (Engelhardt 1986:15).

As Elena was sharing the history of the spiritual pole, Martha walked in with a basketful of family heirlooms. She proudly displayed them and indicated which ones were passed down through the generations and which ones were Santa Inés artifacts that she had collected over the years. I immediately recognized the function of all their heirlooms, because they are the types of objects that have been studied by anthro-

Photograph 45. Elena Gonzalez and My Son, Carlos Valencia. Photograph taken by author.

Photograph 46. Martha Gonzalez and Betty Valencia-Cruz. Photograph taken by author.

pologists and described in *The Handbook of North American Indians* (Grant 1978b). Among the family heirlooms were small balls used for sports, rocks shaped like cigars that were used to perform healing rituals, metates and pestles used for grinding, and huge stone pots used for cooking. Indeed these were wonderful objects for an anthropologist to see outside of a museum context. I was mesmerized.

As we concluded our interview, Elena shared one last comment on racial politics (see Photographs 45 and 46). She stated that today the stigma of being an Indian has been largely erased and people can celebrate their culture publicly. She noted that this has not always been the case, however. Based on family oral histories told by her father, Raymond, in his youth it was still difficult to be an Indian. Ranchers took advantage of their Indian workers and paid them low wages because they knew that families did not want to move to other cities. Consequently, most Chumash families had to hunt deer and quail to have enough food to feed their families. Worst of all, parents were afraid that their children would be taken away to Indian boarding schools if the local teachers complained about their parenting skills. According to Elena, in Santa Inés life is currently easier for Indian people; but what is sad and will never be forgotten is that the Chumash were reduced from being one of California's numerically largest Indian peoples to being one of the smallest tribes in the nation today.

Photograph 48. Pete Crowheart Zavalla, Los Padres National Forest Guide, San Marcos Pass. Photograph taken by author.

Photograph 49. John Carrillo Viewing His Ancestors' Art, San Marcos Pass. Photograph taken by author.

Photograph 47. Chumash Rock Art Heritage Field Trip, San Marcos Pass. Photograph taken by author.

Conclusion

Elena's closing comment on the near extinction of the Chumash tribe is not a myth (see Grant 1978a). If we view the Chumash as an ethnic group and not solely as a tribe, however, Chumash people constitute a sizable population. In Santa Barbara urban people of Chumash descent have established a cultural organization called the Chumash Native American Cultural Center and organized the corporation of the Coastal Band of Chumash Indians. The Coastal Band addresses health, welfare, and political issues faced by urban Indians. For example, in 1986 the Coastal Band of Chumash Indians brought a suit against the federal government to re-

Photograph 50. Chumash Rock Art at San Marcos Pass, A.D. 500. Courtesy of the National Forest Parks. Photograph taken by author.

gain land lost after the Mexican American War (*U.S. v. Ringrose*, 1986). To this date, however, they have been unsuccessful because under *Johnson v. McIntosh* (1823) and similar rulings the U.S. Congress and the courts continue to be the only institutions able to determine when Native Americans have the legal basis to gain back part of the property they lost.

The Chumash Native American Cultural Center also organizes many cultural programs and festivities. The goal is to teach people of Chumash descent and the general public about Chumash culture. During my last research trip to Santa Barbara, when I brought my son Carlos, I was fortunate to be invited on a tour through the mountains of San Marcos Pass. My sister-in-law Betty, who is a board member of the center, organized a visit to the San Marcos Pass Chumash rock art caves. She did this specifically to take Carlos and her grandchildren to see a place associated with their Chumash roots. Pete Crowheart Zavalla, a Comanche Indian whose children are Chumash and Comanche, served as our guide (see Photographs 47–50). We were accompanied by Betty's son, John Carrillo, a fireman. Carlos was mesmerized, and now he understood who were the people his father had told him about, the people who sang the lullaby "Mimi, mimi, tata, lulu, lulu, rata." Indeed, this reminded me of my childhood, when my mother took my brothers and sisters and I to Chicomoztoc and sparked my indigenist identity and love for anthropology and history.

Notes

Introduction

1. Omi and Winant (1986) introduced the concept of racialization and defined it as a process of racial categorization. In this book I develop their idea and propose that categorizing people into distinct racial groups is commonly achieved through the legal system.

2. The northwestern and northeastern coasts of Mexico were inhabited by groups that were not Chichimec (see Alonzo 1998; Spicer 1981).

3. Mexican Americans, like American Indians, are predominantly of White and Indian descent. Since 1810 Mexico's national censuses have estimated that 90 percent of Mexicans are of indigenous descent (cited in Aguirre Beltrán 1946: 237), whereas by 1920 the U.S. Census estimated that 50 percent of American Indians were racially mixed and were one-half or less of Indian descent (cited in Forbes 1982:95).

Chapter 1. Racial Foundations

1. In 1973 historian Jack Forbes wrote *Aztecas del Norte: The Chicanos of Aztlán*, offering a historical analysis of the Mexican Americans' indigenous heritage. He also argued in favor of archaeological theories proposing that Mexican Indian groups had significantly influenced the cultural development of the Indians of the Southwest. In 1982 Forbes wrote *Native Americans of California and Nevada*. The second book no longer supported the Southwest-Mexico connections; nor were Mexican Americans included as part of the indigenous peoples of the Southwest.

2. Aztlán was often spelled "Astatlan" by sixteenth-century scholars (see Tibón 1983).

3. Richard Perry (1991) offers an alternate racial classificatory scheme in his study on the Western Apache. He posits that Athapaskan Indians who reside in Alaska, Canada, the United States, and Mexico (e.g., the largest groups: Apache, Navajo) are racially distinct from the rest of the Indians of the New World. Apparently, only the Athapaskan Indians share a common blood antigen called

"albumin Naskapi" and twenty-four blood group frequencies. Thus, based on this biological information Perry concludes that the Athapaskans may be racially different from other indigenous peoples. Although he claims a separate racial origin for Athapaskan Indians, the governments where these Indians reside (Canada, the United States, and Mexico) do not distinguish these people as racially different from other Indians. For now the dominant perspective continues to be that the indigenous people of the New World belong to one race.

4. In 1936 Emil Haury (1992d:337) introduced the hypothesis that the Hohokam were descendants of the Cochise, a cultural complex located in southern Arizona and dated to approximately 7000 B.C. Although Haury has abandoned this position, it continues to be a popular hypothesis. Due to lack of evidence supporting this hypothesis, William Lipe (1978) and Haury (1992d) caution that at this time no connection between the Cochise and any other Indian group can be made with certainty.

5. It is likely that some Eastern Pueblo groups are also related to the Mogollon or Anasazi (i.e., Tewa, Tiwa, Jemez, Piro, Keresan) (Ortiz 1991:10). Winifred Creamer and Jonathan Haas (1991:95) conclude that there is sufficient archaeological evidence indicating that the Tewa, an Eastern Pueblo branch, descend from the Anasazi.

6. There are two major Jumano subdivisions: the puebloan and the nomadic. This classification is based upon the linguistic findings of sixteenth-century Spanish explorers, who reported that Jumano peoples spoke the same Uto-Aztecan language (Sauer 1934; Scholes and Mera 1940). Although this classificatory scheme continues to be the dominant perspective, William W. Newcomb (1986) proposes that material culture remains cast doubt on a common kinship origin.

7. Julian Steward (1933) proposes that the Mexican–Plains Shoshone debate most likely reflects a misclassification scheme. It is likely that archaeologists classified three unrelated Indian groups in the category Shoshone because they practiced similar forms of material culture.

8. See the Introduction, note 2.

9. On the basis of the similarity of events contained in the myths, Gillespie (1989:44, 115) proposes that Aztlán and Chicomoztoc are synonymous concepts, both referring to the homeland of the Chichimec peoples. Both versions claim that the Chichimec emerged from the earth in a place where seven underground caves were located. They then marched south.

Mexican historian Emilio Rodríguez Flores (1976) offers an alternate interpretation and states that archaeological data and Mesoamerican mythology clearly indicate that Chicomoztoc was founded after Aztlán. Though the origin myth of Chicomoztoc is similar to the myth of Aztlán, it nonetheless is the origin myth of a subdivision of the Chichimec and not the Mexica. Basing his analysis on archaeological data, Rodríguez Flores states that Chicomoztoc was founded around A.D. 1164 in Villa Nueva, Zacatecas, near the old Hacienda de la Quemada. It is the point of origin of the Zacateco and San Luis Obispo Indians. These two peoples were the last Chichimec groups to settle in Mexico and left Aztlán after the Mexica. When they entered Mexico, they ended their migration in Chicomoztoc and subsequently built a well-fortified city, surrounded by a massive stone fence. In the interior of the city they constructed pyramids, houses, and civic buildings (ibid., 43). According to Rodríguez Flores, the origin myth of the state of Zacatecas claims that the people of Chicomoztoc came from Aztlán (ibid., 44–46). This version locates Aztlán in California, around the archaeological zone where Shoshone sites have been discovered. The people who left present-day California were Chichimec. They crossed the Colorado River, migrated toward the Gila River in Arizona, and eventually settled in Culiacán for three years. They then left Culiacán and established a permanent settlement in Chicomoztoc. Some groups later chose to leave Chicomoztoc. Most families stayed in the present states of Zacatecas and San Luis Obispo; as they settled in different areas, they gave birth to new villages. Some of the families continued to migrate further south, however, and founded Tabasco, Jalpa, Juchipilo, Moyahua, El Tuel, and other smaller towns.

10. The Basques may have entered Catalonia as early as 2000 B.C. (Vinces Vives 1972:8). This is uncertain, however, as the sites attributed to them may have belonged to Tartessians.

11. The families and monarchies who ruled Muslim Spain changed over time (Levtzion 1973).

12. King Ferdinand inherited Catalonia and Valencia, and Queen Isabella inherited León. In 1512 Navarre was also annexed to their kingdom (Lynch 1964:4, 33).

13. Altamira (1988) proposes that Muslim cultural influences were insignificant outside of Granada. He alleges that Muslim cultural practices disappeared over time and that it is now difficult to recognize their traces except for historic architecture.

14. By 1526 all citizens practicing Islam or Judaism were forced to convert to Christianity; if they resisted, they were expelled from Spain (Lynch 1964:205).

15. Muslims also influenced Spain's marriage legal system by introducing civil and common-law codes (Bravo Lira 1970).

16. In 1501 the Spanish crown prohibited the introduction of Moors, Jews, Herehes, and Christians as slaves in its New World colonies (Palacios 1988:8; Palmer 1981:3).

17. In Veracruz and the Yucatán Peninsula slaves served as farm workers and servants (Aguirre Beltrán 1946).

18. John Reader (1997:160) argues that agriculture may have started in the Nile region as early as 18,000 years ago.

Chapter 2. Racial Formation: Spain's Racial Order

1. Spaniards used formal schooling as a peaceful acculturating strategy. In 1523 Spain founded the first elementary school in Texcoco, now a district of

Mexico City (Larroyo 1946:595). Within the next twenty years, many Spanish elementary schools were founded in Mexico City, Morelia, and Pátzcuaro.

2. The Laws of Burgos were an extension of the *Siete Partidas* protectionist legislation enacted in 1265 (Cutter 1986:8).

3. Under the Laws of Burgos, additional acculturation policies stipulated that (1) the education of the sons of chiefs must be entrusted to the church; (2) Indians must wear clothes; and (3) Indians must learn a trade (Borah 1983:23; Hanke 1949:24).

4. De Las Casas conceded to his opponents that Indians were culturally inferior and barbarous, a condition easily resolved by Christianizing them. He favored replacing the *encomienda* system with a mission system, in which Indians could live under the tutelage of the friars rather than the *encomenderos* (Gibson 1964; Wagner and Parish 1967). Eventually this recommendation was instituted, in northern Mexico and the southwestern United States (Engelhardt 1929; Polzer 1976).

5. In 1859 the pseudo-scientific school of thought that argued that Indians, Blacks, Asians, and racially mixed peoples were not human was struck its final blow when Charles Darwin published *The Origin of the Species* (Menchaca 1997:30). Darwin advanced an evolutionary theory and supported it with skeletal evidence. He argued that all races were of a modern human stock and had gradually, and in one line, evolved from a common origin. None of the races could be classified as premodern humans, including Indians.

6. The fact that the Aztec in the preconquest period had established Calmecac and Telpochcalli schools influenced the church to determine Indians were humans (León-Portilla 1975; Vigil 1984). Indians also were very instrumental in convincing the clergy of their human origins. The Indians demonstrated that they possessed sophisticated knowledge with respect to government, agriculture, architecture, and the arts and sciences. Two great Indian philosophers, Icazbalceta and Pablo Nazareo, came to the attention of the church and were used as evidence of the Indians' rationality. Icazbalceta and Nazareo also helped Spanish historians reconstruct Mexico's Mesoamerican heritage (Bayle 1931).

Father Zumárraga, a clergyman who believed in the Indians' rationality, influenced the crown to establish a seminary for Indians. In 1536 the first Indian seminary was built in Mexico City (Bayle 1931:216, 218). It was called Santa Cruz and was located in present Tlatelolco.

7. In colonial times the Valley of Mexico included what today is Mexico City as well as unincorporated districts on the outskirts of the city (see Gibson 1964).

8. In 1648 the Yucatán Peninsula experienced several deadly epidemics (Perry and Perry 1988:40). The population was reduced by half and hundreds of villages were abandoned. The process of reallocating land replicated the policies in central Mexico.

9. Gibson (1964:236–256) asserts that the *corregimiento* was a less exploit-

ative land and labor system. Nonetheless, he argues that Indians were exploited by the crown and church, because they were overworked and many died during the construction of bridges and tunnels.

10. Between 1633 and 1821 slaves from Asia were exported to Mexico (Aguirre Beltrán 1946:42, 101–102). Although the number of Asian slaves is unknown, they were brought in ships weighing 600 to 800 tons. Most of them came from the Philippines, Indonesia, China, Japan, Java, and Cambodia.

11. The *mestizo* population in 1646 is estimated at 109,042 (Aguirre Beltrán 1946:221). Scholars propose that it was much larger, however, because many light-complexioned *mestizos* were included as part of the White population (see Cope 1994; Meyer and Sherman 1995; Seed 1988).

12. Parts of this section previously appeared in Menchaca 1993, "Chicano Indianism: A Historical Account of Racial Repression in the United States," *American Ethnologist* 20 (3): 583–603.

13. By the late 1600s, 42 percent of the Indian women in Mexico City were marrying non-Indians and 28 percent of the Indian males were marrying racially mixed women, either *mestizas* or *mulattas* (Cope 1994).

Chapter 3. The Move North: The Gran Chichimeca and New Mexico

1. The Tarascans were from Michoacán and retained their independence during the height of the Aztec Empire. In 1479 the Aztec unsuccessfully tried to colonize the Tarascans and instead generated a legacy of mutual hostility (Meyer and Sherman 1995:65).

2. To the northwest of the Chichimec lived over forty-five indigenous groups which the Spanish categorized into five linguistic families, calling them Piman, Cahitan, Opatan, Serian, and Tarahumaran (Spicer 1981:10). This was a region of small, autonomous local communities, economically and politically independent of one another. On occasion groups who spoke the same dialect temporarily united for purposes of warfare. Their coalitions dissolved when the fighting was over.

The northeast was populated by over three hundred and fifty autonomous indigenous groups categorized into twenty-six ethnic families (Salinas 1990:28–29), the largest being the Comecrudos. This region was also part of the Seno Mexicano, which stretched in an arc from the Pánuco River near Tampico along the coast to the southern limits of Texas (Alonzo 1998).

3. In 1513 Juan Ponce de León set foot on Florida's shores (Weber 1992:2).

4. Scholars disagree on several issues regarding Cabeza de Vaca's account of the Narváez expedition. First, there is disagreement over where they landed in Texas (Bandelier 1990; see Chipman 1992). It may have been near Galveston or somewhere in southeastern Texas. Estimates of the size of the expedition range from 300 to 600 men (see Weber 1992:42–43). Finally, there are different interpretations of Cabeza de Vaca's route in the Southwest. Some scholars propose that

he walked through Texas, New Mexico, and Arizona (Bannon 1970), while others suggest that he walked only through Texas (Bandelier 1990; Chipman 1992).

5. Hernán Cortés is known to have explored Baja California in 1535 (see Engelhardt 1929:20).

6. For a detailed analysis of the exploration of North America, see Weber 1992.

7. Guachichiles, Caxcanes, and Zacatecos frequently intermarried and were related by kinship ties. Their origin was the ancient city of Chicomoztoc located in present Villa Nueva, Zacatecas (Rodríguez Flores 1976:46).

8. "Debéis estar locos, pues sin más que ustedes quieren que los matemos; nosotros por fuerza nos exponemos a la defense de nuestras tierras, pero a ustedes? ¿quién los ha llamado?" (cited in Rodríguez Flores 1976:76).

9. The mining camps of Santa Bárbara and San Bartolomé were founded in Chihuahua in 1566 (Chipman 1992:43–45). The colonists were soldiers, mining barons, and a few paid civilians. These settlements did not boom until after the Gran Chichimeca was stabilized (Powell 1952:29). Furthermore, in 1581 the royal government gave Franciscan missionaries permission to explore New Mexico (see John 1975:24). They were part of the Chamuscado-Rodríguez-López expedition.

Exploration voyages were also launched by sea. During the 1560s to 1570s, the Spanish crown commenced its colonization of Florida (Engelhardt 1929:13). The high point of the colonization of Florida, however, was in 1675 (Weber 1992:101).

10. Unlike Mexico's central valley, where the *repartimiento* system was dismantled in 1633, in the north the crown allowed Spaniards to force Chichimec Indians to work without pay until the late 1600s (Gibson 1964).

11. Engelhardt (1929:13) proposes that the first mission in northern Mexico was established among the Indians of Florida in 1577. Weber (1992:29) suggests that it was founded in 1595. A common point of disagreement is whether a mission began when missionaries started evangelizing the Indians or when a building was erected. For a discussion of this interpretive difference, refer to Polzer (1976).

12. The four hundred families came from the state of Tlaxcala, from the towns of Tlaxcala, Tepeyanco, Altihuetzía, Chiantempan, Huamantla, Ixtacuixtla, Hueyotlopan, Atlangalepec, and Totolac (Hernández Xochitiotzin 1991:4).

13. This information is based upon the official records found in the historical archives of Tlaxcala, Archivo General del Estado, Ave. Juárez #16, Colonia Centro Tlaxcala, Tlaxcala Mexico.

14. In his historical ethnography of the Tlaxcalan Indians of Mexquitic (San Luis Potosí) Frye (1996) concludes that by the mid-seventeenth century Spain had broken most of its agreements with the Tlaxcalans. This occurred after a large number of non-Tlaxcalan settlers arrived in San Luis Potosí. Although most Tlaxcalan land grants were honored, the royal government allowed others to set overlapping claims. The government also broke its promise to exempt the Tlaxcalans from paying tribute.

15. A village by the name of Tacuitapa was also mentioned as part of the first Tlaxcalan pueblos in the far north (Hernández Xochitiotzin 1991). It is uncertain whether such a settlement was established, since other scholars do not refer to this town (Alessio Robles 1934; Frye 1996).

16. The census of 1646 for North Mexico does not include the unconquered indigenous populations.

17. Scholars disagree on the size of Juan de Oñate's colony of 1598. Spicer (1981:156) and Weber (1992:81) agree that around 400 soldiers plus the families of 130 of the men joined the colony. Bannon (1970:36) estimates that 129 heads of households plus their families formed the colony. Gutiérrez (1991:103) states that only 19 of 130 soldiers brought families.

18. Chipman (1992:46) proposes that the trek north began from an outpost called Gerónimo, near Santa Bárbara.

19. Bannon (1970:36) states that the first colonists arrived in New Mexico in mid-June 1598.

20. Villagrá identified the women as the wives of Don Francisco de Peñalosa, Alonso Sánchez, Zubia, Don Luis Gasco, Diego Núñez, Pedro Sánchez Monrroi, Sosa, Pereira, Quesada, Juan Morán, Simón, Pérez, Ascencio de Archuleta, Boca-negra, Carabajal, Romero, Alonso Lucas, San Martín, Cordero, the caudillo Francisco Sánchez, Francisco Hernández, Monzón, Alonso Gómez Montesinos, Francisco García, and Bustillo (Villagrá 1933:224–225).

21. Villagrá (1933:224–225) proposes that the Spanish soldiers did not have to set Acoma on fire because it was only a matter of time before the entire village surrendered.

22. Bannon (1970:38) states that the colonists arriving in 1600 were separated and that only seventy-eight settlers plus several friars arrived at this time. The second part of the colony arrived later, with an undetermined number of settlers.

23. Mission Corpus Cristi de la Ysleta was founded in 1682 (Spicer 1981:163).

24. Don Diego de Vargas was appointed governor and captain-general of New Mexico on 18 June 1688 (Bannon 1970:86).

25. The 1804 census of New Mexico was published in a report written by Don Pedro Bautista Pino (in Carroll and Haggard 1942).

26. Metz (1994:21) states that El Paso Valley remained part of New Mexico until 1824.

27. Don Pedro Bautista Pino reported in 1804 that there were 26 Indian pueblos and 102 settlements in New Mexico (Bautista Pino 1812:217).

28. Bowden (1971:156) states that San Elizario was founded in 1780.

29. Two additional presidios were located near El Paso on what today is the Mexican side of the border (Bowden 1971:156).

30. Hacienda Nuestra Señora de la Soledad de los Tiburcios was founded in 1724 by Antonio Tiburcio Ortega, one of the grandsons of Captain Francisco de Ortega (Hendricks and Timmons 1998:11). Francisco was a *mulatto* from Zacatecas who later moved to New Mexico and became a distinguished person. During the mid-1600s, he was granted many military honors for his bravery. Francisco's

son Pablo became *alcalde* (mayor) of the Jemez district, and after the Pueblo Indian revolt his grandson Diego became justice of the peace for Ysleta, Senecú, and Socorro. In 1762 the *hacienda* had a total population of 210 (ibid., 12). It was abandoned after fifty-three years of continuous occupation due to a series of devastating Apache attacks.

31. See Weber (1992:195) for a demographic description of New Mexico in 1765.

Chapter 4. The Spanish Settlement of Texas and Arizona

1. In Arizona Franciscans replaced the Jesuits in 1767 (Engelhardt 1929: 306), when the Jesuit order was expelled from Mexico.

2. "Tejas Indians" is a general term applied to Indians native to Texas. The Coahuiltecans were the largest subdivision of the Tejas (Salinas 1990).

3. See Beers (1979) for a review of the political reorganization of Texas between 1689 and 1836. Over time, Texas was under the direct command of either the viceroy or the king. Furthermore, its political jurisdiction was reconfigured six times, making Texas a separate province or part of the internal or eastern provinces.

4. Bannon (1970:114) states that only four missions were founded among the Caddo Indians of the northeast.

5. Castañeda (1936:35) proposes that only thirty-eight of the seventy-two settlers in Alarcón's colony were not Indians.

6. Chipman (1992:117) claims that Alarcón's party arrived in San Antonio on 25 April 1718.

7. A villa was a settlement larger than a town and smaller than a city (see Graham 1994; Hendricks and Timmons 1998).

8. After Don Pedro de Rivera's military inspection of 1727, the soldiers stationed at La Bahía were reduced to twenty (Bannon 1970:123). Rivera reported that La Bahía was excessively militarized for a zone surrounded by peaceful Indians.

9. Chipman (1992:180) estimates that only 200 neophytes were regular residents at the missions of La Bahía.

10. After their initial founding, the settlements at La Bahía were moved to different locations. The presidio and Mission Espíritu Santo were moved from the Guadalupe River to the San Antonio River (Beers 1979:96; Chipman 1992:147–150, 201). After three moves, Mission Refugio was established in present Refugio.

11. See Beers (1979) for a history of the political shifts in the governance of the Province of Texas and Nuevo Santander.

12. In 1684 six missions were established on the Mexican side of the border between Texas and Chihuahua, at the conjunction of the Rio Grande and the Concho River (Castañeda 1936:328). This region was known as La Junta. Mission Cíbola was established over half a century later on the U.S. side of the border. It was also part of the La Junta colonization project.

13. The exact date when Mission Cíbola was destroyed is unknown since Captain José Idoyaga arrived at the mission after the inhabitants had been dead for what appeared to be a long time (Castañeda 1938:224). Very little is known about Mission Cíbola because most of the documents concerning the mission were burned.

14. In 1748 several missions were established in present Milam County along the San Gabriel River (Bannon 1970:136; Castañeda 1938:362–387). The missions were later relocated to San Marcos and New Braunfels. Ten years later the mission neophytes and church belongings were transferred to the newly established mission at San Sabá.

15. In 1759 Presidio del Norte was initially founded on the south side of the Rio Grande (Beers 1979:97; Castañeda 1938:223–232). After Apaches destroyed the presidio, it was moved across the river to what is today U.S. soil.

16. Over sixty soldiers and their families lived in Presidio de Los Adaes and thirty-one soldiers and their families in Presidio de San Agustín de Ahumada (Castañeda 1939:34, 39). The missions were also abandoned, and the few neophytes living there were taken to San Antonio (Castañeda 1936:231).

17. The Spanish plaza in Nacogdoches originally stood in the center of town. In the 1930s it was moved near the cemetery. This information was provided by Carolyn Spears, curator of the Stone Fort Museum, Nacogdoches, Texas.

18. No racial or ethnic data were included for 81 persons (Tjarks 1974:324–325).

19. Data were not offered for 62 inhabitants. Percentages are based on a total of 457 inhabitants (Tjarks 1974:325).

20. Spicer (1981:123) states that in the late 1600s *visitas* were also established among the Pima of Arizona in Quiburí, Gaybanipitea, and Gubo.

21. Swanton (1984:363) argues that the first mission buildings in Arizona were erected in 1731.

22. There is disagreement over how many *visitas* were established in Arizona. Engstrand (1992:179) claims there were ten, Kessell (1976:7) fourteen, and Dobyns (1962:23–25) nine.

23. Scholars distinguish between the Upper Pima, who lived in Arizona, and the Lower Pima, who lived in Sonora (see Spicer 1981).

24. In 1776 temporary presidios were established in the Santa Cruz and San Pedro valleys. After a series of sustained attacks, the presidio at Sópori was moved to Sonora and the presidio along the border near San Bernardino was abandoned and later transformed into a ranch (Beers 1979:311; Kessell 1976:98–99, 109, 169, 245).

25. Navajos sometimes also attacked the colonial settlements, but for the most part they remained at a distance and only on occasion migrated south (Officer 1987). Their history is more closely intertwined with the colonial settlements of New Mexico.

26. Often titles were not issued because people abandoned their ranches after Apache attacks and new claimants moved when an area was recolonized (Beers

1979). Allegedly many ranches were not inhabited long enough to merit issuing property deeds.

27. One league amounted to approximately 1,100 varas or 4,438 acres (see Margadant S. 1991:91).

28. Rancho San Bernardino was located on the border between Arizona and Sonora (cf. Beers 1979:310; Engstrand 1992:179; Kessell 1976:10).

29. Dobyns (1976:171–173) claims that census records from Presidio Tucson indicate that the officers' families were Spanish.

30. There is no evidence indicating that the soldiers who married Indian women were issued property deeds.

31. Two missions located on the border between Arizona and California, La Concepción and San Pedro y San Pablo de Bicreñer, lasted a short period (Kessell 1976:7; Weber 1992:259).

32. On the Mexican side of the border between Arizona and Sonora several other *visitas* were converted into mission pueblos (see Kessell 1976).

33. The Tumacácori land grant covered part of the mission land of the abandoned *visita* of Calabasas and part of the nearly dismantled mission at Guevavi.

34. Weber (1992:233) found that in 1793 several Apache *rancherías* settled near Tucson and formed colonial alliances. The number of inhabitants is estimated to have reached 2,000.

Chapter 5. The Settlement of California and the Twilight of the Spanish Period

1. The founding of the Baja California missions began in 1683 (Engelhardt 1930:82–84).

2. Engelhardt (1929:383) proposes that there were a total of eighty-four colonists in the Rivera y Moncada division, while Chapman (1930:222) proposes there were only seventy-two. Engelhardt may have counted the number of people who departed from Mission Velicatá, while Chapman only counted those who arrived.

3. Chapman (1930:221) claims that thirty-eight of the men on the *San Carlos* survived, while Bannon (1970:157) argues that most of the men died.

4. Weber (1992:41) proposes that the Indians who first contacted the Spanish in San Diego were called Ipai, although he recognizes that they were part of the Yuma linguistic family.

5. The Yuma were an ethnic subdivision of the Yuman Indians of Arizona.

6. The Anza expedition also provides information on intertribal relations in Arizona and California (see Bolton 1966). According to Anza in 1774 there were over 3,500 Yuma Indians along the Yuma Crossing (Bolton 1966:94). Most of them were gentle and peaceful. The Gabrileño Indians of Mission San Gabriel, however, considered the Yuma to be their enemies and were not pleased that Chief Palma was a Spanish ally.

7. Chapman (1930:308) argues the Anza's colony arrived in San Gabriel on

4 January 1776; Bannon says that they arrived on 2 January (1970:163). Weber (1992) gives no exact date.

8. Historians disagree on the size of the party brought by Rivera y Moncada in 1781, because the records were destroyed and later reconstructed based on missionary accounts. Weber (1992:259) argues that there were sixty in the party, including families and soldiers; Engelhardt (1930:387) claims there were forty-two soldiers, accompanied by thirty-two families; and Chapman (1930:337–338) believes there were forty families and eleven or twelve soldiers.

9. This information was obtained from Engelhardt (1930) and from El Pueblo de Los Angeles Historic Monument, Los Angeles City Government. The city government of Los Angeles has dedicated a plaque in Plaza Olvera to the founders of Los Angeles, which provides information on their race, gender, and age, based upon the 1781 census of California.

Bancroft claims that most of the people who participated in the founding of Los Angeles were part of the Rivera y Moncada expedition and were *afromestizo* (see Engelhardt 1930:705), while Forbes disputes this and claims that only twenty-six of the forty-six persons who founded Los Angeles were *afromestizos* (cf. Forbes 1968:12). Except for one Chinese and one Spaniard, the rest were Indians and *mestizos*.

10. Chapman (1930:385) offers a slightly larger population estimate of 1,200 for 1793.

11. Bowman uses Bancroft's notes on the missions to estimate the size of the mission Indian population in 1790. Bowman's tabulation differs slightly and totals 7,718 (Bowman 1958:148).

12. Bowman's statistical registry is based upon a revision of the documents used by Hubert Howe Bancroft to reconstruct the size of the neophyte mission population from 1769 to 1774 (see Bowman 1958). Bowman's tabulation is slightly different from Bancroft's. According to Bowman, Bancroft made minor mathematical errors, which he revised.

13. For a comprehensive register of the California *rancherías*, see Merriam (1955:188–225) and Engelhardt (1930:643, 644, 686–689). See also *Byrne v. Alas et al.* (1888:525), for a U.S. legal definition of a Spanish and Mexican *ranchería*. Merriam reconstructed a registry of the *rancherías* of California based on mission records. Although the records are incomplete, they cover the *rancherías* associated with nineteen of the twenty-one missions. Merriam states that the Christian *rancherías* were part of Spanish municipalities, but he does not clarify whether these communities were registered in the presidios. A comparison of this registry with Engelhardt's analysis (1930:638–652) of Father Tapia's 1807 report on the California *rancherías* provides an insightful description of the Indian ally communities. For example, Father Tapia reported that by 1807 all of the Indians of the Santa Bárbara and Santa Inés regions lived in Christian *rancherías*.

14. The missions at Ventura, Santa Bárbara, La Purísima, San Miguel, Santa Inés, and San Fernando were specifically built for the Chumash Indians (see Engelhardt 1913, 1930; Hoover, Rensch, and Rensch 1966; Menchaca 1995). At

San Fernando most of the neophytes were Chumash, but among them were other tribal Indians.

15. The county of San Luis Obispo is on the border between central and northern California (Menchaca 1995). Chumash and Salinan Indians inhabited this territory during the Spanish period.

16. For different interpretations of which settlements functioned as towns, see Bannon (1970:164), Mason (1986:5), Robinson (1948:12), and Weber (1992:262).

17. Regional California censuses indicate that a large percentage of the population was *afromestizo*. In Santa Bárbara 19 percent of the residents in 1785 were *afromestizos*; in San José 24 percent and in Monterey 18 percent in 1790 (Forbes 1966:240, 241). Likewise, the population registry of the founders of Los Angeles indicates that 59 percent were *afromestizos* (El Pueblo de Los Angeles Historic Monument, City of Los Angeles).

18. Sánchez (1986:16) proposes that twenty-five ranches were established during the Spanish period, Engstrand (1991:39) thirty-four, Robinson (1948:49–56) thirty, Rush (1965:1) twenty-four, and Cowan (1977:139) thirty-three.

19. Though the children of Black slaves and Indian women were born free, they were required to pay the same taxes as Indians since legally they belonged to Indian communities (McAlister 1957:43–54).

20. The *corregimiento* system was dismantled in 1786 under the intendancy laws (Gibson 1964:84).

21. Hutchinson (1969:80) offers a different date, stating that Indians were released from paying tribute on 26 May 1810.

Chapter 6. Liberal Racial Legislation during the Mexican Period, 1821–1848

1. In 1823 Sonora and Sinaloa were joined as a state (Officer 1987:18, 117). Between 1823 and 1830 Sonora and Sinaloa were separated, rejoined, and finally declared separate states.

2. At the end of the colonial era, the number of slaves in Mexico is estimated to have ranged from 6,000 to 10,000 (Aguirre Beltrán 1946:236–237; cf. Meyer and Sherman 1995:217).

3. Since the late Spanish period, many have considered the mission system an outdated paternalistic institution. For some liberal thinkers the mission system obstructed the acculturation of the Indians, while others who were unconcerned with the welfare of the Indians considered it an obstacle in the conversion of the Southwest into a large-scale private family agriculturalist or ranching economic system.

4. The secularization orders were originally drafted under the Plan de Iguala in 1821 (Engelhardt 1913:108).

5. Of the five-member committee elected to select a delegate to Congress in California, three were former mission Indians (Engelhardt 1913:150).

6. Vicente Guerrero was born in Tixtla, Mexico. He was of Spanish, Black, and Indian descent. In 1810 he enlisted in José María Morelos's troops fighting in

favor of Mexican independence (Appiah and Gates 1999:882–883). By 1816 he had become a general of the rebels and the main military strategist of the movement for independence (ibid.). In 1821 his troops joined forces with General Agustín de Iturbide; their combined armies successfully defeated the royal troops, winning independence for Mexico (Meyer and Sherman 1995:293–295). Guerrero afterward became one of the major figures in designing the new republic's provisional constitution. In 1829 he became president of Mexico, but was shortly thereafter thrown from office when Anastasio Bustamante, his vice-president, executed a successful coup d'état (Weber 1982:31).

7. Engstrand's Spanish text on racial classifications in Arizona reads:

. . . todo el sistema de clasificación racial había sido bastante arbitrario, y lo fue siendo cada vez más a medida que se aproximaba el fin del periodo colonial. El padre Francisco Iturralde, de la misión de Tubutama, ni siquiera intentó dejar constancia del origen de los habitantes de su jurisdicción a los que calificó bajo el epígrafe de "gente de razón," arguyendo que no disponía de tal información. El censo de Tumacácori [1796] que confeccionó el padre Gutiérrez proporciona una información tan vaga como la anterior. Incluye a 29 personas el la categoría de "vecinos," la mayoría de ellos aparentemente peons y ayudantes. (Engstrand 1992:254)

8. In 1910 the federal government allowed census enumerators to count people on the basis of language in order to determine the size of the aboriginal Indian population (Mörner 1967:145–169).

9. Chapman (1930:384) offers a slightly larger estimate of 3,270 for California's population in 1820.

10. The Papago are related to the Pima and belong to the Pima branch of the Uto-Aztecan linguistic stock (Swanton 1984:357). The Cocomaricopa are closely related to the Yuma and are part of the Yuman linguistic stock, a part of the Hokan family (ibid., 349, 354).

11. For a detailed description and analysis of the Indian communities in New Mexico during the Mexican period, see Carroll and Haggard (1942). They provide a translation and analysis of many Mexican documents containing census and ethnographic descriptions as well as copies of the original Mexican documents.

12. During the Mexican period, the state government in Texas prohibited the use of racial distinctions in enumerating the population (Alonzo 1998:48).

13. Weber (1982:4) estimates that in the 1820s most Mexican citizens were acculturated Texan Indians and less than 2,500 were not of that heritage.

14. The population of El Paso Valley and the surrounding communities is estimated to have grown to 8,000 by the 1820s (Weber 1982:4–5) and Laredo to 2,041 (Alonzo 1998:41).

15. Bolton (1921), Ezzell (1974), Kessell (1976), Doyle (1989), and Johnson (1989) contend that many of the Indians who were Christianized by the Spanish already practiced some form of hierarchical political structure (Deloria and Lytle 1983; Johnson 1989; Merriam 1955).

16. Portions of this history of schooling in the Southwest appeared in an earlier version as "The Treaty of Guadalupe Hidalgo and the Racialization of the Mexican Population," in *The Elusive Quest for Equality: 150 Years of Chicano/Chicana Education,* ed. José F. Moreno (Cambridge, Mass.: Harvard Educational Review, 1999), pp. 3–29. Copyright 1999 by the President and Fellows of Harvard College. All rights reserved.

17. After the 1793 decree, the private schools in San Antonio received greater financial support from the local assembly and were provided school supplies, including books, charts, paper, pencils, and slates (Menchaca 1999:12).

18. Not until the federal government passed the act of 1836 was schooling made compulsory and the local governments made responsible for levying taxes to pay for public education (Tyler 1974:209).

19. A league based on Mexican measurements is 2.6 miles or 4,438 acres (Engstrand 1991:46; Margadant S. 1991:91).

20. José Joaquín Ortega was a government administrator and successful otter-hunter and entrepreneur. He served several terms as justice of the peace of the California ranches. He was the son of José María Ortega, a corporal of the Santa Bárbara company, who upon retirement obtained Rancho Refugio. José María was a distinguished officer.

José Joaquín's grandfather, José Francisco, was also a prominent person. Besides being one of the first pioneers in California, José Francisco was a member of his town assembly and a judge and served several terms as head peace officer of the ranches of California. Throughout his lifetime he served as a military officer stationed in several missions (Bancroft 1964:I-Q 760–761).

Chapter 7. Land, Race, and War, 1821–1848

1. Ysleta was separated from New Mexico in 1823 and annexed to the state of Chihuahua (Bowden 1971:157).

2. After Mexican independence, communities in the Southwest were distinguished based on population size and political organization. A village between 800 to 2,000 people was governed by a justice of the peace, who possibly had assistants (Hendricks and Timmons 1998:41–42; cf. Carroll and Haggard 1942:209–210). A town or city exceeding 2,000 had a town assembly (*ayuntamiento*) consisting of a mayor and six elected officials (Hendricks and Timmons 1998:41–42). Communities of less than 800, called *lugares* (places), were governed by the nearest town with an elected assembly.

3. William W. Morrow's estimate (1923) is based on congressional reports. Morrow was a U.S. Circuit Court of Appeals judge in 1923. This estimate does not include the land grants in Arizona.

4. Sixteen land grants were issued in Arizona during the Spanish and Mexican periods (Mattison 1946).

5. The San Pedro land grant was located along the current Sonora-Arizona border (Officer 1987).

6. Bautista Miller was the first non-Indian to live in what today are Liberty and Orange counties. This area was inhabited by the Orcoquisac Indians. In late 1778 Gil Y'Barbo's exploratory expedition found him living there (Castañeda 1939:324–326). Miller was an English castaway who had fled Jamaica. Under Spanish law it was illegal for foreigners to live in Texas without approval of authorities. Miller relayed to Y'Barbo his account of how he had arrived in Texas. He had boarded a ship in Jamaica with five of his slaves. The captain robbed Miller and forced him to abandon ship at the mouth of the Trinity River. Miller also reported that this was a rest stop for English slave ships (Block 1976).

7. The term "bachelor" appears to have been used in a gender-neutral manner: Article 15 defines as bachelors "all those who are alone, or forming a part of no family" (State of Coahuila and Texas Law of Colonization of 1825, cited in *Laws of Texas, Vol. 1*, p. 101). This interpretation is supported by Texas land grant documents indicating that the Mexican government awarded women land grants (TGLO-SMTT).

8. Among the Indians of Mission Espada who applied and obtained deeds were Juan Gomez, Ascencion Garza, Nanuzal, Josefa de la Garza, Simon Gomez, Gaspar Hone, Vicente Gotarz, Jose Maria Condenar, Franco Arando, Luciano Navarro, Jose Maria Escaleta, Vicente Micheli, Ventura de la Garza, Maria de la Garza, Juan Martin de Bermudez, Victoriano Zepeda, Alexaj, Jose Maria Hernandez, Miguel Triciegin, Maria del Refugio de la Garza, and Josefa Maria Hernandez. When the petitioners met with Saucedo, they brought witnesses to support their claims. Most of the witnesses were petitioners themselves; others also served as witnesses, however, including Gaspar Flores Vicente, Goraceig, Delgados, Maria Cardenas, Clem, Francisco Fuardo, Calena, Felipe Frasinga, Mariano de Cansenas, Sonacio Acchesj, Jose Antonio de la Guera, Francisco Arguello, Francisco Ravier, Buntillo, Jose Viciano Navaro, Jose Maria Anocha, Ignacio Chavez, Jose Maria Asuba, Fernando Rodriguez, Francisco de Fevicado, Fernando Rodriguez, Francisco Javier Bustillo, Jose Maria de Gazares, Jose Maria Axocha, Jose Maria Escalena, Jose Fandoval, and Juan Cortina. Several of the witnesses did not know how to write and instead entered iconic signatures (Texas General Land Office Archives, File 121:45, "Espada Mission Land Records").

9. Article 32 of Texas's Law of 1825 exempted immigrants from paying taxes (cited in *Laws of Texas, Vol. 1*, p. 104).

10. During the Spanish period, land was distributed in South Texas on a seniority basis. The founding settlers received 2 leagues for pasture (8,876 acres) and 1,500 acres for planting (Alonzo 1998:39). Settlers who arrived later received the same amount of land for pasture but only 750 acres for planting. Often, however, exceptions were made for subjects favored by the royal government, who received over 5 leagues.

11. Metz (1994:19) argues that in 1790 a land grant extending from El Paso to Arizona was issued to Francisco García, where he established Rancho de Santa Teresa. I have been unable to find any other source to verify this claim.

12. Plans for the secularization of the California missions were based upon

committee recommendations issued beginning in 1825 and were published in reports titled "Regulation of the Missions" (Hutchinson 1969:255).

13. In contrast to Pío Pico, Figueroa is considered by most historians to have been a fair governor and defender of the Indians. Figueroa was known to be proud of his Indian heritage and throughout his lifetime was an advocate for democracy and a proponent of civil rights. He fought against Spain in the war of independence and served in the ranks of José María Morelos and Vicente Guerrero. He was a member of the Congress which drafted the Constitution of 1824 and a staunch supporter of President Vicente Guerrero when he abolished slavery in Mexico (Hutchinson 1969:154). Though Figueroa was an advocate of the Indians, many colonists in California disliked his liberal Indian policies.

14. Lisbeth Haas posits that territorial officials blocked the assignment of land grants to immigrants. In 1834 they composed the *Manifiesto de la República Mexicana*, in which they asserted the land rights of the Indians and colonists (Haas 1995:36). Though Haas is correct in the interpretation of this document, land grant records indicate that many Anglo Americans were issued grants throughout California (Cowan 1977).

15. In northern California Christian *ranchería* Indians from Capay, Casalamcujomí, and Cotate began the land patent process, but did not complete it (Robinson 1948:71).

16. See note 18 in Chapter 5.

17. This information was obtained by comparing the names of the grantees in Cowan's (1977:115–123) land registry with Bancroft's (1964) abstracts of California's pioneers.

18. The Carrillo, Pico, and Alvarado families intermarried during the Mexican period (see Bancroft 1964; Garrison 1935).

19. Vallejo's and Carrillo's grants were confirmed within a few months after Alvarado left office (Cowan 1977:126–133).

20. Rafael Sánchez received a patent a few months after Micheltorena left office (Cowan 1977:141).

21. From 1832 to 1833 José Maria Echeandía, Agustín Zamorano, and Pío Pico claimed that they were governors of California (Rush 1965:116). Pío Pico obtained federal recognition as interim governor twenty days before the federal government appointed José Figueroa as the new governor.

22. This oral history was collected by Hubert H. Bancroft from Pío Pico (Bancroft 1964:I-Q 778, 779).

23. Santiago's non-*afromestizo* sons Don Patricio, Don Javier, and Don Miguel Pico obtained 100,000 acres in southern California, on the ranch they called San José de Gracia de Simi, and another son, Don Dolores, obtained 35,504 acres (8 square leagues) in Monterey district, in which he established Bolsa de San Cayetano (Garrison 1935:30–31).

Chapter 8. The Treaty of Guadalupe Hidalgo and the Racialization of the Mexican Population

1. The ideas contained in the sections on the Treaty of Guadalupe Hidalgo and citizenship are based upon two of my articles, "Chicano Indianism: A Historical Account of Racial Repression in the United States" (1993) and "The Treaty of Guadalupe Hidalgo and the Racialization of the Mexican Population" (1999).

2. The California legislature passed the Fugitive Slave Law in 1852, prohibiting runaway slaves from settling in the state (Heizer and Almquist 1977:122–124).

3. For an extended discussion on citizenship after the Mexican American War, see my article "Chicano Indianism: A Historical Account of Racial Repression in the United States" (1993). Although the Fourteenth Amendment was passed in 1868 with the intention of legislating a uniform citizenship law and allowing many people of color to become citizens, many states ignored this ruling.

4. The Naturalization Act of 1790, which only allowed "free white immigrants" to apply for naturalization, was finally nullified in 1940 (Hull 1985; Konvitz 1946). For a detailed discussion on the history of naturalization and Mexicans, see Menchaca 1993.

5. Under the Plan de Iguala all free people residing in Mexico in 1821 were declared citizens (Meyer and Sherman 1995). Foreigners who immigrated to Mexico after that date needed to be naturalized before becoming citizens (Weber 1982).

6. David Williams (1998) argues that William Goyen obtained property by a special grant of the Texas legislature. The name of the tract of land is not specified. Allegedly he was rewarded for his services as an Indian agent. I was unable to confirm this information based on Texas General Land Office records. The *New Handbook of Texas History* (1996) states that "Goyen's Hill" was purchased.

7. Mr. Gaylan Greaser, the archivist of the Spanish and Mexican land grant records in the Texas General Land Office, concurs that there are no available records indicating that Christian Indians had their grants confirmed under the Republic of Texas or U.S. occupation.

8. After the U.S.-Mexico boundary was set, following the Mexican American War, the civic buildings of Senecú lay on the Mexican side and a large part of the farm lands on the U.S. side. Those Senecú Indians living on the U.S. side lost their ranch lands during American occupation (see Bowden 1971; Minter 1993). The Texas legislature treated the confiscated property as part of the grant land given to the Ysleta Indians.

9. Garza (1980) is a photocopy of the original study conducted by the Mexican government in 1852.

10. In comparing the list compiled by the General Commission for U.S.-Mexico Relations with the names of the land grantees of Mission Espada I did not find the names of the mission Indian families included in the list of grantees who complained to the Mexican government (Texas General Land Office, archives, File 121:45, "Espada Mission Land Records").

11. After Mexican independence, the towns founded by *genizaros* were classified as Mexican towns and villas (see Chapter 7). See Brayer (1949:149, 205, 210, 253) and Leonard (1943:27) for a discussion of the land confirmation process experienced by the settlers of Abiquiú, Ojo Caliente, Socorro, Anton Chico, and San Miguel del Vado.

12. On 8 February 1887 the General Allotment Act was passed, allowing Indian communities to divide reservation land among tribal members and give each family the authority to sell their parcels (Dale 1951:120). Furthermore, the act authorized the president of the United States to purchase any tract and distribute it among homesteaders. The Pueblo Indians resisted the allotment process and retained their land under the control of their tribal governments.

13. Former circuit court judge of appeals William W. Morrow offers a different estimate of the amount of land involved in the claims, arguing that approximately 30 million acres were reviewed and 20 million rejected (Morrow 1923:23). He excludes from his estimate the acreage that was rejected on the basis that the claims were fraudulent. Ebright's claim includes the acreage identified to be fraudulent.

14. Edward Soza (1994a, 1998) found in a review of the applications submitted under the Homestead Act of 1862 and other state homestead acts that the majority of Mexican applicants were unsuccessful. The reasons given by the land commission included individuals' not being citizens, fraudulent conduct, and people claiming to be Mexican who were actually Indian.

15. After Indians were denied citizenship and protection under the Treaty of Guadalupe Hidalgo, Mexican delegates attempted to obtain some monetary compensation for their anticipated property losses in 1849, during California's first constitutional convention (see Ross Browne 1850:70). In particular, the delegate for Santa Bárbara, Mr. P. Noriega de la Guerra, argued that if Christian Indians were going to be taxed like other California residents they should receive some political privileges and at minimum be paid for the confiscation of their property. He added that it was cruel to rescind the political rights Christian Indians had enjoyed for decades and to treat them as if they were uncivilized. Though the majority of the delegates concurred that Christian Indians should not be treated as nomadic Indians and removed to reservations, they rejected any plan to compensate them. In 1849 California's constitution was endorsed by forty-eight delegates, eight of whom were Mexican (Ross Browne 1850:478–479).

16. In 1876 Simone, an Indian, purchased a land grant in San Gabriel and had the grant validated by the California Land Commission (Ayers 1886:13; Engstrand 1991). He was allowed to keep his land because under federal law Indians could own property if it had been purchased. Property was confiscated when the Spanish or Mexican government had granted the land. This is the only case of a Christian Indian purchasing a land grant and subsequently having it confirmed. The original land grant owner was a Mexican and had a perfect land title.

17. Under *Worcester v. Georgia* (1832, cited in Minter 1993:3) the U.S. Supreme Court reaffirmed the opinion that the federal government had the obliga-

tion to protect Indian territory against the passage of state laws which left Indians homeless.

18. Reservations established between 1851 to 1853 were designed to relocate nomadic Indians who had ceased warring against the state (Hurtado 1988:136–147). Mainly the Indians from Tejón Pass and the San Joaquín Valley were placed on reservation lands.

19. When the U.S. Congress passed the California Land Act of 1851, it placed full authority in a land commission and instructed the district courts to adjudicate land claim appeals. The president appointed a commission of three members to hear testimony and to study land documents. The commission could either confirm or reject the claims, and either side could appeal to the district courts (Engstrand 1991:43, 44).

20. Robinson and Engstrand offer slightly different estimates. Robinson (1948: 106) proposes that 604 grants were confirmed, 190 rejected, and 19 withdrawn. Engstrand (1991:44) states that 603 claims were confirmed, 190 rejected, and 20 withdrawn.

21. The file *Santa Paula Water Works et al. v. Julio Peralta, 1893–1898* is located in the Ventura County Court House. It contains documents pertaining to Peralta's district and state court cases.

22. Mexican elites experienced downward mobility during the 1870s, but most did not lose their homes. For example, though General Vallejo lost his land grants, he was able to send his son to medical school, and one of his daughters married into a wealthy Anglo-American family (Bancroft 1964:R-Z 759).

23. In 1870, a few years after the transatlantic railroad connecting the East and West coasts was completed, thousands of railroad workers and their families settled in California and sought employment. Among this population were over 49,277 Chinese railroad workers, who turned to the ranches and farms in search of work (U.S. Census 1872:20; Takaki 1990).

24. Blacks for unknown reasons did not become part of the preferred farm labor force (Galarza 1964). Instead they were hired for the lowest-paying occupations in the factories and for unskilled jobs, including service and domestic work.

Chapter 9. Racial Segregation and Liberal Policies Then and Now

1. Sections of this chapter are based upon my article "Chicano Indianism: A Historical Account of Racial Repression in the United States" (1993).

2. *United States v. Wong Kim Ark* was argued in March 1897; the final decision was rendered in March 1898.

3. By 1900 the size of the Mexican immigrant population had increased to 103,445 and by 1920 to 486,418 (U.S. Census 1902:61, 1922:299).

4. Bakke filed his suit against the University of California Medical School at Davis in 1974 (Takaki 1994:24).

Bibliography

Acuña, Rodolfo

1972 *Occupied America: The Chicano's Struggle toward Liberation.* San Francisco, Calif.: Canfield Press.

Adams, Richard

1991 *Prehistoric Mesoamerica.* Norman: University of Oklahoma Press.

Agassiz, Louis

1854 Sketch of the Natural Provinces to the Animal World and Their Relation to the Different Types of Man. In *Types of Mankind,* ed. Josiah Clark Nott, pp. viii–xxvi. Philadelphia, Penn.: Lippincott, Grambo and Company.

Aguirre Beltrán, Gonzalo

1991 *Formas de gobierno indígena.* 3rd ed. Obra Antropológica 4. Veracruz, Mexico: Instituto Nacional Indigenista, Universidad Veracruzana.

1946 *La población negra de México, 1519–1810.* Mexico City: Ediciones Fuente Cultural.

1944 The Slave Trade in Mexico. *Hispanic American Historical Review* 24 (3): 412–431.

Aikens, Melvin C.

1978 The Far West. In *Ancient Native Americans,* ed. Jessie David Jennings, pp. 131–181. San Francisco, Calif.: W. H. Freeman.

Alessio Robles, Vito

1934 *Saltillo en la historia y en la leyenda.* Mexico City: A. del Bosque Impresor Pensador Mexicano.

Almaguer, Tomás

1979 Class, Race, and Capitalist Development: The Social Transformation of a Southern California County, 1848–1903. Doctoral dissertation, University of California Berkeley.

Alonso, Ana María

1995 *Thread of Blood: Colonialism, Revolution, and Gender on Mexico's Northern Frontier.* Tucson: University of Arizona Press.

Alonzo, Armando C.

1998 *Tejano Legacy: Rancheros and Settlers in South Texas, 1734–1900.* Albuquerque: University of New Mexico Press.

Altamira, Rafael

1988 *Historia de la civilización española.* Barcelona: Instituto de Estudios "Juan Gil-Albert," Fundación Altamira.

Alurista

1972 *Nationchild/Plumaroja.* San Diego, Calif.: Toltecas en Aztlán, Centro Cultural de La Raza.

1970 Poem in Lieu of Preface. *Aztlán* 1 (1): vi.

1969 "The History of Aztlán." Alurista Papers, 1968–1979. Nettie Lee Benson Latin American Collection, Rare Books, University of Texas at Austin.

Alvarez, Roberto, Jr.

1986 The Lemon Grove Incident: The Nation's First Successful Desegregation Court Case. *Journal of San Diego History* 32 (2): 116–135.

American Anthropological Association

1999 *American Anthropological Association 1998–1999: A Guide to Programs/ A Directory of Members.* Arlington, Va.: AAA.

Anzaldúa, Gloria

1986 *Borderlands/La Frontera: The New Mestiza.* San Francisco: Aunt Lute Press.

Appiah, Anthony Kwame, and Henry Louis Gates

1999 *Africana: The Encyclopedia of the African and African American Experience.* New York: Basic Civitas Books.

Archibald, Richard

1978 Acculturation and Assimilation in Colonial New Mexico. *New Mexico Historical Review* 53 (3): 205–217.

Ayers, James J.

1886 *Spanish and Mexican Grants in California, Complete to February 25, 1886.* Sacramento, Calif.: State Printing.

Baga, Fray Antonio

1690 Relatos acerca de varias misiones de Coahuila y Tejas. General Archives of the State of Tlaxcala, File Diaspora Tlaxcalteca. Tlaxcala, Mexico (reprint).

Bancroft, Hubert Howe

1964 *Register of Pioneer Inhabitants of California 1542–1848.* Los Angeles: Dawson's Book Shop.

Bandelier, Adolph F.

1990 *The Discovery of New Mexico by the Franciscan Monk Friar Marcos de*

Niza in 1539. Trans. and ed. Madeline Turrell Rodack. Tucson: University of Arizona Press. (1st ed. 1886.)

Bannon, John Francis
1970 *The Spanish Borderlands Frontier 1513-1821*. New York: Holt, Rinehart and Winston.

Banton, Michael, and Jonathan Harwood
1975 *The Race Concept*. London: David and Charles.

Barreiro, Antonio
1832 *Ojeada sobre Nuevo México, que da una idea*. Reprinted in *Three New Mexico Chronicles*, ed. H. Bailey Carroll and J. Villasana Haggard, pp. 263–318. Albuquerque, N.M.: Quivira Society, 1942.

Barth, Fredrik
1969 Introduction. In *Ethnic Groups and Ethnic Boundaries*, ed. Fredrik Barth, pp. 9–38. Boston: Little, Brown and Company.

Bautista Pino, Pedro
1812 Exposición sucinta and sencilla de la Provincia del Nuevo México. Reprinted in *Three New Mexico Chronicles*, ed. H. Bailey Carroll and J. Villasana Haggard, pp. 211–261. Albuquerque, N.M.: Quivira Society, 1942.

Bayle, Constantino
1931 España y el clero indígena de América. *Razón y Fe: Revista Quinceñal Hispano Americana* 94 (405): 213–225.

Bean, John Lowell, and Florence C. Shipek
1978 Luiseños. In *Handbook of North American Indians: Vol. 8, California*, ed. Robert F. Heizer, pp. 550–563. Washington, D.C.: Smithsonian Institution.

Beers, Henry Putney
1979 *Spanish and Mexican Records of the American Southwest*. Tucson: University of Arizona Press.

Berdan, Frances F.
1982 *The Aztecs of Central Mexico: An Imperial Society*. New York: Holt, Rinehart and Winston.

Berger, Max
1947 Education in Texas during the Spanish and Mexican Periods. *Southwestern Historical Quarterly* 51: 41–53.

Blackburn, Robin
1998 *The Making of New World Slavery: From Baroque to the Modern 1492-1800*. New York: Verso.

Blauner, Robert
1994 Colonized and Immigrant Minorities. In *From Different Shores: Perspec-*

tives on *Race and Ethnicity in America,* ed. Ronald Takaki, pp. 149–160.
New York: Oxford University Press. (1st printing 1972.)

Blazquez, Jose Maria

1975 *Tartessos y los origenes de la colonizacion fenicia en Occidente.* Spain:
University of Salamanca.

Block, W. T.

1979 Meanest Town in the Coast. *Old West* 16 (2): 10–11, 28–30.

1976 *A History of Jefferson County, Texas: From Wilderness to Reconstruction.*
(Master of arts thesis, Lamar University.) Printed Nederland, Tex.: Nederland Publishing.

Bolton, Herbert E.

1966 *Anza's California Expeditions, An Outpost of Empire, Volume 1.* New
York: Russell and Russell.

1960 *The Mission as a Frontier Institution in the Spanish-American Colonies.*
El Paso: Texas Western College Press for Academic Reprints.

1921 *The Spanish Borderlands.* New Haven, Conn.: Yale University Press.

Bonifaz de Novello, María Eugenia

1975 *La mujer mexicana: Análisis histórico.* Mexico City: Impresa Mexicana.

Borah, Woodrow

1983 *Justice by Insurance: The General Indian Court of Colonial Mexico and
the Legal Aides of the Half-Real.* Berkeley: University of California Press.

Bourdieu, Pierre

1992 *Outline of a Theory of Practice.* Cambridge: Cambridge University Press.

Bowden, Jocelyn J.

1971 *Spanish and Mexican Land Grants in the Chihuahua Acquisition.* El Paso:
Texas Western Press.

Bowman, J. N.

1958 The Resident Neophytes of the California Missions 1769–1834. *Historical
Society of Southern California Quarterly* 40 (2): 138–148.

Bravo Lira, Bernardino

1970 *Formación del derecho occidental: Con especial referencia a la Península
Ibérica.* Santiago, Chile: Editorial Jurídica de Chile.

Brayer, Herbert O.

1949 *William Blackmore: The Spanish-Mexican Land Grants of New Mexico
and Colorado, 1863–1878.* Denver, Colo.: Bradford-Robinson.

Brinton, Daniel Garrison

1890 *Races and Peoples: Lectures on the Science of Ethnography.* New York:
N. D. C. Hodges Publishers.

Bronitsky, Gordon

1987   Indian Assimilation in the El Paso Area. *New Mexico Historical Review* 62 (2): 151–168.

Brumgardt, John R.

1976   *From Sonora to San Francisco Bay: The Expeditions of Juan Bautista de Anza 1774–1776.* Riverside, Calif.: Historical Commission.

Bugbee, Lester G.

1898   Slavery in Early Texas. *Political Science Quarterly* 13 (3): 389–413.

Bustamante, Adrian

1991   "The Matter Was Never Resolved": The *Casta* System in Colonial New Mexico, 1693–1823. *New Mexico Historical Review* 66 (2): 143–163.

Cabeza de Vaca, Alvar Núñez

1922   *Naufragios y comentarios.* Madrid: Calpe. (1st printing 1542.)

California

1849   *Constitution of the State of California, 1849.* Reprinted in original form: San Marino, Calif.: Friends of the Huntington Library, 1949.

California Land Case No. 550

1853   For the Place Named Santa Paula y Saticoy. United States District Court, Southern California. California land cases compiled by Mr. Guadalasca. Archived at Bancroft Library, University of California, Berkeley.

Camarillo, Albert

1984   *Chicanos in California: A History of Mexican-Americans.* San Francisco: Boyd and Fraser Publishing.

Campbell, Thomas Nolan

1977   Ethnic Identities of Extinct Coahuiltecan Populations: Case of the Juanaca Indians. *Pearce Sellars Series* 26: 1–16. Austin: Texas Memorial Museum.

Carpenter, Rhys

1925   *The Greeks in Spain.* New York: Longmans, Green and Company.

Carrico, Richard L.

1987   *Strangers in a Stolen Land: American Indians in San Diego 1850–1880.* Sacramento, Calif.: Sierra Oaks.

Carroll, H. Bailey, and J. Villasana Haggard

1942   *Three New Mexico Chronicles.* Albuquerque, N.M.: Quivira Society.

Cary, Eve, and Kathleen W. Peratis

1977   *Woman and the Law.* New York: National Textbook Company and the American Civil Liberties Union.

Castañeda, Antonia

1993   Presidarias y Pobladoras: The Journey North and Life in Frontier Califor-
       nia. In *Chicana Critical Issues*, ed. Norma Alarcón, Rafaela Castro, Emma
       Pérez, Beatriz Pesquera, Adaljiza Sosa Ridell, and Patricia Zavella, pp. 73–
       94. Berkeley: Third Woman Press.

Castañeda, Carlos Eduardo

1950   *Our Catholic Heritage in Texas 1519–1936, the Transition Period: The Fight
       for Freedom 1810–1836, Vol. 6.* Austin, Tex.: Von Boeckmann–Jones Com-
       pany.

1939   *Our Catholic Heritage in Texas 1519–1936, the Mission Era: The Passing of
       the Missions 1762–1782, Vol. 4.* Austin, Tex.: Von Boeckmann–Jones Com-
       pany.

1938   *Our Catholic Heritage in Texas 1519–1936, the Mission Era: The Missions
       at Work 1731–1761, Vol. 3.* Austin, Tex.: Von Boeckmann–Jones Company.

1936   *Our Catholic Heritage in Texas 1519–1936, the Mission Era: The Winning
       of Texas 1693–1731, Vol. 2.* Austin, Tex.: Von Boeckmann–Jones Company.

Castetter, Edward F., and Willis H. Bell

1951   *Yuman Indian Agriculture: Primitive Subsistence on the Lower Colorado
       and Gila Rivers.* Albuquerque: University of New Mexico Press.

Castillo, Edward D.

1989   The Native American Response to the Colonization of Alta California. In
       *Columbian Consequences, Vol. 1, Archaeological and Historical Perspec-
       tives on the Spanish Borderlands West,* ed. David Hurst Thomas, pp. 377–
       394. Washington, D.C.: Smithsonian Institution Press.

Chalfant, William Y.

1991   *Without Quarter: The Wichita Expedition and the Fight on Crooked Creek.*
       Norman: University of Oklahoma Press.

Chance, John K., and William Taylor

1977   Estate and Class in Colonial City: Oaxaca in 1792. *Comparative Studies in
       Society and History* 19 (4): 454–487.

Chapman, Charles E.

1930   *A History of California: The Spanish Period.* New York: Macmillan Com-
       pany.

1916   *The Founding of Spanish California: The Northward Expansion of New
       Spain, 1687–1783.* New York: Macmillan Company.

Chipman, Donald. E.

1992   *Spanish Texas 1519–1821.* Austin: University of Texas Press.

1977   The Oñate-Moctezuma-Zaldivar Families of Northern Spain. *New Mexico
       Historical Review* 52 (October): 297–310.

Cohen, Ronald

1978 Ethnicity: Problem and Focus in Anthropology. *Annual Review of Anthropology* 7: 379–403.

Collins, Karen Sikes

1970 Fray Pedro De Arriquibar's Census of Tucson, 1820. *Journal of Arizona History* 2 (1): 14–22.

Constitution of the United States

1986 In *United States Code Service Constitution*, p. 18. Washington, D.C.: Government Printing Office.

Contreras, Sheila Marie

1998 Bloodlines: Modernism, Indigenismo, and the Construction of Chicana/o Identity (Mexican Indian). Doctoral dissertation, University of Texas at Austin.

Cook, Sherburne F.

1976 *The Population of the California Indians 1769–1970.* Berkeley: University of California Press.

Cook, Sherburne F., and Woodrow Borah

1974 *Essays in Population History: Mexico and the Caribbean, Vol. 2.* Berkeley: University of California Press.

Cope, R. Douglas

1994 *The Limits of Racial Domination: Plebeian Society in Colonial Mexico City, 1660–1720.* Madison: University of Wisconsin Press.

Corbin, James E.

1989 Spanish-Indian Interaction on the Eastern Frontier of Texas. In *Columbian Consequences, Vol. 1, Archaeological and Historical Perspectives on the Spanish Borderlands West,* ed. David Hurst Thomas, pp. 269–276. Washington, D.C.: Smithsonian Institution Press.

Cornish, Beatrice Quijada

1917 The Ancestry and Family of Juan De Oñate. In *The Pacific Ocean in History,* ed. H. Morse Stephens and Herbert E. Bolton, pp. 452–466. New York: Macmillan Company.

Cortes, Vicenta

1964 *La esclavitud en Valencia durante el reinado de los reyes católicos 1479–1516.* Valencia, Spain: Publicaciones del Archivo Municipal de Valencia.

Costello, Julia G., and David Hornbeck

1989 Alta California: An Overview. In *Columbian Consequences, Vol. 1, Archaeological and Historical Perspectives on the Spanish Borderlands West,* ed. David Hurst Thomas, pp. 303–331. Washington, D.C.: Smithsonian Institution Press.

Cowan, Robert G.

1977   *Ranchos of California.* Los Angeles: Society of Southern California, American Offset Printers.

Creamer, Winifred, and Jonathan Haas

1991   Pueblo: Search for the Ancient Ones. *National Geographic* 180 (4): 84–99.

Cutter, Charles R.

1995   *The Legal Culture of Northern New Spain.* Albuquerque: University of New Mexico Press.

1986   *The Protector de Indios in Colonial New Mexico, 1659–1821.* Albuquerque: University of New Mexico Press.

Dale, Edward E.

1951   *The Indians of the Southwest: A Century of Development and the United States.* Norman: University of Oklahoma Press.

Davis, Stephen, and Merritt Mechem, comps.

1915   *New Mexico Statutes Annotated.* Denver, Colo.: W. H. Courtright Publishing.

Dean, Jeffrey S.

1992   Delineating the Anasazi. In *Emil W. Haury's Prehistory of the American Southwest,* ed. J. Jefferson Reid and Davis Doyle, pp. 407–413. Tucson: University of Arizona Press.

Deavenport, James J., comp.

1856   *Revised Statutes of the Territory of New Mexico.* Santa Fe, N.M.: Santa Fe Weekly Gazette.

de la Peña, Guillermo

1993   Individuo, etnia, nación: Paradojas y antinomias de la identidad colectiva. In *Epistemología y cultura: En torno a la obra de Luis Villoro,* ed. Ernesto Garzón Valdín and Fernando Salmerón, pp. 243–261. Mexico City: Universidad Nacional Autónoma de México, Instituto de Investigaciones Filosóficas.

de la Teja, Jesús

1991   Forgotten Founders: The Military Settlers of Eighteenth-Century San Antonio de Béxar. In *Tejano Origins in Eighteenth-Century San Antonio,* ed. Gerald E. Poyo and Gilbert M. Hinojosa, pp. 27–39. Austin: University of Texas Press.

de León, Arnoldo

1987   *They Called Them Greasers: Anglo Attitudes toward Mexicans in Texas, 1821–1900.* Austin: University of Texas Press.

Deloria, Vine, Jr., and Clifford M. Lytle

1988   *American Indians, American Justice.* Austin: University of Texas Press.

Desmond, Clark J.

1973 Prehistoric Origins of the African Culture. In *Peoples and Cultures of Africa*, ed. Elliott P. Skinner, pp. 34–58. Garden City, N.Y.: National History Press.

Despres, Leo A.

1975 Toward a Theory of Ethnic Phenomena. In *Ethnicity and Resource Competition in Plural Societies*, ed. Leo A. Despres, pp. 187–208. The Hague/Paris: Mouton Publishers.

Díaz del Castillo, Bernal

1963 *The Conquest of New Spain*. 6th ed. Translated by J. M. Cohen. New York: Penguin Classics. (Manuscript written circa 1578.)

Dobyns, Henry F.

1976 *Spanish Colonial Tucson: A Demographic History*. Tucson: University of Arizona Press.

1962 *Pioneering Christians among the Perishing Indians of Tucson*. Lima, Peru: Editorial Estudios Andinos.

Donato, Rubén

1997 *The Other Struggle for Equal Schools: Mexican Americans during the Civil Rights Era*. New York: State University of New York.

Donato, Rubén, Martha Menchaca, and Richard R. Valencia

1991 Segregation, Desegregation, and Integration of Chicano Students: Problems and Prospects. In *Chicano School Failure and Success: Research and Policy Agendas for the 1990s*, ed. Richard R. Valencia, pp. 27–63. New York: Falmer Press.

Doyle, David E.

1989 The Transition to History in Northern Pimería Alta. In *Columbian Consequences, Vol. 1, Archaeological and Historical Perspectives on the Spanish Borderlands West*, ed. David Hurst Thomas, pp. 139–158. Washington, D.C.: Smithsonian Institution Press.

D'Sousa, Dinesh

1995 *The End of Racism*. New York: Free Press.

Dubois, William Edward Burghardt

1975 *The Gift of Black Folk*. Millwood, N.Y.: Kraus-Thomson.

Ebright, Malcolm

1991 Introduction: Spanish and Mexican Land Grants and the Law. In *Spanish and Mexican Land Grants and the Law*, ed. Malcolm Ebright, pp. 3–11. Manhattan, Kans.: Sunflower University Press.

1980 The Embudo Grant: A Case Study of Justice and the Court of Private Land Claims. In *Spanish and Mexican Land Grants in New Mexico and Colo-*

rado, ed. John R. Van Ness and Christine M. Van Ness, pp. 74–85. Special edition of *Journal of the West.*

Engelhardt, Zephyrin

1986 *Mission Santa Ines Virgen y Martir and Its Ecclesiastical Seminary.* Santa Barbara, Calif.: McNally and Loftin Publishers. (1st printing 1932.)

1930 *Missions and Missionaries of California: Upper California, Vol. 2.* 2nd ed. Santa Barbara, Calif.: Mission Santa Barbara.

1929 *Missions and Missionaries of California: Lower California, Vol. 1.* 2nd ed. Santa Barbara, Calif.: Mission Santa Barbara.

1913 *Missions and Missionaries of California: Lower California, Vol. 3, Part 2.* San Francisco, Calif.: James H. Barry Company.

Engstrand, Iris H. W.

1992 *Arizona hispánica.* Madrid, Spain: Editorial Mapre.

1991 An Enduring Legacy: California *Ranchos* in Historical Perspective. In *Spanish and Mexican Land Grants and the Law,* ed. Malcolm Ebright, pp. 36–47. Manhattan, Kans.: Sunflower University Press.

1978 Land Grant Problems in the Southwest: The Spanish and Mexican Heritage. *New Mexico Historical Review* 53 (4): 317–336.

Ezzell, Paul H.

1974 The Hispanic Acculturation of the Gila River Pimas. *American Anthropologist Memoir 90.* Milwood, N.Y.: Kraus Reprint.

Fagan, Brian

1991 *Ancient North American: The Archeology of a Continent.* New York: Thames and Hudson.

Feagin, Joe

1996 *Racial and Ethnic Relations.* Englewood Cliffs, N.J.: Prentice-Hall.

Feagin, Joe, and Clairece Booher Feagin

1999 *Racial and Ethnic Relations.* Upper Saddle River, N.J.: Prentice-Hall.

Fewkes, Walter J.

1902 The Pueblo Settlements near El Paso, Texas. *American Anthropologist* 4: 57–75.

First Legislative Assembly

1851 New Mexico Organic Law [Act] of 1850. In *Laws of the Territory of New Mexico,* pp. 17–24. Santa Fe, N.M.: James L. Collins and Company.

Fish, Susan K., Paul R. Fish, and John H. Madsen

1992 Introduction to Time, Place and Research. In *The Marana Community in the Hohokam World,* ed. Susan K. Fish, Paul R. Fish, and John H. Madsen, pp. 1–19. Tucson: University of Arizona Press.

Fletcher, Richard

1992 *Moorish Spain.* London, England: Weidenfeld and Nicolson.

Forbes, Jack D.

1994 *Apache, Navaho, and Spaniard.* Norman: University of Oklahoma Press.

1982 *Native Americans of California and Nevada.* Happy Camp, Calif.: Nature-graph Publishers.

1973 *Aztecas del Norte: The Chicanos of Aztlán.* Greenwich, Conn.: Fawcett Publications.

1968 *Afro-Americans in the Far West: A Handbook for Educators.* Berkeley, Calif.: Far West Laboratory for Educational Research and Development.

1966 Black Pioneers: The Spanish-Speaking Afroamericans of the Southwest. *Phylon* 27: 233–246.

Fowler, Catherine S.

1972 Some Ecological Clues to Proto-Numic Homelands. In *Great Basin Cultural Ecology,* ed. Don D. Fowler, pp. 105–121. Reno: Desert Research Institute, University of Nevada.

Frye, David

1996 *Indians into Mexicans: History and Identity in a Mexican Town.* Austin: University of Texas Press.

Galarza, Ernesto

1964 *Merchants of Labor: The Mexican Bracero Story.* Santa Barbara, Calif.: McNally and Loftin Publishers.

Ganot, Jaime R., and Alejandro A. Peschard

1995 The Archaeological Site of El Cañón del Molino, Durango, Mexico. In *The Gran Chichimeca: Essays on the Archaeology and Ethnohistory of Northern Mesoamerica,* ed. Jonathan E. Reyman, pp. 146–178. Aldershot, Hampshire, Great Britain: Avebury.

Garrison, Myrtle

1935 *Romance and History of California Ranchos.* San Francisco: Harr Wagner Publishing Company.

Garza, Leonel, comp.

1980 Agencia mexicana ante la Comisión General de Reclamaciones entre México y los Estados Unidos—Reclamaciones mexicanas. Reprint of the original 1852 manuscript. In *Indece [sic] de propetarios [sic] originales con la pagina y numero de reclamacion,* pp. 1–13, 102–157. N.p.: Asociacion de Reclamantes of Texas Land Grant Heirs.

Gibson, Charles

1967 *Tlaxcala in the Sixteenth Century.* New Haven, Conn.: Yale University Press.

1964 *Aztecs under Spanish Rule: A History of the Indians of the Valley of Mexico.* Stanford, Calif.: Stanford University Press.

Gillespie, Susan
1989 *The Aztec Kings: The Construction of Rulership in Mexican History.* Tucson: University of Arizona Press.

Givens, David B., and Timothy Jabloski
1996 Survey of Departments. *Anthropology Newsletter* 37 (6): 5.

Glick, Thomas
1979 *Islamic and Christian Spain in the Early Middle Ages.* Princeton, N.J.: Princeton University Press.

Gómez-Quiñonez, Juan
1978 *Mexican Students Por La Raza: The Chicano Movement in Southern California, 1967–1977.* Santa Barbara, Calif.: Editorial La Causa.

Gonzalez, Gilbert
1990 *Chicano Education in the Era of Segregation.* Philadelphia: Balch Institute Press.

Goodrich, Chauncey Shafter
1926 The Legal Status of the California Indian. *California Law Review* 24 (2): 83–100.

Gordon, Milton M.
1964 *Assimilation in American Life: The Role of Race, Religion, and National Origins.* New York: Oxford University Press.

Gossett, Thomas F.
1977 *Race: The History of an Idea in America.* New York: Schocken Books.

Graham, Joe S.
1994 *El Rancho in South Texas: Continuity and Change from 1750.* Kingsville: University of North Texas Press.

Graham, Richard, ed.
1990 *The Idea of Race in Latin America, 1870–1940.* Austin: University of Texas Press.

Gramsci, Antonio
1988 *An Antonio Gramsci Reader: Selective Writings, 1916–1935.* Comp. David Forgacs. New York: Schocken Books.

Grant, Campbell
1978a Chumash: Introduction. In *Handbook of North American Indians: Vol. 8, California,* ed. Robert F. Heizer, pp. 505–508. Washington, D.C.: Smithsonian Institution.
1978b Eastern Coastal Chumash. In *Handbook of North American Indians:*

Vol. 8, California, ed. Robert F. Heizer, pp. 509-519. Washington, D.C.: Smithsonian Institution.

Grodin, Joseph R., Calvin R. Massey, and Richard B. Cunningham
1993   The California State Constitution: A Reference Guide. Westport, Conn.: Greenwood Press.

Guest, Francis F.
1978   An Examination of the Thesis of S. F. Cook on the Forced Conversion of Indians in the California Missions. Southern California Quarterly 61 (1): 1-77.

Gutiérrez, Nelly Solana
1992   Códices de México. Mexico City: Panorama Editorial.

Gutiérrez, Ramón A.
1991   When Jesus Came, the Corn Mothers Went Away: Marriage, Sexuality, and Power in New Mexico, 1500-1846. Stanford, Calif.: Stanford University Press.

Haas, Lisbeth
1995   Conquests and Historical Identities in California 1769-1936. Berkeley: University of California Press.

Hall, Thomas D.
1989   Social Change in the Southwest, 1350-1880. Lawrence: University Press of Kansas.

Hall, Thomas D., and David J. Weber
1984   Mexican Liberals and the Pueblo Indians, 1821-1829. New Mexico Historical Review 59 (1): 5-32.

Hammond, George P.
1953   Introduction. In Don Juan de Oñate: Colonizer of New Mexico, 1595-1628, Volume 5, ed. George P. Hammond and Agapito Rey, pp. 1-38. Albuquerque: University of New Mexico Press.

Hammond, George P., and Agapito Rey, eds.
1953   Don Juan de Oñate: Colonizer of New Mexico, 1595-1628, Volume 5. Albuquerque: University of New Mexico Press.

Hanke, Lewis
1949   The Spanish Struggle for Justice in the Conquest of America. Philadelphia: University of Pennsylvania Press.

Haring, Clarence H.
1963   The Spanish Empire in America. New York: Harbinger.

Haury, Emil Walter
1992a The Mogollon Culture of Southwestern New Mexico. In Emil W. Haury's

Prehistory of the American Southwest, ed. J. Jefferson Reid and David E. Doyle, pp. 305–404. Tucson: University of Arizona Press.

1992b Roosevelt 9:6: A Hohokam Site of the Colonial Period. In *Emil W. Haury's Prehistory of the American Southwest*, ed. J. Jefferson Reid and David E. Doyle, pp. 211–294. Tucson: University of Arizona Press.

1992c Speculations on Prehistoric Settlement Patterns in the Southwest. In *Emil W. Haury's Prehistory of the American Southwest*, ed. J. Jefferson Reid and David E. Doyle, pp. 422–431. Tucson: University of Arizona Press.

1992d Thoughts after Sixty Years as a Southwestern Archaeologist. In *Emil W. Haury's Prehistory of the American Southwest*, ed. J. Jefferson Reid and David E. Doyle, pp. 435–464. Tucson: University of Arizona Press.

Hechter, Michael

1977 *Internal Colonialism: The Celtic Fringe in British National Development, 1536–1966.* Berkeley: University of California Press.

Heizer, Robert F., and Alan F. Almquist

1977 *The Other Californians: Prejudice and Discrimination under Spain, Mexico, and the United States.* Berkeley: University of California Press.

Hendrick, Irving G.

1977 *The Education of Non-Whites in California 1849–1970.* San Francisco: R & E Associates.

Hendricks, Rick, and W. H. Timmons

1998 *San Elizario: The Spanish Presidio to Texas County Seat.* El Paso: University of Texas at El Paso.

Hernández Xochitiotzin, Desiderio

1991 *Crónica de 400 de las familias tlaxcaltecas, 1591–1991.* Tlaxcala, Mexico: H. Ayuntamiento de Tlaxcala, General Archives of the State of Tlaxcala, File Diaspora Tlaxcalteca.

Hester, Thomas

1989a Perspectives on the Material Culture of the Mission Indians of Texas Northeastern Borderlands. In *Columbian Consequences, Vol. 1, Archaeological and Historical Perspectives on the Spanish Borderlands West*, ed. David Hurst Thomas, pp. 213–229. Washington, D.C.: Smithsonian Institution Press.

1989b Texas and Northeastern Mexico: An Overview. In *Columbian Consequences, Vol. 1, Archaeological and Historical Perspectives on the Spanish Borderlands West*, ed. David Hurst Thomas, pp. 191–211. Washington, D.C.: Smithsonian Institution Press.

Higham, John

1987 Strangers in the Land: Nativism and Nationalism. In *From Different*

Shores: Perspectives on Race and Ethnicity in America, ed. Ronald Takaki, pp. 78–82. New York: Oxford University Press.

Hinojosa, Gilbert

1991 The Religious Indian Communities: The Goals of the Friars. In *Tejano Origins in Eighteenth-Century San Antonio*, ed. Gerald E. Poyo and Gilbert M. Hinojosa, pp. 61–83. Austin: University of Texas Press.

1983 *A Borderlands Town in Transition: Laredo 1755-1870*. College Station: Texas A & M University Press.

Hodge, Frederick Web

1953 Pueblo Names in the Oñate Documents. In *Don Juan Oñate: Colonizer of New Mexico, 1595-1628, Volume 5*, ed. George P. Hammond and Agapito Rey, pp. 365–374. New Mexico: University of New Mexico Press.

Hoffman, Paul E.

1973 Diplomacy and the Papal Donation 1493–1585. *Americas* 30: 151–183.

Hoover, Mildred Brooke, Hero Eugene Rensch, and Ethel Grace Rensch

1966 *Historic Spots in California*. 3rd ed. Revised by William N. Abeloe. Stanford, Calif.: Stanford University Press.

Hoover, Robert L.

1989 Spanish-Native Interaction and Acculturation in the Alta California. In *Columbian Consequences, Vol. 1, Archaeological and Historical Perspectives on the Spanish Borderlands West*, ed. David Hurst Thomas, pp. 395–406. Washington, D.C.: Smithsonian Institution Press.

Horcasitas, Fernando

1992 *The Aztecs: Then and Now*. Mexico City: Editorial Minutiae Mexicana.

Hornbeck, David

1989 Economic Growth and Change at the Missions of Alta California, 1769–1846. In *Columbian Consequences, Vol. 1, Archaeological and Historical Perspectives on the Spanish Borderlands West*, ed. David Hurst Thomas, pp. 423–433. Washington, D.C.: Smithsonian Institution Press.

1978a Land Tenure and *Rancho* Expansion in Alta California, 1784-1846. *Journal of Historical Geography* 4 (4): 371–390.

1978b Mission Population of Alta California, 1810-1830. *Historical Geography* 8 (Supp.): 1–9.

Howe, Nicholas

1989 *Migration and Mythmaking in Anglo-Saxon England*. New Haven, Conn.: Yale University Press.

Hoyt, John P., comp.

1877 *The Compiled Laws of the Territory of Arizona*. Detroit: Richmond, Backus and Company.

Hull, Elizabeth

1985 *Without Justice for All: The Constitutional Rights of Aliens.* Westport, Conn.: Greenwood Press.

Hurtado, Albert

1988 *Indian Survival on the California Frontier.* New Haven, Conn.: Yale University Press.

Hutchinson, Cecil Alan

1969 *Frontier Settlement in Mexican California: The Hijar-Padres Colony and Its Origins, 1769–1835.* New Haven, Conn.: Yale University Press.

Hyman, Harold M., and William M. Wiecek

1982 *Equal Justice under Law: Constitutional Development, 1835–1875.* New York: Harper and Row Publishers.

Jackson, Helen Hunt

1903 *Glimpses of California and the Missions.* Boston: Little, Brown and Company. (1st ed. 1883.)

Jackson, Jack

1986 *Los Mesteños: Spanish Ranching in Texas, 1721–1821.* College Station: Texas A & M University Press.

Jackson, Robert H.

1987 Patterns of Demographic Change in the Missions of Central Alta California. *Journal of California and Great Basin Anthropology* 9 (2): 251–272.

John, Elizabeth A. H.

1991 Independent Indians and the San Antonio Community. In *Tejano Origins in Eighteenth-Century San Antonio,* ed. Gerald E. Poyo and Gilbert M. Hinojosa, pp. 123–135. Austin: University of Texas Press.

1975 *Storms Brewed in Other Men's Worlds: The Confrontation of Indians, Spanish, and French in the Southwest, 1540–1795.* College Station: Texas A & M University Press.

Johnson, John

1989 The Chumash and the Missions. In *Columbian Consequences, Vol. 1, Archaeological and Historical Perspectives on the Spanish Borderlands West,* ed. David Hurst Thomas, pp. 365–375. Washington, D.C.: Smithsonian Institution Press.

Jones, James

1981 The Concept of Racism and its Changing Reality. In *Impact of Racism on White Americans,* ed. Benjamin P. Bowser and Raymond G. Hunt, pp. 27–49. Beverly Hills, Calif.: Sage Publications.

Judd, Cornelius D., and Claude Y. Hall

1932 *The Texas Constitution: Explained and Analyzed*. Dallas: Banks, Upshaw and Company.

Kansas, Sidney

1941 *U.S. Immigration: Exclusion and Deportation, and Citizenship of the U.S. of America*. 2nd ed. New York: M. Bender.

Keefe, Susan, and Amado Padilla

1987 *Chicano Ethnicity*. Albuquerque: University of New Mexico Press.

Keller, Gary

1972 Alurista, Poeta-Antropologo, and the Recuperation of the Chicano Identity. In *Return: Poems Collected and New Alurista*, pp. xi–xlix. Ypsilanti, Mich.: Bilingual Press/Editorial Bilingüe.

Kelley, Charles J.

1995 Trade Goods Traders and Status in Northwestern Greater MesoAmerica. In *The Gran Chichimeca: Essays on the Archaeology and Ethnohistory of Northern MesoAmerica*, ed. Jonathan Reyman, pp. 102–145. Glasgow, Scotland: Averbury Ashgate Publishing.

Kelley, Charles J., and Ellen Abbott Kelley

1971 *An Introduction to the Ceramics of the Chalchihuites Culture of Zacatecas and Durango, Mexico, Part I: The Decorated Wares*. Carbondale: University Museum, Southern Illinois University.

Kessell, John L.

1989 Spaniards and Pueblos: From Crusading Intolerance to Pragmatic Accommodation. In *Columbian Consequences, Vol. 1, Archaeological and Historical Perspectives on the Spanish Borderlands West*, ed. David Hurst Thomas, pp. 127–138. Washington, D.C.: Smithsonian Institution Press.

1976 *Friars, Soldiers, and Reformers: Arizona and the Sonora Mission Frontier 1767–1856*. Tucson: University of Arizona Press.

Kibbe, Pauline

1946 *Latin Americans in Texas*. Albuquerque: University of New Mexico Press.

King, Chester

1990 *Evolution of Chumash Society: A Comparative Study of Artifacts Used for Social Systems Maintenance in the Santa Barbara Channel Region before A.D. 1804*. New York: Garland Publishing.

Klor de Alva, J. Jorge

1988 Sahagún and the Birth of Modern Ethnography: Representing, Confessing, and Inscribing the Native Other. In *The Work of Bernardino de Sahagún: Pioneer Ethnographer of Sixteenth-Century Aztec Mexico*, ed. J. Jorge Klor de Alva, H. B. Nicholson, and Eloise Quiñones Keber, pp. 31–52. Institute for Mesoamerican Studies, Studies on Culture and Society, Vol. 2. Albany, N.Y.: University at Albany, State University of New York.

Knowlton, Clark S.

1991 The Mora Land Grant: A New Mexican Tragedy. In *Spanish and Mexican Land Grants and the Law*, ed. Malcolm Ebright, pp. 59–73. Manhattan, Kans.: Sunflower University Press.

Konvitz, Milton R.

1946 *The Alien and the Asiatic in American Law*. Ithaca, N.Y.: Cornell University Press.

Kutsche, Paul, ed.

1979 *The Survival of Spanish American Villages*. Colorado Springs: Research Committee, Colorado College.

Kutsche, Paul, and John Van Ness

1986 *Cañones: Values, Crisis, and Survival in a Northern New Mexican Village*. Albuquerque: University of New Mexico Press.

Lafaye, Jacques

1974 *Quetzalcoatl and Guadalupe*. Chicago: University of Chicago Press.

Lagum, David J.

1987 *Law and Community on the Mexican Frontier: Anglo-American Expatriates and the Clash of Legal Traditions, 1821–1846*. Norman: University of Oklahoma Press.

Lamar, Howard Roberts

1966 *The Far Southwest 1846–1912: A Territorial History*. New York: W. W. Norton and Company.

Lamb, Sydney M.

1964 The Classification of the Uto-Aztecan. *University of California Publications in Linguistics* 34: 106–125.

1958 Linguistic Prehistory in the Great Basin. *International Journal of American Linguistics* 29: 95–100.

Larroyo, Francisco

1946 La educación. In *México y la cultura*, ed. Arturo Barocio et al., pp. 584–625. Mexico City: Secretaría de Educación Pública.

Larson, Daniel O., John R. Johnson, and Joel C. Michaelsen

1994 Missionization among the Coastal Chumash of Central California: A Study of Risk Minimization Strategies. *American Anthropologist* 96 (2): 263–299.

Larson, Robert

1968 *New Mexico's Quest for Statehood 1846–1912*. Albuquerque: University of New Mexico Press.

Leal, Luis

1985 *Aztlán y México: Perfiles literarios e históricos.* Binghamton, N.Y.: Bilingual Press/Editorial Bilingüe.

LeBlanc, Steven A.

1992 Development of Archaeological Thought of the Mimbres Mogollon. In *Emil W. Haury's Prehistory of the American Southwest,* ed. J. Jefferson Reid and David E. Doyle, pp. 297–304. Tucson: University of Arizona Press.

Leonard, Olen E.

1943 The Role of the Land Grant in the Social Organization and Social Processes of a Spanish-American Village in New Mexico. Doctoral dissertation, Louisiana State University.

León-Portilla, Miguel

1975 *Pre-Columbian Literatures of Mexico.* Norman: University of Oklahoma Press.

1972 The *Norteño* Variety of Mexican Culture: An Ethnohistorical Approach. In *Plural Society in the Southwest,* ed. Edward Spicer and Raymond H. Thompson, pp. 77–101. New York: Weatherhead Foundation.

Lévi-Strauss, Claude

1982 *Elementary Structures of Kinship.* Boston: Beacon Press.

Levtzion, Nehemia

1973 *Ancient Ghana and Mali.* Bungay, Suffolk, Great Britain: Richard Clay.

Lipe, William

1978 The Southwest. In *Ancient Native Americans,* ed. Jesse Jennings, pp. 327–401. San Francisco, Calif.: W. H. Freeman.

Liss, Peggy K.

1975 *Mexico under Spain, 1521–1556: Society and the Origins of Nationality.* Chicago: University of Chicago Press.

Livermore, Harold Victor

1971 *The Origins of Spain and Portugal.* London: George, Allen and Unwin.

Lockhart, James

1991 *Nahuas and Spaniards: Postconquest Central Mexican History and Philosophy.* Palo Alto, Calif.: Stanford University Press.

Lomawaima, Hartman H.

1989 Hopification: A Strategy for Cultural Preservation. In *Columbian Consequences, Vol. 1, Archaeological and Historical Perspectives on the Spanish Borderlands West,* ed. David Hurst Thomas, pp. 365–375. Washington, D.C.: Smithsonian Institution Press.

Lopéz [sic] de Guana, Martín

1591 Letter from Tlaxcala Governor Martín Lopéz de Guana, 1591 to Viceroy Don Luis de Velasco. General Archives of the State of Tlaxcala, File Diaspora Tlaxcalteca. Tlaxcala, Mexico.

Love, Edgar F.

1971 Marriage Patterns of African Descent in a Colonial Mexico Parish. *Hispanic American Historical Review* 51: 79–91.

1970 Legal Restrictions on Afro-Indian Relations in Colonial Mexico. *Journal of Negro History* 55 (2): 131–139.

Lynch, John

1964 *Spain under the Habsburgs: Empire and Absolutism, 1516–1598, Vol. 1.* New York: Oxford University Press.

Margadant S., Guillermo

1991 Mexican Colonial Land Law. In *Spanish and Mexican Land Grants and the Law*, ed. Malcolm Ebright, pp. 85–99. Manhattan, Kans.: Sunflower University Press.

Mason, William M.

1986 Alta California during the Mission Period, 1769–1835. *Masterkey* 60 (2/3): 4–14.

Mattison, Ray H.

1967 The Tangled Web: The Controversy over the Tumacácori and Baca Land Grants. *Journal of American History* 8 (2): 71–90.

1946 Early Spanish and Mexican Settlements in Arizona. *New Mexico Historical Review* 21 (4): 273–327.

May, Geoffrey

1929 *Marriage Laws and Decisions in the United States: A Manual.* New York: Russell Sage Foundation.

McAlister, Lyle

1963 Social Structure and Social Change in New Spain. *Hispanic American Historical Review* 43 (Aug.): 349–370.

1957 The Privileges of the Pardos. In *The Fuero Militar in New Spain, 1764–1800*, 43–54. Gainesville: University of Florida Press.

McDowell, Bart

1980 The Aztecs. *National Geographic* 158 (6): 714–751.

McIntosh, Susan Keech

1995 Conclusion: The Sites in Regional Context. In *Excavations at Jenné-jeno, Hambarketolo, and Kaniana (Inland Niger Delta, Mali): The 1981 Season*, ed. Susan Keech McIntosh, pp. 360–411. Anthropology, Vol. 20. Berkeley: University of California Press.

McWilliams, Carey

1968 *North from Mexico.* New York: Greenwood Press.

Meade de Angulo, Mercedes

n.d. *Apuntes para la colonización tlaxcalteca en el norte de México.* Tlaxcala, Mexico: H. Ayuntamiento de Tlaxcala, General Archives of the State of Tlaxcala, File Diaspora Tlaxcalteca.

Menchaca, Martha

1999 The Treaty of Guadalupe Hidalgo and the Racialization of the Mexican Population. In *The Elusive Quest For Equality: 150 Years of Chicano/Chicana Education,* ed. José F. Moreno, pp. 3–29. Cambridge, Mass.: Harvard Educational Review.

1997 Early Racist Discourses: The Roots of Deficit Thinking. In *The Evolution of Deficit Thinking: Educational Thought and Practice,* ed. Richard R. Valencia, pp. 13–40. Stanford Series on Education and Public Policy. London: Falmer Press.

1995 *Mexican Outsiders: A History of Marginalization and Discrimination in California.* Austin: University of Texas Press.

1993 Chicano Indianism: A Historical Account of Racial Repression in the United States. *American Ethnologist* 20 (3): 583–603.

1989 Chicano-Mexican Assimilation and Anglo-Saxon Cultural Dominance. *Hispanic Journal of Behavioral Sciences* 11 (3): 203–231.

Merriam, Clinton Hart

1955 *Studies of California Indians.* Berkeley: University of California Press.

Metz, Leon C.

1994 *El Paso Chronicles: A Record of Historical Events in El Paso, Texas.* El Paso, Tex.: Mangan Books.

Meyer, Michael, and William L. Sherman

1995 *The Course of Mexican History.* New York: Oxford University Press.

Miller, Robert R.

1985 *Mexico: A History.* Norman: University of Oklahoma Press.

Minter, Alan H.

1993 Indian Land Claims in Texas during the Twentieth Century. Paper archived at the Texas General Land Office, Austin.

Molitor, Martha

1981 *Hohokam-Toltec Connection.* Occasional Publications in Anthropology and Archaeology, Series No. 10. Greeley: University of Northern Colorado, Museum of Anthropology.

Monroy, Douglas

1990 *Thrown among Strangers: The Making of Mexican Culture in Frontier Cali-fornia.* Berkeley: University of California Press.

Montejano, David

1987 *Anglos and Mexicans in the Making of Texas, 1836–1986.* Austin: University of Texas Press.

Morfí, Father Juan Agustín

1977 *Account of Disorders in New Mexico.* Trans. and ed. Marc Simmons.Ysleta Pueblo, N.M.: St. Augustine Church, by Rev. James T. Burke. (1st ed. 1778.)

1935 *Historia de la Provincia de Texas, 1673–1779.* With annotations by Carlos E. Castañeda. Albuquerque, N.M.: Society Publications. (1st ed. 1783.)

1780 Notas de las memorias para la historia de Texas. Manuscript located at the University of Texas at Austin, Benson Latin American Collection, Rare Book Unit, No. WBS 2065.

Mörner, Magnus

1967 *Race Mixture in the History of Latin America.* Boston: Little, Brown and Company.

Morrow, William W.

1923 *Spanish and Mexican Private Land Grants.* San Francisco: Bancroft-Whitney Company.

Murphy, James

1970 *Laws, Courts, and Lawyers: Through the Years in Arizona.* Tucson: University of Arizona Press.

Nacogdoches Archives. University of Texas at Austin. Center for American History. Texas Collection.

Newcomb, William W.

1986 *The Indians of Texas: From Prehistoric to Modern Times.* Austin: University of Texas Press.

New Handbook of Texas History, Vol. 3. Ed. Ron Tyler. Austin: Texas State Historical Association, 1996.

Nott, Josiah Clark, and Geo. R. Gliddon

1857 *Indigenous Races of the Earth.* Philadelphia, Penn.: Lippincott and Company.

1854 *Types of Mankind.* Philadelphia, Penn.: Lippincott, Grambo and Company.

Officer, James E.

1987 *Hispanic Arizona, 1536–1856.* Tucson: University of Arizona Press.

Oliver, Roland, and Brian Fagan

1975 *Africa in the Iron Age: c. 500 B.C. to A.D. 1400.* Cambridge: Cambridge University Press.

Olmstead, Virginia Langham, comp.

1981 *Spanish and Mexican Censuses of New Mexico 1750-1830.* Albuquerque: New Mexico Genealogical Society.

Omi, Michael, and Howard Winant

1994 *Racial Formation in the United States: From the 1960s to the 1990s.* New York: Routledge. (1st ed. 1986.)

Orfield, Gary, and Franklin Monfort

1992 *Status of School Desegregation: The Next Generation.* Cambridge, Mass.: Harvard University, Metropolitan Opportunity Project.

Ortiz, Alfonso

1991 Through Tewa Eyes: Origins. *National Geographic* 180 (4): 5-13.

Padilla, Fernando

1979 Early Chicano Legal Recognition in 1846-1897. *Journal of Popular Culture* 13 (3): 564-574.

Palacios Preciado, Jorge

1988 *La esclavitud de los africanos y la trata de negros: Entre la teoría y la práctica.* Tunja, Boyaca, Colombia: Magister en Historia, Escuela de Posgrado de la Facultad Educación, Universidad Pedagógica y Tecnológica de Colombia.

Palmer, Colin

1981 *Human Cargoes: The British Slave Trade to Spanish America, 1700-1739.* Urbana: University of Illinois Press.

Paredes, Américo

1978 The Problem of Identity in a Changing Culture: Popular Expressions of Culture Conflict along the Lower Rio Grande Border. In *Views across the Border: The United States and Mexico,* ed. Stanley Ross, pp. 68-94. Albuquerque: University of New Mexico Press.

Paschal, George W.

1874 *Digest of Decisions, Vol. 2.* Washington, D.C.: W. H. Morrison Publishers.

Perry, Richard J.

1991 *Western Apache Heritage.* Austin: University of Texas Press.

Perry, Richard, and Rosalind Perry

1988 *Maya Missions: Exploring the Spanish Colonial Churches of Yucatan.* Santa Barbara, Calif.: España Press.

Persons, Billie

1958   Secular Life in the San Antonio Missions. *Southwestern Historical Quarterly* 62 (1): 45–62.

Pertulla, Timothy

1992   *The Caddo Nation: Archeology and Ethnohistoric Perspectives.* Austin: University of Texas Press.

Pi-Sunyer, Oriol

1957   Historical Background of the Negro in Mexico. *Journal of Negro History* 42 (4): 237–246.

Pitt, Leonard

1970   *The Decline of the Californios: A Social History of the Spanish-Speaking Californians, 1846–1890.* Berkeley: University of California Press.

Polzer, Charles W.

1976   *Rules and Precepts of the Jesuit Missions of Northwestern New Spain.* Tucson: University of Arizona Press.

Powell, Philip Wayne

1952   *Soldiers, Indians and Silver: The Northward Advance of New Spain, 1550–1600.* Berkeley: University of California Press.

Poyo, Gerald E.

1991a The Canary Islands Immigrants of San Antonio: From Ethnic Exclusivity to Community in Eighteenth-Century Béxar. In *Tejano Origins in Eighteenth-Century San Antonio,* ed. Gerald E. Poyo and Gilbert M. Hinojosa, pp. 41–60. Austin: University of Texas Press.

1991b Immigrants and Integration in Late Eighteenth-Century Béxar. In *Tejano Origins in Eighteenth-Century San Antonio,* ed. Gerald E. Poyo and Gilbert M. Hinojosa, pp. 85–103. Austin: University of Texas Press.

Poyo, Gerald E., and Gilbert M. Hinojosa, eds.

1991   *Tejano Origins in Eighteenth-Century San Antonio.* Austin: University of Texas Press.

Prince, Bradford L.

1915   *Spanish Mission Churches of New Mexico.* Cedar Rapids, Ia.: Torch Press.

Rangel, Jorge C., and Carlos Alcala

1972   Project Report: De Jure Segregation of Chicanos in Texas Schools. *Harvard Civil Rights–Civil Liberties Law Review* 1: 307–391.

Reader, John

1997   *Africa: A Biography of the Continent.* London: Hamish Hamilton.

Recopilación de leyes de los reynos de las Indias

1774   Vol. 1. Books 1 and 2. 3rd ed. Compiled and published by Andres Ortega, under the royal orders of Don Carlos II, King of Spain. Vol. 2. Books 3, 4, 6, and 7. 3rd ed. Compiled and published by Antonio Perez de Soto, under the royal orders of Don Carlos II, King of Spain. Madrid: n.p. (1st ed. 1681.)

Reed-Donahay, Deborah E.

1997 *Auto/Ethnography: Rewriting the Self and the Social.* New York: Berg.

Reisler, Mark

1976 *By the Sweat of Their Brow: Mexican Immigrant Labor in the United States, 1900–1940.* Westport, Conn.: Greenwood Press.

Rendón, Armando

1971 *Chicano Manifesto.* New York: Macmillan Company.

Residents of Texas 1782–1836. Reprint of the Spanish and Mexican censuses made in 1984. University of Texas Institute of Texan Cultures. St. Louis, Mo.: Ingmire Publications.

Reyman, Jonathan E.

1995 *The Gran Chichimeca: Essays on the Archaeology and Ethnohistory of Northern Mesoamerica.* Aldershot, Hampshire, Great Britain: Avebury.

Richardson, Rupert, Ernest Wallace, and Adrian Anderson

1970 *Texas the Lone Star.* Englewood Cliffs, N.J.: Prentice-Hall.

Ríos-Bustamante, Antonio

1986 The Barrioization of Nineteenth-Century Mexican Californians: From Landowners to Laborers. *Masterkey* 60 (2/3): 26–35.

Robinson, William W.

1948 *Land in California.* Berkeley: University of California Press.

Rock, Michael J.

1976 The Change in Tenure New Mexico Supreme Court Decisions Have Effected upon the Common Lands of Community Land Grants in New Mexico. *Social Science Journal* 13 (3): 53–63.

Rodríguez Flores, Emilio

1976 *Compendio histórico de Zacatecas.* Zacatecas, Mexico: Academia Comercial Heroes del 64.

Romano-V, Octavio I.

1968 The Anthropology and Sociology of the Mexican-Americans: The Distortion of Mexican-American History. *Voices: Readings from El Grito* 2 (1): 13–26.

Roncal, Joaquín

1944 The Negro Race in Mexico. *Hispanic American Historical Review* 24 (3): 530–540.

Rosaldo, Renato
1985 Chicano Studies, 1970–1984. *Annual Reviews of Anthropology* 14: 405–427.

Ross, Ivy B.
1974 *The Confirmation of Spanish and Mexican Land Grants in California.* San Francisco: R & E Associates.

Ross Browne, J., comp.
1850 *Report of the Debates in the Convention of California, on the Formation of the State Constitution, in September and October, 1849.* Washington, D.C.: John J. Towkes Printers.

Rubel, Arthur
1966 *Across the Tracks.* Austin: University of Texas Press.

Rush, Philip S.
1965 *Some Old Ranchos and Adobes.* San Diego, Calif.: Neyenesch Printers.

Sahlins, Marshall
1985 *Islands of History.* Chicago: University of Chicago Press.

Said, Edward
1979 *Orientalism.* New York: Vintage Books.

Salinas, Guadalupe
1973 Mexican Americans and the Desegregation of Schools in the Southwest. In *Voices: Readings from El Grito,* ed. Octavio I. Romano-V, pp. 366–399. Berkeley, Calif.: Quinto Sol.

Salinas, Martín
1990 *Indians of the Rio Grande Delta: Their Role in the History of Southern Texas and Northwestern Mexico.* Austin: University of Texas Press.

Sánchez, Federico A.
1986 Rancho Life in Alta California. *Masterkey* 60 (2/3): 15–25.

Sánchez, George I.
1976 *Forgotten People: A Study of New Mexicans.* Albuquerque, N.M.: Calvin Horn.

Sánchez, Jane
1983 Spanish-Indian Relations during the Otermín Administration, 1677–1683. *New Mexico Historical Review* 58 (2): 133–151.

Santa Paula Water Works et al. v. Julio Peralta, 1893–1898. Reel no. 38, case no. 001458. Superior Court, Ventura County, California.

Sauer, Carl

1934 The Distribution of Aboriginal Tribes and Languages in Northwestern Mexico. *Ibero-Americana* 5: 65–74.

Schoen, Harold

1937a The Free Negro in the Republic of Texas: The Free Negro and the Texas Revolution. *Southwestern Historical Quarterly* 40 (1): 26–34.

1937b The Free Negro in the Republic of Texas: The Law in Practice. *Southwestern Historical Quarterly* 40 (4): 267–289.

Scholes, France V.

1937 Troublous Times in New Mexico, 1659–1670. *New Mexico Historical Review* 12 (2): 134–174.

Scholes, France V., and Harry P. Mera

1940 Some Aspects of the Jumano Problem. *Carnegie Institution Contributions to American Anthropology and History* 6: 265–299.

Schwartz, Rosalie

1975 *Across the Rio to Freedom: United States Negroes in Mexico.* El Paso: University of Texas at El Paso.

Seed, Patricia

1988 *To Love, Honor, and Obey in Colonial Mexico: Conflicts over Marriage Choice, 1574–1821.* Stanford, Calif.: Stanford University Press.

1982 Social Dimensions of Race: Mexico City, 1753. *Hispanic American Historical Review* 62 (4): 569–606.

Sickels, Robert J.

1972 *Race, Marriage, and the Law.* Albuquerque: University of New Mexico Press.

Simmons, Marc

1964 Tlascalans in the Spanish Borderlands. *New Mexico Historical Review* 34 (2): 101–110.

Simpson, J. H. Brevet Brig.-General

1986 Great Basin of Utah. In *A Great Basin Shoshonean Source Book,* ed. David Hurst Thomas, pp. 1–58. New York: Garland Publishing Inc. (1st ed. 1869.)

Smith, Ralph

1962a Apache Plunder Trails Southward, 1831–1840. *New Mexico Historical Review* 37 (1): 20–42.

1962b Apache "Ranching" below the Gila, 1841–1845. *Arizonian* 3 (4): 1–17.

Soza, Edward, comp.

1998 Affidavits of Contest vis-à-vis Arizona Hispanic Homesteaders 1880–1908. Arizona General Land Commission Publication. Archives and Correspondence. Altadena, California.

1994a Hispanic Homesteading in Arizona 1870 to 1908, under the Homestead Act of May 20, 1862, and Other Public Land Laws. Arizona General Land Commission Publication. Archives and Correspondence. Altadena, California.

1994b Mexican Homesteading in the San Pedro River Valley and the Homestead Act 1862, 1870, 1908. Arizona General Land Commission Publication. Archives and Correspondence. Altadena, California.

Spicer, Edward

1981 *Cycles of Conquest: The Impact of Spain, Mexico, and the United States on the Indians of the Southwest 1533-1960.* 7th rpt. Tucson: University of Arizona Press.

Spier, Leslie

1933 *Yuman Tribes of the Gila River.* Chicago: University of Chicago Press.

Stallings, Williams Sidney, Jr.

1932 Notes on the Pueblo Culture in South-Central New Mexico and in the Vicinity of El Paso, Texas. *American Anthropologist* 34: 67-78.

Stanton, William

1966 *The Leopard's Spots: Scientific Attitudes toward Race in America 1815-59.* Chicago: University of Chicago Press.

Steward, Julian

1933 Ethnography of Owens Valley Paiute. *University of California Publications in American Anthropology and Ethnology* 33 (3): 233-350.

Stocking, George W., Jr.

1968 *Race, Culture and Evolution.* New York: Free Press.

Stuart, George E.

1995 The Timeless Vision of Teotihuacán. *National Geographic* 188 (6): 2-35.

Stuart, James

1879 *Arguments and Points and Authorities on Appeal to the Honorary Secretary of the Interior: In the Case of the Southern Pacific Railroad Company vs. the Settlers on Land.* San Francisco: Bacon and Company Book and Job Printers.

Swadesh, Frances Leon

1974 *Los Primeros Pobladores: Hispanic Americans of the Ute Frontier.* Notre Dame, Ind.: University of Notre Dame Press.

Swanton, John R.

1984 *The Indian Tribes of North America.* 4th rpt. Bureau of American Ethnology, No. 45. Washington, D.C.: Smithsonian Institution Press. (First printed 1952.)

Takaki, Ronald

1994 Reflections of Racial Patterns in America. In *From Different Shores: Perspectives on Race and Ethnicity in America*, ed. Ronald Takaki, pp. 24–35. 2nd ed. New York: Oxford University Press.

1990 *Iron Cages: Race and Culture in Nineteenth-Century America*. 2nd ed. New York: Alfred A. Knopf.

Tate, Bill

1969 *Guadalupe Hidalgo Treaty of Peace 1848 and the Gadsden Treaty with Mexico 1853*. Truchas, N.M.: Tate Gallery and Rio Grand Sun Press.

Texas General Land Office

n.d.a Espada Mission Land Records. File 121:45. Austin: Texas General Land Office.

n.d.b File Afro-Americans in Austin's Colony. Austin: Texas General Land Office.

n.d.c Guide to Department of Béxar/Texas Records. Austin: Texas General Land Office.

n.d.d Guide to Spanish and Mexican Titles in Texas. Austin: Texas General Land Office.

1988 *Guide to Spanish and Mexican Land Grants in South Texas.* Austin: Texas General Land Office, Gary Mauro, Land Commissioner.

Thompkins, Walker

1967 *Old Spanish Santa Barbara*. Santa Barbara, Calif.: McNally and Loftin.

Thompson, Seymour D.

1878 *A Treatise on Homestead and Exemption Laws*. St. Louis, Mo.: F. H. Thomas and Company.

Thornton, John

1996 *Africa and Africans in the Making of the Atlantic World, 1400–1680*. Cambridge: Cambridge University Press.

Tibón, Gutierre

1983 *El jade de México: El mundo esotérico del "Chalchihuite."* Mexico City: Panorama Editorial, S.A.

Tjarks, Alicia

1974 Comparative Demographic Analysis of Texas, 1777–1793. *Southwestern Historical Quarterly* 77 (Jan.): 291–338.

Torres Ramirez, Bibiano

1973 *La Compañía Gaditana de Negros*. Sevilla, Spain: Escuela de Estudios Hispano-Americanos de Sevilla Consejo Superior de Investigaciones Científicas.

Triem, Judith

1985 *Ventura County: Land of Good Fortune.* Northridge, Calif.: Windsor Publications.

Trouillot, Michel-Rolph

1995 *Silencing the Past: Power and the Production of History.* Boston: Beacon Press.

Tyler, Daniel

1991 Ejido Lands in New Mexico. In *Spanish and Mexican Land Grants and the Law,* ed. Malcolm Ebright, pp. 24–35. Manhattan, Kans.: Sunflower University Press.

1974 The Mexican Teacher. *Red River Valley Historical Review* 1 (3): 207–221.

Union Republican Congressional Committee

n.d. *Homes for the Homeless: What the Republican Party Has Done for the Poor Man.* Washington, D.C: Government Printing Office. (Circa 1870s.)

United States Census

1922 *U.S. Bureau of the Census Abstracts.* Washington, D.C.: Government Printing Office.

1902 *Abstracts of the Twelfth Census of the United States 1900.* Washington, D.C.: Government Printing Office.

1894 *Population of the United States 1890.* Washington, D.C.: Government Printing Office.

1882 *Tenth Census of the United States 1880, Vol. 1.* Washington, D.C.: Government Printing Office.

1872 *A Compendium of the Ninth Census of the United States 1870.* Washington, D.C.: Government Printing Office.

1864 *Population of the United States in 1860, Compiled from the Original Returns of the Eighth Census.* Washington, D.C.: Government Printing Office.

1854 *Population of the United States in 1850, Compiled from the Original Returns of the Seventh Census.* Washington, D.C.: Government Printing Office.

Valdez, Luis

1972 *Aztlán: An Anthology of Mexican American Literature.* New York: Knopf.

Valencia, Richard, ed.

1991 *Chicano School Failure and Success: Research and Policy Agenda for the 1990s.* New York: Falmer Press.

Valencia, Richard, and Daniel B. Solorzano

1997 Contemporary Deficit Thinking. In *The Evolution of Deficit Thinking: Educational Thought and Practice,* ed. Richard R. Valencia, pp. 160–210. Stanford Series on Education and Public Policy. London: Falmer Press.

Van Ness, John

1976 Spanish Americans vs. Anglo American Land Tenure and the Study of Economic Change in New Mexico. *Social Science Journal* 13 (3): 45–52.

Van Ness, John R., and Christine M. Van Ness

1980 Introduction. In *Spanish and Mexican Land Grants in New Mexico and Colorado*, ed. John R. Van Ness and Christine M. Van Ness, pp. 3–11. Special edition of *Journal of the West*.

Vigil, James Diego

1984 *From Indians to Chicanos: The Dynamics of Mexican American Culture*. Prospect Heights, Ill.: Waveland Press. (1st ed. 1980.)

Villagrá, Gaspar Pérez de

1933 *History of New Mexico*. Trans. Gilberto Espinosa. Los Angeles: Quivira Society. (1st printing 1610.)

Vinces Vives, Jaime

1972 *Approaches to the History of Spain*. Berkeley: University of California Press.

Wagner, Henry R., and Helen R. Parish

1967 *The Life and Writings of Bartolomé de las Casas*. Albuquerque: University of New Mexico Press.

Wagoner, Jay J.

1970 *Arizona Territory 1863–1912: A Political History*. Tucson: University of Arizona Press.

Walker, Phillip L., and Travis Hudson

1993 *Chumash Healing: Changing Health and Medical Practices in an American Indian Society*. Banning, Calif.: Malki Museum Press.

Weber, David J.

1992 *The Spanish Frontier in North America*. New Haven, Conn.: Yale University Press.

1982 *The Mexican Frontier, 1821 to 1846: The American Southwest under Mexico*. Albuquerque: University of New Mexico Press.

Weinberg, Meyer

1977 *A Chance to Learn: The History of Race and Education in the United States*. Cambridge: Cambridge University Press.

Weiss, Michael

1978 Education, Literacy and the Community of Los Angeles in 1850. *Southern California Quarterly* 60 (1): 117–142.

Wetterau, Bruce

1994 *World History: A Dictionary of Important People, Places, and Events from Ancient Times to the Present.* New York: Henry, Holt and Company.

White, Hayden

1992 *Tropics of Discourse: Essays in Culture Criticism.* Baltimore: Johns Hopkins University Press.

White, Owen

1923 *Out of the Desert: A Historical Romance of El Paso.* El Paso, Tex.: McMath Company.

Williams, David A.

1998 *Bricks without Straw: A Comprehensive History of African Americans in Texas.* Austin, Tex.: Eakin Press.

Wollenberg, Charles

1974 *Mendez v. Westminster:* Race, Nationality and Segregation in California Schools. *California Historical Society Quarterly* 53: 317–332.

Yanagisako, Sylvia, and Carol Delany

1995 Introduction. In *Naturalizing Power: Essays in Feminist and Cultural Analysis,* ed. Sylvia Yanagisako and Carol Delany, pp. 1–22. New York: Routledge.

Ybarra-Frausto, Tomás

1979 Alurista's Poetics: The Oral, the Bilingual, the Pre-Columbian. In *Modern Chicano Writers,* ed. Joseph Sommers and Tomás Ybarra-Frausto, pp. 117–130. Englewood Cliffs, N.J.: Prentice-Hall.

1978 The Chicano Movement and the Emergence of a Chicano Poetic Consciousness. In *New Directions in Chicano Scholarship,* ed. Ricardo Romo and Raymundo Paredes, pp. 81–109. Chicano Studies Monograph Series. La Jolla, Calif.: Chicano Studies Program, University of California, San Diego.

Newspapers

Austin American-Statesman
Santa Barbara News Press

Court Cases

Botiller v. Dominguez, 130 U.S. 238–256 (1889).
Brown v. the Board of Education of Topeka, 347 U.S. 483–496 (1954).
Byrne v. Alas et al., 16 Pacific Reporter 523–529 (Supreme Court of California 1888).
Cook v. Garza, 5 Texas Reports 358–363 (Supreme Court of Texas 1853).

Davidson et al. v. United States Government, 328 District Court of Southern California. County of Santa Barbara. Archived at Bancroft Library, University of California Berkeley (1857).

Elk v. Wilkens, 112 U.S. 94 (1884).

Independent School District v. Salvatierra, 33 South Western Reporter, 2nd Series 790–796 (Texas Civic Appellate, San Antonio 1930).

In re Ah Yup, 5 Sawy 155–160 (District Court, California 1878).

In re Camille, 6 Federal Reporter 256–259 (District Court, Oregon 1880).

In re Kanaka Nian, 21 Pacific Reporter 993–994 (Supreme Court of Utah 1889).

In re Rodriguez, 81 Federal Reporter 337–356 (District Court, W. D. Texas 1897).

Johnson v. McIntosh, 21 U.S. 543–695 (1823).

Lewis v. San Antonio, 7 Texas Reports 288–322 (Supreme Court of Texas 1851).

Loving v. Virginia, 388 U.S. 1010–1018 (1967).

Lueras v. Town of Lafayette, 100 Colorado State Supreme Court 124–127 (1937).

McMullen v. Hodge and Others, 9 Texas Reports 34–87 (Texas State Supreme Court 1849).

Mendez v. Westminster, 64 Federal Supplement (S.D. Cal) 544–554, (1946); aff'd 161 Federal Reporter 2nd Series 774–785 (Ninth Circuit Court of Appeals, San Francisco, 1947).

People v. Juan Antonio, 27 California 404–406 (Supreme Court of California 1865).

People v. Pablo De La Guerra, 40 California 311–344 (Supreme Court of California 1870).

Perez v. Sharp, 32 California 2nd Series 711–763 (Supreme Court of California 1948).

Phillips v. Martin Marietta Corporation, 411 Federal Reporter, 2nd Series 1–5 (U.S. Court of Appeals, Fifth Circuit 1969); 400 U.S. 542 (1971).

Pico v. United States, 2 U.S. (2 Wallace) 279–282 (1864).

Plessy v. Ferguson, 163 U.S. 537–564 (1896).

Regents of the University of California v. Bakke, 438 U.S. 265–421 (1978).

Roberto Alvarez v. Lemon Grove School District, Petition for Writ of Mandate no. 66625 (Superior Court of the State of California, County of San Diego 1931).

Robinson and Wife v. Memphis and Charleston Railroad Company, 109 U.S. 3–62 (1883).

Rosenfeld v. Southern Pacific Company, 444 Federal Reporter, 2nd Series 1219–1228 (U.S. Circuit Court of Appeals, Ninth Circuit 1971).

Santa Paula Water Works et al. v. Julio Peralta, Case no. 001458 (Superior Court, Ventura County, California 1893).

Santa Paula Water Works et al. v. Julio Peralta, 5 California 239 (Supreme Court of California 1895).

Santa Paula Water Works et al. v. Julio Peralta, 113 California 38–45 (Supreme Court of California 1896).

Sprogis v. United Air Lines, 444 Federal Reporter, 2nd Series 1194–1207 (U.S. Court of Appeals, Seventh Circuit 1971), Cert. denied 404 U.S. 999 (1971).

State of Nevada v. Ah Chew, 16 Nevada Supreme Court 50–61 (1881).

Suñol v. Hepburn, 1 California 254–294 (Supreme Court of California 1850).

Terrell Wells Swimming Pool v. Rodríguez, 182 South Western Reporter, 2nd Series 824 (Texas Civic Appellate, San Antonio 1944).

United States v. Andres Pico, 22 U.S. 406–416 (1859).

United States v. Francisco Pico and Others, 23 U.S. 321–326 (1859).

United States v. Joseph, 1 Territory of New Mexico 593–602 (Supreme Court of New Mexico 1874).

United States v. Joseph, 94 U.S. 614–619 (1876).

United States v. Lucero, 1 Territory New Mexico 423–458 (Supreme Court of New Mexico 1869).

United States v. Ringrose, 788 Federal Reporter 2nd Series 638–648 (U.S. Court of Appeals, Ninth Circuit 1986).

United States v. Ritchie, 17 U.S. 525–541 (1854).

United States v. Rogers, 4 U.S. 567–574 (1846).

United States v. Sandoval, 231 U.S. 28–49 (1913).

United States v. Vallejo, 22 U.S. 416–422 (1859).

United States v. Vallejo, 1 U.S. 283–285 (1861a).

United States v. Vallejo, 1 U.S. 541–565 (1861b).

United States v. Wong Kim Ark, 169 U.S. 649–732 (1898).

Statutes

California Statutes 1851. The Statutes of California, 2nd Session of the Legislature, 6 January 1851 to 1 May 1851 at the City of San Jose. State Printer Eugene Cassey.

Civil Rights Act of 1866, Chap. 31, Secs. 1–6.

Eighteen United States Statutes at Large, 1873–1875 (1875).

Four United States Statutes at Large, 1789–1845 (1850).

Laws of Texas, Vol. 1 (1898).

Laws of Texas, Vol. 2 (1898).

Laws of Texas Supplement, 1822–1897 (1898).

Naturalization Act of 1790, Chap. 3, Sec. 1.

Naturalization Act of 1795, Chap. 20, Stat. 2, Sec. 1.

Naturalization Act of 1802, Chap. 28, Stat. 1.

Naturalization Rev. Stat. of 1870, Sec. 2169.

Nine Statutes at Large and Treaties of the United States of America, 1845–1851 (1862).

Penal Code of the State of Texas, Vol. 1 (1952).

Twelve Statutes at Large, Treaties, and Proclamations of the United States of America, 1859–1863 (1865).

Twenty-five Statutes at Large, Treaties, and Proclamations of the United States of America, 1887–1889 (1889).

Two United States Statutes at Large, 1789–1845 (1845).

Index

—New Mexico: Santa Fe, 164
—Texas: Bejar, 104; Del Norte at La
   Junta, 110, 114–115, 174; El Paso del
   Norte, 92, 94, 203; Nuestra Señora
   de la Bahía del Espiritu Santo, 106–
   107; Nuestra Señora del Pilar de Los
   Adaes, 106; San Elizario, 92, 94–95,
   164, 202–203; San Francisco, 106;
   San Luis de Las Amarillas, 108
Presidio, Texas: Cabeza de Vaca, 70;
   mission, 108
Pueblo Indians: Acoma conquest,
   86–88; citizenship under U.S., 224–
   225; ethnic divisions, 312n.5; Great
   Pueblo Indian Rebellion, 90–92;
   land under U.S., 247–248, 274; after
   Mexican Independence, 175–176;
   reconquest, 93. See also Anasazi;
   General Law of Colonization 1824;
   Mogollon; Tewa; Tiwa

Quetzalcoatl, 34

racial dictatorship, 3
racialization: theory 3, 311n.1; after
   Treaty of Guadalupe Hidalgo, 217–
   246, 252, 256–258, 274–275, 328n.15
Ramón, Captain Domingo, 102
ranchería, defined, 101
Regents of the University of Califor-
   nia v. Bakkee (1978), 294–295
repartimiento: dismantled, 316n.10;
   during epidemics, 58–59. See also
   slavery
Río Abajo (New Mexico), 91
Río Arriba (New Mexico), 91
Rivera y Moncada, Captain Fernando,
   128–131, 135–136, 138–140
Robinson, William W., 263–264
Robinson and Wife v. Memphis and
   Charleston Railroad Company
   (1883), 286, 294–295
Rodríguez-Cabrillo, Juan, 72
Rodriguez Flores, Emilio, 8, 312–313

Romano-V, Octavio, 14–15
Romans, 39–40
Romero, Evarista, 298–300
Rosenfeld v. Southern Pacific Com-
   pany (1971), 294
Royal Order of 1790, 123
Rubí, Marques de (Cayetano María
   Pignatelli Rubí Corbera y San Cli-
   ment), 114–115, 121
Ruiz, Verónica, 299–301

Sahlins, Marshall, 67
San Antonio, 104, 105, 109–111, 113,
   115–117, 194, 276; schools, 178, 180.
   See also land grants
San Diego, 128, 130–133, 136, 141,
   152–153, 266; schools, 178, 180
San Elizario, 92, 94–95, 164, 171,
   202–203, 317n.30
San Francisco, 131, 137; homesteaders,
   264, 266–267; schools, 178
San Gabriel (Yukewingge), 88
Sanhaja, 46
San José, 147, 264, 322n.17; founding,
   137; schools 179
San Juan de los Caballeros (Caypa),
   86–87
San Luis Obispo, 170
San Pedro Valley, 119–120, 126
Santa Bárbara (Calif.), 131–132, 138,
   146–147, 149, 170, 206, 221, 276,
   298–299, 301, 308–309, 322n.17;
   schools 178, 180
Santa Bárbara (Chihuahua): during
   Chichimec Wars, 76–77; founded,
   316n.9; Oñate's colony, 83, 86
Santa Cruz (Calif.), 147, 264
Santa Cruz Valley (Arizona), 119–120,
   125–126
Santa Fe, 89–92, 94, 164, 171; schools,
   179
Santa Inés: city, 259, 298, 305–306;
   mission, 206–207, 302; reservation,
   10, 301

ish allies, 42, 49; in Texas, 102–105, 107, 109
Tolosa, Juan de, 75
Tolosa Cortés Moctezuma, Isabel de, 82–83
Toltecs: Aztlán, 25–26; Mixcóatl, 33, 35
Tompiros, 92
Treaty of Guadalupe Hidalgo, 215, 218, 274; Arizona (see Gadsen Purchase), 255; California, 221–222, 260–263; land, 233–237; naturalization, 284–285; New Mexico, 224–226, 246–247, 249; Texas, 241. See also racialization
Trouillot, Michel-Rolph, 84–85
Tubac, 120–121, 124, 134–135, 192–193, 254
Tucson, 118, 124–125, 192–193, 253, 255
Tupatú, Luis, 93

United States Indian removal policies: Arizona, 228; California, 218, 222–223, 257–258, 261, 329n.18; New Mexico, 224; Texas, 229–230. See also Indian Intercourse Act of 1834
United States naturalization laws, 281–285
United States v. Joseph (1874, 1876), 248
United States v. Lucero (1869), 224–225, 247
United States v. Sandoval (1913), 279
United States v. Wong Kim Ark (1898), 280
Uolla, Lope de, 83, 85
Urrea, Lieutenant Mariano de, 125
Ute, Aztlán, 25

Valdez, Fred, 1–2, 14
Valencia, Carlos, 307–309

Valencia, Richard, 10, 259, 297–299, 301
Valencia-Cruz, Betty, 298–299, 301, 305, 307–308
Vallejo, Guadalupe Mariano, 203–205, 207, 210, 265–266
Vargas, Governor Diego de, 93
Vásquez de Coronado, Francisco, 72
Velasco, Viceroy Luis de, 81–82
Velázquez, Governor Diego, 42
Ventura, 170, 183, 268–272; last full blooded Chumash in Ventura, 300
Veracruz, 27. See also Olmec
Vigil, James Diego, 14–15
Visigoths, 40
Vitoria, Father Francisco de, 52–53
Vizcaíno, Sebastián, 128; map, 131; route, 133

Walker, Phillip L., 300, 304
Weber, David, 10, 15–16, 18–19, 117, 136
Winant, Howard, 2–3, 311n.1
Wolof, 45, 60

Y'Barbo, Antonio Gil, 111, 115, 325n.6
Ysleta, 92, 94, 171, 202–203; under United States, 230, 240–242
Yucatan Peninsula: conquest, 55; and Hernán Cortés, 42; Toltec-Chichimec, 34. See also Teotihuacán
Yuma, 125, 132–133, 138, 140, 152, 320n.6
Yuma Crossing, 132–140

Zacatecas, 4–5, 8, 75–77, 312–313
Zaldívar, Captain Juan de, 86–87
Zumárraga, Father Juan de, 78
Zuñi, 25, 93
Zuñiga y Acevedo, Viceroy Gaspar de, 82